The International Rule of Law Movement

The International Rule of Law Movement

A Crisis of Legitimacy and the Way Forward

Edited by David Marshall

Human Rights Program Series
Harvard Law School

DISTRIBUTED BY HARVARD UNIVERSITY PRESS

Human Rights Program
Harvard Law School
6 Everett Street
Third Floor
Cambridge, MA 02138
United States of America

hrp@law.harvard.edu
http://www.hup.harvard.edu

ISBN: 978-0-6743657-0-4

Library of Congress Cataloging-in-Publication Data

The international rule of law movement : a crisis of legitimacy and the way
forward / Edited by David Marshall.
    p. cm. -- (Human rights program series)
  Includes bibliographical references.
  ISBN 978-0-674-36570-4
1. Rule of law. 2. International law. I. Marshall, David, (lawyer), author
editor of compilation.
  K3171.I59 2014
  340'.11--dc23

                              2014013831

Printed by Signature Book Printing, http://www.sbpbooks.com

Contents

Foreword

Is international rule of law assistance a waste of time and resources because we do not generally achieve expected results? As institutions that were invited to contribute financially to this volume,[1] we believe it is not. Nonetheless, based on our experience, we support the call to rethink strategy and implementation methods of international rule of law assistance and to identify a new way forward. Most importantly, we believe that the dialogue between conflict-affected societies, international assistance providers, field practitioners, and researchers needs to be strengthened.

The rule of law field is the subject of an intense debate. Our institutions believe that there are two chief reasons for this. First is the seriousness of the matter at hand. As a principle of governance, the rule of law has a direct bearing on how political actors and public employees exercise power and are held accountable. The rule of law therefore involves issues of justice and impunity, often in relation to societies divided by ethnic or sectarian rifts and where these matters are contentious and violently fought over. The second reason for scrutinizing rule of law assistance has to do with volume. There is simply more rule of law assistance now than ever before.[2] There are no exact figures, but a quick scan of AidData and similar databases shows an increase in and diversification of interventions in the last two decades.

Some of the contributions to this volume paint a seemingly bleak picture, concluding that the "field" is performing poorly. Some attribute weak performance to donors' tendency to work with institutions rather than with "ends" or "outcomes": institution-building rather than problem solving. Several authors also suggest interesting approaches that might counterbalance the field's poor track record—for instance, working at the community level and with broader justice issues. We appreciate the expertise and insights brought to bear on the rule of law in these chapters; they give us case studies, which may not be amenable to "scaling up." We might know that assistance of a certain kind in some countries, or for some sectors, has failed to achieve expected results; but for the field as a whole, more is needed.

While we recognize that these conclusions represent distinct perspectives on unique events, we demur from a wholesale dismissal of rule of law programs, reforms, and similar interventions absent more generalizable studies—by which we mean comprehensive, longitudinal empirical studies that might be dispositive of which factors, levers, and sorts of interventions are most effective in promoting and realizing the rule of law. Such studies no doubt are difficult to design and quite expensive. Yet this sort of empirical data, even with its limitations, may allow for the identification of patterns over time, between countries, and between different challenges. Moreover, it is in all likelihood not a matter of failure or success, since the rule of law is not a binary system that can be started, paused, or stopped. All stakeholders involved in rule of law assistance have to adjust their expectations regarding what is achievable and within what timeframe: the *World Development Report 2011* states that it took the fastest reforming countries in the twentieth century up to forty-one years to make significant progress on institutional transformation in the rule of law sector.[3]

Other chapters in this volume despair less, and suggest a revised form of rule of law assistance—one that is incremental and experimental, that works through trial and error, and that is smaller in scale but broader in terms of values (e.g., by encompassing human rights). This has some appeal, but might not be an easy sell to the constituencies in war-stricken, poor, and transitional countries expecting a quick response and for whom the "rule of law" has symbolic, if not actual, value. People in conflict-affected and fragile states may have different expectations and hopes about the rule of law, and they will have this whether we reconfigure rule of law assistance or not. Thus, the approaches to rule of law that we identify may not be the approaches sought by end users.

We recognize that rule of law assistance is never a mere technical activity but a highly sensitive political process about ideas, attitudes, and human behavior that affects elite privileges. Considering the tall order of changing behavior where such change may entail great personal loss, we should also be aware of political will, or lack thereof, when discussing failure or success. Rule of law interventions are in many ways games played by local rules, and we should not overemphasize the role of externally driven reform. While there is sometimes talk of "windows of opportunity" for external actors, past experience gives reason to be skeptical about what can be achieved by outsiders. Rule of law assistance is no longer the purview of Western donors, and the moral authority and legitimacy of organizations such as the United Nations is in some parts of the world questioned and contested.

Notwithstanding our different perspectives on the "field," linking practice with research is an important step forward, and we would like to sincerely thank the editor and the contributors to this volume for taking that step.

Richard Zajac Sannerholm and *Jennifer Schmidt*
Folke Bernadotte Academy

Britta Madsen
ZIF – Center for International Peace Operations

Colette Rausch and *Vivienne O'Connor*
United States Institute of Peace

Notes

1. The United States Institute of Peace (USIP), Folke Bernadotte Academy (FBA), and Center for International Peace Operations (ZIF) offer specialized training on the rule of law. FBA and USIP work in the field. FBA and ZIF select and recruit civilian experts to be deployed to peace operations and civilian crisis management missions worldwide. While funding this volume, all three organizations also participated in the expert panel and in the review of articles.

2. For UN rule of law commitments in peace operations, see, for example, Richard Zajac Sannerholm, Frida Möller, Kristina Simion, and Hanna Hallonsten, *UN Peace Operations and Rule of Law Assistance in Africa 1989–2010: Data, Patterns and Questions for the Future* (Stockholm: Folke Bernadotte Academy, 2012).

3. World Bank, *World Development Report 2011: Conflict, Security and Development* (Washington, DC: World Bank, 2011), 11.

Acknowledgments

This book brings together the research of individual experts in the area of rule of law whose focus is predominately on postconflict and fragile states. The volume grew out my time as a visiting fellow with the Human Rights Program at Harvard Law School, while on sabbatical leave from the United Nations. During that time, I had a rich discussion with Robert O. Varenik on the meaning, if any, of the latest pronouncement by member states of the United Nations on the centrality of the rule of law to solving most of the world's ills. Their pronouncement came at a time when there is actually evidence to the contrary. We discussed whether anything new could be said about the reasons for the failure of the global rule of law movement that had not been said a decade ago by Thomas Carothers, Erik G. Jensen, Brian Z. Tamanaha, and many others.

That discussion led, in turn, to a workshop on the rule of law, convened in November 2013 by the Human Rights Program. There, scholars presented papers that were eventually transformed into the chapters of this volume. Special thanks are owed to the authors for sacrificing considerable time and energy on this initiative. Deep gratitude also goes to the members of the expert panel, Rachel Kleinfeld, Robert O. Varenik, and William O'Neill, and to commentators Juan Carlos Botero, Erik G. Jensen, and Ahmed Ghanem.

I would particularly like to thank Harvard Law School faculty members Gerald L. Neuman, co-director of the Human Rights Program, and Mindy J. Roseman, academic director of the Human Rights Program, for hosting the review meeting and supporting this initiative. I am also grateful to the Visiting Fellows Program at the Human Rights Program for providing an institutional environment that encourages deeper learning and innovation in addressing global injustice. This publication would not have been possible without the generous support of both my employer, the Office of the High Commissioner for Human Rights, and the United Nations Sabbatical Leave Programme, which allowed me to explore in greater depth the challenges facing the United Nations in its efforts to bring lasting peace and justice to fragile states.

I am indebted to Naz Modirzadeh for carefully reviewing and providing comments on earlier drafts and for her friendship sealed during a rule of law–related endeavor in Kandahar, Afghanistan, in 2002.

Deep gratitude is also due to the three organizations that funded this initiative: the Center for International Peace Operations, the Folke Bernadotte Academy, and the United States Institute of Peace. The representatives of these organizations—Britta Madsen, Richard Zajac Sannerholm, Jennifer Schmidt, Colette Rausch, and Vivienne O'Connor—also read and provided comments on many of the chapters.

Thanks to Morgan Stoffregen for copyediting the book and to Catlin Rockman for designing it and laying it out. I would also like to recognize Bryan Chadwick for his support and insights.

Finally, I want to thank Giorgia for her extraordinary patience following my return from South Sudan and my immediate subsequent departure to Harvard Law School. The burdens were many. There are currently no plans to leave the New York area—unless for Rome.

David Marshall
March 2014
Cambridge, MA

Introduction

David Marshall

Today, unprecedented international attention is being placed on state-building in postconflict and fragile states, with a primary focus on rule of law reform. Enormous amounts of money[1] and effort have gone into rebuilding and often changing entire justice systems, with modest success. This attention raises profound questions about the objective, approach, methodology, and consequences of these efforts.

The drivers that cause state collapse or dissolution are often multifaceted, with each situation having its own history, contingencies, and specificities. It stands to reason that each may require a unique approach to rebuilding the state and respect for state authority, laws, and institutions. That said, the international community prefers to see commonalities—such states aspire to be nation-states; all nation-states need functioning legal systems predicated on the rule of law; and, due to a rule of law deficit, these countries have "failed." The restoration (or *de novo* construction) of legal systems is the solution.

The encounter between the international rule of law movement and fractured and distant countries that very few outsiders understand has resulted in great disappointment and disillusionment. Persistent state-building failures—such as in Afghanistan, the Democratic Republic of Congo, Haiti, Iraq, and South Sudan—have not deterred the international community. Though the evidence suggests that trying to change such legal systems is an unproductive endeavor, the international community continues to attempt to reengineer institutions, laws, and legal processes, perhaps because there is no accountability for such meager results.

It once seemed incontrovertible that the Western rule of law model was a "good thing." The end of the Cold War provided new opportunities for the international community to help rebuild shattered states in the developing world. At the time, the rule of law movement was generally considered an adjunct to broader democratization efforts. But it has now taken center stage, accompanied by bold assertions that it will alleviate poverty, secure human rights, and prevent conflict. These goals have proved elusive because the rule of law does not have special abilities to deliver them.

The causes of the movement's failure have remained constant—unrealistic objectives, misplaced doctrinal approaches, insufficient expertise, poor planning and execution, and a lack of deep contextual knowledge. The lessons learned suggest a need to calibrate goals and objectives so that they take account of the negligible impact that international rule of law assistance has had to date. Although the seminal works of Thomas Carothers (1998, 2006), Erik G. Jensen and Thomas C. Heller (2003), and Brian Z. Tamanaha (2011) call for focus and modesty, the international rule of law movement remains undeterred from adopting "comprehensive," whole-system approaches. Indeed, the movement has morphed into an "industry" in that there is considerable business activity around it—though not much of a product.

The past decade has seen an explosion of entities in the rule of law field. They encompass academic institutions, governments, government-funded bodies, journals, nonprofit organizations, private-sector initiatives, and professional associations. At last count, over 1,300 rule of law organizations were listed in the International Bar Association's Rule of Law Directory.[2] The output is enormous—courses and academic programs,[3] research centers, publications, guidance and lessons-learned materials,[4] networks,[5] workshops, training programs, projects, awards,[6] online platforms and forums, blogs, tweet-a-thons,[7] indexes, campaigns, summits, and conferences. In addition to a growth in rule of law entities, there are global rule of law "professionals," mainly Western, ready to deploy "rapidly" to foreign lands to assist in this grand state-building exercise.

A striking development over the past decade has been the increased attention paid by the United Nations (UN) to state-building, particularly rule of law assistance. The UN has since become, probably next to the United States, one of the world's major global actors in rule of law assistance. As described in one of the chapters to this volume, in 2002, a total of eight UN entities provided rule of law expertise. By 2008, the number had grown to forty. Today, UN entities provide rule of law assistance in more than 150 countries; in 70 of these, a minimum of three UN entities provide such expertise.

Though recent international outputs—such as the Global Rule of Law Business Principles and the LexisNexis Rule of Law Business Code—suggest a broadening of the field into commercial interests, the international rule of law movement has been predominately focused on the reform of criminal justice systems through a state-centric, top-down approach. Perhaps this is because manifestations of dysfunctional justice systems are more easily identified when seen through the lens of crumbling court houses, overcrowded prisons, and limited numbers of police. But deficiencies in the criminal justice system are often a reflection of social and cultural attitudes, political inequalities, distributional disparities, and the power dynamics between elites and the populations they serve. The international rule of law movement has been slow to recognize this.

It is with this critical eye toward the movement's past decade of endeavors that I engaged in discussions with scholars and practitioners while on sabbatical from the United Nations. Those discussions ultimately formed the basis for this volume. The authors all have a mixture of scholarship and practice, rooted in fieldwork. Three major rule of law research entities—the Center for International Peace Operations, the Folke Bernadotte Academy, and the United States Institute of Peace—all of whom are deeply invested in the movement, have provided financial support for this volume and the scholarship therein that is critical of the status quo.

Chapter Review

Authors were asked to address a multitude of conceptual and operational questions. Conceptually: What are the assumptions underlying rule of law? In what way does the technocratic positioning of the rule of law blind us to the problematic aspects of creating law for others? In what ways does rule of law reform work clash with state sovereignty? What does it mean to seek to rebuild a justice system from the ground up? Is rule of law reform antidemocratic? Is the enterprise so flawed that it is impossible, or is it morally and ethically sound but hobbled by poor systems and flawed processes? And operationally: How can identifying goals and being clearer about how we know when they have been achieved help us improve rule of law work? How can we better capture and manage our rule of law knowledge, including an understanding of historic cultural attitudes about the nature of law, the role of law in society, and the way that law should be made and applied? What have been the successes of locally driven, "light footprint" interventions? And how can we best identify and support local priorities, initiatives, and solutions?

This volume reflects a diversity of interpretations of the international rule of law movement. It is intended to raise questions—not to provide definitive answers—regarding the way forward. We hope that it lays a foundation for future debate and, potentially, radical change concerning the way the international rule of law movement does business. Though most of the chapters speak to one another, some of the contributions reveal competing approaches and, to some extent, generate tension rather than harmony.

Central to that tension is whether the focus should be about renewal and improvement or about recognizing failure and stopping the cycle of "tinkering" with the existing levers of justice reform in postconflict and fragile states. These two approaches promise radically different outcomes. The latter approach essentially promises to destroy entire areas of the "industry," declare them fatally flawed, and reimagine the entire enterprise. The former assumes that the international rule of law industry (either because it is too big to fail or because it is actually a good thing) is here to stay, and that its size, ambition, and scope are not things that can (or should) be questioned. Rather, we must commit ourselves to improving what already exists, whether by incorporating customary systems, increasing funding, or linking the rule of law to the post-2015 development agenda.

A second theme that emerges from these chapters is the extent to which the failure of rule of law is a failure of international organizations as "institutions." Do these organizations possess certain characteristics that make them the appropriate and legitimate purveyors of rule of law theory and vision? Or is it inappropriate and illegitimate for these organizations to represent the global rule of law movement? Should the organizations instead invest in playing more of a convening role, supporting "cultural affinity" initiatives, such as that being undertaken in South Sudan by the Intergovernmental Authority on Development in East Africa?

Moreover, is the rule of law about law and institutions? Is it about binding law? Would rule of law be better if it were grounded in things that states must do as a matter of law (as opposed to, say, having a flourishing defense bar, which is not a legal obligation)? Many in the rule of law field believe that law and institutions are the solution to problems, based on the assumption that the state has a monopoly on law. But customary law and religious, tribal, and community bodies are already providing solutions in much of the world. Does resolving a dispute always have to engage state institutions? If informal processes are providing essential services to communities, albeit with inequalities and unfairness, is this not "good enough," particularly given the deficits in state responses? And would the international rule of law movement not be better if it were run and staffed by anthropologists, sociologists, and linguistic and cultural experts? Is the rule of law about understanding and working with societies, or is it about understanding and building institutions around law and legal practice?

The rule of law is a work in progress everywhere, at home and abroad. An exploration of how the rule of law is working at "home"—particularly an analysis of the easy assumptions that are often made about "model" justice systems in some states, in which laws and institutions can be easily transported and replicated abroad—is a missing piece of this publication. Recent research in one of the most well-resourced and sophisticated legal regimes in the world, the United States, indicates deep and disturbing problems, particularly in the criminal justice system (Stuntz 2011; Bibas 2012). The system's main achievements appear to be the mass incarceration of millions and an emphasis on process and procedure rather than principles of fairness and equality. And despite layers of judicial review and other protections, there is increasing evidence of the wrongful convictions of innocent persons, including those serving death sentences. Though this volume calls for the international rule of law movement to move beyond a myopic focus on criminal justice reform, the research and experiences in this area nevertheless have serious implications that go well beyond the shores of the United States and are worthy of further exploration by the international rule of law movement. If states wish to improve the prospects of the rule of law in the world, they must first fix the rule of law at home.

Most of the contributions to this volume address rule of law reform in the context of postconflict and fragile states because that is where there is considerable international attention. Two of the authors focus on more developed states. The majority of contributors believe that nothing short of a new paradigm is required for the international rule of law movement.

In **Beyond Deficit and Dysfunction: Three Questions toward Just Development in Fragile and Conflict-Affected Settings**, Louis-Alexandre Berg, Deborah Isser, and Doug Porter suggest that donors must reorient the way they understand justice and their role in promoting it. To date, justice reform efforts have been detached from emerging knowledge about the need to embed justice work within a broader understanding of sociopolitical trajectories, and to more deeply engage with the realities found in unstable and crisis-ridden environments. Donor preoccupation with law and order creates blind spots around justice needs and challenges—from land and property ownership to access to basic services—in which grievances and disputes occur that contribute to conflict and fragility. The authors suggest shifting away from emphasizing institutional deficits and dysfunctions and moving toward focusing on issues related to conflict, perceptions of justice, and barriers to development. These are identified in a problem-solving approach through a series of questions: What is the justice problem? How is this problem being governed? And what is the appropriate role for external assistance in constructively facilitating these contests?

In **Reboot Required: The United Nations' Engagement in Rule of Law Reform in Postconflict and Fragile States**, I call for radical change in the way that the UN engages this field. The UN must reexamine the purpose, approach, methodology, and results of its rule of law assistance, understanding that much good can be done, but on a smaller scale. Though central to the development of the international legal framework and normative human rights and criminal justice principles, on which rule of law work is based, the UN was historically a modest actor when it came to the provision of technical rule of law assistance to its member states. This profoundly changed in 2003, with the Security Council's decision to establish multidimensional peacekeeping missions in postconflict and fragile states. These missions had mandates to "comprehensively" reform justice systems, with a particular focus on police and prisons. The chapter suggests that the premise was based on a flawed understanding of the justice problem, and that, in any event, the UN was ill-suited to play this role because of deficits in its knowledge, capacities, and skills. The chapter recommends that the UN adopt a modest, focused, and incremental approach, moored in international human rights law, in which the organization uses its moral and normative authority and convening power to better identify and support local priorities, initiatives, and solutions.

Haider Ala Hamoudi's chapter, **Decolonizing the Centralist Mind: Legal Pluralism and the Rule of Law**, suggests that the international rule of law movement needs to unshackle itself from the conception of state centrality that has permeated its legal consciousness so it can imagine a different set of solutions for addressing problems related to rule of law. The chapter examines the deficiencies associated with the legal centralist approach in the context of rule of law efforts through an exploration of the "legal order" in the Republic of Iraq. It explores the failure to heed the lessons of legal pluralism, which indicate that, in any social field, there is more than one legal system in operation and that state law by no means reigns supreme. The author rejects the suggestion that law should ultimately derive from, or be delegated by, the state and challenges the notion that the exclusive role of the state is to manage legal disputes. The chapter, while careful not to romanticize religious or tribal "legal order," highlights the important advantages of these processes—they command loyalty, are familiar and accessible to their participants, and are undertaken in a language that is understood. It argues that that the state should be simply one of many players in a multi-faceted and multidimensional system.

While calls for the international rule of law movement to consider the local "context" become more ubiquitous, in **Policy of Government and Policy of Culture: Understanding the Rules of Law in the "Context" of South Sudan's Western Equatoria State**, Mareike Schomerus suggests that "context" is in fact a dynamic interplay between changing, symbolic, and imagined realities and histories. The question of how international rule of law assistance might navigate nonstatic belonging, tradition, and rule setting is thus more complex than even a context-sensitive rule of law intervention might envision. Rule of law reform efforts in South Sudan are mainly an international endeavor focusing on the rule of law as "legal certainty," while local requirements, manifest in how the Azande kingdom is imagined, seek flexible interpretation of a broad range of governance and cultural issues. The chapter challenges widely held assumptions that see context-sensitive justice provision as requiring a clear set of rules, institutions, and authorities, with context acknowledged through an extension of those into so-called informal processes. Instead, the chapter suggests, the international rule of law movement needs to adjust its understanding of "context specific" and "culturally sensitive" as meaning to engage in surroundings that are permanently evolving and to reimagine social realities, with notions of democracy, rules of law, and justice profoundly different from those of the international rule of law movement.

Deval Desai's chapter, **In Search of "Hire" Knowledge: Donor Hiring Practices and the Organization of the Rule of Law Reform Field**, highlights a strange dynamic in the world of rule of law reform: money spent on rule of law projects has increased, even as a strong sense of consensus has emerged that the international community does not really know what to do in this "field." He argues that the idea that the field does not really know what it is doing is not only unproblematic for the field's continued existence but has in fact become constitutive of it. People working in rule of law reform are not grouped together, nor do they share a common sense of purpose or an approach to reform. Rather, they are bound together by the very idea they do not know what to do. Desai argues that the rule of law field exists because the field states that it does, through an ongoing restatement of its existence and reinvention of its history. In light of these circumstances, how can the field be "organized"? How is it possible to learn and move forward if we are constantly reinventing the past and restating our existence in the present? The author suggests that we perhaps remain too concerned at the conceptual level with trying—and always failing—to find some clear content that can bind us together as rule of law reformers. Instead, we should turn to practice to see how we deal with and ignore the indeterminacy of what we do. The chapter looks specifically at the characteristics of rule of law personnel enumerated in the hiring statements of international organizations and donors to see how they engage with what it means to be a rule of law reformer.

In **New Rules for the Rule of Law**, James A. Goldston explores why the rule of law's moment of relevance has arrived and what can be done to give the concept greater meaning in practice. The chapter describes the rule of law's new rhetorical popularity among politically diverse states, which embrace the breadth of its reach and the legitimacy it bestows, including on controversial policies, perhaps because they perceive it as content free. This, the author argues, may explain some states' preference for the rule of law over human rights. The chapter calls for a vision of the rule of law grounded as much in the experiences and struggles of ordinary people as in the adoption of laws and the building of institutions. The rule of law's new ascendancy in official discourse has implications for donors and practitioners, including the implication that rule of law reform, while often presented as a technical challenge, is an inherently political act. Finally, the chapter recommends that advocates seize on a time-bound opportunity—the negotiation of the post-2015 development agenda—to promote the rule of law as a value integral to more inclusive and effective human development.

Other chapters discuss innovations that the international rule of law movement needs to better understand and explore. In **From HiPPOs to "Best Fit" in Justice Reform: Experimentalism in Sierra Leone**, Margaux Hall, Nicholas Menzies, and Michael Woolcock explore the use of experimentation in the World Bank's Justice for the Poor program in Sierra Leone to improve justice and accountability outcomes relating to the delivery of health services. Given the inherent state of uncertainty in complex environments, the authors posit, justice reform efforts could be improved by crafting such responses through a conscious stance of experimentation. Such an approach would design projects that allow data to be collected in real time from an evolving set of activities, using the most encouraging empirical findings to identify locally legitimate, context-specific solutions. Though admittedly radical in the field of justice reform, continually testing and refining operational alternatives based on ongoing data collection is common in the web-based tech world. This approach, the authors suggest, would engage different actors and remedy injustices at different levels.

In **Legal Empowerment and the Land Rush: Three Struggles**, Vivek Maru examines potential innovations relating to grassroots efforts to pursue justice in the context of community rights to land and natural resources. Globally, vast amounts of land are held under customary tenure, with no formal documentation and no clear governance arrangements for making land-use decisions. Exploitation, conflict, and shortsighted decisions are occurring because increased investment interest is colliding with the fact that most people who live and depend on the land do not have secure tenure. The chapter explores three struggles: community efforts to secure tenure in Liberia, Uganda, and Mozambique; rural landowners' efforts to renegotiate a large-scale land lease in Sierra Leone; and coastal communities' efforts to seek environmental compliance from a massive port and coal plant in India. Together, the three stories illustrate the spectrum of interactions between industrial firms and communities practicing traditional livelihoods. The chapter suggests that paralegals, with quality training and supervision, are able to succeed in surmounting power imbalances and remedying injustice—and if not eliminating the disparities in power, at least narrowing them. Moreover, the chapter argues that this approach strengthens citizens' ability to understand and use law.

Humility and help for existing operations are explored as strategies of peer assistance in Todd Foglesong's chapter, **The Rule of Law in Ordinary Action: Filing Legal Advice in Lagos State**. The chapter demonstrates how ostensibly banal accomplishments—such as improving the process by which prosecutors decide whether to charge a suspect being investigated by the police for a grave criminal offense—can exemplify the rule of law and catalyze changes to the governance of the justice system as a whole. It also describes the contribution to that change made by the use of "indicators" that measure the pace of prosecution, exploring the operating principles behind these indicators and focusing on their dependence on the collective identity of "state counselors" in the Directorate of Public Prosecution and the organizational authority of its leaders.

Despite some strong criticisms found in this volume, the message is not to turn away from the rule of law. Every society requires an effective legal order that can manage basic safety and security, ensure accountability, and oversee state authority and economic order. Rule of law *is* the legal restraint on government behavior. But significantly reducing the overheated rhetoric about what the rule of law can actually achieve would be an important start.

Without a doubt, international organizations and donors will likely continue their involvement and investment in rule of law activities in postconflict and fragile states. And with no accountability mechanisms in place, it is conceivable that the movement will continue with the status quo, recycling old ideas that fail to address the core problems identified in this volume. But I remain hopeful that modest objectives, increased learning, and a degree of experimentation will help ensure that justice institutions and services are more inclusive, innovative, and accessible to all.

References

American Bar Association. 2014. "Annual Rule of Law Award Luncheon." Accessed March 23. http://www.americanbar.org/advocacy/rule_of_law/newsroom_events/rule_of_law_award.html.

Bibas, Stephanos. 2012. *The Machinery of Criminal Justice*. Oxford: Oxford University Press.

Carothers, Thomas. 1998. "The Rule of Law Revival." *Foreign Affairs*. March 1. http://www.foreignaffairs.com/articles/53809/thomas-carothers/the-rule-of-law-revival.

———, ed. 2006. *Promoting the Rule of Law Abroad: In Search of Knowledge*. Washington, DC: Carnegie Endowment for International Peace.

Jensen, Erik G., and Thomas C. Heller. 2003. *Beyond Common Knowledge: Empirical Approaches to the Rule of Law*. Palo Alto: Stanford University Press.

LexisNexis. 2014. "Rule of Law Event and Awards." Accessed March 23. https://www.lexisnexis.com/en-us/about-us/rule-of-law/event-and-awards.page.

Special Inspector General for Afghanistan Reconstruction. 2014. *Quarterly Report to the United States Congress*. January 30. Arlington: SIGAR.

Stuntz, William J. 2011. *The Collapse of American Criminal Justice*. Cambridge, MA: Belknap Press of Harvard University Press.

Tamanaha, Brian Z. 2011. "The Primacy of Society and the Failures of Law and Development." *Cornell International Law Journal* 44: 209–47.

United Nations Development Programme. 2012. "United Nations Tweet-a-Thon on the Rule of Law." Accessed March 23, 2014. http://www.undp.org/content/undp/en/home/ourwork/get_involved/live/rol4peace.html.

United Nations Secretary-General. 2008. "The Rule of Law at the National and International Levels." UN doc. A/63/64.

Notes

1. According to the US Special Inspector General for Afghanistan Reconstruction (2014, 79), the United States' twelve-year effort in Afghanistan has cost more than US$100 billion, 40% of which was allocated for rule of law programs.

2. The directory, launched in 2002, is available at http://www.roldirectory.org.

3. For example, Loyola University Chicago offers an LLM in Rule of Law for Development for those seeking a "career in rule of law advising" (http://www.luc.edu/prolaw) and Ohio Northern University offers an LLM in Democratic Governance and Rule of Law (https://law.onu.edu/llm_program).

4. The UN's Department for Peacekeeping Operations has produced over 1,000 rule of law documents (United Nations Secretary-General 2008, para. 459).

5.   The International Network to Promote the Rule of Law (http://www.inprol. org) comprises "some 2,000 rule of law practitioners from 120 countries and 300 organizations."

6.   These include the American Bar Association's (2014) Annual Rule of Law Award and the LexisNexis (2014) Rule of Law Award.

7.   For example, the United Nations Development Programme (2012) hosted an international tweet-a-thon in September 2012.

Abstract

While the idea of the "rule of law" has a long history, only in recent years has it achieved talismanic status as the answer to some of the international community's greatest policy challenges—from armed conflict to poverty, from corruption to dictatorship. Many reasons underlie this growing popularity, including the rule of law's conceptual breadth, its solid brand name, and its purported neutrality. This chapter explores some of the definitional challenges that underlie the concept and argues for a vision of the rule of law grounded as much in the experiences of ordinary people as in the pronouncements of courts, political leaders, and academic theorists. It begins to articulate some of the possible implications—for donors, practitioners, and others in the field—of an understanding of the rule of law rooted in social culture and practice. And it recommends that advocates seize on a fortuitous and time-sensitive political opportunity—the negotiation of the post-2015 development agenda—to capitalize on the recent fascination with the rule of law in a manner that can enhance its impact.

1 New Rules for the Rule of Law

James A. Goldston

Introduction

Since 2006, tens of thousands of people have been killed in Mexico, and many more disappeared, as a war between narcotics gangs and government security forces engulfs civilians. Few perpetrators have been brought to justice. In Equatorial Guinea, a country with a per capita gross domestic product greater than those of Italy and South Korea, 60% of the population survives on less than US$1 a day, as oil revenues are siphoned off by widespread corruption. Throughout Central and Eastern Europe, Roma children are condemned to second-class education because of the color of their skin.

A common problem underlies each of these tragedies: the failure of the rule of law.

In recent years, the concept of the rule of law has been gaining increased attention in academic and political circles. A "rule of law revival" was identified fifteen years ago,[1] and the trend has only accelerated since.

Since the end of the Second World War, rule of law promotion abroad has become an increasingly common, and sometimes controversial, tool of foreign and development policy. As decolonization gathered force in the war's aftermath, successive British governments funded law schools in

I am grateful to a number of colleagues who offered helpful comments on earlier versions of this chapter (one of which was delivered in April 2013 at a panel of the American Bar Association)—in particular, Jonathan Birchall, Peter Chapman, Tracey Gurd, Shawn Sebastian, Harshani Dharmadasa, and Leah Wissow (who also undertook essential research). I am also grateful to Stephen Humphreys, as well as to the participants from the workshop sponsored by the Harvard Human Rights Program in November 2013, who offered trenchant commentary on this and other papers.

former colonies, offered scholarships for students from former colonies to study law at British universities, built courthouses and other legal infrastructure, provided technical assistance in legal drafting, and engaged in police and military training.

In the 1960s and 1970s, the rule of law was adopted as a core component of the US government's "law and development" programs in Africa and Latin America. Ultimately, these programs lost support when some of their underlying assumptions—for example, the ease and desirability of adapting US legal institutional models to other contexts, the contribution of legal education to attitudinal change, and the role of lawyers and other legal actors in leading social reform—were not borne out by experience.

The current wave of transnational rule of law promotion began in the 1980s, when the US Agency for International Development launched a series of "administration of justice" programs in Central America. These programs trained prosecutors and investigators, built and equipped prisons, and fostered cross-border efforts to combat transnational crime. A major motivation was to secure congressional support for the Reagan administration's military-dominated policies in the region.

With the transitions in Eastern Europe, Latin America, and southern Africa in the late 1980s, rule of law promotion emerged as a key element of a renewed impetus at the World Bank and a number of bilateral institutions to develop a free-market-enabling environment for private investment. Development, according to this view, depended more on markets than on aid. Although the demise of the Washington Consensus after the economic crisis in Mexico and other countries in the 1990s dented the appeal of this strategy, it retains many adherents.

In recent years, the idea of the rule of law has achieved talismanic status as the answer to many of the international community's greatest policy challenges—from armed conflict to poverty and from corruption to dictatorship. According to the United Nations' (UN) Commission on Legal Empowerment of the Poor, "[F]our billion people around the world are robbed of the chance to better their lives and climb out of poverty, because they are excluded from the rule of law." For Robert Zoellick, former president of the World Bank, "The most fundamental prerequisite for sustainable development is an effective rule of law" (Dombey 2008).

In 2012, heads of state and governments from around the world came together to "reaffirm [their] commitment to the rule of law." According to the declaration from this UN gathering, the "rule of law . . . is the foundation of friendly and equitable relations between States and the basis on which just and fair societies are built" (United Nations General Assembly 2012).[2]

In short, the rule of law has had several prior incarnations, many of them premised on the unlikely—and, to date, not wholly successful—transposition of laws and institutions as a means to other ends, whether economic development, national security, or democracy promotion. But throughout this experience, the concept has been repeatedly if perversely disentangled from the real political constraints and possibilities that shape it. Perhaps not unrelatedly, even as many rule of law practitioners have developed an "institutional checklist" of "what the rule of law is supposed to look like in practice, . . . they are less certain what the essence of the rule of law is" (Carothers 2003, 8).

This chapter begins by examining why the rule of law has attracted increasing attention and (at least rhetorical) affirmation in recent years. The second section explores some of the definitional challenges that underlie the concept. Thereafter, the third section argues for a more holistic vision of the rule of law grounded as much in the thoughts and practices of people in everyday life as in the pronouncements of courts, political leaders, and academic theorists. The fourth section then articulates some of the possible implications—for donors, practitioners, and others who seek to promote it—of an understanding of the rule of law rooted in political struggle, social culture, and practice. Finally, the chapter concludes by identifying a time-sensitive political opportunity to capitalize on the recent fascination with the rule of law: the post-2015 development agenda.

Why the Rule of Law?

Why this growing popularity of an idea that, by some accounts, has been around since the ancient Greeks?[3]

First, rule of law matters. Rule of law shortages produce more violence, less security, and diminished economic capacity. Around the world, those with the least legal protection in practice—often women, children, and ethnic, racial, and religious minorities—are condemned to the informal economy, cheated by employers, driven from their land, preyed upon by the corrupt, and victimized by violence.[4]

Yet another reason various development agencies and international actors are attracted to the concept of the rule of law is its conceptual breadth. Indeed, the term "rule of law" is sometimes so broad that anyone can embrace it.[5] This is, as others have noted, both a strength and a weakness.[6] Thus, the rule of law is praised by leaders of different persuasions who may wish to convey entirely different ideas. If US president Barack Obama and former Iranian president Mahmoud Ahmadinejad could agree on nothing else, they could both praise the rule of law.[7] Even Gambian president Yahya Jammeh (2009), who infamously threatened in September 2009 to "kill" human rights workers who criticized his government, nonetheless saw fit in a speech delivered weeks later to hail "the rule of law" as a means of addressing "the complexities of today's world."

Third, by invoking the rule of law, governments and policy makers may seek to bestow legitimacy on controversial policies. When, after years of litigation, the UK finally succeeded in mid-2013 in deporting accused terrorist Abu Qatada to Jordan with the blessing of the European Court of Human Rights, the home secretary went out of her way to

> make it clear that the Government have succeeded in deporting Qatada by respecting the rule of law at each and every stage of the process. We did not ignore court judgments we did not like. We did not act outside the law. We did what was right. And for a civilized nation, that is something of which we should be immensely proud. (May 2013)

Notwithstanding the UK government's hostility to certain decisions of the European Court[8] and its general questioning of the very architecture of European human rights protection (Chorley 2013), the home secretary considered it both important and valuable to underscore the government's commitment to "the rule of law" (May 2013).

Fourth, the rule of law carries the veneer of neutrality, of rising above partisanship. As one scholar suggests, "It is as though the association between something called 'the rule of law' and contemporary ideas of the good life has grown so strong as to inoculate efforts undertaken in its name against serious scrutiny" (Humphreys 2010, 8). Absent association with the rule of law, development projects aimed at beefing up state security agencies or promoting investment climates for private business risk sounding ideological. At its best, the rule of law's perceived neutrality serves as a foundation for discussion, if not agreement, among disparate actors. At its worst, it can be used to mask the pursuit of private interests at odds with the common good.

Fifth, even for those who see the rule of law as a means of legitimizing interference with national sovereignty, the concept serves a valuable purpose in highlighting—and offering a platform to redress—global power imbalances. The very name of the UN General Assembly's 2012 high-level meeting—"on the rule of law at the national *and international* levels"—reflects this tension (Pillay 2012). After all, some ask, if the rule of law constrains powerful individuals, should it not also limit powerful states? Thus, the 2012 UN Declaration on the Rule of Law affirms that "the rule of law applies to all States equally, and to international organizations, including the United Nations and its principal organs" and calls for "reform" of the famously unequal UN Security Council (United Nations General Assembly 2012, paras. 2, 35).

Finally, the rule of law is attractive to many because it is different from (even if intimately related to) human rights. On the one hand, for those hostile to human rights, the rule of law offers a blander, milder, and less pointed alternative. In one of its many narratives, the rule of law is understood to be primarily about matters with which many elites are comfortable—foreign investment, security, and public order. Under this view, law plays an important role in the service of power—it reinforces unequal relationships between ruler and ruled, and between rich and poor. At its narrowest, rule of law becomes rule by law (Hille 2013). By contrast, human rights are often seen as too controversial, too threatening to state sovereignty, too much about individuals, and not enough about states. Many governments allergic to the concept of rights are prepared to accept at least a state-centric conception of the rule of law. Indeed, the 2012 UN Declaration on the Rule of Law affirms such a view when it supports "all efforts to uphold the sovereign equality of all States," pledges "non-interference in the internal affairs of States," and goes so far as to bestow a right to nondiscrimination not just on individuals but also on "the State itself" (United Nations General Assembly 2012, paras. 2, 3).

Conversely, for rights advocates, the rule of law is a source of complementary strength. Whereas the rights discourse has traditionally (and productively) prioritized naming and shaming tactics, rule of law reform deploys a range of tools that span the spectrum of confrontation and collaboration. Whereas rights are about, well, rights, the rule of law is about rights, responsibilities, and enforcement concerning a broader range of issues—for example, corruption, economic inequality, climate change, foreign investment, and the law of the sea. These issues, although they have rights dimensions, extend beyond them as well.

For all of the above reasons, the rule of law is a concept whose time has come.

The Rule of Law: What Does It Mean?

When it comes to defining the rule of law, the converse of Potter Stewart's notorious description of obscenity may be true—we know it when we *don't* see it.[9] When the Hungarian prime minister casually disregards laws against the expropriation of private property in an effort to seize an attractive building on a whim, that is not the rule of law (Dempsey 2013). When a Chinese customs rule mandates the payment of a tax on every iPad brought into the country, including by Chinese tourists returning home with their own iPads purchased in China, and public officials offer no helpful information about how Chinese residents can avoid the tax, that is not the rule of law (Hua 2013). When the police force in Thailand "is an organized crime gang," or judges in Cambodia act as "proxies for the ruling political party," that is not the rule of law (Thi 2008). When a man is detained in Nigeria for more than nine years without being charged with any crime, that is not the rule of law (Open Society Justice Initiative 2011). When "[d]rug traffickers and street gangs act unimpeded as the National Police look the other way, or even run their own criminal rackets" in a country—Honduras—"believed to have the highest peacetime murder rate in the world," that is not the rule of law (Malkin 2013).

But if it is reasonably clear what the rule of law is *not,* it is less clear what the rule of law is.

If we are to give content to the rule of law, we must look beyond the 2012 UN declaration, which does not offer a definition for the concept, apart from noting, correctly, that "the independence of the judicial system, together with its impartiality and integrity, is an essential prerequisite for upholding the rule of law" (United Nations General Assembly 2012, para. 13).[10]

Some argue for a purely formalist rule of law, stripped of substantive content. Joseph Raz (1979, 211, 221) has famously written:

> A non-democratic legal system, based on the denial of human rights, on extensive poverty, on racial segregation, sexual inequalities and religious persecution, may, in principle conform to the requirements of the rule of law better than any of the legal systems of the more enlightened Western democracies. . . . It will be an immeasurably worse legal system, but it will excel in one respect: in its conformity to the rule of law. . . . The law may . . . institute slavery without violating the rule of law.

The United States in the pre-*Brown* era of state-sanctioned racial segregation, South Africa under apartheid, and Chile during the Augusto Pinochet dictatorship have been cited as examples of states that violated the rights of many citizens while upholding certain aspects of the rule of law (Barros 2003; Tamanaha 2012, 2).

Less controversially, Brian Tamanaha (2012, 233) argues that "the rule of law means that government officials and citizens are bound by and abide by the law." As he notes, this definition "does not include human rights" (ibid.). In so arguing, Tamanaha cites no lesser authority than John Rawls, who explained that, by rule of law,

I mean that its rules are public, that similar cases are treated similarly, that there are no bills of attainder, and the like. These are all features of a legal system insofar as it embodies without deviation the notion of a public system of rules addressed to rational beings for the organization of their conduct in the pursuit of their substantive interests. This concept imposes, by itself, no limits on the content of legal rules. (Rawls 1999, 118–19, quoted in Tamanaha 2012, 235)

The core of the rule of law, according to Tom Bingham (2010, 8), the widely respected British jurist who wrote a book on the topic, is that "all persons and authorities within the state, whether public or private, should be bound by and entitled to the benefit of laws publicly made, taking effect (generally) in the future and publicly administered in the courts." But Bingham "roundly reject[s]" what "some economists have called a 'thin' definition of the rule of law . . . in favour of a 'thick' definition, embracing the protection of human rights within its scope" (ibid., 67).[11]

Prior to 2012, the UN developed its own notion, defining the rule of law as

a principle of governance in which all persons, institutions and entities, public and private, including the State itself, are accountable to laws that are publicly promulgated, equally enforced and independently adjudicated, and which are consistent with international human rights norms and standards. It requires, as well, measures to ensure adherence to the principles of supremacy of law, equality before the law, accountability to the law, fairness in the application of the law, separation of powers, participation in decision-making, legal certainty, avoidance of arbitrariness and procedural and legal transparency. (United Nations Secretary-General 2004, para. 6)

"The rule of law," as the UN High Commissioner for Human Rights has observed, "constitutes the backbone for the legal protection of human rights. In addition, the rule of law itself must be grounded in human rights. . . . [R]ule of law without human rights is only an empty shell" (Pillay 2012).[12] The 2012 UN Declaration on the Rule of Law similarly "affirm[s] that human rights, the rule of law and democracy are interlinked and mutually reinforcing" (UN General Assembly 2012, para. 5).[13]

Louise Arbour (2012), former UN High Commissioner for Human Rights, has argued:

The real rule of law is substantive and encompasses many human-rights requirements. It reflects the idea of equality in a substantive way: not just that no one is above the law, but that everyone is equal before and

under the law, and is entitled to its equal protection and equal benefit.
. . . Under this substantive understanding, rules serve a higher purpose
than the mere orderly regulation of human conduct; laws must also
enhance liberty, security and equality and strive to attain a perfect balance between law and justice.

Many governments seem to agree that the rule of law has a wide thematic
remit. Or so it would seem upon examination of the list of voluntary pledges
made by states from around the world in 2012, on the occasion of the UN Declaration on the Rule of Law, to further "the rule of law at the national and international levels." To take just a few examples: Argentina pledged to "strengthen
regional atrocity prevention mechanisms"; Denmark, "to strengthen and protect
women's sexual and reproductive rights"; the European Union (EU), "to publish every two years an EU Anti-Corruption report," "to develop a framework
for raising issues of statelessness with third countries," "to pursue a civilian
approach addressing counter-terrorism globally," to "fight against the manufac-
ture of drugs and its trafficking," to counter "illicit transnational trafficking in
firearms," and "to support efforts to counter piracy and armed robbery at sea";
Kenya, to "enhance equitable access to justice," including by "operationalizing
small claims courts"; Liberia, to "establish a civilian oversight board for the
Liberian National Police"; Mexico, to train judges, magistrates, and prosecutors
"for the adequate implementation of international standards related to human
rights"; Rwanda, to "build the capacities of security organs (including community policing)"; Thailand, to ratify the Optional Protocol to the Convention
on the Rights of the Child allowing for individual communications; and the
United States, to "reduce domestic violence homicides" and "increase women's
ability to get quality evidence collection following a sexual assault."[14] This list
hardly reflects a "thin" version of the rule of law.

And yet, even arguments for a "thick" version of the rule of law must
acknowledge that the rule of law is at times in tension with human rights.
This tension was reflected in the famous assessment by the Independent International Commission on Kosovo of the 1998 NATO military intervention
in that country undertaken for humanitarian purposes. In the words of the
commission, NATO's action was "illegal but legitimate" (Independent International Commission on Kosovo 2000, 4). Similarly, in the recent debate over
Syria, the desire to end, minimize, or punish those responsible for the deaths
of tens of thousands of civilians has come up against the international legal
prohibition against military intervention except in self-defense or with UN
Security Council authorization.[15] In the view of some, the tension between,
on the one hand, the importance of military intervention to safeguard human
rights and, on the other, the absence of legal authorization is so great that, in

8

the words of former French foreign minister Bernard Kouchner, "Sometimes you have to break the law to change it" (Lowe 2013).

This tension manifests itself in many other situations as well. The September 2013 ruling by the Dominican Republic's Constitutional Court—the country's highest judicial authority—that, contrary to the American Convention on Human Rights, thousands of persons of Haitian descent must be placed in a separate registry, stripped of their Dominican nationality, and rendered stateless is only one of numerous court rulings from around the world that, while setting forth the "rules of law" on particular issues, contradict fundamental human rights norms.[16]

Similarly, the rule of law, though often seen as complementary to democracy, is at times at odds with it. The EU, a rule-based society if ever there was one, has long suffered from a perceived democratic deficit. Thus, it is commonly noted that the European Commission, the administrative arm of the EU, is "the impartial 'guardian of the treaties' that pursues the broad European interest" (Grabbe and Lehne 2013, 2)—whether in monitoring fiscal discipline by EU member states or in enforcing conditions on debtor countries that receive international assistance. This role of the European Commission, "vital to the EU's system of rule of law" (ibid., 2), demands a high degree of public trust in the institution's "impartiality" (ibid., 3)—which would, in the view of some, be endangered by efforts to make the commission more democratically accountable.[17]

Also, on occasion, the rule of law is in tension with justice. The Rome Statute of the International Criminal Court provides that one of the three different routes through which a "situation" may come before the court is through referral by the United Nations Security Council.[18] As of October 2013, two of the situations before the court—in Libya and Sudan—were referred by the Security Council. And yet many have noted the patent injustice of a mechanism that allows members of the Security Council who have not ratified the Rome Statute—and thus who have not subjected themselves to the jurisdiction to the court—to refer to the court situations from other countries that have made a similar choice.[19]

While popular understandings of the phrase "the rule of law" vary from place to place, four of them have broad resonance across many cultures. First is the rule of law as the opposite of anarchy. In this sense, the rule of law is a state of basic security and order in which people can live without constant fear. Second is the rule of law as the antipode of arbitrary power. This conception of the rule of law is captured in the Lockean formulation that "wherever law ends, tyranny begins" (Locke [1689] 1988, sec. 202). In this sense, the rule of law provides clarity and predictability, which serve as helpful guides for human behavior. Third is the rule of law as a guarantee that no one is above the law. Where the same law applies to everyone equally, the most senior perpetrators are prosecuted for abuses and the most vulnerable accused are guaranteed due process. Finally, implied in each of the foregoing are certain building blocks of legal process—access to counsel and legal advice; an independent, impartial judiciary; and, just as important, an acceptance of judicial decisions as legitimate and authoritative, even when we disagree with them.

The Cultural Dimension of the Rule of Law

Is it possible to choose from among these different versions of the rule of law? If so, how?

Some propose, for strategic or political reasons, confining the rule of law to its more limited elements. To ensure the widest possible acceptance of the rule of law, they suggest, one must discard its most controversial features, such as human rights.[20] But how does this search for universal application account for the ever-changing nature of our understanding of the rule of law over time? Why confine the rule of law to formalism if a growing portion of the world's population invests the rule of law with substantive meaning?

Alternatively, why not continue to tolerate a range of interpretations, in hopes of preserving a fragile consensus on the rhetorical value of the phrase "the rule of law"? Or should we move beyond the ambiguity of language and theory to the realm of practice in giving additional meaning to a concept that offers much unexploited potential for human well-being?

A first step might be to recall that, at its root, the rule of law is about power—or more precisely, the willingness of those with power to resolve disputes through law. Altruism is not typically the origin of the rule of law. Rather, it arises when those with the resources and ability to employ other tools to defend their interests—military force, economic bribery, political subterfuge—decide instead to resolve conflicts through recourse to law and legal institutions. Why do the powerful restrain themselves even when they do not have to? As reasoned by Machiavelli and others, they do this in order "to obtain a sustained, voluntary cooperation of well-organized groups commanding valuable resources" (Maravall and Przeworski 2003, 3). In exchange for such cooperation, "rulers will protect the interests of these groups by legal means" (ibid.).

This insight—that the rule of law is, on one level, a means of purchasing political cooperation—has a long and distinguished pedigree. It is embedded in the preamble of the Universal Declaration of Human Rights, which presciently warns: "[I]t is essential, if man is not to be compelled to have recourse, as a last resort, to rebellion against tyranny and oppression, that human rights should be protected by the rule of law."[21] As Mary Ann Glendon (2004, 1) has written, "This clause, with its allusion to the right to revolt against tyranny, emphasizes the fragility as well as the importance of the rule of law. It reminds the powerful that they ignore human rights at their peril."

Viewed in this way, the rule of law is not so much a fixed, unchanging concept as a set of cultural understandings and practices that vary depending on the organization and collective power of interests in society. In 1215, the relative sway of baronial interests extracted from King John the Magna Carta as an embodiment of what the rule of law meant at that time and in that place. Until recently, even a thin notion of the rule of law—under which government officials, like all other citizens, are accountable to the law—may have been a bridge too far for many in official circles in the Arab world. But political realities are, to say the least, changing. As a result of the courageous, rebellious acts of thousands of individuals from Cairo to Tunis, it is and will be increasingly "essential"—as a matter of both political survival and morality—"that human rights should be protected by the rule of law."[22]

The notion of a rule of law as a set of cultural understandings and practices implies a relationship between the traditional objects of rule of law promotion—laws and institutions—and the world of public consciousness and action. As many commentators have noted, too many rule of law "reforms" driven by donors and governments have suffered from a debilitating "tunnel vision" perspective that overlooks the social fabric and power relations within which laws and institutions are embedded (Golub 2003; Kleinfeld 2005).[23] Kenya is only the most recent example of a country that has reformed its laws and institutions—including a progressive new constitution, a transformed judiciary, and a revived electoral system—only to find itself continuing to struggle with problems (such as ethnic division, allegations of election fraud, and the taint of judicial corruption) rooted in inequalities of power. Even in the UK, where the 1998 Human Rights Act ushered in a revolution in legal and judicial circles previously resistant to European law, insufficient efforts at public consultation and education have meant that the act "has limited legitimacy and is vulnerable to constant attack because the people do not feel that they made the law" (Amos 2013, 400).[24] In many other places, a narrow focus on laws and institutions with little attention to the wider reality in which they exist has resulted in technical and logistical enhancements—such as new and computerized courtrooms and security agencies equipped with the latest technology—that do little to deliver more justice on the ground. Such reforms fail to address the popular aspiration for law to improve lives in concrete ways. As a journalist in Ukraine protesting repressive policies recently declared, ""I

want to live in a country where the law is not just a word in the dictionary'"
(Herszenhorn 2013).

To state the obvious, laws are adopted and institutions created, in part, because of how people think and act. And, in turn, people's behavior, as well as their assumptions of what is possible, may be influenced by the existence and shape of certain laws and institutions. While the different "tools" commonly used to promote the rule of law—such as litigation, legal advocacy, legal education, and capacity building—produce a variety of results, at least some of them, some of the time, generate changes in social thought and practice.

To take one example, until the late 1990s, bribes paid by corporate representatives to foreign government officials were tax-deductible in a number of Western democracies, including France and Germany. Over the past two decades, those provisions have been largely abolished,[25] and bribery in most places is now a penal offense. That change in the law both reflects and accentuates shifts in public attitudes toward bribery and corruption.

Similarly, over the past half century, views toward political violence have changed, such that what was once deemed the prerogative of political and military leaders is increasingly considered a crime.[26] To be sure, the causes are many. But the rapidly accruing body of international standards and jurisprudence—along with the creation of institutions such as the International Criminal Tribunal for the Former Yugoslavia, the International Criminal Tribunal for Rwanda, and the permanent International Criminal Court, themselves the result of dedicated advocacy on the part of many—has played a role.

The cultural dimension of rule of law is also seen in the impact of high court decisions on everyday reality. Volumes have been written about the range of social effects—intended and unintended, positive and negative—flowing from the US Supreme Court ruling in *Brown v. Board of Education*.[27] Changes in American attitudes toward race over the past sixty years have many roots. And yet it would be hard to deny that *Brown* contributed significantly to the delegitimation of white supremacy in American public life.

More recently, the two landmark decisions of the US Supreme Court upholding same-sex marriage,[28] both handed down in June 2013, have had important practical consequences. However, perhaps their most important effect has been, according to one commentator, "deeply emotional, potently symbolic and impossible to measure—but arguably much more sweeping. . . . [T]he court's actions set a tone. They send a signal. They alter the climate of what's considered just and what's not, of what's permissible and what's intolerable" (Bruni 2013).

To take another example, in Guatemala in May 2013, an unprecedented trial of former dictator José Efraín Ríos Montt—the first former head of state to be tried at the national level on charges of genocide—put to the test the rule of law's intention to protect the most vulnerable while holding to account the most powerful. The closely followed proceedings resonated widely outside the courtroom: "Images broadcast on national television of the ex-dictator facing witnesses from one of the poorest indigenous communities vividly demonstrated the principle that all citizens are equal before the law" (International Crisis Group 2013, i). When the Constitutional Court, just ten days after the trial court's conviction of Ríos Montt, annulled the verdict on legally questionable grounds under vocal political pressure, it reinforced what has long prevailed in Guatemala: a culture not of the rule of law but rather "of impunity in which powerful criminals have little fear of justice and victims little faith in it" (ibid., 2).

Massive human rights violations have been found to generate "spillover effects" on public expectations; these effects touch not just direct victims of murder or rape but potentially anyone living in a society where once-accepted norms have been shattered. By publicly and authoritatively reaffirming the continuing relevance of such norms, court rulings, like legislation and executive decrees, can help restore civic trust in legal rules and bodies (de Greiff 2010).[29]

> Judicial institutions, particularly in contexts in which they have traditionally been essentially instruments of power, show their trustworthiness if they can establish that no one is above the law. . . . [C]riminal trials that offer sound procedural guarantees and that do not exempt from the reach of justice those who wield power illustrate nicely the generality of law. (ibid., 3)

Even cases that do not result in final convictions of perpetrators of grave crimes can have a major impact. The arrest of former Chilean dictator Augusto Pinochet in London in 1998 and the House of Lords' vindication of the principle of accountability galvanized the filing of numerous criminal complaints in Chile, where Pinochet returned in 2000 after a prolonged legal struggle. He eventually died in 2006 without having been tried. But before his death, a significant shift in legal culture—in the sense of what the law permitted—made prosecutions of past crimes not just feasible but routine. As a result, since 2000, more than 750 members or former members of the Chilean state security forces have been prosecuted for human rights violations (Burt 2009; Roht-Arriaza 2013, 543). In retrospect, Pinochet's prolonged legal struggle had a major impact on public attitudes about the potential for law to provide redress for serious abuses.

Staff members at the Extraordinary Chambers in the Courts of Cambodia (ECCC)—the UN-backed tribunal created to prosecute and try those most responsible for the crimes of the Khmer Rouge—point to the "empowering" impact, on both lawyers and members of the public, of the visible model of professional legal practice at the ECCC. According to one staffer, before the ECCC came into existence,

> it was relatively rare for a defense lawyer to speak up on behalf of the accused in a criminal case. But that is changing. Highly competent lawyers in our court vigorously represent their clients. And that is being noticed, not just by other lawyers, but by ordinary people. This is not about the text of law, but about a deeper sense of professionalism and entitlement and the definition of roles.[30]

To be sure, not all impacts of rule of law promotion are positive. The very same ECCC project has been criticized by many, including my own organization, for offering a model of judicial independence unduly compromised by internal corruption, donor fatigue, and, most tellingly, open Cambodian government opposition to any but a small number of politically convenient prosecutions and trials.[31] More generally, a critical weakness of the contemporary international human rights system is the dismal record of state implementation of and compliance with the judgments of regional human rights tribunals, the "views" of UN treaty bodies, and the orders of international criminal courts.[32] The cumulative effect of court judgments that are routinely ignored or defied is the depreciation of the very notion that law rules. Repeated judicial condemnations of rights violations that yield no change in practice undermine the rule of law by demonstrating its powerlessness.

And, of course, the relationship between institutional or legal change and shifts in public practices and attitudes is neither linear nor one-way. Nor is the notion of "culture" a panacea—for law or other phenomena. Indeed, "culture" is frequently deployed to disparage entire communities through the use of stereotypes—whether in the modern American conservative critique of social welfare policies for purportedly creating a "culture of dependency" among the poor,[33] the common European trope associating Roma "culture" with crime, or the British attorney general's recent warning that politicians must "wake up" to the "favour culture" of corruption that allegedly afflicts "the Pakistani community" and other immigrant communities ("Corruption Problem among Some UK Minorities" 2013).

Nonetheless, for good and ill, the rule of law's cultural manifestations are many and diverse. Around the world, grassroots and other actors are giving meaning to the concept of the rule of law in ways that are rooted in local context, with effects that may be felt more widely. In Liberia, paralegals have helped clients secure the return of corruptly confiscated assets, pressed for the prosecution of perpetrators responsible for violent crimes, and obtained the enforcement of a law granting women inheritance rights (Carter Center 2013). From Indonesia (Haryanto 2012) and the Philippines (Open Society Justice Initiative 2012) to Mozambique (Birchall 2012) and Uganda (International Fund for Agricultural Development 2013), community advocates with some legal training have protected or expanded rights of access to land (Knight et al. 2012). Public interest lawyers in South Africa have won health care for people living with HIV,[34] and others in Latin America have extended public access to government-held information and secured legal recognition of the right to truth about past abuses (Mendel 2009).

Each of these efforts concerns specific issues—access to land, health care, education, and citizen security. But they are also about the use of law as a tool to secure and defend these interests. As one member of a community in Sierra Leone remarked about a nongovernmental organization founded to provide legal assistance, "Before [the organization existed], people who didn't have money to sue to the chiefs or court resorted to either fighting or swearing or sorcery as a way of investigating or satisfying their desire to seek justice" (Dale 2009).

In short, "the rule of law is both a product of, and a contributor to, a culture of respect for law and reason that is nurtured as much in local communities as in international courts" (Glendon 2004, 2). Action by civil society—through public complaints, petitions, and lawsuits—is often necessary to bring legal principles to life.[35] To take one example, for years, the European Convention on Human Rights contained a clear guarantee of nondiscrimination in access to education that went largely unenforced.[36] For Roma children in particular, the disproportionate assignment to—indeed, segregation in—ethnically separate and educationally substandard schools and classes was the accepted norm. Only when, in the late 1990s, Roma children and parents, supported by civil society organizations, filed formal complaints with the authorities to challenge such practices, and then went to court to seek redress, did many people—in government, the courts, and the private sector—take note of the disconnect between the convention's legal guarantee and the reality for thousands of schoolchildren. Bridging that gap between law and reality remains an incomplete task. But from the Czech Republic to Hungary, from Croatia to Greece, the discussion about educational policy, racial discrimination, and equal opportunity has been engaged, and the rule of law has become, for some, more than a lofty and unattainable ideal.[37]

Over time, the repeated recourse to law and legal institutions as a source of redress will, it is hoped, increase respect for, and the legitimacy of, law itself. The process will be more successful in some places, and less so in others. And it will take decades, if not generations.[38] But wherever it is pursued, this struggle must be at least as much about the way people think and act as about the adoption of laws and the building of institutions, important though they are.

Putting a More Meaningful Rule of Law into Practice

What are some of the possible implications of an understanding of the rule of law rooted in social culture and practice for practitioners, policy makers, donors, and others who seek to promote it?

First, a more holistic vision of the rule of law rejects the false but common perception that rule of law promotion "abroad"—that is, in countries other than where donor institutions are based—is fundamentally different from the search for rule of law "at home." The rule of law is a work in progress everywhere.[39] While history remains a relevant indicator, no country or region has a monopoly on the rule of law—or its absence. In this regard, it is heartening that, in September 2012, the European Commission announced the introduction of a "Justice Scoreboard" as an "effective mechanism . . . to enforce respect for the rule of law" (General Secretariat of the Council, 2012). The scoreboard is intended to assess and compare justice systems among the twenty-seven member states of the EU on the basis of "strength, efficiency and reliability" (Nielsen 2012). Similarly, the World Justice Project (2013)—an organization that monitors the rule of law worldwide—has noted problems in Europe and North America, just as it has in parts of Africa, Asia, and Latin America (see also Dumas 2012). Organizations that work on different aspects of the rights and justice agenda in their own countries—for example, the American Civil Liberties Union in the United States, the Center for Legal and Social Studies in Argentina, the Egyptian Initiative for Personal Rights, and the Legal Resources Centre in South Africa—are, in substance if not always in name, promoting the rule of law.

Second, in this field, doing is often the best way to teach and to learn. While training, skills building, and institutional modeling can be useful when undertaken with adequate attention to context, some of the most effective rule of law promotion occurs through the demonstrative effect of direct action—monitoring, litigation, and advocacy—in support of the rule of law. The arrest and charge of former Peruvian dictator Alberto Fujimori (Burt

2009); the adoption, following a ten-year-long civil society campaign, of a national law guaranteeing public access to government-held information in Nigeria (United States Agency for International Development 2012); and a US Supreme Court decision affirming the judiciary's purview to rule on the constitutionality of military tribunals[40] were all events of significance in their own right, which communicated to justice actors and the wider public not only the meaning of the rule of law but also the fact that it is possible to achieve. At a more micro level, using legal and other tools to secure a child's admission to school, to document a person's legal residence, or to release an unjustly detained individual can have similar resonance and meaning—both for the persons at issue and the broader communities in which they live.

Third, a vigorous, enabled, and secure civil society sector is often a key factor in sustainable rule of law promotion over the long term. Government is far from monolithic, and numerous well-intended, highly capable persons enter public service. But they often require assistance from external allies—in business, labor, religion, the bar, and the nonprofit sector—in contending with the shifting vagaries of political reality to foster enduring rule of law reforms.

Fourth, to ensure that a vision of the rule of law grounded in practice and local context has impact, governments and other donors must put their money where their mouths are. The louder the official rhetoric on behalf of the rule of law, the starker the gap in funding to support it. Though the US Agency for International Development budgeted close to US$300 million to foster "rule of law and human rights" overseas in fiscal year 2010, it spent far more on other items: close to $6 billion on health; over $1 billion each on education, infrastructure, and agriculture; over $500 million on "private sector competitiveness"; and over $400 million on counternarcotics.

Government spending on the judiciary is insufficient in many countries.[41] International and regional rights tribunals are starved for resources. As a result, victims must frequently wait between five and seven years for judgments to be handed down.

While resources alone are not the answer to rule of law deficits, such penury is counterproductive. If the rule of law is not itself a sufficient reason to fund justice mechanisms, the cost of unremedied abuses to good governance and global development should be. Injustice without remedy can lead to violence and instability. As a recent World Bank report concludes, poverty rates are 20% higher in countries affected by repeated cycles of violence (de Greiff 2010, 5).[42] Investing in lawyers and judges on the front end—and developing more nuanced understandings of the sources of injustice and of appropriate responses—is often more cost-effective than providing soldiers and peacekeepers on the back end. Even in wealthier countries, over time, the failure to prevent and, where necessary, redress rights violations corrodes public faith in the government.

And while more resources are needed, investment in justice need not be expensive. In the Democratic Republic of the Congo, mobile courts have fairly tried and convicted army soldiers for mass rape in far less time and at a fraction of the cost of international tribunals (Open Society Justice Initiative 2013c). In Nigeria, recent law graduates placed in police stations have freed hundreds of persons who otherwise faced months, if not years, languishing needlessly in pretrial detention (Ibe 2012). In Sierra Leone, members of rural communities trained as paralegals for far less than the price of a lawyer have resolved land disputes and won community access to roads, electricity, and environmental cleanup (Open Society Justice Initiative 2013a; see also Maru, this volume).

Fifth, rule of law reformers must address the growing perception of double standards in the application of the rule of law—in other words, the perception that there is not one rule of law but two: one for the powerful and another for everyone else (National Intelligence Council, 2012).

The widespread perception of partiality impairs the rule of law's appeal.

Thus, many ask what allegiance is owed a norm—whether the Kyoto Treaty or the International Criminal Court's Rome Statute—from which some of the most powerful governments exempt themselves. Why should some governments hold to account perpetrators of serious crimes when others have made clear that they will not? And why, many have asked, should we heed the decisions of courts that address abuses in only some places (such as Kenya, Sudan, or the Democratic Republic of the Congo) while ignoring other situations of commensurate gravity (as in Gaza or Syria)?

The perception of double standards in applying the rule of law internationally is exacerbated by both the structure of international aid—dominated by Western donors and implementers applying Western models—and the funding practices of the international donor community. For too long, foreign policy and political interests (whether fostering a better climate for investment, gathering intelligence, or promoting legal practices or institutional models specific to one national tradition) have unduly influenced government decisions about how to allocate scarce resources. It is not at all clear that the rise of new funders, including Brazil and China, is fundamentally changing this dynamic. The perceived bias of rule of law promotion at the national level is heightened further by the resistance of the most powerful states to an international legal regime that more closely approximates evenly and impartially applied rules, whether through binding judgments of the International Court of Justice or reform of the unequal UN Security Council.

This perceived bias is particularly damaging given the centrality of concepts such as universality, independence, and impartiality to the rule of law. And the inconsistency between aspiration and practice is all the more apparent and unacceptable in a world that is rapidly becoming multipolar. Arguments about the "indispensable" quality of certain countries' contributions to global stability—which have been used to justify (in some eyes) individualized exemptions from international agreements on accountability (Dobbs and Goshko1996)[43]—hold less water as other powers increasingly share responsibility for keeping the peace.

Finally, and relatedly, rule of law promotion requires attention not just to capacity building but also to the generation and maintenance of political will. If the rule of law is fundamentally about constraining the exercise of power, technical fixes will not be sufficient. The fight for an independent judiciary, for the right to counsel, and for the presumption of innocence is a political act.

The Rule of Law and the Post-2015 Development Agenda

The pursuit of a rule of law grounded in the reality of everyday problems, animated by universal aspirations yet capable of curbing the exercise of arbitrary power by the highest officials, must take place at many levels. From a police stop to a courthouse hearing, from town halls to UN headquarters, from Sidi Bouzid to the streets of New York, the rule of law is present—both as it is and as it could be. Though frustration with law's impotence and unfulfilled promise is widespread, it is impossible to say precisely when or where the next explosion of collective anguish will erupt—only that it will. And yet, a major opportunity to capitalize on the recent fascination with the rule of law is on the horizon: the post-2015 development agenda.

In September 2000, world leaders came together to proclaim, in the Millennium Declaration, that "the central challenge we face today is to ensure that globalization becomes a positive force for all the world's people" (United Nations General Assembly 2000, para. 5). The declaration pledged the UN General Assembly's commitment to a set of ambitious, time-bound, measurable goals to promote development and reduce poverty. But it also identified a number of other "key objectives" (ibid., para. 7), including to further peace and security, protect the environment, and "promote democracy and strengthen the rule of law, as well as respect for all internationally recognized human rights and fundamental freedoms" (ibid., para. 24).

In 2001, when the declaration was operationalized into the Millennium Development Goals, the rule of law, human rights, democracy, and the environment were left out. Nonetheless, the MDGs, as they have become known, have had a substantial impact in their respective fields. By 2010, five years before their deadline, the overarching goal of halving extreme poverty had been met. In part as a result of MDG-linked funding, primary education enrollment rates have increased measurably, particularly in South Asia and sub-Saharan Africa. MDG-related health gains with regard to malaria and HIV/AIDS have led to big reductions in child mortality, from Cambodia to Rwanda to Senegal (McArthur 2013, 160).

At the same time, the absence of the rule of law has been telling. Conflict-affected states—those, by definition, where the rule of law is lacking—account for disproportionately high percentages of the developing world's poor and uneducated, as well as of infant deaths (Robinson, Rudd, and Cheng-Hopkins 2013). In advanced economies, too, those portions of the population denied access to justice suffer from higher levels of discrimination in education and other public services.

How might both the popular ascendancy and a richer understanding of the rule of law encourage its inclusion in the post-2015 development framework? And how can this framework avoid instrumentalizing the rule of law as simply a means to developmental ends, instead promoting it as a value both integral to sustainable human development and important in its own right?

First, one might look to theory. The rule of law has become more directly relevant to development, in part because development concepts have broadened in recent years beyond purely economic concerns. Development theory—whether through the "capabilities approach" of Amartya Sen (1999) and Martha Nussbaum (2011), the notion of "human development" embodied in annual United Nations Development Programme *Human Development Reports* and the World Bank's 2011 *World Development Report*, or the "rights-based approach to development" pursued within UN agencies (see generally Office of the High Commissioner for Human Rights 2006; United Nations Development Group 2003; United Nations Children's Fund 2003)—is increasingly tackling questions of governance, peace and security, and indicators of human well-being. In short, the rule of law is increasingly seen as an essential foundation for human development.

Second, this conceptual evolution reflects recent experience. The eruptions in the Arab world since 2011 offer further evidence of the interrelated nature of the rule of law and development in practice. A common slogan of the popular revolt in Egypt that led to the downfall of Hosni Mubarak—"bread, dignity, and social justice"—underscored that, in many people's minds, the rule of law and development are not unrelated goods but different aspects of a comprehensive aspiration for a better life. Today, even as the military reconsolidates power following the Morsi government's abortive, troubled democratic experiment, popular demands for the prosecution of police violence persist alongside economic discontent.[44]

Recent developments further question the continuing relevance of notions of development divorced from concerns for justice and the rule of law. As the UN Special Rapporteur on the promotion of truth, justice, reparation and guarantees of non-recurrence has observed:

> Some of the countries in the Middle East and North Africa region were widely seen to be successfully progressing in the achievement of the [Millennium Development Goals] . . . . In Tunisia, national income trebled in the three decades to 2010; almost all Tunisian children attended school; child mortality was significantly lower and life expectancy significantly higher than the average for countries at a similar income level. . . . Tunisia is the most obvious example of a dilemma within the original Millennium Development Goal framework: rapid Millennium Development Goal progress completely failed to predict widespread popular discontent. (de Greiff 2013, paras. 12–13)

Nor has stunning progress in traditional measures of economic development forestalled eruptions of social discontent and instability in other countries.[45]

In the past, efforts to ground economic growth in the development of effective institutions capable of protecting property rights, resisting or combating corruption, insuring functioning commercial law, and fostering fair arbitration procedures have been "mostly based on guesses and assumptions and remain[] largely unproven" (Kleinfeld 2012, 53). But evidence of the linkages between efforts to promote the rule of law and development outcomes is slowly accumulating. A study presented during the September 2013 "Global Dialogue on the Rule of Law and the Post-2015 Development Agenda," sponsored by the United Nations Development Programme, found that "the components of rule of law" as defined in the annual survey of the World Justice Project, "powerfully predict development."[46] Gradually (albeit unevenly), policy makers are increasingly appreciating the positive impacts of the rule of law on fostering more inclusive and effective human development.[47]

Increasing opportunities for members of marginalized communities to understand and utilize legal tools yields tangible developmental impact. Institutions run efficiently and effectively when people have information about, and the agency to utilize, the laws and regulations that govern their lives. For example, civil society efforts focused on raising women's awareness of rights and responsibilities around marriage have been reported to help decrease the size and frequency of illegal dowry payments in Bangladesh (Asian Development Bank 2001, 135, 141, 145). In Ecuador, the expansion of access to legal information and advice helped address physical violence against women, enabling many to live more secure lives (Rodríguez 2003).

Similarly, enhanced awareness of legal tools has positively affected health delivery outcomes in several ways: by providing a framework for partnerships among affected communities, government institutions, and service providers; by expanding access to essential information about what services are available, where, and when; and by enhancing accountability through the establishment of redress mechanisms (Open Society Justice Initiative 2013b). In Uganda, a World Bank partnership with the government and civil society that employed legal empowerment and education techniques reportedly improved both the quality of service delivery and user health outcomes (Björkman and Svensson 2009).

A judicially enforceable right to information (RTI) also plays a critical role in ensuring government accountability. People in many countries have used such a right to monitor public spending and advocate for change. In Chiapas, Mexico, rural community members found out through RTI requests that a government sewage project had been contaminating local water. With that information, they successfully advocated for authorities to halt the project and install proper filter systems (Dokeniya 2013). Slum dwellers in India have also used RTI requests to ensure the equitable delivery of state entitlements. According to a recent study, 94% of ration-card applicants in New Delhi who filed RTI inquiries into the status of their applications received their cards within a year, as opposed to the 21% of those who did not file an RTI petition (Open Society Foundations 2013).

Legal identity is similarly crucial for people to participate meaningfully in public life. Basic legal protections often are not effective for those who lack identity documents. Legal identity documentation has been found by the Inter-American Development Bank to be a "determining and aggravating factor for social, economic, and political exclusion—for men and women alike" (Harbitz and Tamargo 2009). Several projects underway—involving Nubians in Kenya (Namati 2013), persons of Haitian descent in the Dominican Republic (see Open Society Justice Initiative 2013e), and Roma in Macedonia[48] and Serbia (see United Nations High Commissioner for Refugees 2011)—successfully deploy low-cost, community-based paralegal schemes to secure legal identity documents, including birth certificates and identification cards, essential for access to citizenship, education, and health care.

For many of the world's poor, land is their greatest asset. Some research suggests that rule of law programs, by helping secure or consolidate land rights, have contributed to environmental sustainability, slowed deforestation, and enhanced food security. In Mozambique, Liberia, and Uganda, paralegal-facilitated community land-titling programs have been shown to improve the accountability of local officials, promote more sustainable land governance, and foster more secure land tenure for communities (Knight et al. 2012). A study of eighty forest areas across Africa, Asia, and Latin America found that greater rule-making autonomy at the local level was associated with high carbon storage and livelihood benefits (Chatre and Agrawal 2009, 17667–70).

And the use of legal tools to combat discrimination and segregation in education has, though slowly and unevenly, improved educational access for minority children in certain contexts.[49]

The case is far from definitively proven. And yet across a growing range of fields, rule of law tools and methods have, apparently, contributed to enhanced development outcomes.

The debate over the next generation of MDGs is underway. In June 2013, a high-level UN panel, cochaired by British prime minister David Cameron, Liberian president Ellen Johnson Sirleaf, and Indonesian president Susilo Bambang Yudhoyono, offered a set of ambitious recommendations under-scoring the fundamental roles of "open and accountable institutions for all"—which "encourage," among other goods, "the rule of law"—as "ends as well as means" of a new development agenda (United Nations 2013a, executive summary). The panel's report makes clear that "[p]ersonal security, access to justice, freedom from discrimination and persecution, and a voice in the decisions that affect their lives are development outcomes as well as enablers" (ibid., 9). The report offers a set of illustrative targets to foster "good gover-nance and effective institutions," as well as "stable and peaceful societies," including in the areas of universal legal identity, freedom of speech and asso-ciation, the right to information, combating corruption, and reductions in violence (ibid., 31). Further reflecting the underlying vision of development as rooted in a vigorous rule of law, the report calls on states to "ensure justice institutions are accessible, independent, well-resourced and respect due pro-cess rights" (ibid., 31).

In July 2013, the UN Secretary-General (2013, para. 95) put forth a vision for a post-2015 development agenda, reminding states that

> [t]here can be no peace without development and no development with-out peace. Lasting peace and sustainable development cannot be fully realized without respect for human rights and the rule of law. Trans-parency and accountability are powerful tools for ensuring citizens' involvement in policymaking and their oversight of the use of public

resources, including to prevent waste and corruption. Legal empowerment, access to justice and an independent judiciary and universal legal
identification can also be critical for gaining access to public services.

In September 2013, the UN General Assembly underscored "the need for a
coherent approach" to the post-2015 development agenda, which, among other
aims, should "promote peace and security, democratic governance, the rule of
law, gender equality and human rights for all" (United Nations 2013b, 3).

The General Assembly's debate will continue through 2015. There are
many good reasons to include the rule of law—whether under its own name
or that of a sister moniker, such as "access to justice"—in the next generation of MDGs. These include its contributions not just to the more effective
implementation of human rights but also to sustainable development, poverty
reduction, and citizen security and empowerment. And not unimportantly,
bringing the rule of law into the global development framework would go a
long way toward reviving the unified framing of rights and human development, which, with such promise, underpinned the Millennium Declaration.

And there are many ways to do so. It could be a goal in its own right,
reflecting the fact that, as world leaders reaffirmed in 2012, the rule of law is
of "fundamental importance for political dialogue and cooperation among all
States and for the further development of the three main pillars upon which
the United Nations is built: international peace and security, human rights
and development" (United Nations General Assembly 2012). The rule of law
also could be integrated into concrete and measurable targets, such as dou-
bling, over the next decade, the number of people who enjoy access to legal
advice at low or no cost, or halving the number of people who have no legal
identity. In addition, rule of law indicators—measuring, for example, whether
national legislation authorizes the provision of medication necessary to treat
certain health conditions or the education of all children of a certain age;
whether legal frameworks are in place to resolve disputes over access to medicine or education; and whether provisions guaranteeing access to health care
or schooling are enforced equally and without discrimination—could be used
to facilitate progress toward other goals, whether with respect to education,
health care, or poverty reduction.[50]

But perhaps the most important reason to include the rule of law in the
post-2015 development framework is that it is the right thing to do. A culture of respect for the rule of law remains both an essential foundation for
human well-being and a distant goal in many places. Since the first MDGs
were promulgated a dozen years ago, rule of law emergencies have continued

to arise—from the terrorist violence of 9/11 to the overreaction of rendition and torture; from civil war in Syria to the collapse of social order in parts of Iraq, Pakistan, and the Democratic Republic of the Congo; and from worsening underdevelopment in parts of the developing world to growing exclusion and inequality in the global North. Failure to incorporate the rule of law into the post-2015 MDGs would signal that these phenomena are acceptable. As the idea of a more vibrant and resilient rule of law gains currency, states have a chance to give more concrete meaning to this elusive, and increasingly attractive, phrase.

Conclusion

The rule of law embodies the enduring tension between hope and reality in the realm of justice. Neither mere politics nor pristine principle, the rule of law rests in a contested space in between.[51] The contest is complicated by the concept's dual nature as a simultaneous instrument of and constraint upon state power. As E. P. Thompson has written:

> The essential precondition for the effectiveness of law, in its function as ideology, is that it shall display an independence from gross manipulation and shall seem to be just. It cannot seem to be so without upholding its own logic and criteria of equity; indeed, on occasion by actually *being* just. (1975, 262–63, emphasis in original)

It is in the working out, in particular places at particular times, of the dialectic relationship between law and justice that the promotion of the rule of law acquires its meaning in practice. Advancing the agenda for rule of law promotion involves breaking down artificial walls between the rule of law at home and abroad, mustering and efficiently deploying the necessary economic resources, removing from the rule of law discourse the double standards that unfairly privilege some parties at the expense of others, enabling civil society to play a central role in the construction of the rule of law, and acknowledging the inherently political nature of the struggle to secure an ideal grounded in the myth of independence from politics.

This is a project at once local and global, urgently needed yet generational in scale, engaging the highest authorities and the common citizen. And though it will continue to inhabit lofty promises and sweeping visions, its progress will be measured less in grand rhetoric than in the everyday experiences of ordinary people across all walks of life.

References

Abel, Richard. 1995. *Politics by Other Means: Law in the Struggle Against Apartheid, 1980-1994.* New York: Routledge.

Ahmadinejad, Mahmoud. 2012. "Piers Morgan Tonight: Interview with President Mahmoud Ahmadinejad." *CNN*, September 24. http://transcripts.cnn.com/TRANSCRIPTS/1209/24/pmt.01.html.

Aldridge, Alex. 2011. "Can 'physically ill' David Cameron find a cure for his European law allergy?" *The Guardian*, May 6. http://www.theguardian.com/law/2011/may/06/david-cameron-european-law-allergy.

Amos, Merris. 2013. "Transplanting Human Rights Norms: The Case of the United Kingdom's Human Rights Act." *Human Rights Quarterly* 35:386–407.

Aptel, Cecile. 2012. "Prosecutorial Discretion at the ICC and Victims' Right to Remedy: Narrowing the Impunity Gap." *Journal of International Criminal Justice* 10:1357–75.

Arbour, Louise, 2012. "The Rule of Law." *The New York Times*, September 26. http://www.nytimes.com/2012/09/27/opinion/UN-general-assembly-on-the-rule-of-law.html?_r=0.

Aristotle. 1941. "Politics." In *The Basic Works of Aristotle*, edited by Richard McKeon, 1127–325. New York: Random House.

Asian Development Bank. 2001. *Legal Empowerment: Advancing Good Governance and Poverty Reduction.* Manila: Asian Development Bank.

Barros, Robert. 2003. "Dictatorship and the Rule of Law: Rules and Military Power in Pinochet's Chile." *Democracy and the Rule of Law* 5:188–219.

Bingham, Tom. 2010. *The Rule of Law.* London: Penguin Group.

Birchall, Jonathan. 2012. "Reverence and Transformation: Q&A on Legal Empowerment with Vivek Maru of Namati." *Open Society Foundations*, February 13. http://www.opensocietyfoundations.org/voices/reverence-and-transformation-qa-on-legal-empowerment-with-vivek-maru-of-namati.

Björkman, Martina, and Jakob Svensson. 2009. "Power to the People: Evidence from a Randomized Field Experiment on Community-Based Monitoring in Uganda." *The Quarterly Journal of Economics* 124:735–69.

Bruni, Frank. 2013. "The Court's Immeasurable Impact." *New York Times*, June 26. http://www.nytimes.com/2013/06/27/opinion/bruni-the-courts-immeasurable-impact.html?_r=0.

Burt, Jo-Marie. 2009. "Guilty as Charged: The Trial of Former Peruvian President Alberto Fujimori for Human Rights Violations." *International Journal of Transitional Justice* 3:384–405.

Cameron, David. 2012. "Combating Poverty at Its Roots." *The Wall Street Journal*, November 1. http://online.wsj.com/article/SB10001424052970204712904578090571423009066.html.

Carothers, Thomas. 1998. "The Rule of Law Revival." *Foreign Affairs*, March 1. http://www.foreignaffairs.com/articles/53809/thomas-carothers/the-rule-of-law-revival.

———. 2003. "Promoting the Rule of Law Abroad: The Problem of Knowledge." Working Paper 34. Carnegie Endowment for International Peace Rule of Law Series.

Carter Center. 2013. "Liberia: Improving Access to Justice." Accessed December 2. http://www.cartercenter.org/peace/conflict_resolution/liberia-access-justice. html.

Chatre, Ashwini, and Arun Agrawal. 2009. "Trade-Offs and Synergies between Carbon Storage and Livelihood Benefits from Forest Commons." *PNAS* 106:17667–70.

"Chipping at the Foundations." 2012. *The Economist*, June 9. http://www.economist. com/node/21556599.

Chorley, Matt. 2013. "Cameron Reveals Britain Could Leave Human Rights Convention." *Daily Mail*, September 29. http://www.dailymail.co.uk/news/article-2437179/We-able-chuck-people-threaten-country-Cameron-reveals-Britain-leave-human-rights-convention.html#ixzz2n22jQREG.

Commission on Legal Empowerment of the Poor. 2008. *Making the Law Work for Everyone: Volume II*. New York: Commission on Legal Empowerment of the Poor and United Nations Development Programme.

"Corruption Problem among Some UK Minorities, Says MP." 2013. *BBC News*, November 23. http://www.bbc.co.uk/news/uk-politics-25062450.

Dale, Pamela. 2009. *Delivering Justice to Sierra Leone's Poor: An Analysis of the Work of Timap for Justice*. Washington, DC: World Bank.

de Greiff, Pablo. 2010. Transitional Justice, Security, and Development. World Development Report 2011 Background Paper.

———. 2013. Promotion of Truth, Justice, Reparation and Guarantees of Non-recurrence. UN doc. A/68/345.

Dempsey, Judy. 2013. "A Bus Ride with Viktor Orban." *The International Herald Tribune*, May 13.

Devarajan, Shantayanan, and Wolfgang Fengler. 2013. "Africa's Economic Boom." *Foreign Affairs*, May/June.

Dicker, Richard. 2012. "A Flawed Court in Need of Credibility." *New York Times*, May 21. http://www.nytimes.com/2012/05/22/opinion/a-flawed-court-in-need-of-credibility.html.

Dobbs, Michael, and John Goshko. 1996. "Albright's Personal Odyssey Shaped Foreign Policy Beliefs." *The Washington Post*, December 6. http://www.washington-post.com/wp-srv/politics/govt/admin/stories/albright120696.htm.

Dokeniya, Anupama. 2013. "Implementing Right to Information: Lessons from Experience." Washington, DC: World Bank.

Dombey, Daniel. 2008. "World Bank Chief Calls for Rethink over Failed States." *Financial Times*, September 12.

"DR Congo: UN Officials Cite Progress in Rule of Law, but Also Continued Rights Abuses in the East." 2013. *UN News Centre*, September 25. http://www.un.org/apps/news/story.asp?NewsID=45999#.UqDw7dKkrcB.

"Draft Declaration on British ECHR Reform Plans Leaked—Antoine Buyse."
2012. *UK Human Rights Blog*, February 29. http://ukhumanrightsblog.
com/2012/02/29/draft-declaration-on-british-echr-reform-plans-leaked-
antoine-buyse.

Dumas, Claudia. 2012. "Taking Stock of Corruption in the U.S. and Worldwide: TI's
Corruption Perceptions Index." *World Justice Project Blog*, December 12. http://
www.worldjusticeproject.org/blog/taking-stock-corruption-us-and-worldwide-
ti's-corruption-perceptions-index.

Gateway Corruption Assessment Index. 2014. "World Bank's Country Policy and
Institutional Assessment." http://gateway.transparency.org/tools/detail/225.

General Secretariat of the Council. 2012. "Council and Commission Statements: Political Situation in Romania." September 13. http://register.consilium.europa.eu/
pdf/en/12/st13/st13780.en12.pdf.

Glaberson, William. 2013. "Justice Denied: Inside the Bronx's Dysfunctional Court
System." *New York Times*, April 13. http://www.nytimes.com/2013/04/14/
nyregion/justice-denied-bronx-court-system-mired-in-delays.html?_r=0.

Glendon, Mary Ann. 2004. "The Rule of Law in the Universal Declaration of Human
Rights." *The Northwestern Journal of International Human Rights* 2:1–19.

Goldsmith, Jack. 2003. "The Self-Defeating International Criminal Court." *The University of Chicago Law Review* 70:89–104.

———. 2013. "What Happened to the Rule of Law?" *The New York Times*, August 31.

Goldston, James A. 2011. "Justice Delayed and Denied." *The International Herald Tribune*, October 13.

Golub, Stephen. 2003. "Beyond Rule of Law Orthodoxy: The Legal Empowerment
Alternative." Working Paper 41. Carnegie Endowment for International Peace
Rule of Law Series.

Grabbe, Heather, and Stefan Lehne. 2013. *The 2014 European Elections: Why a Partisan Commission President Would Be Bad for the EU*. London: Centre for European
Reform.

Harbitz, Mia, and Maria del Carmen Tamargo. 2009. *The Significance of Legal Identity
in Situations of Poverty and Social Exclusion: The Link between Gender, Ethnicity, and
Legal Identity*. Washington, DC: Inter-American Development Bank.

Haryanto, Ulma. 2012. "For Indonesia's Poor, Paralegals Pave the Way for Justice."
Jakarta Globe, January 25. http://www.thejakartaglobe.com/home/for-indone-
sias-poor-paralegals-pave-the-way-to-justice/493419.

Herszenhorn, David. 2013. "Ukraine in Turmoil After Leaders Reject Major E.U.
Deal." *New York Times*, November 26. http://www.nytimes.com/2013/11/27/
world/europe/protests-continue-as-ukraine-leader-defends-stance-on-europe.
html?hpw&rref=business.

Hille, Kathrin. 2013. "Putin Tightens Grip on Legal System." *Financial Times*, November 27. http://www.ft.com/cms/s/0/a4209a42-5777-11e3-b615-00144feabdc0.
html#axzz2mE55dZXU.

Holmes, Stephen. 2003. "Lineages of the Rule of Law." In *Democracy and the Rule of
Law*, edited by José María Maravall and Adam Przeworski, 19–61. Cambridge:
Cambridge University Press.

Hua, Yu. 2013. "In China, Power Is Arrogant." *New York Times*, May 8.

Humphreys, Stephen. 2010. *Theatre of the Rule of Law: Transnational Legal Intervention in Theory and Practice.* Cambridge: Cambridge University Press.

Ibe, Stanley. 2012. "Making Legal Aid Work in Nigeria's Police Stations." *Open Society Justice Initiative Voices*, November 7. http://www.opensocietyfoundations.org/voices/making-legal-aid-work-nigerias-police-stations.

Independent International Commission on Kosovo. 2000. *The Kosovo Report.* Oxford: Oxford University Press.

International Bar Association and International Legal Assistance Consortium. 2009. *Rebuilding Courts and Trust: An Assessment of the Needs of the Justice System in the Democratic Republic of Congo.* London and Stockholm: International Bar Association and International Legal Assistance Consortium.

International Criminal Court. 2013. "Situations and Cases." Accessed December 2. http://www.icc-cpi.int/en_menus/icc/situations%20and%20cases/Pages/situations%20and%20cases.aspx.

International Crisis Group. 2013. *Justice on Trial in Guatemala: The Rios Montt Case.* Brussels: International Crisis Group.

International Fund for Agricultural Development. 2013. "International Land Coalition: Knowledge Programme; Uganda." Accessed December 2. http://www.ifad.org/program/kpulalric.htm.

Jammeh, Yahya. 2009. "Statement at the General Debate of the 64th Session of the United Nations General Assembly." September 24. http://www.un.org/en/ga/64/generaldebate/pdf/GM_en.pdf.

Johnson, Rucker C. 2011. "Long-Run Impacts of School Desegregation and School Quality on Adult Attainments." National Bureau of Economic Research Working Paper 16664.

"Justice Sequestered." Editorial. *New York Times,* July 20, 2013.

Karsten, Sjoerd. 2010. *Equal Opportunities? The Labour Market Integration of the Children of Immigrants.* Paris: Organisation for Economic Co-operation and Development.

Keating, Joshua. 2013. "Why Hasn't Assad Been Charged with War Crimes?" *Slate,* September 5. http://www.slate.com/blogs/the_world_/2013/09/05/assad_s_war_crimes_why_hasn_t_he_been_charged_with_war_crimes_by_the_international.html.

Kirkpatrick. David D. 2014. "Clashes Kill 29 Egyptians on Uprising's Anniversary." *The New York Times*, January 25.

Kirp, David. 2012. "Making Schools Work." *The New York Times*, May 19.

Kleinfeld, Rachel. 2005. "Competing Definitions of the Rule of Law: Implications for Practitioners." Working Paper 55. Carnegie Endowment for International Peace Rule of Law Series.

———. 2012. *Advancing the Rule of Law Abroad: Next Generation Reform.* Washington, DC: Carnegie Endowment for International Peace.

Knight, Rachael, Judy Adoko, Teresa Auma, Ali Kaba, Alda Salomao, Ailas Siakor, and Issufo Tankar. 2012. *Protecting Community Lands and Resources: Evidence from Liberia, Mozambique and Uganda.* Rome: International Development Law Organization.

Kohn, Sebastian. 2013. "For Roma, Justice Is Sometimes the Best Medicine." *Open Society Justice Initiative Voices*, November 13. http://www.opensocietyfoundations.org/voices/roma-justice-sometimes-best-medicine.

Locke, John. (1689) 1988. *Two Treatises of Government*. Edited by Peter Laslett. Cambridge: Cambridge University Press.

Lowe, Rebecca. 2013. "Syria: Military Intervention is Illegal: But May Be Legitimate." *IBA Global Insight*, September 6. http://www.ibanet.org/Article/Detail. aspx?ArticleUid=26cfd2b2-e6cf-4209-903c-9327c76c9bd4.

Malkin, Elisabeth. 2013. "Political Doubt Poses Risk to Honduras, Battered by Coup and Violence." *The New York Times*, November 23. http://www.nytimes. com/2013/11/23/world/americas/precarious-honduras-fears-another-bout-of-electoral-uncertainty.html.

Maravall, José María, and Adam Przeworski. 2003. "Introduction." In *Democracy and the Rule of Law*, edited by José María Maravall and Adam Przeworski, 1–18. Cambridge: Cambridge University Press.

May, Theresa. 2013. "Statement in Commons on Deportation of Abu Qatada." July 8. http://www.publications.parliament.uk/pa/cm201314/cmhansrd/cm130708/ debtext/130708-0001.htm#13070810000003.

McArthur, John W. 2013. "Own the Goals: What the Millennium Development Goals Have Accomplished." *Foreign Affairs*, March/April.

Mendel, Tobey. 2009. *The Right to Information in Latin America: A Comparative Legal Survey*. Quito: United Nations Educational, Scientific and Cultural Organization.

Mendes, Errol. 2010. *Peace and Justice at the International Criminal Court: A Court of Last Resort*. Cheltenham: Edward Edgar Publishing.

Namati. 2013. "Realizing Citizenship Rights." Accessed December 2. http://www. namati.org/work/realizing-citizenship-rights.

National Intelligence Council. 2012. *Global Trends 2030: Alternative Worlds*. Washington, DC: National Intelligence Council.

Nielsen, Nikolaj. 2012. "EU Keen to Rank Justice Systems in Member States." *EU Observer*, September 13. http://euobserver.com/justice/117535.

Nussbaum, Martha. 2011. *Creating Capabilities: The Human Development Approach*. New York: Belknap Press.

Obama, Barack. 2009. "Remarks by the President on National Security." May 21. http://www.whitehouse.gov/the-press-office/remarks-president-national-security-5-21-09.

Office of the High Commissioner for Human Rights. 2006. *Frequently Asked Questions on a Human Rights-Based Approach to Development Cooperation*. New York: Office of the High Commissioner for Human Rights.

Open Society Foundations. 2013. "Justice 2015: Justice Plays a Fundamental Role in Eliminating Poverty." Fact sheet. http://www.opensocietyfoundations.org/ sites/default/files/fact-sheet-justice-2015-21030319.pdf.

Open Society Justice Initiative. 2010. *From Judgment to Justice: Implementing International and Regional Human Rights Decisions*. New York: Open Society Foundations.

———. 2011. "Alade v. The Federal Republic of Nigeria." Last modified July 7. http:// www.opensocietyfoundations.org/litigation/alade-v-federal-republic-nigeria.

———. 2012. "Grassroots Justice: Philippines." April. http://www.opensocietyfoundations.org/multimedia/grassroots-justice-philippines.

———. 2013a. "The Global Campaign for Pretrial Justice: Improving Pretrial Justice in Sierra Leone." Fact sheet. http://www.opensocietyfoundations.org/fact-sheets/fact-sheet-pretrial-justice-and-paralegals-sierra-leone.

———. 2013b. "Justice 2015: How Justice Impacts Development." Fact sheet. http://www.opensocietyfoundations.org/fact-sheets/justice-2015-how-justice-impacts-development.

———. 2013c. *Justice in DRC: Mobile Courts Combat Rape and Impunity in Eastern Congo.* New York: Open Society Foundations.

———. 2013d. *Recent Developments at the Extraordinary Chambers in the Courts of Cambodia.* New York: Open Society Justice Initiative.

———. 2013e. "We Are Dominicans." *Open Society Justice Initiative Videos.* Accessed December 2. http://www.opensocietyfoundations.org/multimedia/we-are-dominicans.

Orentlicher, Diane F. 2008. *Shrinking the Space for Denial: The Impact of the ICTY in Serbia.* New York: Open Society Justice Initiative.

Organisation for Economic Co-operation and Development. 2008. "Budget Practices and Procedures Survey." Accessed March 23, 2014. http://webnet.oecd.org/budgeting/Budgeting.aspx.

———. 2011. "Update on Tax Legislation on the Tax Treatment of Bribes to Foreign Public Officials in Countries Parties to the OECD Anti Bribery Convention." June. http://www.oecd.org/tax/crime/41353070.pdf.

Orkin, Mark. 2013. "The Linkages Between Rule of Law and Development: An Empirical Intimation." Paper prepared for Global Dialogue on Rule of Law and Post-2015 Development Agenda, New York, September 26–27.

Pillay, Navanethem. 2012. "Statement by Ms. Navanethem Pillay, High Commissioner for Human Rights at the High Level Meeting on the Rule of Law at the National and International Level." September 24. http://www.ohchr.org/en/NewsEvents/Pages/DisplayNews.aspx?NewsID=12572&LangID=E.

Public Expenditure and Financial Accountability. 2014. "Public Expenditure and Financial Accountability." Accessed March 12. http://www.pefa.org.

Rawls, John. 1999. "Legal Obligation and the Duty of Fair Play." In *Collected Papers*, edited by John Rawls and Samuel Freeman, 118–19. Boston: Harvard University Press.

Raz, Joseph. 1979. *The Authority of Law: Essays on Law and Morality.* Oxford: Oxford University Press.

Right2Info.org. 2014. "Good Law and Practice." Accessed March 12. http://right2info.org.

Rivera, Ray. 2013. "Bronx Courts Trim Big Backlog, with Outside Judge at the Helm." *The New York Times*, July 29.

Robinson, Mary, Kevin Rudd, and Judy Cheng-Hopkins. 2013. "Same Millennium, New Goals: Why Peace, Security, Good Governance and the Rule of Law Must Be Included in the New MDGs." *Huffington Post*, March 12. http://www.huffingtonpost.com/mary-robinson/millenium-development-goals_b_2862059.html.

Rodríguez, Marcela. 2003. *Empowering Women: An Assessment of Legal Aid Under Ecuador's Judicial Reform Project. World Bank.* Washington, DC: World Bank.

Roht-Arriaza, Naomi. 2013. "Just a 'Bubble'? Perspectives on the Enforcement of International Criminal Law by National Courts." *Journal of International Criminal Justice* 11:537–43.

Ryan, Paul. 2013. "Meet the Press: Interview with David Gregory." *NBC*, January 27. http://www.nbcnews.com/id/50605316.

Sen, Amartya. 1999. *Development as Freedom.* New York: Alfred A. Knopf.

Shklar, Judith. 1998. *Political Thought and Political Thinkers.* Chicago: University of Chicago Press.

Sikkink, Kathryn, and Hun Joon Kim. 2013. "The Justice Cascade: The Origins and Effectiveness of Prosecutions of Human Rights Violations." *Annual Review of Law and Social Science* 9:269–85.

Simons, Marlisle. 2013. "U.S. Grows More Helpful to International Criminal Court, a Body It First Scorned." *The New York Times*, April 2. http://www.nytimes.com/2013/04/03/world/europe/us-assists-international-criminal-court-but-still-has-no-intention-of-joining-it.html.

Summers, Robert S. 1993. "A Formal Theory of the Rule of Law." *Ratio Juris* 6:127–42.

Tamanaha, Brian Z. 2004. *On the Rule of Law: History, Politics, Theory.* Cambridge: Cambridge University Press.

———. 2012. "The History and Elements of the Rule of Law." *Singapore Journal of Legal Studies* 2012:232–47.

Thi, Awzar. 2008. "Rule of Lords: Asia Needs a New Rule-of-Law Debate." *Prachatai English*, August 16. http://www.prachatai.com/english/node/751.

Thomas, Melissa A. 2009. "What Do the Worldwide Governance Indicators Measure?" *European Journal of Development Research* 22(1):31–54.

Thompson, Edward P. 1975. *Whigs and Hunters: The Origins of the Black Act.* New York: Pantheon Books.

Transparency International. 2014. "Global Corruption Barometer." Accessed March 12. http://www.transparency.org/gcb2013.

Tsokodayi, Cleophas. 2010. "Zimbabwe: SADC Tribunal Suspended Pending Review of Functions and Terms of Reference." *The Examiner*, September 1. http://www.examiner.com/article/zimbabwe-sadc-tribunal-suspended-pending-review-of-functions-and-terms-of-reference.

United Nations. 2013a. *A New Global Partnership: Eradicate Poverty and Transform Economies through Sustainable Development.* New York: United Nations.

———. 2013b. "Special Event 25 September: Outcome Document." September 25. http://www.un.org/millenniumgoals/pdf/Outcome%20documentMDG.pdf.

United Nations Children's Fund. 2003. "The Human Rights-Based Approach: Statement of Common Understanding." http://www.unicef.org/sowc04/files/AnnexB.pdf.

United Nations Department of Public Information. 2013. "Security Council Stresses Conflict Prevention in Africa Must Address Root Causes: Poverty, Poor Governance, Political Exclusion." Press release, April 15. http://www.un.org/News/Press/docs/2013/sc10970.doc.htm.

United Nations Development Group. 2003. "The Human Rights Based Approach to Development Cooperation Towards a Common Understanding Among UN Agencies." http://www.undg.org/archive_docs/6959-The_Human_Rights_Based_Approach_to_Development_Cooperation_Towards_a_Common_Understanding_among_UN.pdf.

United Nations General Assembly. 2000. United Nations Millennium Declaration. UN doc. A/RES/55/2.

———. 2012. Declaration of the High-Level Meeting of the General Assembly on the Rule of Law at the National and International Levels. UN doc. A/RES/67/1.

United Nations High Commissioner for Refugees. 2011. *Persons at Risk of Statelessness in Serbia*. New York: United Nations High Commissioner for Refugees.

United Nations Office on Drugs and Crime. 2014. "Country Profiles." Accessed 11 February. http://www.unodc.org/unodc/en/treaties/CAC/country-profile/index.html.

United Nations Rule of Law. 2012. "Voluntary Pledging by Member States." Accessed March 23, 2014. http://www.unrol.org/article.aspx?article_id=170.

United Nations Secretary-General. 2004. The Rule of Law and Transitional Justice in Conflict and Post-Conflict Societies. UN doc. S/2004/616.

———. 2011. The Rule of Law and Transitional Justice in Conflict and Post-Conflict Societies. UN doc. S/2011/634.

———. 2013. A Life of Dignity for All: Accelerating Progress towards the Millennium Development Goals and Advancing the United Nations Development Agenda beyond 2015. UN doc. A/68/202.

United States Agency for International Development. 2012. "Nigeria's Information-Freedom Triumph." *Frontlines*, January/February. http://www.usaid.gov/news-information/frontlines/democracy-human-rights-governance/nigeria%E2%80%99s-information-freedom-triumph.

World Bank. 2011. *World Development Report 2011: Conflict, Security and Development*. Washington, DC: World Bank.

World Justice Project. 2013. "The Rule of Law Index." Accessed December 2. http://worldjusticeproject.org/rule-of-law-index.

Notes

1. Carothers (1998) called the rule of law "a venerable part of Western political philosophy enjoying a new run as a rising imperative of the era of globalization."

2. In November 2012, in the *Wall Street Journal*, British prime minister David Cameron (2013), cochair of the High-Level Panel on the Post-2015 Development Agenda, chimed in, calling for "a radical new approach" to combating poverty grounded in support for "the rule of law, the absence of conflict and corruption, and the presence of property rights and strong institutions." And in its most recent survey of global trends, the premier official political forecaster of the US government—the National Intelligence Council (2012, 48)—projected that over the next two decades, the "global middle class" is likely to expand throughout the

developing world, and, with it, "demand for rule of law and government accountability is likely to increase."

3. Aristotle is reported to have observed that "the rule of law" is "preferable to that
of any individual" (Aristotle 1941).

4. According to the UN Secretary-General (2011, para. 6):

> It is increasingly recognized that States marked by ineffective governance, repres-
> sive policies, poverty and high rates of violent crime and impunity pose significant
> threats to international peace and security. Deep capacity deficits in State justice
> and security institutions, exacerbated by widespread corruption and political inter-
> ference, lead to diminishing levels of citizen security and economic opportunity.
> Resentment, distrust or outright hostility towards the State grows. Radicalized ideo-
> logical movements often stand ready to harness these sentiments . . . to challenge the
> established order through violent means. Transnational organized crime emerges
> in parallel with increasing instability, stoking new forms of violence, while further
> undermining the legitimacy and competency of State institutions.

5. For example, Shklar (1998, 21) argues that "[i]t would not be very difficult to
show that the phrase 'the Rule of Law' has become meaningless thanks to ideological abuse and general over-use."

6. I am grateful to Erik Jensen for highlighting the "fatal attraction" of the rule of
law's conceptual breadth in the course of his extensive and helpful comments on
an earlier draft of this chapter. See also Maru (this volume).

7. For example, in the words of Ahmadinejad (2012), "We have been condemned
for a great many things. Because we said justice for all, the rule of law for all,
the right of peaceful nuclear energy for all." And Obama (2009): "From Europe
to the Pacific, we've been the nation that has shut down torture chambers and
replaced tyranny with the rule of law."

8. In reaction to the European Court of Human Rights' decision in *Hirst v. United
Kingdom*, which ruled that the UK's refusal to allow British prisoners to vote was
contrary to the European Convention on Human Rights, Prime Minister Cameron declared that the prospect of compliance made him "physically ill" (Aldridge
2011).

9. *Jacobellis v. Ohio* 378 U.S. 184 (1964) (Stewart, J., concurring).

10. Important though the independence of the judiciary is, rule of law enthusiasts
may and often do acknowledge the reality that law is not entirely neutral and that
judges are human beings with moral, political, and institutional interests.

11. Bingham (2010, 66–67) sets forth eight distinct "ingredients of the rule of law,"
which include concepts such as equality before the law, fair adjudicative proce-

dures, and affordable means of dispute resolution. Along similar lines, de Greiff (2010, 12), currently the UN Special Rapporteur for the promotion of truth, justice, reparation and guarantees of non-recurrence, has written:

> If the notion of the rule of law is to have any critical purchase, it has to take seriously the idea that legitimacy does not depend just on formal characteristics of the law, but also on characteristics of the very process of making laws and on the substance of the laws thus produced.

12. The Commission on Legal Empowerment of the Poor (2008, 3), an independent body established under the auspices of the United Nations Development Programme, used the following formulation: "All citizens should enjoy effective protection of their basic rights, assets and livelihoods, upheld by law. They should be protected from injustice, whether caused by their fellow citizens or government officials, all of whom—high and low—must be bound by the law."

13. "What many of today's internationalists have forgotten, or chosen to ignore, is that Roosevelt, Malik, and Cassin saw the rule of law at the national level as the best and surest legal means for protecting human rights" (Glendon 2004, 1).

14. All of the voluntary pledges can be found in United Nations Rule of Law (2012).

15. See, e.g., Goldsmith (2013), who argues that American military action in Syria would be "in clear violation of international law," and Keating (2013), who asserts that "international law is once against protecting Assad's violations of international law."

16. See Constitutional Court of the Dominican Republic, September 23, 2013, Judgment TC/0168.

17. Grabbe and Lehne (2013), for example, describe the costs of a proposal to allow political parties in the European Parliament to put forward their own candidates for commission president.

18. Rome Statute of the International Criminal Court, art. 13(b), July 17, 1998, 2187 UNTS 90. The other two routes are through self-referral by a state party (art. 13[a]) and through an investigation initiated by the prosecutor and approved by the Pre-Trial Chamber (art. 130[c]).

19. For example, see Mendes (2010, 160); Dicker (2012); Goldsmith (2003, 92).

20. "[A] relatively formal theory is itself more or less politically neutral, and because it is so confined, it is more likely to command support on its own terms from right, left and center in politics than is a substantive theory which not only incorporates the rule of law formally conceived but also incorporates much more controversial substantive content" (Summers 1993, 135). "If there is to be an enduring interna-

tional rule of law, it must be seen to reflect the interests of the entire international community. Otherwise there is little prospect of persuasively entrenching the requisite belief that international law is worthy to rule" (Tamanaha 2004, 136).

21. Universal Declaration of Human Rights, G.A. Res. 217A(III), UN doc. A/810 at 71 (1948).

22. Ibid., preamble.

23. The dichotomy is illustrated by a recent statement of the UN High Commissioner for Human Rights. On the one hand, the statement celebrated "progress . . . in the Democratic Republic of the Congo in putting in place a legal regime to combat impunity for human rights violations" while, on the other, it "deplor[ed] the 'significant deterioration' of the human rights situation in the east of the country" ("DR Congo" 2013).

24. Amos (2013, 402) elaborates:

> During the drafting of the HRA, no elaborate process of public consultation or drafting of rights and procedures occurred; therefore, the potential educational function those processes could have served was missing. . . . Overnight, the UK legal system took on fifty-seven years of jurisprudence flowing from the ECtHR and the now-extinct European Commission of Human Rights. A full understanding of the HRA's operation and application also requires an excellent command of Strasbourg jurisprudence. It is not surprising that the result is uncertainty and limited knowledge of the HRA.

25. For a comprehensive list of recently enacted laws that prohibit tax deductibility for bribes, see Organisation for Economic Co-operation and Development (2011).

26. According to Sikkink and Kim (2013, 269):

> A new trend in world politics toward accountability for past human rights violations is taking place simultaneously in international courts, foreign courts, and domestic courts of the country in which the human rights violations occurred. These international, foreign, and domestic human rights trials are all part of an interrelated trend. . . . The justice cascade is a rapid and dramatic shift in the legitimacy of the norms of individual criminal accountability for human rights violations and an increase in actions (such as trials) on behalf of those norms.

27. 347 U.S. 483 (1954).

28. *Hollingsworth v. Perry*, 133 S. Ct. 2652 (2013); *United States v. Windsor*, 133 S. Ct. 2675 (2013).

29. See also Aptel (2012, 1358), who argues that "when those responsible for the hei-
nous crimes are held accountable, international criminal justice signals to victims
that their suffering is acknowledged by the international community as a whole."

30. Deputy administrator, ECCC, interview with the author, Phnom Penh, October
2013. In a different context, the work of the International Criminal Tribunal for
the Former Yugoslavia helped lay the foundation for Serbia to "deal with the burden of war crimes in all its dimensions," in part through the establishment in 2003
of the War Crimes Chamber as a specialized component of the Belgrade District
Court (Orentlicher 2008, 25–26). The tribunal further affected public attitudes by
"shrinking the public space" within which political leaders could "credibly deny
key facts about notorious atrocities" (ibid., 24).

31. In an op-ed, I argue that the "Cambodian government's public opposition to the
two remaining cases under investigation … threatened the very independence of
the court" (Goldston 2011). See also Open Society Justice Initiative (2013d).

32. Even the European Court of Human Rights—which has the longest history and
the most substantial financial backing from its membership—struggles to get
states to do what it says. By the end of 2012, more than 10,000 decisions were
still awaiting implementation. In Russia, petitioners who dare take their government to Strasbourg have been beaten, kidnapped, and even killed. Elsewhere,
though filing a lawsuit will not likely result in violence, hostility to European
judges abounds.

   In another context, as of December 6, 2013, twelve of the twenty-five public
warrants for arrest issued by the International Criminal Court remained outstanding (International Criminal Court 2013). In yet another forum, the views of UN
treaty bodies—the expert committees that oversee state performance under the
various UN rights conventions—are widely ignored. A recent study by the Open
Society Justice Initiative revealed that of the 500-plus cases in which the UN
Human Rights Committee has found violations of the International Covenant
on Civil and Political Rights, fewer than one-fifth have received a satisfactory
response from the state (Open Society Justice Initiative 2010, 27). Many states
never respond.

   Worse yet, some states are pushing back against the institutional architecture
of human rights. Since 2010, we have witnessed the shutdown of the Southern
African Development Community tribunal, a hostile turn by a number of states
against the Inter-American Commission on Human Rights, and a government-
led effort to compromise the independence of the European Court of Human
Rights in the guise of preserving it (Tsokodayi 2010). The Economist reports,
"On June 4th and 5th, in Bolivia, the [Organization of American States] held its
annual meeting. Ecuador, Venezuela, Bolivia and Nicaragua all threatened to pull
out of the [Inter-American Commission on Human Rights] if it is not reformed to

their liking" ("Chipping at the Foundations" 2012). And the UK Human Rights Blog observes that UK-backed "proposals seem to present a very mixed bag . . . of efficiency enhancing measures and potentially dangerous ideas which would undermine human rights protection by curtailing the Court and access to it for victims" ("Draft Declaration on British ECHR Reform Plans Leaked" 2012).

33. See, e.g., NBC News quoting US Representative Paul Ryan (2013) as saying, "We don't want a dependency culture."

34. *Minister of Health and Others v. Treatment Action Campaign and Others*, 5 SA 721 (2002).

35. As Holmes (2003, 35–37, 59) writes:

> [A]ctive and even boisterous citizenship is essential for the rule of law. . . . In a democratic society . . . a certain degree of initiative from ordinary citizens, beyond a willingness to stand in line on election day, is a precondition for law to function as it should. The right to sue abusive officials on the basis of a statute requires just as much activism on the part of the individual rights holder as the right to vote.

36. See, e.g., Council of Europe, Convention for the Protection of Human Rights and Fundamental Freedoms, November 4, 1950, ETS 5, art. 14 ("The enjoyment of the rights and freedoms set forth in this Convention shall be secured without discrimination on any ground such as sex, race, colour, language, religion, political or other opinion, national or social origin, association with a national minority, property, birth or other status."); Council of Europe, Protocol 1 to the European Convention for the Protection of Human Rights and Fundamental Freedoms, March 20, 1952, ETS 9, art. 2 ("No person shall be denied the right to education.").

37. See *DH and Others v. Czech Republic*, App. No. 57325/0, European Court of Human Rights (November 13, 2007); *Horváth And Kiss v. Hungary*, App. No. 11146/11, European Court of Human Rights (January 29, 2013); *Oršuš and Others v. Croatia*, App. No. 15766/03, European Court of Human Rights (March 16, 2010); *Sampanis v. Greece*, App. No. 32526/05, European Court of Human Rights (June 6, 2008).

38. In the words of the World Bank (2011, 108–9):

> Historically, the fastest transformations have taken a generation. Well-known institutional indices are relevant to reducing the risk of violence—the rule of law, corruption, human rights, democratic governance, bureaucratic quality, oversight of the security sectors, and equity for the disadvantaged. How much time has it taken to move from current average levels in fragile states around the world to a threshold of "good enough governance"? The results are striking. It took the 20 fastest-

moving countries an average of 17 years to get the military out of politics, 20 years to achieve functioning bureaucratic quality, and 27 years to bring corruption under reasonable control. This did not mean perfection, but rather adequacy.

39. For just two recent examples from the United States, see the impact of across-the-board budget cuts in "undermining the sound functioning of the courts and . . . imperiling the delivery of effective legal representation to poor people accused of federal crimes" ("Justice Sequestered" 2013) and the fire-sale nature of plea bargains in Bronx County, New York, designed to reduce "a backlog of felony cases that had swelled to crisis proportions" (Rivera 2013).

40. *Hamdan v. Rumsfeld*, 548 U.S. 557 (2006).

41. See, e.g., International Bar Association and International Legal Assistance Consortium (2009), reporting that, in 2007, 0.03% of the annual state budget, or roughly US$1.2 million, was allocated to the justice sector in the Democratic Republic of the Congo. This was "not sufficient to cover the salaries of the judiciary for even one month." For an example of the consequences of an under-financed judiciary in an advanced economy, see Glaberson (2013):

> At a time of slashed judicial budgets across the country, the Bronx offers a stark picture of what happens when an overwhelmed justice system can no longer keep pace: Old cases pile up, prosecutions fail at alarming rates, lives stall while waiting for court hearings and trust in the system and its ability to protect the public evaporates. . . . These problems worsened after two reorganizations left the Bronx criminal courts with fewer judges, a smaller budget and a bigger backlog of cases.

42. More recently, Secretary-General Ban Ki Moon told the UN Security Council that "[c]onflicts breed where there is poor governance, human rights abuses and grievances over the unequal distribution of resources, wealth and power" (United Nations Department of Public Information 2013).

43. For general US posture toward the International Criminal Court, see Goldsmith (2003, 89–104). But see also Simons (2013).

44. See, e.g., Kirkpatrick (2014), quoting a shopkeeper carrying a poster of a son killed by security forces during the 2011 uprising, who "said he believed General Sisi would 'turn Egypt from a third-world country to a first-world country' while bringing justice for the revolution's 'martyrs.' 'He will hold the police accountable and put them on trial, as soon as they get rid of the terrorism of the Muslim Brotherhood,' Mr. Shehab said."

45. Devinfo.org, which contains data compiled from UN agencies and governments, reveals significant statistical indicators of economic development in countries

that recently experienced mass protests and political upheavals. For example, Brazil and Turkey experienced major social protests in 2013 notwithstanding outstanding progress in reducing infant mortality rates, child mortality rates, and undernourished populations.

46. According to Orkin (2013, 119):

> RoL is conceived by the World Justice Project (WJP) to have eight components, of which four may be taken as core to RoL (limited government powers, regulatory performance, civil justice, and criminal justice), and four may be taken as cognate, in that they are equally well regarded as aspects of good governance (absence of corruption, order and security, fundamental rights and open government). Development is measured by the UNDP's Human Development Index, which compounds measures of education, life expectancy and gross national income.

47. This impact is the flip side of the growing recognition that, in too many areas—from infrastructure to water and electricity to other public services—"the obstacles to durable growth . . . are primarily political" (Devarajan and Fengler 2013, 81).

48. Kohn (2013) notes that "the work of Roma paralegals is having a profound impact on Roma health in their communities," including by helping "Roma obtain personal identification documents, without which they cannot get health insurance to subsidize their care."

49. See Kirp (2012), citing economic studies that "consistently conclude that African-American students [in the United States] who attended integrated schools fared better academically than those left behind in segregated schools"; Johnson (2011), finding that black students who went to desegregated schools in the United States not only achieved greater educational outcomes but earned higher incomes later in life and their children performed better than the children of those who attended segregated schools; and Karsten (2010, 193), analyzing Organisation for Economic Co-operation and Development countries that employ legal tools to counter the socioeconomic effects of residential and cultural segregation in order to achieve greater levels of school integration and concluding that, across all countries, ethnic composition of the classroom is "a major factor, particularly for children from disadvantaged environments, who are almost entirely dependent on the school for the acquisition of their human capital."

50. A commonly voiced objection to including the rule of law within the post-2015 development framework is the challenge of attaching a quantifiable measure to such a broad and politically rooted concept. See, e.g., Thomas (2009, 31–54). Without addressing this concern in any detail, it may be useful to note that a number of existing indicators of different aspects of the rule of law could serve as a model or foundation for the creation of measureable proxies within the post-2015 agenda. See, e.g., United Nations Office on Drugs and Crime (2014), concerning whistleblower protection and disclosure of public officials' incomes, assets, and

conflicts of interest; Organisation for Economic Co-operation and Development (2008), Public Expenditure and Financial Accountability (2014), and Gateway Corruption Assessment Index (2014), concerning country performance on public financial management surveys and procurement integrity; Right2info.org (2014), concerning freedom-of-information legislation; and Transparency International (2014), concerning perceptions of judicial and other forms of corruption.

51. See Abel (1995, 523), arguing that "[a] pure theory of law—logically coherent, universally valid, uncontaminated by the messiness of life—is a misguided dream. At the same time, we cannot simply 'read off' a superstructural element like law from the material base."

Abstract

This chapter establishes and explores a paradox at the heart of much contemporary writing on rule of law reform and its implications for the sharing and generation of knowledge. Contemporary rule of law reform seems to be a coalescing around a professional field. Yet underdetermining the "rule of law"—or, indeed, rendering it indeterminate—remains a legitimate (but not universal) professional position within this field: in other words, observing that "no one knows what it is" without trying to offer determinate content (as Carothers and others have done) is considered to be justifiable.

This chapter explores how writers struggle to organize the field while constantly being confronted with the conditions of their own unmaking. It argues that their organizing moves fall into one or more baskets of concepts, epistemologies, or tools that form the basis for their prescriptions to donors. These moves are predicated on an assumption that the correct terrain on which the field can be organized—and thus knowledge circulated—is one of uncovering determinate content in the rule of law.

This chapter argues that the correct terrain is instead the field itself: the emerging field will shape how development institutions conceive of objectives and realize (or fail to realize) them. Moreover, development institutions themselves are generating organizing principles for the field by inserting themselves through their hiring practices. This chapter studies the job descriptions and personnel specifications for rule of law specialists in four institutions—the World Bank, the United Nations Development Programme, the Australian aid program within the Department of Foreign Affairs and Trade, and the UK Department for International Development—to explore how these institutions organize the field, what skills they privilege, the implications for experimentation that result, and (embedded within this) how they understand useful knowledge to be shared.

2   In Search of "Hire" Knowledge: Donor Hiring Practices and the Organization of the Rule of Law Reform Field

Deval Desai

[The rule of law] is not a field if one considers a requirement for such a designation to include a well-grounded rationale, a clear understanding of the essential problem, a proven analytic method, and an understanding of results achieved.

—Carothers (2006, 28)

Introduction

Thomas Carothers' lament for rule of law reform, its coherence, and its aspirations resonates as strongly today as it did when it was first published. In recent years, a veritable cottage industry of dirges has sprung up, decrying the inadequacies of reform efforts (e.g., Trubek and Santos 2006; Trebilcock and Daniels 2008; Palombella and Walker 2009; Hatchard and Perry-Kessaris 2009; Heckman, Nelson, and Cabatingan 2010; Humphreys 2010; Kleinfeld 2012) while remarking on the persistent allure of the rule of law ideal (e.g.,

I am grateful to Lisa Kelly and Rob Varenik for their sustained engagement and to Todd Foglesong, Rachel Kleinfeld, Nicholas Menzies, Rebecca Tapscott, Michael Woolcock, Freddie Carver, Daniel Woods, Aparna Basnyat, and the participants from the Harvard Human Rights Program "International Rule of Law Movement" workshop for their comments and support. All errors remain my own.

Tamanaha 2004; Krygier 2009; Kennedy 2003; Jensen and Heller 2003; Desai and Woolcock forthcoming). It is possible to read Carothers as a diagnosis of a failed and incoherent set of practices, something rotten in the state of Denmark.[1] Indeed, this is the tack taken by many of these subsequent critics of reform (Armytage 2012, 5; Peerenboom, Zurn, and Nollkaemper 2012, 308–9; Golub 2003). At their strongest, they follow Carothers in denying the very existence of a rule of law field (whatever they might consider a "field" to be). For example, eliding rule of law reform and "law and development" (the latter presumably being a broader category, but one that is substantially constituted by the former; Tamanaha 2011, 216–19), Brian Tamanaha adds his voice to the chorus of field-deniers:

> Many who write on law and development appear to consider it a "field." . . . Conceiving of law and development as a field, I will argue, is a conceptual mistake that perpetuates confusion. The multitude of countries around the world targeted for law and development projects differ radically from one another. No uniquely unifying basis exists upon which to construct a "field"; there is no way to draw conceptual boundaries to delimit it. Law and development work is more aptly described as an agglomeration of projects advanced by motivated actors and supported by external funding. Law and development activities are driven and shaped by the flow of money that supports it and by the agendas of the people who secure this funding [citation omitted]. This is offered as an accurate description, not a cynical characterization. (ibid., 220)

These negating accounts offer little salve for putative reformers of rule of law reform. Based on analytical moves that examine the aspirations and internal consistency of a self-proclaimed rule of law field, they reflect a desire to collapse the field under the weight of its own claims, to press down on what they see as its analytically indeterminate foundations. In this view of rule of law reform, learning and progress are at best challenging and at worst hopeless; the field is at best marshy or stagnant and at worst nonexistent.

Despite these critiques, efforts at rule of law reform have not just persisted but expanded. Official development assistance disbursed for "legal and judicial development" suggests an upward trajectory of rule of law reform (to say nothing of all the other funding themes that might fall under a rule of law rubric). From 2002 (when data from the Organisation for Economic Co-operation and Development are first available) to 2006 (when Carothers published his edited volume), this assistance increased from around US$175 million to over $710 million. In 2007, this jumped to over $1.3 billion, and by 2011 (the last year for which data are available), it stood at $3.2 billion. While a significant amount of this money was disbursed in Afghanistan and

Iraq by the United States Agency for International Development (over $840 million in 2010 and $750 million in 2011), expenditure in other countries by bilateral and multilateral donors has also expanded by billions of dollars.[2] Even in simple financial terms, the stakes of the existence and nature of the field—how the idea of the field shapes what can and cannot be done in rule of law reform—have increased significantly in recent years.

In this chapter, I propose an inverted reading of the field-deniers' claims. Rather than seeing Carothers' negation as a lament, it is possible to view it as a full-throated statement of the self-confidence of the rule of law reform field. As expenditure has boomed and "rule of law" has emerged as its own professional identification (along with the accoutrements of a profession, such as degree programs and academic journals), the field's ability to subject itself to such sustained critique from one of its grandees can be seen as a mark of independence. I argue that we can interpret subsequent laments and prescriptions for rule of law reform (see, e.g., Kleinfeld 2012; Trebilcock and Daniels 2008; Rodriguez, McCubbins, and Weingast 2010) as a continued assertion of the field's independence encased in a jeremiad. Where writers such as Carothers and Tamanaha attempt to stand outside the field to examine—and undermine—its consistency in an analytical fashion, I base my reading on a performative and institutional approach to the field. I rely on the self-articulation of actors as rule of law professionals—thereby performatively constituting a rule of law field—and the institutions that give this self-articulation material weight, from donors to journals to job postings.

This chapter examines the body of literature that has arisen in the 2000s seeking to define and organize the rule of law reform field—a body that is marked by a blend of theory, policy, and practice, and, indeed, of which this volume is a part. I categorize much of this "field-overview literature" as a series of attempts to organize the field while constantly being confronted with the conditions of its own unmaking or collapse. This literature is faced with a central problem. How can a professional field organize itself and move forward when a legitimate—perhaps even constitutive—position in the field is one that negates the field's very existence by exposing an analytic indeterminacy at its core: that no one knows what the rule of law is nor how to do it? I argue that the organizing moves in this literature fall into one or more baskets of concepts, epistemologies, or tools, which form the basis for prescriptions to donors. These moves are predicated on an assumption that the correct method for organizing the field—and thus circulating knowledge—is to uncover determinate content in the rule of law. Furthermore, the organizing principles are to be found by reaching outside the field for conceptual, epistemological, or tool-based inspiration or substance.[3] These external sources are thought to provide content and structure for the field. These, I argue, misunderstand the contemporary nature of the rule of law field. Rather than engaging with the field as "thing," or product of the Real, capable of being analyzed, I focus on the community of agents and institutions that state that the field exists. In doing so, I suggest that the field might better be understood in terms of these actors and their utterances, and that they will determine the nature and scope of rule of law reform—the projects embarked on, resources allocated, and the resultant winners and losers.

I argue that a firmer terrain on which to organize rule of law reform is the field itself. Starting an analysis of the rule of law field not through definitional attempts but *in medias res* means that the ways in which participants in the field position themselves and the practices they generate will shape how objectives are conceived of and realized (or missed). In particular, given that I understand the field to be performative and institutional, I turn to the hiring practices—specifically, the job descriptions and personnel specifications—of development institutions as performative statements of the nature of the field. I contend that these statements can be seen as organizations' expressions of commitment to the types of knowledge they want generated, transmitted, and restated by their actors. I look at four institutions—the World Bank, the United Nations Development Programme (UNDP), the Australian aid program within the Department of Foreign Affairs and Trade (DFAT), and the UK Department for International Development (DFID)/UK government— to explore how they organize the field, what skills they privilege, and (embedded within this) how they understand useful knowledge to be shared.

The chapter proceeds as follows. The next section, which briefly outlines my understanding of the curious nature of the rule of law field, is framed by a short intellectual and social history of the rule of law profession. I argue that the field exists simply because a group of actors—a group that subsequently struggles to position itself within that very field—says it does. Thereafter, the third section details the three types of outward-reaching organizing moves made in the recent field-overview literature (concepts, epistemologies, and tools) and highlights the specter of indeterminacy with which each does battle. It then explores the inward-reaching organizing moves of "expert politics" and "context," arguing that they simply represent a nesting of this specter. Finally, it examines the move to privilege "experimentation" as a recent response. I suggest that the performative nature of the field means that the impacts of this move might oscillate between stasis and fragmentation. In other words, the problem may be not that there is too little experimentation (an idea on which the move to experimentation is predicated) but that there is also the possibility of being overwhelmed by the vast potential for experimentation. The fourth section turns to actual practice, examining hiring documents from the World Bank, UNDP, DFAT, and DFID/the UK government to explore whether and how this move to "experimentation" plays out in practice, the ways in which these institutions seek to organize the field, and the sorts of skills and knowledge that are privileged as a result. Finally, the last section argues that these institutions provide a sophisticated articulation of the field and offers some suggestions concerning how they might continue to take "experimentation" seriously in the context of a broader trend toward experimentation in development (see Hall, Menzies, and Woolcock, this volume).

The Field

I will not spend much time here delving into the social theory of the field. My concern in this chapter is with the practical and organizational implications for the transmission of knowledge among those who inhabit it.[4] Nevertheless, Pierre Bourdieu's widely adopted notion of a field is a useful starting point for trying to comprehend the complex dynamics of rule of law reform and its agents. A "structured field of forces, and also a field of struggles to conserve or transform this field of forces," a field describes a network of positions occupied by agents who, through their relationships, create "the very space that determines the[se agents]" (Bourdieu 2004, 33). Individuals who share specific logics and beliefs compete for primacy in their field, having succumbed to the *illusio* or the act of getting "caught up in and by the game, of believing . . . that playing is worth the effort" (Bourdieu 1998, 76–77). In seeking to exert power in their field, they structure and change the boundaries of the field and, as a result, themselves. These acts, in Bourdieu's terms, are not unfettered. They arise out of the interaction between two accumulated histories. First is the agent's *habitus*, or series of dispositions. This is "the durably installed generative principle of regulated improvisations" that generates practices (Bourdieu 1977, 78). In other words, the *habitus* is the embodied, accumulated history of how things are done in the field—the basis for "reasonable" and "common-sense" behavior (Bourdieu 1990, 55)—that has been internalized by its agents and has become second nature. Second is the structure of the field, which is an "objectified" history of all of those interactions to be found in institutions, objects, texts, formulae, and so on (Bourdieu 2004, 35). Innovation resides in the creative act of adopting new positions to one's advantage in the field of struggles, bounded by the limits of objectified history and fettered by the chains of internalized dispositions. Understanding the nature of the field matters, then, because it structures and limits the positions we can take regarding what rule of law reform is, how it is best done, and

47

where new ideas may come from. For my purposes, the structuring role of the history of positions and dispositions for the field is key.

A Bourdieusian approach is particularly helpful in light of Yves Dezalay and Bryant G. Garth's application of it to the rule of law field (2002; and in a long series of subsequent, well-cited studies looking at the exportation of legal expertise in the context of global governance). Referring to that recent research in a contemporaneous article, Garth (2002, 384) offers an early lament for the failings of rule of law reform but puts them in a temporal context: "All this activity, however, comes with a strong current of disappointment [citation omitted]. We are trying hard, but the results are not what we had hoped. So far this disappointment is attributed mainly to the relative immaturity of the field, implying that we need more practice and more learning." This sense of disappointment, of unmet aspirations, resonates with Carothers, Tamanaha, and much of the recent literature on rule of law reform (e.g., Kleinfeld 2012; Trebilcock and Daniels 2008; Rodriguez, McCubbins, and Weingast 2010). In the least-charitable stories of reform, we are faced with a field of stasis, not struggle; of history repeated, not accreted; of reproduction, not learning.[5]

Yet in another sense—Garth's suggestive use of "immaturity" when describing the field—we are presented with the beginnings of a story of its transformation, a story not of the evolution (or otherwise) of rule of law reform as a series of disjointed practices or interventions, but of the emergence of a field. Garth draws a sharp distinction between the "old" law and development of the 1960s and 1970s and the "new" one of the 1990s.[6] In his view, the latter achieved consensus among a range of transnational actors from different disciplines—economists, political scientists, lawyers, and development practitioners—around "reform and the legal approaches identified with the United States, including the core idea of a strong and independent judiciary" (Garth 2002, 385). Dezalay and Garth (2002, 17–30) expand on this point, suggesting that (rule of) law reform became a field of ideas in which actors from different disciplines (particularly "gentlemen lawyers" and economic "technopols") brought the political, social, cultural, and intellectual capital that their backgrounds and disciplines afforded them in order to struggle for position. In their story of the field, we would understand the turns to the rule of law as a facet of governance and development, of democracy promotion and human rights, and of state-building[7] (ibid., 163–86) as different vernaculars in which participants in the rule of law field might seek to implement this "consensus" in national contexts.

However, today this story seems to have been inverted: in place of a range of disciplines orbiting around a core set of ideas, we now see a self-articulated rule of law profession confronting an indeterminacy at its core. The strong sense of ideational consensus has been replaced by the idea that "we know how to do a lot of things, but deep down we don't really know what we are doing," even as we can speak of "rule-of-law aid practitioners" (Carothers 2006, 15) implementing the significant increase in aid allocated to the rule of law.[8] Indeed, this new story of the field is being embraced as a positive phenomenon rather than a reason for collapse. Writing in response to the field-slayers, Randall Peerenboom asserts the existence of a rule of law field as part of the "law and development industry" (2009, 13), which actually adopts this conceptual indeterminacy as a motif:

> As the field has expanded, so have definitions of rule of law and the normative goals that rule of law is supposed to serve. . . . It is time to give up the quest for a consensus definition or conception of rule of law and to accept that it is used by many different actors in different ways for different purposes. But rather than seeing this as a disadvantage, we should turn this into an advantage by using the different definitions and ways of measuring rule of law to shed light on more specific questions. (ibid., 7)

Today, we might observe a group of individuals asserting that they are rule of law[9] professionals operating in the context of a series of institutions that reinforce this claim. Institutions require these professionals to have experience in rule of law reform, without specifying the content of reform or a specific institutional approach. UNDP (2013b) might seek candidates whose disciplinary competencies are "in the area of [r]ule of [l]aw"; the World Bank (2012a) has "justice reform specialists" on its books; and DFAT (2013), DFID (2014), and the UK government's Stabilisation Unit (2014b, 2014c) all—in different ways—see the rule of law as a discrete subspecialty of governance. These professionals might enter the field (or teach others as part of the same process) through specialized degree courses.[10] They might then write about their experiences in a journal aimed at the field—for example, the *Hague Journal on the Rule of Law* inaugurated in 2009—while participating in networks of rule of law specialists: "The Hague Institute for the Internationalisation of Law has established a network of academics and practitioners to meet on a regular basis to discuss recent development and key issues" (Peerenboom 2009, 13).

The field, then, can be understood performatively: it constantly utters itself into being without referring to—and sometimes even acknowledging the absence of—a determinate analytic core. These utterances are then given weight through particular institutions. This performative view of the field does not sit easily with a Bourdieusian analysis. Critiquing Jean-Paul Sartre's sketch of a cafe waiter's *mauvaise foi* in *Being and Nothingness*, Bourdieu writes:

> [T]he agents [in a field]—who do not thereby become *actors* perform-
> ing *roles*—enter into the spirit of the social character which is expected
> of them and which they expect of themselves (such is a vocation) . .
> . . The café waiter does not play at being a café waiter, as Sartre sup-
> poses. When he puts on his white jacket, which evokes a democratized,
> bureaucratized form of the dutiful dignity of the servant in a great
> household, and when he performs the ceremonial of eagerness and con-
> cern, which may be strategy to cover up a delay or an oversight, or to
> fob off a second-rate product, he does not make himself a thing . . . .
> His body, which contains a history, espouses his function, i.e. a history,
> a tradition which he has only ever seen incarnated in bodies, or rather,
> in those habits "inhabited" by a certain *habitus* which are called café
> waiters. . . . *He cannot even be said to take himself for a café waiter; he is too
> much taken up in the job which was naturally (i.e. socio-logically) assigned to
> him* (e.g. as the son of a small shopkeeper who needs to earn enough
> to set up his own business) even to have the idea of such role-distance.
> (1981, 309, emphasis added)

In other words, Bourdieu asserts that being an actor in a field goes beneath
the skin. However, it appears that rule of law reformers are in fact able "to
take themselves" as such—to give themselves their professional title without a
clear substance to that profession.

This perhaps helps explain the dynamics of simultaneous assertion and
dirge that characterize the field: if the field exists because we say it exists,
changing the field's positioning does not necessarily require a changed relationship to its history but rather an ongoing need for that history's invention
in the absence of a shared basis on which to do so. Amanda Perry-Kessaris
expresses this concisely in her introduction to another lament: "I have been
struck by the absence of a shared analytical framework, a *set of reference points*,
for this *field* of ours" (2009, 3, emphasis added). A story of the evolution of
the field—from Garth through Carothers and to today—may not be one of
accreted history, but nor is it one of repeated history (as Carothers and Tamanaha might have it). It might be one of *repeat performance*: the field constituting
itself through an ongoing restatement of its existence and reinvention of its
history.[11] Thus, Chantal Thomas (2010) tells a history of the field marked by
a series of high-level intellectual and policy statements (predominantly by the
World Bank); by contrast, Stephen Golub (2003) draws on a brief survey of
projects to discuss a "rule of law orthodoxy," and Vivek Maru (2010) explicitly incorporates the history of social accountability projects into rule of law
reform as a way of telling a new history of the field and setting out possible
new directions.

This relationship to positioning and history makes the rule of law field somewhat unusual. How can a field that is constantly rearticulating itself and its history be organized? More pertinently, how is it possible to learn and move forward if we are constantly reinventing the past and restating our existence in the present? The next section will map out the conceptual challenges that such organization entails, while the section after that will examine how certain institutions tackle these challenges and use their power to organize the field performatively through their hiring practices.

Negation and Organization

Having sketched out the way in which the rule of law field appears to articulate itself, I will now explore more deeply the field's ideas about and reactions to the indeterminacy of the rule of law. I do not seek to make any claims about the inherent determinacy of the rule of law as a concept. Rather, by examining recent literature purporting to give an overview of the field, I explore the ways in which actors within the field approach its potential indeterminacy and their responses. I then consider how this affects the constitution and nature of the field, particularly the organizing strategies its actors adopt in response.

Negation

On one level, contest around the meaning of the rule of law is unsurprising. Contingency is the hallmark of any field, enabling contests and positioning to take place. A field is

> to some extent, at least potentially informed by an alternative set of principles on which agents can draw when disputes arise over what is considered proper or legitimate activity. . . . [Agents] will . . . be aware at some level that this context is contingent and open to negotiation. (Schirato and Webb 2002, 265)

Scientists, for example, might dispute methods or attempt to introduce new paradigmatic ways of understanding the problem at hand. Yet on another level, expressions of the rule of law's contingency and the significance of this contingency for the field are more radical. Rather than the field simply being structured—and its bounds determined and negotiated—by competing argumentative moves articulating alternative principles, it also appears to be a *legitimate* position within the rule of law field to deny any determinate content. Carothers' (2006, 15) idea that "deep down we don't

51

really know what we are doing" is powerful in part because he uses the device of a faceless rule of law reform practitioner to say this: it becomes a specter of anyone and everyone who constitutes the field.

Actors often embark on projects offering different ways of organizing the field (while others may simply ignore the question of indeterminacy). Yet I argue that the combination of indeterminacy and performativity has profound structural effects on the field. Overview projects that attempt to organize the field frequently begin with—and are often haunted by—the possibility of their own unmaking, as any concept of the rule of law might fall apart at the foundations. Perry-Kessaris sees the specter of radical indeterminacy thus, in this case attempting to tame "the absence of a shared . . . set of reference points" (2009, 3) by turning it into a technical challenge:

> [D]o we—practitioners and academics at the intersection of law and development—have an ABC, an index or a map for our field? If we do, it has not yet, to my knowledge, been articulated. We address the same well-trodden paths, circling around issues such as the rule of law . . . . But we do not have a systematic way of classifying our discussions. As a result, we do not always notice how our work fits together; we do not allow ourselves to build upon each others' work as effectively as we might; we unconsciously block those who concentrate their efforts in other fields from drawing on and contributing to our work, and we spend not insignifcant amounts of time reinventing various wheels. The nature of the concerns at the heart of our field—poverty, drought, humiliation, desolation, violence, injustice, death—demand that we do the best we can. Might we not be more effective if we were better organised? (ibid., 4, internal citations omitted)

The radical nature of this indeterminacy is important. Dezalay and Garth (2012, 166) take to heart Bourdieu's notion that "texts circulate without their contexts," meaning that a "consensus" on the rule of law can be taken and redeployed in the service of power struggles in different levels of contest (from the United States to Chile, for example). According to this view, rule of law reformers act as "translators" of ideas in national contexts (Dezalay and Garth 2011, 3). Such action requires and presumes a determinate-enough "text" for actors to translate. Yet if this determinacy slips—if the "text" becomes unstable—it is no longer sufficient simply to shine a light on the nature and practices of these translators, these rule of law "professionals" (Kratochwil 2009) or institutions. They are implicated not just in how they translate the field but also in how they negate and reorganize it.

The operation of indeterminacy as a negating agent in the field is complex. We might situate its roots and its structure in theory. Writing in response

52

the US Supreme Court's decision in *Bush v. Gore*, Jeremy Waldron (2002, 160) extends Walter Bryce Gallie's notion of the "essentially contested concept" to the rule of law, arguing that it is not determinacy but essential "contestedness [that is] understood to be part of the very meaning of the concept." He posits the very debate it engenders as a political good, generative of dialogue, debate, and participation (a notion that Peerenboom [2009, 7] translates into a good among the practitioners of the field themselves). Desmond Manderson (2012) casts this political-philosophical idea in literary and deeply human terms. Drawing on Walter Benjamin's phenomenal sense of "the curious and at first discouraging experience of the ultimate undecidability of all legal problems" (ibid., 499),[12] he adopts lessons from modernist literature to argue that in relation to the rule of law, a "'determinate oscillation' swings us between two irreconcilable poles—general and particular, prior rules and new circumstances—forcing us to rethink our rules, the meaning we give our words, the imagined 'essences' of those words, and the purposes that are served by them" (ibid., 500). This oscillation is never resolved; rather, we as modern humans inhabit the undecidability of law, a condition Manderson calls polarity: "an endless polarity . . . ensures that we *never stop deciding*" (ibid., 501, emphasis in original). This polarity, he believes, sets in motion conversations that form the basis of social relations; in this sense, an indeterminate rule of law is "the framework for a social and human dialogue" (ibid., 503). Even recent attempts from theoreticians in the field to lay out a determinate or unipolar rule of law recognize and must grapple with its undecidability. Tamanaha (2004, 82–84, 86–90; 2009, 10) spends several pages expressly dealing with the indeterminacy question as part of a move to establish "basic principles" of the rule of law. Gianluigi Palombella (2009, xii, 24) relies on an intellectual history to tackle what he translates as rule of law's "elusiveness."

We might also turn to policy and practice to see this indeterminacy play out in the world. Despite Peerenboom's calls for practitioners to embrace the fundamental contest in the field, "polarity" in practice is understood not as generative but as frustrative or confusing. When working to achieve concrete outcomes, it is hard to emphatically enjoy indeterminacy. In the rule of law overview literature, authors tip their hats to the unknowability of the rule of law in theory and practice, before proceeding to try to know it. Rachel Kleinfeld and Kalypso Nicolaidis (2009, 144–51) detail a notion of the rule of law for European Union interventions as constraints on executive power in the "legal, institutional, cultural and structural" spheres. Before doing so they assert that, for the "armies of rule of law soldiers trekking the world," "there is great confusion . . . as to the battle that they wage," in particular as "law ceases to uncontroversially enjoy the aura of universality as its specificity"—in other words, its conversion into policy—"is increased" (ibid., 143). Kleinfeld (2012, 2–3)[13] is even stronger in her problematizing moment preceding her prescriptions for sorting out the field: "the field of rule-of-law reform has remained in conceptual infancy, unaware of its own history, and as the saying goes, bound to repeat it." Michael Trebilcock and Ronald Daniels (2008, 12–14) preface their "procedural" definition of the rule of law with nods to Tamanaha, Kleinfeld, Carothers, and Peerenboom's own acknowledgments of rule of law's "great uncertainty," and go on to quote an "academic China law expert" as saying that "[r]ule of law has no meaning" (13, citing Stephenson 2006). All of these authors are placed in the unusual position of prefacing their attempts to organize the field not simply with counterarguments to be overcome but with the very conditions of their own unmaking. They remove the bottom from the vessel before attempting to fill it.

This challenge ought to be taken seriously: the ways in which it shapes the field have implications for learning and progress. I argue that current attempts to deal with the challenge of indeterminacy struggle as they reach outside the field for grounds on which to array the field and the possibilities for learning. This leaves them vulnerable to the specter of negation. I suggest that they instead turn to the field itself, which articulates its own principles that might help us construct a framework for learning and moving forward.

Organization

For those concerned with policy and practice, frustration with the field's constitutive "essential contest" has led to a profound "anxiety of content" and to a concomitant proliferation of attempts to organize the field. Perhaps in recognition of the lack of solid ground beneath, these attempts look beyond the field for a place on which to found their arguments and projects. They tend to fall into one or more of three general categories: concepts, epistemologies, and tools.[14]

By concepts, I mean a turn to concepts around which the rule of law might be organized. These concepts range from principles of political philosophy to descriptive statements of the form and content of institutions (or Martin Krygier's [2009] "teleology" and morphology). Trebilcock and Daniels (2008, 29–36) take a morphological approach, attempting to define what key (mainly formal) legal institutions should look like on the basis of "process values," such as transparency; "institutional values," such as "independence" and "accountability"; and "legitimacy values," such as "social acceptance." By contrast, Kleinfeld (2006, 62–64) identifies five "ends": a government bound by law; equality before the law; law and order; a predictable and efficient government; and human rights. Amichai Magen (2009, 53–54) sits somewhere in between, "adopti[ng] a more operational, policy-oriented approach to the rule of law; one that is . . . inextricably linked to the institutions and norms of liberty" and that consists of "[e]stablishing basic conditions of security . . . ; [c]reating legal certainty, secure property rights and private spheres . . . ; [e]nsuring free and fair electoral transitions"; and fostering institutional change for liberal democratic transitions. All preface their search for an organizing concept with statements on the problem of indeterminacy (Trebilcock and Daniels 2008, 12–14; Kleinfeld 2006, 31–33; Magen 2009, 54–55), asserting, to varying degrees, that we must find some core or "epicentre" (Magen 2009, 55) for practical purposes.

Yet such assertions, such reaching out for conceptually determinate ground, are constantly in danger of being destabilized from within the field. Alternative concepts may be drawn on (for example, Joseph Raz's [1977] formalist view of the rule of law that counters the incorporation of human rights). More radically, these concepts can simply be undone by the idea that rule of law "has no meaning." Thus, Friedrich Kratochwil (2009, 172) is able to downplay the utility of the move to concepts as an organizing strategy, arguing that

> [t]he initial bewilderment caused by this brief historical reflection [on the meaning of the rule of law] has some methodological implications. It casts doubt on the viability of our usual means of clarifying the meaning of concepts, that is of ascertaining to which events, objects or actions this term "refers."

A second, similar set of organizing moves consists of reaching out to other epistemologies or methods of knowing the rule of law. These attempt to organize the field through the insights of anthropology, economics, sociology, and so on. The new institutional economics-inflected approach of Douglass North et al. (2007) and North, John Joseph Wallis, and Barry Weingast (2009) attempts to organize the rule of law around the calculation of the distribution of political and economic outcomes of laws, rules, and institutions. This enables a high-level yet methodologically individualist account of the formation of organizations and the generation of legal institutions that many sociologists might contest (Gauri, Woolcock, and Desai 2013). By contrast, a legal pluralist account of the rule of law might draw on (legal) anthropological and sociological method and theory (Merry 1988; Tamanaha, Sage, and Woolcock 2012, 7; see Hamoudi [this volume] for a short history of legal pluralism) to organize the rule of law in relational terms of complexity, context, and culture. Take, for example, Jean and John Comaroff's (2004, 192) notion of the role of law in development as the process of carving "concrete realities" out of the complex and "fragile fictions" by which we live our lives in a "policultural" modernity. The limits of the move to method are well expressed in an exchange between Krygier (2012) and Marc Hertogh (2013). While Krygier argues for a sociological approach (as opposed to a legal one) to rule of law reform, Hertogh (2013, 43) argues that a move to organize by method and not concept still does not help us—method remains an approach, and we still have no way of organizing the method to ascertain the right questions to ask, collapsing the methodological moves back into conceptual indeterminacy.

A third set of moves is the appropriation of particular tools as a way of organizing the field. Hernando de Soto's (2000, 73–74) promotion of land titling as a tool organizes the field inasmuch as he argues that people's social and economic organization is inextricably linked to the prevailing legal regime for land. Golub's (2003, 7) notion of the "legal empowerment alternative" expressly rejects the concepts that he sees as foundational of the "rule of law orthodoxy," including "security for foreign and domestic investment, property and contract rights, international trade, and other vehicles for advancing economic growth." It also expressly rejects attempts to organize the field epistemologically: he sees the "orthodoxy" as beholden to "lawyers" and their ways of seeing the world, and as leading to "a tendency to define the legal system's problems and cures narrowly, in terms of courts, prosecutors, contracts, law reform, and other institutions and processes in which lawyers play central roles" (ibid., 9, 22). This critique paves the way for a much more practical turn to tools or the focused "use of legal services and related development activities" for the express purpose (resonating with Krygier's teleology) of "increas[ing] disadvantaged populations' control over their lives" (ibid., 25). Golub attempts to present his move to tools as somewhat contingent, suggesting that it is not "the correct path to pursue under all circumstances" and that one should not be "absolutist" (ibid., 6). However, the tenor of the piece is one of reorienting the field away from the "orthodoxy." Such a turn to tools is subject to the same undoing as concepts and epistemologies. Critiques that problematize the idea of the "use of legal services" as a neutral suite of tools put empowerment approaches in the political context and power dynamics of the communities in which they operate. Doing so allows them to highlight the risk of capture by powerful interests (Hayat and Ahmed 2008) or the accountability of facilitators (such as paralegals) to target beneficiaries (von Broembsen 2012, 15). In essence, these critiques rearticulate empowerment as a set of concepts and presumptions about the rule of law (as human rights compliance, accountability, and so on) embedded in "legal services." These presumptions shape the power dynamics of legal service providers themselves, suggesting that the delivery of "empowerment" as a suite of tools is contingent on a set of indeterminate concepts around the rule of law.

In contrast to these external efforts, another set of organizing projects uses process-oriented arguments focused on the operation of the field itself, in place of arguments that reach beyond the field. These include calls to interrogate the politics of "experts" and to analyze the "contexts" in which actors pursue rule of law reform. The arguments around expert politics tend to try to show rule of law reform as a set of supposedly depoliticized techniques. They then attempt to unmask the latent or express "politics" of the reformers and their tools—in other words, the technical as political. The literature urging a turn to context mainly tells a similar story of technologization but asks us to take seriously the "context" of the objects of reform—the place and its people. I argue that neither move offers concrete foundations for the field; rather, they reproduce the question of indeterminacy within the operation of the field itself.

Attempts to "unveil" expert politics have proliferated in recent years. Thomas (2010), for example, painstakingly sets out an intellectual history of the interaction between images of law in development and neoclassical and new institutionalist economics. She attempts to unveil the ideological underpinnings of the approach to law taken by the main institutions of development (namely, the International Monetary Fund and the World Bank). Kerry Rittich (2006, 247), in calling for a new politics of contest and engagement between social justice activists and development policy makers, emphasizes the importance of adumbrating and contesting "the manner in which social objectives are framed and conceptualized" by international financial institutions. Some writers have conducted a close ethnographic analysis of experts themselves in order to unveil their political commitments: Galit Sarfaty (2009) explores the ways in which distinct practice groups in the World Bank understand and use the term "human rights"; while Alvaro Santos (2006) analyzes how the term "rule of law" is understood and used by the World Bank and certain subgroups, including the Doing Business project and rule of law reform teams in Latin America.

This move to unveil the politics of experts is aptly summarized by Kratochwil, for whom

> any analysis of this *problematique* [of what the rule of law is and means] must always be historical as well as analytical and must be alert to its

"ideological" dimension. Because it addresses practical issues, the rule
of law is bound to deal with political projects, and these, in turn, always
transcend the world as observed from an (allegedly) "objective" point of
view. (2009, 173, internal citations omitted)

Such an approach to organizing the field problematizes the objectivity
of technique as a foundation for some neutral statement of the rule of law;
rather, the object of study becomes the "political projects" of the experts and
practitioners, offering new sets of actors to analyze and new tools with which
to analyze them. This resonates with Dezalay and Garth's (2002) effort to
unpick the social and ideological motors behind the application of expertise.
And this resonance suggests that the move to expert politics does not offer
an organizing principle. The move presumes that the techniques, or "texts"
(to return to Dezalay and Garth's appropriation of Bourdieu), of rule of
law reform are stable enough on their own to allow an excavation that goes
beyond the purely personal: that is, these texts are capable of being studied
in an analytic, rather than a performative, register. While Santos and Sarfaty
show that this can be done within the constraints of a particular institution,
the very nature of the rule of law field is to utter itself into being beyond these
institutional boundaries: a rule of law expert is a rule of law expert, irrespective of the institution to which she belongs. To unpick her "political project"
requires an individual-level determination of her view of the rule of law at
any given moment. This effort reproduces, or "nests" (Kennedy 1994, 344),
the question of indeterminacy within the politics of the expert.

Calls to context have also proliferated in recent years. These reflect an
unease with the notion that the content of the rule of law can transcend the
bounds of time and space—the various normative, institutional, and cultural
processes that take place within (and construct) a polity over time such that
a set of legal institutions eventually emerges. Erik Jensen (2003, 341), in a
survey of legal and judicial reform projects, simply states that "[l]egal and
judicial reform projects cannot succeed without a stronger understanding of
the actual function and scope of the legal system, and related institutions, in a
particular local context." This is proposed as an organizing move at the policy
level as well. Jethro Pettit and Joanna Wheeler (2005, 1) ask of donors: "How
do the generalised directives of aid agencies relate to context-specific struggles
for rights, rooted historically in experiences of exclusion and marginalisa-
tion?" Caroline Sage, Nicholas Menzies, and Michael Woolcock (2010) speak
at length of the "missing context" in justice reform efforts at the World Bank,
perhaps reflecting the evolution of a view from 1995 when, in a review of its
own efforts in what was then called "legal technical assistance," the World
Bank concluded that "[i]n order for legal technical assistance to have a lasting

impact on a country, it is imperative to include training activities which needs to be adjusted to local conditions" (World Bank Legal Department 1995, 26). This organizing move is well expressed by Tamanaha (2011). Reviewing the historical trajectories of "law and development," he finds among its failings a "connectedness of law principle" (an idea reiterated by Kleinfeld [2012, 217]):

> Legal institutions and cultural attitudes toward law exist inseparably within a broader milieu that includes the history, tradition, and culture of a society; its political and economic system; the distribution of wealth and power; the degree of industrialization; the ethnic, language, and religious make-up of the society (the presence of group tension); the level of education of the populace; the extent of urbanization; and the geo-political surroundings (hostile or unstable neighbors). (Tamanaha 2011, 214)

In other words, *everything* matters.

Such contextualization nests anew the indeterminacy underpinning the field within and across spatial, temporal, and jurisdictional frameworks. As a result, context-based attempts at organization have to pull off a complex double-move of decontextualized contextualization to allow for some non-relativistic value. Peerenboom's (2009, 7–8) attempt to survey and direct the field again provides a helpful example:

> While nowadays there is greater sensitivity to the need to tailor reforms to the particular conditions in developing countries, the overall tendency is still to treat rule of law and rule of law promotion as a single entity or enterprise, and to rely on generally applicable, and hence overly simple, highly reductive and exceedingly abstract, international best practices. . . . A more refined typology of ideal types or patterns of developing countries and rule of law challenges is needed.

The move to context is balanced here by the quest for necessarily decontextualized "refined typologies" and "ideal types." This is exemplified by contemporary development professionals' frequent translation of "context" into "nonstate" or "informal" justice institutions, which can then be systematized in some way to make them an object of development intervention (Wojkowska 2006; Isser [2011] offers a more sober account of the struggles between context and the need for systematization).

In analyzing these organizing moves and attempts to overcome or tame indeterminacy, I am neither suggesting bad faith on the part of rule of law reformers nor impugning deeply held moral or ethical positions. While Krygier (2013, 47)—in responding to Hertogh (2013)—refers to Waldron to acknowledge the essential contestability of the rule of law, he cites his experience of "despotism, violence, anarchy, and other such calamities" in support of his belief in the rule of law as constraining the arbitrary exercise of power. Still, such belief need not necessarily translate into a quest for a strong determinate base for the rule of law. Writing on indicators as a tool,[15] Todd Foglesong and Christopher Stone (2012, 15) recognize the deep difficulty in articulating what the rule of law is and how to do it;[16] however, at the same time they still find value in pursuing some dimensions of it: "If we are never to see justice fully realised or the rule of law permanently established, at least we should be able to see the police solving more crimes with less intrusion on our liberties, and courts able to reduce the time that un-convicted suspects spend in detention." This attempt to grapple with the rule of law appears to resonate with Manderson's polarity—seeking some determinate ground, situated in the particular, in full acknowledgment of the slipperiness of the broader principle.

This is a valuable shift in emphasis. Embracing the simultaneous need for and contingency of determination in a policy setting appears to provide a basis for exploring how a shift to the practical is possible around a core of uncertainty. It is in this light that we might understand David Kennedy's (2003) intervention, in which contest around law in development is manifested in practice through the revelation of political and distributive implications behind the ordering of the rule of law in a particular (for him, technologized) array. It leads him to conclude that the space for political and distributive experimentation around the rule of law is needed. Such a call for more experimentation is reflected in Deval Desai, Deborah Isser, and Michael Woolcock (2012).[17] Experimentation clearly resonates with the idea of making the indeterminate determinate, of exploring possibilities in concrete terms.

Yet both Kennedy and Desai, Isser, and Woolcock contrast experimentation with an account of the field that emphasizes the replication of techniques and tools (and critiques them as political instruments in apolitical coverings, akin to the foundations of the "expert politics" move). This enables an argumentative chiaroscuro in which techniques and tools provide background shading against which experimentation comes to the fore as an appealing set of brushstrokes. While it may be valuable to speak of particular techniques and tools as driven by the incentives and structures within specific development institutions (for example, Santos 2006; Wade 1996; Pritchett and Woolcock 2004), in a field that utters itself into being around an indeterminate core it is difficult to assert such a shared set of techniques and tools and a common framework around which they might coalesce.

Stephen Humphreys (2010, 224) uses the absence of this shared basis to argue that a tools-and-techniques-based view of the field masks the forceful application of ideology by development institutions to create a liberal subject in developing countries:

> [T]oday rule of law is public policy, breaking down into a set of identifiable prescriptions that states everywhere are exhorted, and often required, to implement. . . . And therein lies the rub. For to query what is or is not "rule of law" today is to run immediately into the complex reality of a term of art that saturates contemporary political life and accommodate increasingly broad political desires. The rule of law is an open-ended concept subject to a barrage of motivated deployments, many of which, as we have seen, are disseminated globally from capable centres of global norm-generation and discourse-shaping.

Humphreys' argument is structured around the ways in which the rule of law in practice deviates from a rule of law "ideal" (ibid., 45), through which he attempts to inscribe a stronger sense of betrayal into the "motivated deployments" of the rule of law. Irrespective of the merits of this sense of betrayal, we might take his insight here—the rule of law as a series of open-ended deployments—on its own terms. Doing so suggests that the politics of technique in the rule of law field is not so hidden and that experimentation does not have to be such a challenge. The rule of law's open-endedness (as understood by the field) suggests that the terrain for experimentation is vast.

The problem, then, is not necessarily the propensity of tools and techniques to foreclose the possibilities of reinvention. Rather, the inverse may be true: the possibilities are so broad that we have no common basis on which to adjudge the desirability of experimentation, a point that Linn Hammergren (2002a, 2002b, 2003a, 2003b) drives home in her critiques of the monitoring-and-evaluation methods of rule of law projects. It is in the absence of such a common basis that we might understand risk aversion, the prominence of institutional constraints (such as the overemphasis on disbursement in relation to impact at the World Bank, as highlighted by Andrews, Pritchett and Woolcock [2012, 5–6]), and repetition rather than learning: stasis as a strategic response to the inability to assess and order new approaches to "what works." The field may "oscillate" (to go back to Manderson's term) between the extreme poles of stasis and fragmentation through *sui generis* experimentation,[18] both products of the particular predilections of the reformer, including his disciplinary lenses and his relationship to the organizational constraints within which he might operate.

I have described the field thus far in terms of performativity, negation, and meaning deferred through reaching out or nesting. So far, so postmodern. Where does this leave the institutions and agents that constitute the rule of law field? My sketch of the field has brought out three related "oscillations" resulting from its performative nature: (i) between indeterminacy and determinacy; (ii) between a vast terrain of experimentation and a narrow technologized space of intervention; and (iii) between fragmentation and stasis. The ways in which institutions and agents position themselves in relation to these oscillations would appear to structure how we might translate "polarity" into a sensibility for effective experimentation—that is, experimentation not for its own sake but within a framework of accreted knowledge and learning in which the field can move forward without constantly being unmade. In other words, making sense of the field does not require looking beyond the field for a stable point; rather, it calls for turning our gaze inward, drilling down to a series of microprocesses within the field—the ways in which experiments and projects are chosen, framed, evaluated, learned from, and shared.

Humphreys (2010) turns to projects (albeit within the context of their development institutions, limiting the scope for an analysis of the field). An ongoing project at Australian National University (2013) is attempting to pull together an "empirical mapping" of the field's actors. I argue in the next section that we might instead look within the field to the different ways the field can utter itself. In other words, if saying can make the field so, perhaps we might turn to the different ways of "saying" to see what organizing moves are emerging and whether they might offer a basis for learning and experimentation. My analysis of these moves does not rely on any sort of external justification. I simply read these statements of the field on their own terms. This means downplaying the quest for the (external) *substance* of the rule of law and taking seriously its *form*, or the ways of talking about the rule of law that prove powerful. To that end, I turn to donors as strong voices within the performative field; specifically, I turn to these institutions' hiring statements—whether articulated sets of competencies to be used for all rule of law hiring or competencies derived from specific job postings. This is a move from the level of "field overviews" as providing an insight into the field's constitution to the field's emergence at the practical level.

Hiring Documents as Statements of the Field

In a field constituted not by external touchstones but by the statements of the field's agents themselves, hiring documents are valuable sources. They are, of course, products of the sorts of microprocesses that we might seek to explore ethnographically, documentary artifacts whose singular texts reflect many voices, contests, or mishaps (Riles 2006; Wade 1996). Yet they are also, in the context of the field, highly public institutional utterances setting out a view of the field as an organized space and the sorts of characteristics that might enable one to make field-constituting statements. In examining donors' hiring statements, I focus on large institutions: ones with the resources and power to shape the field while continually uttering it into being.[19] I do not suggest here that donors constitute the field specifically through the agents they hire, nor do I suggest that there is a direct link between these hiring statements and the kind of person who actually gets hired. Rather, I explore hiring statements themselves as insights into how institutions see the field.

To that end, I examine the most recent set of documents from four organizations engaged in significant rule of law work: DFID/the UK government, DFAT, the World Bank, and UNDP. After the US government, these are four of the biggest donors in recent years.[20] All four have clear statements about the rule of law in their hiring documents. The two bilateral agencies have developed a general set of "core competencies" for all rule of law hires, while the two multilateral agencies produce specifications on a job-by-job basis. I look at the emphasis they place on the *form* of knowledge in relation to its *substance*. This has implications for the sort of knowledge that gets shared, the ways in which that happens, and the knowledge and skills required. As a result, this section explores a different "problem of knowledge" from the one identified by Carothers (2006): rather than lamenting the state of knowledge, I am interested in how this lament itself—this statement of indeterminacy—has come to be operationalized by institutions. I am also interested in the experimentation and learning that it does or does not support.

These hiring statements tend to do three things to different degrees. First, they look to hire people with rule of law experience (rather than looking for lawyers, economists, and so on) without necessarily specifying what that is. This reinforces the idea that we have moved on from the rule of law as a site of disciplinary contest to the asserted existence of a rule of law field. Second, they generally (although weakly) seek some sort of determination of the rule of law from beyond the field through concepts, epistemologies, or tools. There is a tension here between appeals to external determinations that cut across the field (such as legal empowerment) and ones that turn to institution-specific approaches. The former places the focus squarely on the field but raises the question of determinacy; the latter resolves the question of determinacy by relying on the weight of the particular institution to underpin an articulation of the rule of law, but it fragments the field by making it contingent on the politics of the institution. Thus, when UNDP (2012b) advertises for a "Programme Specialist, Access to Justice" in New York, it enacts this tension by articulating a "legal empowerment" approach that is simultaneously general and UNDP's own: "Taking a Legal Empowerment of the Poor (LEP) approach, UNDP supports people's socio-economic potential through legal recognition, strengthening housing, land and property rights, labour and employment rights, and economic empowerment." Third, these hiring statements focus on the form of agents' voice rather than an externally underpinned substance. Here, we see some indication of the value of synthesis and the ability to inhabit a debate as characteristics of the rule of law field. I turn now to the documents of each institution to draw these elements out in greater detail.

DFID and the UK Government

DFID (2014, 5) recruits "Security, Justice, Rule of Law and Human Rights" specialists as part of its cadre of "governance advisers."[21] The UK government's Stabilisation Unit, a "uniquely integrated civil-military operational unit . . . designed to . . . operate in high threat environments" (2014a) and overseen by three different government departments, recruits "deployable civilian experts" into a "function area" on "security and justice," which incorporates competencies on "justice," "security and justice sector oversight and accountability," and "local security and justice," among others (2014d).

The DFID competencies are broken down into desirable knowledge and experiences and their corresponding uses. The competencies for many other governance specialists begin with clear statements of the specialism's content: "[c]ore governance concepts (such as capacity, accountability, responsiveness, legitimacy, empowerment, rights)"; "democratic and accountable governance (including elections, parliaments, political parties and the media)"; "[t]he public sector budget cycle from formulation to execution . . . [and] [f]inancial information systems, public procurement and audit"; and "[d]ifferent types of corruption (grand; petty; bribery; fraud; money laundering etc.)." The rule of law competencies, however, begin not with a statement of the rule of law (nor its relationship to security and justice) but with a requirement that candidates have "knowledge and experience" of how it "contribute[s] to development and peace building and state building goals." They then proceed to attach the rule of law to a series of external approaches, goods, and outcomes: the "political-economy drivers" of rule of law reform; its "links to political governance and human rights"; "rule of law for growth, including civil and commercial law"; "rule of law and property rights for the development of the private sector"; and so on. Interestingly, there are two moments in which the competencies attempt to give rule of law some internal content. The first requires governance advisers to recognize a plural institutional view of the rule of law: "[d]ifferent security and justice institutions (state/non-state) and legal systems (common/civil/ religious/traditional)." The second requires a knowledge of "[d]ifferent approaches to strengthening oversight and account-ability of security and justice institutions." The forms of knowledge related to the rule of law here—the voices being privileged—are those that can encom-pass difference.

Of the Stabilisation Unit's three sets of competencies mentioned above, the "security and justice sector oversight and accountability" competencies give the rule of law clear sectoral and institutional content. Oversight consists of the strengthening of institutions to ensure "democratic accountability," parliamentary oversight, and civil society oversight. These are coupled with generic programmatic skills, such as institutional analysis, program design, and monitoring and evaluation. By contrast, the "justice" and "local security and justice" competencies open with statements on the complexity of the rule of law. The former requires an understanding of how to work with a "range of different justice systems, often characterised by legal pluralism," and experi-ence in "[h]olistic approaches to justice sector reform, including cross-sectoral linkages, interdependence and the role of non-state actors in justice delivery." The latter requires knowing how to work with "[n]on-state, informal and tra-ditional security and justice actors and mechanisms[,] [c]ommunity security/ safety processes and actors," and the "[l]inkages between the formal/state and informal/non-state security and justice actors and mechanisms." For both, the specific technical and programmatic competencies then turn to a shop-ping list of goods ("human rights"; "gender equality") and tools (alternative dispute resolution; "paralegals"). Yet "local security and justice" has as a behavioral competency "contextual and cultural awareness and sensitivity." The Stabilisation Unit thus appears to assert that doing "justice" entails a great deal of "holism" as an intellectual exercise—again, this is knowledge as the ability to engage with difference. "Local security and justice" makes a less strong point about knowledge—there, complexity is tied to the range of actors and institutions that straddle the formal/informal divide, as with the DFID competencies—but ties complexity into a behavioral story. In this light, the rule of law field is not just about knowing difference but about inhabiting it: the ability to be "polar" rather than to just think it.

DFAT

DFAT's "Governance Capability Requirements" (2013) are a competency framework for governance that "lay out [DFAT's] understanding of, and approach to, governance"—in other words, a statement of what governance and its components mean to DFAT. The requirements provide guidance to staff on the governance capabilities and depth of knowledge and skill necessary for positions with a significant governance component. "Law and Justice" is one of three themes that cuts across the three core capabilities of "Governance and Institutions"; "Political Systems and Political Economy Analysis"; and "State Building, Fragility and Conflict." These capabilities are further broken down into three levels of expertise: "awareness," "operational," and "expert." There are no behavioral competencies: they are all statements of knowledge or experience.

Several of DFAT's governance capabilities entail specific bodies of knowledge around concepts, epistemologies, and tools: "[the] importance of elites and coalitions"; "why the historical foundations of the state are critical to nation and state building"; and "how enhanced human rights reduces wealth inequality, promotes equity and social stability and contributes to improved democratic governance, and particularly how human rights protection impacts on disadvantaged and marginalised groups and development outcomes." Yet as the competencies move up the three levels of expertise, almost all capabilities require knowledge of "complex issues" or complexity in governance more generally. More specifically, some require detailed knowledge not just of complexity but of the debates around governance issues, such as the "contested relationship between governance and growth." In relation to laws and norms, DFAT stresses the importance of knowing "approaches to understanding how legal rules and social norms shape behaviour and institutional frameworks (including the New Institutional Economics (NIE)) and the potential of these to influence policy direction." While DFAT frames human rights issues in much more determinate and universal terms (for example, by presuming a clear link between rights and development), its statements around laws and legal institutions highlight the importance of knowledge of the complexity of law and justice (for example, "how communities access justice and resolve disputes in legally pluralistic environments" and "how justice is delivered by the state and non-state actors, including through formal and informal justice institutions"); and, for the "expert" level, DFAT's statements call for knowledge of "complex issues" associated with this complexity (for example, "complex issues associated with how justice is delivered by the state and non-state actors").

While DFAT's institutional statements demonstrate at least some attempt to give universal determinate content to the rule of law, in general these statements seem to entail pluralism and complexity. The key to recognizing and operationalizing this complexity appears to reside not in specific subject matter but in a set of intellectual approaches, particularly the ability to straddle debates.

UNDP

Unlike DFID, the Stabilisation Unit, and DFAT, UNDP does not have a set of core competencies for the rule of law. Rather, it produces specific terms of reference (TORs) tailored to specific openings. As a result, UNDP provides no prima facie indication that it sees "rule of law" as a field of practice in which professionals calling themselves rule of law reformers might move from context to context. To explore this a little deeper, I turn to a series of recent TORs for positions characterized as "rule of law" jobs: a "Rule of Law Project Coordinator" in Haiti (UNDP 2013b); a "Technical Specialist (Access to Justice)" in Nepal (UNDP 2013c); a "Programme Manager, Governance and Rule of Law" in Somalia (UNDP 2013a); a "Programme Specialist, Access to Justice" in New York (UNDP 2012b); and "International Consultants to assist the Ministry of Justice in drafting of [sic] the new Strategy for the reform of judiciary" in Montenegro (UNDP 2012a).

None of the TORs require a specific degree, such as a law degree. Instead, they simply require degrees in one of a range of relevant fields (often law, political science, development studies, and the social sciences) and require a certain number of years of experience in "rule of law" (Haiti); "rule and law, access to justice, justice sector coordination, legislative reform and human rights" (Nepal); "[g]overnance and [r]ule of [l]aw" (Somalia); "rule of law, access to justice and legal empowerment issues " (New York); and "relevant professional experience . . . [along with] [e]xtensive knowledge of the rule of law reform process in Montenegro." The TORs thereby assert the field. Save in Montenegro, the required "experience" is not geographically contingent; the TORs merely call for experience in "rule of law"—without offering further content on what that might mean.

The sections in the TORs offering "background" on the job are usually short statements of the rule of law dimensions of the United Nations' engagement in country. As such, they are programmatic rather than policy statements about the rule of law, detailing the specific rule of law project components underway: "support to the judiciary" (Haiti); "legal aid reform" (Nepal); "local governance, institution building, parliament, access to justice, police and community safety" (Somalia); and "[i]ndependence and autonomy of the judiciary, . . . [e]fficiency of the judiciary, . . . [a]ccess to justice and . . . [r]aising of public trust in the judiciary" (Montenegro). As noted above, the background section concerning the job in UNDP's New York headquarters (2012b) offers a much more detailed statement of UNDP's vision of the rule of law, with a specific aim: "ensuring that poor and marginalized people are able to seek and obtain justice, in its widest understanding, through formal or informal processes and in conformity with international human rights standards." The use of "widest understanding" appears to be an acknowledgment of definitional contest, reinforced by the caveat that "the rule of law remit is broad and comprehensive, and varies depending on country and regional challenges"—in other words, a move to context. The TORs then attempt to get around this definitional contest by simply offering a list of interventions that exemplify UNDP's approach: "the reform and development of [states'] constitutional and/or legal frameworks, justice and security services, and accountability and oversight mechanisms, including transitional justice processes" and "legal recognition, strengthening housing, land and property rights, labour and employment rights, and economic empowerment."

As a result, the skills and knowledge required by the TORs vary, creating a complex picture when read together. All TORs call for experience in the rule of law, with the New York job being the only one to define it. The New York job posting refers to a defined set of technical knowledge that derives from this definition (albeit hedged with references to the breadth of the concept of the rule of law): "[s]ubstantive knowledge and understanding of access to justice and legal empowerment as well as more broadly, rule of law, with an emphasis on the provision of coordinated support and management of strategic programmes to advance law and justice; [s]ubstantive knowledge and experience in management of rights based programmes." By contrast, the Somalia posting appears to place much more emphasis on the job's managerial dimension than its rule of law aspect. Almost all of the required competencies are managerial. Indeed, under the subheading "[e]xpert knowledge of own discipline," the posting states in general terms, "[p]ossesses expert knowledge of advanced concepts in primary discipline, a broad knowledge of related disciplines, as well as an indepth knowledge of relevant organizational policies and procedures." The Nepal job posting also lists a series of soft skills as competencies; however, in the list of required skills and experience, it calls for "[s]pecialized knowledge in the areas of legal aid, including indepth familiarity with the international legal and policy framework and comparative international models and 'best practices.'" This job description would appear to require content, situating it not within UNDP but within the field itself—the international technocratic order around legal aid becomes the site of determinate purchase. In other words, this TOR states not only that the field exists but that it is organized; the role of the agent is not to inhabit debate but to find "best practices." In the Montenegro posting, by contrast, there is a resonance with the Stabilisation Unit's behavioral take on rule of law reform. While the TOR gives a programmatic statement of the rule of law, it is the only TOR to identify specific behavioral competencies: "[r]emains calm, in control and good humored even under pressure; [d]emonstrates openness to change and ability to manage complexities." If we choose to read those two competencies together, we might see this TOR as suggesting that rule of law reform requires more than an intellectual engagement with complexity and contest (as in DFAT) and a behavioral commitment to it (as in the Stabilisation Unit). Rather, it requires a set of attitudes—calm, control, and humor—that allows that sort of behavioral and intellectual commitment to take place.

It is difficult to tell a coherent story about the way in which UNDP organizes the rule of law field through its TORs. However, we can draw out a few strands. All TORs recognize the "rule of law" as a discrete field in which agents can work; indeed, one of the conditions of the Nepal job is the ability to go to that field (and not UNDP) to define what "best practices" in rule of law reform look like. Where there is recognition of determinate content in the field (in the New York job), there is also an attempt to underdetermine that content, recognizing the breadth of the rule of law and making a shift to context ("rule of law . . . varies depending on country and regional challenges"). And even the specific country TORs dedicate little space to defining the rule of law, focusing instead on the programmatic content that already exists. They place a greater emphasis on soft skills, to the extent that the Montenegro TOR suggests that a key part of "doing" the rule of law is possessing a set of attitudes and behaviors that enable one to know its complexity.

World Bank

As with UNDP, the World Bank has no centralized set of competencies for its rule of law work. I turn to two recent TORs for "Program Officers" for the Justice for the Poor program in Sierra Leone and Papua New Guinea (both national hires) (World Bank n.d.). I also turn to the TORs for two international hires: a "Public Sector Specialist" (focusing on justice reform) for the Poverty Reduction and Economic Management Unit for Europe and Central Asia (ECA) (World Bank 2012b)[22] and a "Project Officer" for the Justice for the Poor program in Washington, DC (World Bank 2010).[23] Finally, I refer to anonymized versions of the interview and assessment frameworks for the Sierra Leone job.

None of the TORs require candidates to have training in a specific discipline. The ECA job looks for experience "in justice reform with in-depth knowledge in justice reform in a development context." The Washington job requires past experience "working on justice sector reform/social development and/or governance issues in a development context" and "managing programs focusing on legal empowerment, access to justice, local governance, and/or civil society development." The Sierra Leone and Papua New Guinea jobs do not even have this requirement. The ECA job provides no further elaboration on what justice reform might entail. Rather, it describes the position in highly institutional terms, requiring, for example, that the candidate have knowledge and experience of "[World] Bank[] projects and trust funds Operation Rules." As with UNDP, the World Bank here does appear to be sensitive to the importance of recognizing the field (and perhaps thus the risk of its fragmentation through an overemphasis on institution-specific approaches): one of the duties mentioned is to "[c]onduct related research for and support the teams' preparation for presentations, and for collaboration with members of the donor community, [justice reform] experts and other international organizations."

The Washington job provides a little more background regarding what it sees as justice reform, stressing pluralism and complexity: "[The Justice for the Poor program] seeks to understand how plural governance and justice systems function, and how individuals and communities navigate those systems in order to resolve disputes and make claims to (or against) state- and non-state authorities." The Papua New Guinea job turns to the specific programmatic context, but provides a conceptual overview rooted in the World Bank's *World Development Report 2011*:

> The Program aims to support sustainable and equitable development processes that manage grievance and conflict stresses effectively . . . by . . . [i]nvesting in empirical research to build an evidence base about the way justice and security play out in context, particularly from citizens' perspectives; [a]nimating citizen voice by supporting the creation of space for contestation; and [c]onnecting voice and evidence to policy reform and operational activities.

Rule of law reform here is associated with a particular view of the relationship between voice and grievances; but it is animated as much by a view of the importance of empirical research into grievances and conflict as by a set of knowledge-practices. The Sierra Leone job repeats verbatim this statement but follows it up with specifics around two projects: "accountability for [essential] services" and "extractives governance." This fleshes out the rule of law *qua* knowledge-practices: it cuts across other sectors of development.

The notion of the rule of law as a mode of cross-sectoral research tied to the complexity of particular contexts is prevalent in the interview and assessment frameworks for Sierra Leone. Alongside general skills such as critical thinking, motivation, experience working with governments, and written skills, candidates are assessed on their "experience with mixed-methods research" and knowledge of the specific project topic areas (health and extractives). Specifics on the rule of law are absent. The emphasis on contextual crosscutting research continues in the written exercise given to candidates. They are asked to comment on the initial design and objectives of a hypothetical research study on the relationship between Sierra Leone's decentralization law, local governance actors (including traditional power holders, such as paramount chiefs), and local health service delivery. And in the interview framework, candidates are faced with extremely contextual questions about research methodology, such as "Should you invite the chief and/or [the District Health Management Team] to the meetings? Why? What are the drawbacks of inviting them?"

There are also sets of behavioral competencies, such as "[s]trong interpersonal skills, including the ability to engage in dialogue with a range of state and non-state stakeholders, including government officials, civil society, research institutes, donors and traditional authorities" (Papua New Guinea and Sierra Leone); a "proven ability to take the initiative and lead teams in a cross-cultural, multi-disciplinary environment" (Washington); and a "[d]emonstrated ability to develop and maintain productive relationships with government counterparts and donors . . . [e]xcellent team skills, a diplomatic approach, and ability to respond flexibly to challenges" (ECA). The ECA TOR seems to be articulating competencies designed to support the view of the position as predominantly intra-institutional while (perhaps performatively) recognizing the broader field. Given the strong emphasis on rule of law as research in the other three TORs, the ECA TOR appears more in line with the Stabilisation Unit's recognition of the importance of inhabiting an intellectual approach (in the Stabilisation Unit's case, a holistic understanding of justice) than with the set of enabling attitudes demonstrated in UNDP's Montenegro posting.

Summary

All four institutions assert, to some degree, the existence of a rule of law field independent of them. In line with the notion of a performative field, they often do not give a significant amount of determinate content (with UNDP New York being a notable exception). Where they do offer some determinate content, they blend a claim to universal and institution-specific determination, the latter often found in relation to specific programmatic ends in a particular country or region rather than at the global level. Yet all institutions share a common move to an appreciation of context and complexity, along with a concomitant move to privilege the ability to engage in the debate around the rule of law as important to the way they organize the field. In this way, they differ from the moves to context outlined above: rather than simply nesting indeterminacy in a generic call to context, they use context as a launching point to examine the forms that knowledge can take and in which it can be shared. And these donors have rather forceful ideas about the nature of these forms: both mind (DFAT) and personality (the Stabilisation Unit and World Bank) geared towards (or even enabling, as in the case of UNDP Montenegro) the rule of law as a set of intellectual approaches (holism, inhabiting debates) and knowledge-practices (contextual, crosscutting, mixed-methods empirical research).

Conclusion

Despite the best efforts of a disenchanted cadre of participants in and thinkers about rule of law reform, the field persists. Attempts to sow the field with the salt of indeterminacy have led to the blooming of strange flowers. The legitimacy of an indeterminacy argument within the field has had a complex distortive effect. Without a core, the field persists performatively, its agents and institutions affirming its existence. Yet this also shapes the field's progress: overviews pay enough heed to the idea that we do not know what the rule of law is nor how to do it that it looms over attempts to organize the field. As a result, such attempts—usually moves to concepts, epistemologies, or tools— either explicitly preface their arguments with the conditions of their own undoing or have those conditions hover over them. Attempts to talk about "expert politics" and "context" can be seen in this light: they nest the specter of indeterminacy inside and outside the field, respectively.

How, then, do we move forward? If the field is to continue (and there is no reason that it must), how might we learn and, on that basis, experiment productively? In the face of essential contest, one way—drawing on Manderson—would be to inhabit this indeterminacy, to let it constantly generate a sensibility for experimentation. This sits uneasily with the practice of policy making, a practice driven by the need to make concrete determinations, to allocate resources and power. The field-overview literature has continued to struggle with this problem at a theoretical level. Yet in practice, institutions undertaking rule of law reform are coming up with functional answers in their hiring statements. They reiterate the essential contest around the rule of law (often in terms of complexity and context, as well as in the absence of concrete definitions), balancing substance (with its risk of field unmaking) and form of knowledge (or the ways in which the field can be uttered). Although heterogeneous (particularly between bilateral and multilateral institutions), they offer a sophisticated picture of the field as being constituted by a set of intellectual approaches and knowledge-practices. They suggest an intellectual approach marked by debate, holism, and synthesis, coupled with a commitment to knowledge-practices constituted by contextual, crosscutting, mixed-methods empirical research. We might stylize this approach as follows: rule of law reform—as forms of knowing—expresses ways of *telling stories*[24] about law that work in the service of an end. These stories are often written in the genre of concepts, epistemologies, and tools, and are expressed through the vernacular of methods.

Such an approach suggests a useful reconfiguration of the move to experimentation in development, one enabled by the rule of law field's confrontation with its own radical indeterminacy. Dani Rodrik (2000, 2010); Gráinne de Búrca, Robert O. Keohane, and Charles Sabel (2013); and others attempt to determine something as innately inchoate as experimentation as a means of a domesticizing (Bauman 1991, 71) the limitations of the modernist projects they are committed to (development economics, global governance, and so on). They do so by articulating new processes by which the substance of their project might emerge. In the context of the rule of law, I suggest that in the face of indeterminacy we might shift the focus instead to forms of knowledge—the nature of the storytelling—thereby leaving open to political contestation the substance of the rule of law. Such an approach implies a fluency in other disciplines and ideas: for example, articulating the rule of law in terms of the new institutional economics and legal pluralism (DFAT). Rodrik (2010, 25) expresses an anxiety that mixed methods may not leave us with a shared vernacular in which to have an organized conversation: "The bad news is the accentuation of the methodological divergence, which threatens to overshadow the convergence on policy." Yet the behavioral components of the hiring statements, such as the World Bank's ECA TOR, suggest an ongoing commitment to an ability to share stories—something fundamentally necessary for maintaining a performative field. Experimentation in the rule of law field—a shared basis on which to learn—would be well served by jettisoning the anxieties of substantive content and committing to a set of skills and attitudes, as well as forms and styles, that allows us to package and unpackage knowledge about law and tell its story across a range of sectors.

References

Andrews, Matt, Lant Pritchett, and Michael Woolcock. 2012. "Escaping Capability Traps through Problem-Driven Iterative Adaptation (PDIA)." Center for Global Development Working Paper 299.

Armytage, Livingston. 2012. *Reforming Justice: A Journey to Fairness in Asia*. Cambridge: Cambridge University Press.

Australian National University. 2013. "Responsive Rule of Law." Last modified January 14. http://regnet.anu.edu.au/responsive-rule-law/home.

Bauman, Zygmunt. 1991. *Modernity and Ambivalence*. Cambridge: Polity Press.

Bourdieu, Pierre. 1977. *Outline of a Theory of Practice*. Cambridge: Cambridge University Press.

———. 1981. "Men and Machines." In *Advances in Social Theory and Methodology: Toward an Integration of Micro- and Macro-Sociologies*, edited by Karin Knorr-Cetina and Aaron V. Cicourel, 304–17. Boston: Routledge and Kegan Paul.

———. 1990. *The Logic of Practice*. Translated by Richard Nice. Cambridge: Polity Press.

———. 1998. *Practical Reason: On the Theory of Action*. Redwood City: Stanford University Press.

———. 2004. *Science of Science and Reflexivity*. Cambridge: Polity Press.

Carothers, Thomas. 2006. "The Problem of Knowledge." In *Promoting the Rule of Law Abroad: In Search of Knowledge*, edited by Thomas Carothers, 15–30. Washington, DC: Carnegie Endowment for International Peace.

Comaroff, Jean, and John Comaroff. 2004. "Criminal Justice, Cultural Justice: The Limits of Liberalism and the Pragmatics of Difference in the New South Africa." *American Ethnologist* 31:188–204.

de Búrca, Gráinne, Robert O. Keohane, and Charles Sabel. 2013. "New Modes of Pluralist Global Governance." *NYU Journal of International Law and Politics* 45:723–86.

de Soto, Hernando. 2000. *The Mystery of Capital: Why Capitalism Triumphs in the West and Fails Everywhere Else*. London: Bantam Press.

Department for International Development (DFID). 2014. "Governance Adviser Technical Competencies." https://www.gov.uk/government/uploads/system/uploads/attachment_data/file/236512/governance1.pdf.

Department of Foreign Affairs and Trade (DFAT). 2013. "Governance Capability Requirements." Draft of January 29. On file with the author.

Desai, Deval, Deborah Isser, and Michael Woolcock. 2012. "Rethinking Justice Reform in Fragile and Conflict-Affected States: Lessons for Enhancing the Capacity of Development Agencies." *Hague Journal on the Rule of Law* 4:54–75.

Desai, Deval, and Michael Woolcock. Forthcoming. "The Politics—and Process—of Rule of Law Systems in Developmental States." In *The Politics of Inclusive Devel-*

opment: Interrogating the Evidence, edited by Badru Bukenya, Samuel Hickey, and Kunal Sen. Oxford: Oxford University Press.

Dezalay, Yves, and Bryant G. Garth. 2002. *The Internationalization of Palace Wars: Lawyers, Economists, and the Contest to Transform Latin American States.* Chicago: University of Chicago Press.

———. 2010. "Marketing and Selling Transnational 'Judges' and Global 'Experts': Building the Credibility of (Quasi)judicial Regulation." *Socio-Economic Review* 8:113–30.

———. 2011. "Introduction: Lawyers, Law, and Society." In *Lawyers and the Rule of Law in an Era of Globalization*, edited by Yves Dezalay and Bryant G. Garth, 1–16. Abingdon: Routledge.

———. 2012. "Marketing Professional Expertise by (Re)inventing States: Professional Rivalries between Lawyers and Economists as Hegemonic Strategies in the International Market for the Reproduction of National State Elites." In *Development and Semiperiphery: Postneoliberal Trajectories in South America and Central Eastern Europe*, edited by Renato Boschi and Carlos Henrique Santana 165–80. London: Anthem Press.

Duffield, Mark. 2007. *Development, Security and Unending War: Governing the World of Peoples*. Cambridge: Polity Press

Ellerman, David. 2002. "Should Development Agencies Have Official Views?" *Development in Practice* 12:285–97.

Europa Nu. 2010. "Project Officer." Application process closed May 10. http://www.europa-nu.nl/id/vier7erm49zr/project_officer.

Foglesong, Todd, and Christopher Stone. 2012. "Strengthening the Rule of Law by Measuring Local Practice, One Rule at a Time." In *Innovations in Rule of Law*, edited by Juan Carlos Botero, Ronald Janse, Sam Muller, and Christine S. Pratt, 12–15. The Hague: Hague Institute for the Internationalization of Law and the World Justice Project.

Garth, Bryant G. 2002. "Building Strong and Independent Judiciaries through the New Law and Development: Behind the Paradox of Consensus Programs and Perpetually Disappointing Results." *DePaul Law Review* 52:383–400.

Gauri, Varun, Michael Woolcock, and Deval Desai. 2013. "Intersubjective Meaning and Collective Action in Developing Societies: Theory, Evidence and Policy Implications." *Journal of Development Studies* 49:160–72.

Ginsburg, Tom. 2011. "Pitfalls of Measuring the Rule of Law." *Hague Journal on the Rule of Law* 3:269–80.

Golub, Stephen. 2003. "Beyond Rule of Law Orthodoxy: The Legal Empowerment Alternative." Carnegie Endowment for International Peace Working Paper 42.

Hammergren, Linn. 2002a. *Assessments, Monitoring, Evaluation, and Research: Improving the Knowledge Base for Judicial Reform Programs*. Washington, DC: United States Agency for International Development.

———. 2002b. "Latin American Criminal Justice Reform: Evaluating the Evaluators." *Sistemas Judiciales* 3:59–66.

———. 2003a. "International Assistance to Latin American Justice Programs: Towards an Agenda for Reforming the Reformers." In *Beyond Common Knowl-*

edge: *Empirical Approaches to the Rule of Law*, edited by Erik Jensen and Thomas Heller, 290–335. Redwood City: Stanford University Press.

———. 2003b. *Uses of Empirical Research in Refocusing Judicial Reforms: Lessons from Five Countries*. Washington, DC: World Bank.

Hatchard, John, and Amanda Perry-Kessaris, eds. 2003. *Law and Development: Facing Complexity in the 21st Century*. London: Cavendish.

Hayat, Hooria, and Khola Ahmed. 2008. "Legal Empowerment: An Impossible Dream." DFID and Women's Empowerment in Muslim Contexts Working Paper.

Heckman, James, Robert Nelson, and Lee Cabatingan. 2010. *Global Perspectives on the Rule of Law*. London: Routledge.

Hertogh, Marc. 2013. "A Sociology of the Rule of Law: Why, What, Where? And Who Cares?" *Recht der Werkelijkheid* 34:42–46.

Humphreys, Stephen. 2010. *Theatre of the Rule of Law: Transnational Legal Intervention in Theory and Practice*. Cambridge: Cambridge University Press.

Isser, Deborah. 2011. "Conclusion: Understanding and Engaging Customary Justice Systems." In *Customary Justice and the Rule of Law in War-Torn Societies*, edited by Deborah Isser, 325–67. Washington, DC: United States Institute of Peace.

Jensen, Erik. 2003. "The Rule of Law and Judicial Reform: The Political Economy of Diverse Institutional Patterns and Reformers' Responses." In *Beyond Common Knowledge: Empirical Approaches to the Rule of Law*, edited by Erik Jensen and Thomas Heller, 336–81. Redwood City: Stanford University Press.

Jensen, Erik, and Thomas Heller, eds. 2003. *Beyond Common Knowledge: Empirical Approaches to the Rule of Law*. Redwood City: Stanford University Press.

Kennedy, David. 2003. "'Laws and Developments.'" In *Law and Development: Facing Complexity in the 21st Century*, edited by John Hatchard and Amanda Perry-Kessaris, 17–26. London: Cavendish.

Kennedy, Duncan. 1994. "A Semiotics of Legal Argument." In *Collected Courses of the Academy of European Law*, vol. 3, bk. 2, edited by the Academy of European Law, 309–65. Amsterdam: Kluwer Academic Publishers.

Kleinfeld, Rachel. 2006. "Competing Definitions of the Rule of Law." In *Promoting the Rule of Law Abroad: In Search of Knowledge*, edited by Thomas Carothers, 31–74. Washington, DC: Carnegie Endowment for International Peace.

———. 2012. *Advancing the Rule of Law Abroad: Next Generation Reform*. Washington, DC: Carnegie Endowment for International Peace.

Kleinfeld, Rachel, and Kalypso Nicolaidis. 2009. "Can a Post-colonial Power Export the Rule of Law? Elements of a General Framework." In *Relocating the Rule of Law*, edited by Gianluigi Palombella and Neil Walker, 139–70. Oxford: Hart.

Kratochwil, Friedrich. 2009. "Has the 'Rule of Law' Become a 'Rule of Lawyers'? An Inquiry into the Use and Abuse of an Ancient *Topos* in Contemporary Debates." In *Relocating the Rule of Law*, edited by Gianluigi Palombella and Neil Walker, 171–96. Oxford: Hart.

Krygier, Martin. 2009. "The Rule of Law: Legality, Teleology, Sociology." In *Relocating the Rule of Law*, edited by Gianluigi Palombella and Neil Walker, 45-70. Oxford: Hart.

————. 2012. "Why the Rule of Law Is Too Important to Be Left to Lawyers." *Prawo i Więź* 2:30–52.

————. 2013. "Still a Rule of Law Guy." *Recht der Werkelijkheid* 34:47–55.

Latour, Bruno. 1988. "The Politics of Explanation: An Alternative." In *Knowledge and Reflexivity, New Frontiers in the Sociology of Knowledge*, edited by Steve Woolgar, 155–76. London: Sage.

Magen, Amichai. 2009. "The Rule of Law and Its Promotion Abroad: Three Problems of Scope." *Stanford Journal of International Law* 45:51–116.

Manderson, Desmond. 2012. "Modernism, Polarity, and the Rule of Law." *Yale Journal of Law and the Humanities* 24:475–505.

Martin, John Levi. 2003. "What Is Field Theory?" *American Journal of Sociology* 109:1–49

Maru, Vivek. 2010. "Allies Unknown: Social Accountability and Legal Empowerment." *Health and Human Rights* 12:83–93.

Merry, Sally Engle. 1988. "Legal Pluralism." *Law and Society Review* 22:869–96.

North, Douglass, John Joseph Wallis, Steven Webb, and Barry Weingast. 2007. "Limited Access Orders in the Developing World: A New Approach to the Problems of Development." World Bank Policy Research Working Paper 4359.

North, Douglass, John Joseph Wallis, and Barry Weingast. 2009. *Violence and Social Orders: A Conceptual Framework for Interpreting Recorded Human History*. Cambridge: Cambridge University Press.

Organisation for Economic Co-operation and Development. 2014. "Query Wizard for International Development Statistics." Accessed January 1. http://stats.oecd.org/qwids.

Pahuja, Sundhya. 2004. "Power and the Rule of Law in the Global Context." *Melbourne University Law Review* 28:232–53.

Palombella, Gianluigi. 2009. "The Rule of Law and its Core." In *Relocating the Rule of Law*, edited by Gianluigi Palombella and Neil Walker, 17–42. Oxford: Hart.

Palombella, Gianluigi, and Neil Walker, eds. 2009. *Relocating the Rule of Law*. Oxford: Hart.

Peerenboom, Randall. 2009. "The Future of Rule of Law: Challenges and Prospects for the Field." *Hague Journal on the Rule of Law* 1:5–14.

Peerenboom, Randall, Michael Zürn, and André Nollkaemper. 2012. "Conclusion: From Rule of Law Promotion to Rule of Law Dynamics." In *Rule of Law Dynamics in an Era of International and Transnational Governance*, edited by Michael Zürn, André Nollkaemper, and Randall Peerenboom, 305–24. Cambridge: Cambridge University Press.

Perry-Kessaris, Amanda. 2009. "Introduction." In *Law in the Pursuit of Development: Principles into Practice?*, edited by Amanda Perry-Kessaris, 1–9. Abingdon: Routledge.

Pettit, Jethro, and Joanna Wheeler. 2005. "Developing Rights? Relating Discourse to Context and Practice." *IDS Bulletin* 36:1–8.

Pritchett, Lant, and Michael Woolcock. 2004. "Solutions When the Solution Is the Problem: Arraying the Disarray in Development." *World Development* 32:191–212.

Raz, Joseph. 1977. "The Rule of Law and Its Virtue." *Law Quarterly Review* 93:195–202.

Riles, Annelise. 2006. "Introduction: In Response." In *Documents: Artifacts of Modern Knowledge*, edited by Annelise Riles, 1–41. Ann Arbor: University of Michigan Press.

Rittich, Kerry. 2006. "The Future of Law and Development: Second-Generation Reforms and the Incorporation of the Social." In *The New Law and Economic Development: A Critical Perspective*, edited by David Trubek and Alvaro Santos, 203–52. Cambridge: Cambridge University Press.

Rodriguez, Daniel, Matthew McCubbins, and Barry Weingast. 2010. "The Rule of Law Unplugged." *Emory Law Journal* 59:1455–94.

Rodrik, Dani. 2000. "Institutions for High-Quality Growth: What They Are and How to Acquire Them." NBER Working Paper 7540.

———. 2010. "The New Development Economics: We Shall Experiment, but How Shall We Learn?" In *What Works in Development? Thinking Big and Thinking Small*, edited by Jessica Cohen and William Easterly, 24–47. Washington, DC: Brookings Institution Press.

Sage, Caroline, Nicholas Menzies, and Michael Woolcock. 2010. "Taking the Rules of the Game Seriously: Mainstreaming Justice in Development in the World Bank's Justice for the Poor Program." In *Legal Empowerment: Practitioners' Perspectives*, edited by Stephen Golub, 19–37. Rome: International Development Law Organization.

Santos, Alvaro. 2006. "The World Bank's Use of the 'Rule of Law' Promise in Economic Development." In *The New Law and Economic Development: A Critical Perspective*, edited by David Trubek and Alvaro Santos, 253–300. Cambridge: Cambridge University Press.

Sarfaty, Galit. 2009. "Why Culture Matters in International Institutions: The Marginality of Human Rights at the World Bank." *American Journal of International Law* 103:647–83.

Schirato, Tony, and Jen Webb. 2002. "Bourdieu's Notion of Reflexive Knowledge." *Social Semiotics* 12:255–68.

Stabilisation Unit. 2014a. "About the Unit." Accessed January 1. http://www.stabilisationunit.gov.uk/about-us.html.

———. 2014b. "Justice." Accessed January 1. www.stabilisationunit.gov.uk/attachments/article/178/Justice.doc.

———. 2014c. "Profile for Security and Justice Function: Local Security and Justice." Accessed January 1. http://www.stabilisationunit.gov.uk/attachments/category/61/Non-state%20security%20and%20justice.doc.

———. 2014d. "Security and Justice Profiles: Border Management." Accessed January 1. www.stabilisationunit.gov.uk/attachments/article/645/SecurityandJusticeProfiles.doc.

Stephenson, Matthew. 2006. "A Trojan Horse in China?" In *Promoting the Rule of Law Abroad: In Search of Knowledge*, edited by Thomas Carothers, 191–216. Washington, DC: Carnegie Endowment for International Peace.

Tamanaha, Brian Z. 2004. *On the Rule of Law: History, Politics, Theory*. Cambridge: Cambridge University Press.

———. 2009. "A Concise Guide to the Rule of Law." In *Relocating the Rule of Law*, edited by Gianluigi Palombella and Neil Walker, 1–16. Oxford: Hart.

———. 2011. "The Primacy of Society and the Failures of Law and Development." *Cornell International Law Journal* 44:209–47.

Tamanaha, Brian, Caroline Sage, and Michael Woolcock, eds. 2012. *Legal Pluralism and Development: Scholars and Practitioners in Dialogue.* Cambridge: Cambridge University Press.

Thomas, Chantal. 2010. "Law and Neoclassical Economic Development in Theory and Practice: Toward an Institutionalist Critique of Institutionalism." *Cornell Law Review* 96:967–1024.

Trebilcock, Michael, and Ronald Daniels. 2008. *Rule of Law Reform and Development: Charting the Fragile Path of Progress.* Northampton: Edward Elgar.

Trubek, David, and Marc Galanter. 1974. "Scholars in Self-Estrangement: Some Reflections on the Crisis in Law and Development Studies in the United States." *Wisconsin Law Review* 4:1062–102.

Trubek, David, and Alvaro Santos, eds. 2006. *The New Law and Economic Development: A Critical Perspective.* Cambridge: Cambridge University Press.

United Nations Development Programme (UNDP). 2012a. "International Consultants to Assist the Ministry of Justice in Drafting of the New Strategy for the Reform of Judiciary in Montenegro (2013–2018): Two Positions." Application process closed August 9. http://jobs.undp.org/cj_view_job.cfm?cur_job_id=31662.

———. 2012b. "Programme Specialist, Access to Justice." Application process closed September 19. http://jobs.undp.org/cj_view_job.cfm?cur_job_id=32536.

———. 2013a. "Programme Manager, Governance and Rule of Law." Application process closed June 17. http://jobs.undp.org/cj_view_job.cfm?cur_job_id=37930.

———. 2013b. "Rule of Law Project Coordinator." Application process closed September 27. http://jobs.undp.org/cj_view_job.cfm?cur_job_id=40423.

———. 2013c. "Technical Specialist (Access to Justice)." Application process closed June 26. http://jobs.undp.org/cj_view_job.cfm?cur_job_id=37890.

UNjobs. 2012. "Public Sector Specialist, Washington." Application process closed April 16. http://unjobs.org/vacancies/1332798043278.

von Broembsen, Marlese. 2012. "Legal Empowerment of the Poor: The Re-emergence of a Lost Strand of Human Rights?" Rapoport Center Human Rights Working Paper 1/2012.

Wade, Robert. 1996. "Japan, the World Bank, and the Art of Paradigm Maintenance: The East Asian Miracle in Political Perspective." *New Left Review I* 217:3–36.

Waldron, Jeremy. 2002. "Is the Rule of Law an Essentially Contested Concept (in Florida)?" *Law and Philosophy* 21:137–64.

Wojkowska, Ewa. 2006. *Doing Justice: How Informal Justice Systems Can Contribute.* Oslo: United Nations Development Programme Oslo Governance Center.

World Bank. 2010. "Project Officer." Application process closed May 10. On file with the author.

———. 2011. *World Development Report 2011: Conflict, Security and Development.* Washington, DC: World Bank.

———. 2012a. "Justice for the Poor Management Team." Last modified June 21. http://web.worldbank.org/WBSITE/EXTERNAL/TOPICS/EXTLAWJUS-

TICE/EXTJUSFORPOOR/0,,contentMDK:23010306~menuPK:8172406~pa
gePK:210058~piPK:210062~theSitePK:3282787,00.html.

———. 2012b. "Public Sector Specialist, Washington." Application process closed April 16. On file with the author.

———. n.d. "Terms of Reference for Program Officer (Sierra Leonean National), Justice for the Poor Program, World Bank, Sierra Leone" and "Terms of Reference for Program Officer (National Hire), Justice for the Poor Program, World Bank, Papua New Guinea." On file with the author.

World Bank Legal Department. 1995. "The World Bank and Legal Technical Assistance: Initial Lessons." World Bank Working Paper 1414.

Notes

1. Alluding to Pritchett and Woolcock's (2004) diagnosis of bureaucratic rationality in development as "getting to Denmark."

2. All data are drawn from Organisation for Economic Co-operation and Development (2014).

3. It is important to bear in mind that these are a relatively narrow set of claims. I am dealing simply with the rule of law reform field as an object of analysis. I am not dealing with the rule of law as a coalesced set of concepts; the rule of law as a rhetoric for legitimating the exercise of power and performance of exploitation (Pahuja 2004, 237–46); the rule of law as a global discourse used to define, order, and control people and states (Duffield 2007, 6–15); or other similar global contextualizations of the term. I do not suggest that my explorations of the nature of the rule of law have validity beyond the field and its operations.

4. See Martin (2003, especially 15–34) for a short historical overview of field theory in the social sciences. He also traces the emergence and impact of Bourdieu on the study of the field.

5. Many accounts of the history of rule of law reform, or law and development more generally, use Trubek and Galanter (1974) as a touchstone from which to organize a temporal narrative of rule of law practices or moments of intervention (Trubek and Santos 2006, 13). Yet the notion that this narrative can constitute a history in the Bourdieusian sense—a structuring of positions—is challenged by the laments that we have experienced repetition rather than progress in the field; see, for example, Kleinfeld's (2012, 2) suggestion that "rule-of-law practitioners and scholars keep waking up to the same predicaments, noting the same things in the same working papers, and then going back to do the same things."

6. It is important to distinguish between the history of practices and a history of a self-aware field. The former is reflected in the various attempts to taxonomize the history of law and development into "waves" (e.g., Magen 2009; Tamanaha 2004; Santos 2006). The latter, marked by a struggle to understand what might and might not count as part of the rule of law field, is captured by Kleinfeld (2006). She speaks of "twenty years of . . . fevered activity toward ambiguous ends" and footnotes it with the difficulty of finding an "easy start date" for rule of law reform activities, suggesting that we might go as far back as "the era of Rome, or even ancient Greece" to see how developed countries affected reforms of weaker states; or that we start with the law and development movement of the 1960s or post-Soviet transitions in the 1980s (ibid., 64, 73 n. 91). In essence, this history of practices offers no resolution to the idea that in the context of the field we do not know what the rule of law is nor how to do it.

7. Interestingly, the idea of rule of law as security and a counterweight to state fragility does not appear in this analysis, nor in most of their subsequent oeuvre (although it briefly appears in Dezalay and Garth 2010, 118).

8. *Supra* n. 2 and accompanying text.

9. In keeping with the laments about a lack of conceptual clarity, the terminology around the rule of law—including its relationship to "justice"—is fraught with definitional complexity, especially regarding which word encompasses what norms, institutions, systems, and so on. I use the terminology roughly in line with my diagnosis of the indeterminacy of the field's core infra, understanding it to be taken "infra-reflexively"—in other words, by a knowing set of readers (Latour 1988).

10. See, e.g., PROLAW at Loyola University (http://www.luc.edu/prolaw/about_prolaw.shtml) or the LLM in Democratic Governance and Rule of Law at Ohio Northern University (http://llm.onu.edu). There are also graduate courses cropping up in which the rule of law, justice, and law and development are significant and separately articulated subspecialities—for example, at Australian National University (http://law.anu.edu.au/masters-program/requirements-0) and, more recently, at the University of Manchester (http://www.manchester.ac.uk/postgraduate/taughtdegrees/courses/atoz/07063/law-and-development-llm/course-details).

11. I do not make a causal claim here: ascertaining whether notions of indeterminacy created the self-articulating field or vice versa may not be possible for a field that is constantly inventing its own history anew; more importantly, is not relevant to the dynamics by which they continue to constitute each other and to the possibilities for new learning.

12. Manderson relies on Giorgio Agamben's translation in *State of Exception* of the original German phrase in Benjamin's *On the Critique of Violence* ("die seltsame und zunächst entmutgende Erfahrungvon der letzlichen Unentscheidbarkeit aller Rechtsprobleme").

13. A serious enough review of the field to be named one of *Foreign Affairs* magazine's best foreign policy books of 2012.

14. Peerenboom (2009, 6) suggests organizing the field around concept, method, empirical tools, and disciplines. I see moves to organize around method and discipline as reflecting an epistemological dissatisfaction with prevailing regimes of knowledge.

15. Indicators could be understood as epistemologies of—or modes of knowing—the rule of law (Ginsburg 2011) and as subject to similar undetermining moves. The process of developing indicators could also be expressed as a tool for doing the rule of law—for generating legal institutional change, for example (Foglesong and Stone 2012).

16. In one sense, they pass that responsibility to (and thus organize the field around) the national level: "The goal [of rule of law reform] should be the establishment of such a professional culture and the promotion of officials and citizens adept at the invention of new measures suited to their own needs" (Foglesong and Stone 2012, 15).

17. While retaining the particularities of the rule of law field's complex relationship to indeterminacy, we might situate this within the broader trend in recent literature toward formalizing "experimentalist" or "experimental" approaches to development (Hall, Menzies, and Woolcock [this volume] problematize the conflation of these two terms) as a counterpoint to "blueprint" (Rodrik 2000) or technologized practices (Ellerman 2002; de Burca, Keohane, and Sabel 2013).

18. The operation of this pole in the field can be seen in the often cynical accounts of the instrumentalization of the term "rule of law" to justify any sort of project: Stephenson (2006, 196) cites a Chinese legal academic as saying, "Everyone uses the phrase [rule of law] because everyone can get behind it and it might make it easier to get funding."

19. I do not seek to propagate the idea that major institutional donors are the only ones that matter in the rule of law field; indeed, Maru (this volume) and Goldston (this volume) make a clear case for the value of the work of other actors. However, the hiring statements of large donors with numerous rule of law staff and consultants offer heuristic value in the context of a field uttered into being by its institutions and agents.

20. Other donors who have contributed similar amounts of ODA in recent years include the Japanese (mainly on the back of a US$240 million infusion into the Law and Order Trust Fund for Afghanistan in 2011), the Germans (again, infusions into this trust fund and other Afghanistan-related activities), the European Union, and the Dutch.

21. Other specialisms include "Governance, Political and Institutional Analysis"; "Political Systems and Accountable Governance"; "Public Sector Governance and Institutional Reform"; "Public Financial Management and Taxation"; and "Corruption."

22. The TOR is accurately reproduced in UNjobs (2012).

23. The TOR is accurately reproduced in Europa Nu (2010).

24. Manderson (2012, 491–93) explicitly relates Benjamin's idea of the mythic register of law to the ability to inhabit and employ contradiction in modernist story writing.

Abstract

This chapter recommends that the United Nations reexamine its purpose, approach, methodology, and results in relation to its rule of law assistance in postconflict and fragile states. Above all, the United Nations needs to return to the human rights-based "roots" of its rule of law engagement with member states, which date back to 1955. Sixty years later, the organization has lost its groove—it pursues overly broad, complex goals; adopts increasingly unrealistic Security Council mandates to "strengthen justice systems"; finds itself entrenched in a law and order narrative; and, most importantly, shows little evidence of success. The organization also appears disengaged from the immense body of literature detailing the conceptual and operational challenges and exploring new approaches.

A more nimble organization needs to emerge—one that avoids the overheated rhetoric of the rule of law as an "applicable fix for society as a whole" (Humphreys 2010), concentrates on fewer goals, cherishes learning, and utilizes the leverage of the international human rights framework to support states in alleviating injustice in its broadest sense.

3   Reboot Required: The United Nations' Engagement in Rule of Law Reform in Postconflict and Fragile States

David Marshall

Introduction

In mid-January 2014, I was in an armored vehicle, being driven down the main road of the destroyed town of Bentiu in Unity State, South Sudan. Protected by armed United Nations (UN) peacekeepers from Mongolia, our convoy was on its way to meet the newly installed government official responsible for the area. En route, we passed civilians and a policeman lying butchered in the street (Office of the High Commissioner for Human Rights 2014). Those civilians able to flee after the explosion of violence on December 15, 2013, had headed to the local UN compound, where they were receiving protection, along with food, safe water, and medical attention. By the end of January 2014, the UN was protecting approximately 80,000 displaced civilians from harm (ibid.).

There were credible allegations of mass atrocities committed by both sides of the conflict, including "reports of mass killings, extrajudicial killings, arbi-

The views expressed herein are mine alone and do not necessarily reflect the views of the United Nations. I am grateful to the UN Sabbatical Leave Programme for providing an opportunity to explore the issues raised in this chapter and to the Visiting Fellows Program at Harvard Law School's Human Rights Program. I would like to thank Jennifer Poon and Zoe Brennan-Krohn for their helpful research assistance.

trary detention, enforced disappearances, sexual violence, the widespread destruction of property and the use of children in the conflict" (Office of the High Commissioner for Human Rights 2014). Particularly disturbing was news of an atrocity that allegedly occurred in a police station in the nation's capital, Juba. According to the UN and Human Rights Watch, hundreds of civilians were reportedly rounded up, taken to a building, and killed because of their ethnicity (ibid.; see also Human Rights Watch 2014). The allegation was of potentially profound consequence because the perpetrators included national police and soldiers, both of whom had received years of mentoring and training from the international community. Even if the perpetrators had been arrested, it was unclear whether South Sudan's justice system was credible enough to ensure a degree of accountability (see Human Rights Watch 2012). This was despite the fact that the UN has been providing rule of law assistance to the country's justice sector since 2005 (Security Council 2005, paras. 4 [vii]–[viii]).

Unlike the UN's humanitarian assistance efforts, the UN's robust role in institution-building in postconflict and fragile states is a fairly recent endeavor: it did not gather steam until 2003, when large peacekeeping missions were deployed to support the reform of local institutions. The center of attention for UN efforts in this regard has become the justice sector—police, prisons, and the judicial system (including the courts and prosecutors).

After more than a decade of providing "comprehensive" rule of law assistance, the UN has been struggling to identify progress, as has the rest of the international community. Of course, the challenges faced in postconflict and fragile states are profound. The settings for interventions are characterized by deep gaps in capacities, rampant corruption, little political will, a lack of trust in institutions, and economic and political inequality. In addition, most of these states have legacies of injustice that extend well beyond the criminal justice system, which is often the focus of international rule of law assistance.

Though the UN must bear some responsibility for the lack of progress, much criticism can also be placed on an international rule of law "industry" that the UN has inevitably been drawn into. The international community remains enamored with the notion that "strengthened justice systems" are the fix for most ills that face states emerging from crisis, despite the lack of evidence of success. A functioning justice system is believed to "solve problems of corruption, violence, sickness, ignorance and poverty" (American Bar Association 2008). According to the Commission on Legal Empowerment of the Poor (2008, 1), "[F]our billion people around the world are robbed of the chance to better their lives and climb out of poverty because they are excluded from the rule of law." In 2012, at the conclusion of the UN General Assembly's "High-Level Meeting on the Rule of Law," member states issued a declaration stating that the "advancement of the rule of law at the national and international levels is essential for sustained and inclusive economic growth, sustainable development, the eradication of poverty and hunger and the full realization of all human rights and fundamental freedoms" (General Assembly 2012, para. 7), despite not having any evidence to support this assertion.

This chapter suggests that the UN's approach suffers from profound problems and is in need of radical change. There is a lack of clarity of purpose with regard to the core objectives of the organization's rule of law assistance. What began decades ago as the UN Centre for Human Rights' provision of fairly small "technical advisory services" based on human rights, democracy, and values to requesting member states has morphed into formidable Security Council mandates that demand "comprehensive" and "rapid" approaches to rule of law reform efforts in postconflict and fragile states. But such approaches appear to be centered on a very narrow field of the rule of law. Since 2000, the Security Council has tasked virtually all new peacekeeping operations with assisting host-country authorities in "strengthening the rule of law," with a primary focus on criminal justice institutions. This narrow perspective is also reflected in UN headquarters.

This chapter does not suggest a diminished role for support to coercive institutions (defined as those institutions tasked with ensuring safety and public order). This is a core function of the UN's "peace and security authority" under the Charter of the United Nations. It has most recently, and visibly, been seen in the Democratic Republic of Congo, where the UN Force Intervention Brigade was deployed with a mandate to use deadly force to protect civilians. But coercive institutions have remained the default entry point for the UN and much of the international rule of law industry, even in countries that are inching toward peaceful transitions. The consequence is that there appears to be little regard for supporting local initiatives or innovations not connected to state institutions, as well as little interest in understanding or engaging informal justice systems, which are often the main providers of justice.[1]

The role of international human rights law and its machinery is absent from much of the UN's work in this field. Linkages with UN human rights bodies—such as the Human Rights Council, treaty-monitoring bodies, the

Office of the High Commissioner for Human Rights (OHCHR), and independent experts (e.g., special rapporteurs)—are not explored. Over the past five decades, international human rights have undergone a widespread revolution, and they offer a potent set of rules and standards regarding the protection of the individual. Some scholarship suggests a strong connection between the international human rights machinery and improved domestic practice (Sikkink 2011; Simmons 2009). Of course, while a rights-based approach is not the "elixir" for addressing profound rule of law deficits in postconflict and fragile states, leveraging international legal obligations and strengthening the interconnectedness among the various components of the UN human rights machinery are useful tools that should be more heavily employed.

Particularly striking is the disconnect between the UN's approach and the literature exploring the reasons for a lack of progress within the international rule of law industry (see Carothers 1998, 2006; Humphreys 2010; Jensen and Heller 2003; Kleinfeld 2012; Samuels 2006; Tamanaha 2011). While some members of the international rule of law industry are assessing why its endeavors are not working and examining possible innovations (Samuels 2006), the UN is not engaging in any meaningful introspection. Rule of law literature is bereft of articles and research from UN field staff exploring their endeavors—what worked and why, as well as lessons learned—because there are few institutional incentives to do so.

The lack of progress raises profound conceptual and operational questions for the UN, particularly the Security Council, member states, and the entities responsible for rule of law delivery. This chapter attempts to explore those questions at length. I draw primarily on published reports, as well as my own observations collected while working on rule of law programs in postconflict and fragile states. The first section lays out the UN architecture and present-day mandates regarding who is responsible for what in the field of rule of law assistance, both at headquarters and in field operations. The second section looks briefly at recent UN field operations. This is followed, in the third and fourth sections, by an exploration of the UN's rule of law experience in Haiti specifically and UN peacekeeping doctrine generally. The fifth section then focuses on the degree to which the organization's knowledge management is effectively capturing what it is actually doing in this field. The suitability of the "rapid deployment" of rule of law expertise is explored in the sixth section. The seventh section explores the assertions regarding the actual rule of law capacity of the UN. Following this section is an examination of how the rule of law is considered by the two key organs of the UN—the General Assembly and the Security Council. The penultimate section highlights the possible leverage that may be gained by utilizing human rights law and its machinery. Finally, the conclusion reflects on how the UN can better engage in promoting the rule of law abroad.

The UN System: An Overview

To the uninitiated, the UN system can seem impenetrable. The system includes the United Nations (an intergovernmental organization founded in 1945 and currently consisting of 193 member states) and its subsidiary bodies, specialized agencies,[2] and affiliated organizations.[3] In terms of structure and organization, it consists of six principal organs established by the Charter of the United Nations: the General Assembly, the Security Council, the Economic and Social Council, the Trusteeship Council (inactive since 1994), the International Court of Justice, and the Secretariat.[4] The Secretariat, headed by the Secretary-General and assisted by a staff of international civil servants, provides administrative support to the other organs and carries out tasks mandated by these organs, primarily the Security Council and the General Assembly.

The UN is the international community's principal instrument for the management of armed conflict, both as a primary response mechanism and as a coordinator of wider international efforts. Central to the UN's mission to "maintain peace and security" is its capacity to prevent conflict and consolidate peace after conflict. With the evolving nature of conflict—including terrorism, regional and localized violence, organized crime, and the increasing power of nonstate actors—the demand for UN assistance remains strong.

The Security Council authorizes UN field operations when there are threats to international peace and security.[5] Peacekeeping ranges from traditional peacekeeping missions, which primarily monitor ceasefires, to complex multidimensional operations, which seek to undertake peacebuilding tasks and address the root causes of conflict.

Virtually every part of the UN is engaged in some form of "peacekeeping" or "peacebuilding," helping build the structures of peace and the foundations for democratic institutions. The departments responsible for planning and managing UN field operations are the Department of Peacekeeping Operations (DPKO) and the Department of Political Affairs. These field operations, authorized by the Security Council, consist of thousands of staff serving in difficult locations and exposed to great dangers in performing their duties.[6] The budgets for UN field operations, which are approved by the General Assembly, cover only "operations" (the establishment of the mission and its day-to-day running, including staffing costs); they do not cover *activities*.[7] This may come as a surprise to many, but it is the situation faced by all components of UN field operations, including those focused on human rights and on civil and political affairs—the budgets approved by the General Assembly provide no funds for local initiatives or programs.

DPKO, based in the Secretariat and answerable to the Secretary-General, is the primary provider of rule of law assistance in postconflict and fragile states, with a focus on police, prisons, and the judicial sector (see United Nations Peacekeeping 2014). In UN field operations, DPKO has 315 judicial affairs officers, 370 corrections officers, and over 14,000 police officers (ibid.). The rule of law components in these field operations focus on law reform; police, justice, and corrections reforms; and support to core government functions. Though these components have traditionally fallen within the domain of DPKO-managed missions, they have increasingly become part of the Department of Political Affairs' "political missions." In his report on the role of special political missions, the Secretary-General notes that of the fifteen "field based" special political missions, 60% have mandates related to the rule of law (Secretary-General 2013a, para. 38).

The United Nations Development Programme is the other major rule of law provider. Though it, too, operates in the same contexts as DPKO, its presence extends well beyond postconflict and fragile states.[8] Its authority derives from the General Assembly, which has established a number of programs and funds to address particular humanitarian and development concerns. The United Nations Development Programme is governed by an executive board (comprising member states of the UN). It develops country programs, including for rule of law activities, and also fundraises. It does not receive funds from the General Assembly or Security Council.

Other UN entities provide varying degrees of rule of law expertise in UN field operations. These include the United Nations Children's Fund and UN Women—both of which are funded through voluntary contributions and whose programs are approved by an executive board consisting of member states—as well as UN Secretariat entities, OHCHR, and the Office of Drugs and Crime.[9]

Recent UN Field Operations

The Security Council is deploying to more volatile and complex environments around the world. Somalia and Mali are the latest in a long line of multidimensional missions with "comprehensive" rule of law mandates. In Somalia, the Security Council has requested that the Secretariat provide "strategic policy advice on peacebuilding and statebuilding, including on: [g]over-

nance[,] . . . rule of law[,] . . . disarmament, demobilization and reintegration
. . . and mine action" (Security Council 2013c, para. 2[b]). In addition, it has
asked UN entities to provide capacity-building support to help "strengthen
Somalia's justice institutions" (ibid., para. 2[d][iv]). The UN had previously
provided rule of law assistance to the country, in 1993, with a mandate from
the Security Council to assist in reestablishing institutions and civil administration "in the entire country," as well as to "assist in the re-establishment of
Somali police . . . [and] to assist in the restoration and maintenance of peace,
stability and law and order" (Security Council 1993a, para. 4[c]–[d]).

In Mali, the Security Council has established the United Nations Multidimensional Integrated Stabilization Mission, whose mandate is to "support national and international efforts towards re-building . . . the police and
gendarmerie, through technical assistance, capacity-building, co-location and
mentoring programmes, as well as the rule of law and justice sectors," and to
assist efforts to bring to justice those responsible for war crimes and crimes
against humanity in Mali (Security Council 2013b, para. 16).

In 2011, after the Republic of South Sudan gained independence from
Sudan, the Security Council established a mission in the new country to
"support[] the development of strategies for security sector reform, rule of
law, and justice sector development" (Security Council 2011b, para. 3[c][i]).
In addition, the Security Council added a new component to its rule of law
assistance, requesting that the mission assist the government "in developing
a military justice system that is complementary to the civil justice system"
(ibid., para. 3[c][iv]).[10] The UN Mission in South Sudan took over responsibilities from the UN Mission in Sudan, which had been providing rule of law
assistance in southern Sudan since 2005.

Many of these missions continue a long-term UN practice of "co-location," whereby international justice, police, and prison experts are placed with
national counterparts with the aim of building capacities and transferring
skills.[11] Co-location may be physical co-location or daily interaction. Most of
these international experts are not regular UN staff but "government-provided
personnel" who are sent, often in large numbers, by national governments to
support UN peacekeeping or peacebuilding missions.[12] They generally serve
for two years before returning to their respective countries.

Two features about co-located personnel are important. First, very little
is done to ensure that international expertise meets local needs. Second, little is known about whether the international personnel are actually transferring skills to their national counterparts. They are not obligated to produce
final reports at the end of their assignments, and there is little oversight of
their activities.[13]

UN Rule of Law in Practice in Haiti

Of course, over the past decade, nation-building has proved extremely difficult (as demonstrated by a decade's worth of efforts in Afghanistan[14] and long-term engagement in the Democratic Republic of Congo[15]). The many obstacles to achieving economic development, political reform, and lasting, meaningful peace are profound. Though not addressing rule of law reform per se, research by the RAND Corporation on twenty postconflict nation-building missions (led by the UN, NATO, and ad hoc coalitions) over the past twenty-five years suggests some success in terms of "improved security, progress in democratisation, modest increases in government effectiveness, significant economic growth, and advances in human development" (Dobbins and Miller 2013, 119). The study relies on a variety of indices—Freedom House's Freedom in the World survey, the World Bank's index for government effectiveness, International Monetary Fund figures on increases in per capita income, and the United Nations Development Programme's Human Development Index.[16]

As the UN enters new, complex terrain, it is worth exploring the Secretariat's endeavors by reference to the experiences of a UN field operation. This section, through an analysis of the Secretary-General's reports to the Security Council, explores the UN's large, multidimensional mission in Haiti, which has a robust rule of law mandate. The reports highlight that the mission—despite having been in operation for approximately ten years and having spent billions of dollars—has demonstrated little success, a very narrow theory of the rule of law that revolves around state institutions and the criminal justice system, and significant focus on the co-location of international experts in police prisons, and justice. The reports reveal very little actual "learning" and certainly little progress in strengthening the justice system in accordance with international human rights standards.

It is likely that no other country in the world has received as much attention in rule of law reform as Haiti, a country that has endured chronic political instability and violence. State institutions have been dysfunctional for many years, with profound deficits in qualified personnel. This small island, with a population of nearly ten million—the majority of whom are under twenty-five (see Index Mundi 2013)—has been at the receiving end of international assistance, particularly regarding the rule of law, for decades.[17] Nevertheless, it remains a deeply troubled state ("Haiti, Unfinished and Forsaken" 2014). It currently ranks eighth on the Fund for Peace's (2013) Failed States Index.

The UN has had some form of field operation in the country since 1993, when the Organization of American States and the UN established the International Civilian Mission in Haiti (MICIVIH) (see "International Civilian Mission in Haiti" 1995)· Created as a human rights observation mission, MICIVIH's terms of reference included assisting "the judicial system to reinforce the legal means guaranteeing the exercise of human rights and the respect of legal procedures" and contributing "to institution-building, particularly judicial and penal reform" (ibid.). Also in 1993, the Security Council authorized UN assistance in modernizing the armed forces of Haiti and establishing a new police force. This was to be carried out by the UN Mission in Haiti (Security Council 1993b), though, following violence and the removal of the country's president, mission staff were evacuated later that year. The UN Mission in Haiti returned in 1995 to provide training to local police throughout the country. Its mandate ended in 1996, when it was replaced by the UN Support Mission in Haiti, whose mandate was to assist the government in professionalizing the police and to coordinate institution-building efforts. This mission lasted one year and was replaced by another UN mission, the UN Transition Mission in Haiti, which lasted four months.

An August 1995 assessment by MICIVIH of the human rights situation concluded that "conditions of detention have . . . improved greatly," acknowledging "improvements . . . by the Haitian Government, aided by the international community, to train and deploy a new and professional civilian police force and to carry out judicial and penal reform" ("International Civilian Mission in Haiti" 1995). In 1997, the head of MICIVIH stated that the mission had "contributed to laying the foundations, institutional and cultural, of the rule of law and of democracy" (Granderson 1997). MICIVIH's mandate ended in 1998.

In 2004, the UN Stabilization Mission in Haiti (MINUSTAH) was established to provide a secure and stable environment, promote the political process, strengthen Haiti's government institutions and rule of law structures, reestablish the prison system, and promote and protect human rights (Security Council 2004b). The resolution establishing the mission endorsed the Secretary-General's recommendations for how the mission should implement the mandate (ibid.; see also Secretary-General 2004a). These recommendations included adopting comprehensive approaches to police reform, improving the delivery of justice, combating impunity, enhancing access to justice, and providing anticorruption measures, among others (Secretary-General 2004a, paras. 33, 38).

The mission's police presence would consist of 1,622 staff, 872 of whom would be co-located with national police "24 hours a day, 7 days a week, as needed" (ibid., para. 92). The Secretary-General's report recommended that the mission's operations "incorporate[] lessons learned from past and ongoing Missions" (ibid., para. 89), though it is unclear how previous experiences fed into the strategic planning for MINUSTAH (ibid., paras. 38, 40).

The reform of the Haitian National Police has been the primary rule of law activity for MINUSTAH—understandably, given the country's lack of an army, its limited national police capacity, ever-present security threats from armed groups, and the surge of violence in the capital. In 2006, the government adopted a five-year reform plan for the national police force, whose aggregated estimated cost was US$700 million. The reform plan included "training, transportation, infrastructure, non-lethal police equipment, weapons and ammunition and communications" (Office of Internal Oversight Services 2012, para. 4; see also Secretary-General 2006b, para. 66). UN police officers were responsible for implementing the plan. By 2006, UN police staffing had increased to include 3,598 officers (Office of Internal Oversight Services 2012, para. 5).[18] It is important to recall that these officers are not regular UN staff but personnel who rotate in, then out, of UN field operations, returning to their home country after two years.

In addition to police reform, the MINUSTAH rule of law strategy was heavily focused on state institutional reform, partnering with the Ministry of Justice, the High Council of the Judiciary, the Court of Cassation, and the prison sector. The main "institutional" problems identified between 2004 and 2013 were corruption, a lack of accountability, professional misconduct, a lack of judicial independence, political instability, and a profound lack of political will (see Berg 2013).

In 2005, the "lack of strong and professional rule-of-law institutions remained one of the biggest challenges facing Haiti" (Secretary-General 2005, para. 36). The national police were guilty of serious misconduct, and the judicial system suffered from "serious technical deficiencies, which undermine[d] public confidence" (ibid., para. 39). That year, the minister of justice published a work plan that prioritized twelve areas for action (ibid., para. 40). The mission was also preparing

> a set of recommendations on how the Mission and the wider international community could assist in strengthening the Haitian judicial and correctional systems, on the basis of, inter alia, the findings of a criminal justice advisory team that was deployed in June. These recommendations w[ould] draw from the lessons learned from prior engagements in Haiti, including the need for a balanced approach to strengthen the police, judicial and corrections institutions in parallel. (ibid., para. 41)

In 2006, "professional, technical and logistical shortcomings continued to inhibit the effectiveness of the Haitian National Police and limit public confidence in it" (Secretary-General 2006a, para. 29). Of major concern was the "criminal behavior and the brutality of some of its members" (Secretary-General 2006b, para. 64). In response, the mission was to undertake a program of "monitoring, mentoring and field training" (ibid., para. 68). A major focus of the program was to eliminate unsuitable candidates for police work, a process that was to be conducted by "50 investigative teams" composed of personnel from the UN and the Haitian National Police (ibid.).[19] These investigative teams identified 139 candidates unsuitable for police work and submitted their names to national authorities, who took no action (Office of Internal Oversight Services 2012, para. 23).

To strengthen national justice institutions, the Secretary-General recommended that MINUSTAH co-locate "qualified experts" in the Ministry of Justice to "assist the [ministry] in developing a comprehensive plan for the reform and institutional strengthening of the justice sector" (Secretary-General 2006b, para. 71). With regard to prison reform, the Secretary-General called for MINUSTAH to provide sixteen corrections officers to mentor local staff and thus "strengthen national capacity to address key security issues in all prisons" (ibid., para. 74).

In 2007, the reform of rule of law institutions was identified as a Haitian presidential priority (Secretary-General 2007a, para. 39). An ad hoc committee on judicial reform was created, which included relevant ministries, civil society, lawyers' associations, human rights organizations, and MINUSTAH. The committee produced a list of recommendations to initiate the reform process, along with "a road map, with timelines, for the implementation of the 18 recommendations" (ibid.) In addition, a working group was established to produce "an overall strategic plan for judicial reform" (ibid., para. 40). In response to the prison conditions described as "unacceptable" by the UN, national authorities established a new commission, the Consultative Commission on Prolonged Pretrial Detention, along with a comprehensive five-year strategic plan for prison reform (ibid., paras. 43–45).

In 2009, though "further progress was made in enhancing the capacity of the police, justice and corrections systems[,] . . . significant additional efforts [were] required . . . to enable Haiti to attain the minimum level of institutional capability" (Secretary-General 2009b, para. 31). A presidential commission on justice reform was established (Secretary-General 2009a, para. 9). Its working group provided thirteen short-term recommendations "on immediate measures to advance the judicial reform process" (ibid., para. 42). With regard to the treatment of detainees, "limited progress" was made in the implementation of the five-year strategic plan (ibid., para. 44). Prolonged pretrial detention remained a serious concern, and, in late 2008, a second commission—the National Commission on Prolonged Pretrial Detention—was established (ibid., para. 47).

Following the earthquake in 2010, and recognizing the "absence of any significant progress in the Rule of Law field in Haiti," MINUSTAH launched a major initiative, the Rule of Law Compact, which was intended to serve as "the cornerstone of any reform strategy" (United Nations 2010, 5). The compact was an agreement between the mission, the government, civil society, and donors "to reinforce a comprehensive police, judiciary and correctional systems reform programme" (ibid., 53). A presentation of the compact was made by a senior MINUSTAH official to a group of member states called the "Group of Friends" of Haiti (Mulet 2010) According to the UN official, "[O]ne may legitimately wonder why, after several international missions, and billions of dollars being allocated into governance projects, the rule of law had remained almost constantly for two decades so weak in Haiti" (ibid.) He continued by explaining that the international response should include the building of infrastructure and the initiation of law reform and capacity building, with "simultaneous" reform of rule of law institutions. The compact suggested key benchmarks, which, if met, would "create an environment conducive to investments, job creations [sic] and long term national development." The official concluded his presentation by stating that without significant progress in the rule of law, "MINUSTAH's efforts to implement its mandate w[ould] be in vain" (ibid.)

The government did not act on the MINUSTAH proposal and, in 2012, launched a presidential commission "to study and propose appropriate measures for the reform of the justice system" (Forst 2012, para. 15). By 2012, the Haitian National Police, though "gradually improving, [were] not yet in a position to assume full responsibility for the provision of internal security" (Secretary-General 2012, para. 11). The UN and the national police agreed on a new five-year strategic plan for the police force, which included the co-location of international police experts (Secretary-General 2013b, para. 27). The new president also announced the establishment of a working group "with a mandate to propose appropriate measures for the implementation of justice reform" (Secretary-General 2012, para. 36). The presence of co-located MINUSTAH corrections officers "allowed for improvements across . . . priority areas," though "Haiti's prisons continued to suffer from overcrowding, deficient management, excessive pretrial detention and food and water shortages" (ibid., para. 38).

A 2012 audit report by the UN concluded that during the period under review (August 2006–June 2011), UN police in the mission had "not been able to establish an effective working relationship with HNP [the Haitian National Police] as adequate delegation of authority had not been designated to HNP managers" (Office of Internal Oversight Services 2012, para. 16). Over the course of the reviewed period, UN police officers were supposed to train thousands of national police officers, and training materials were to be approved by a joint UN-Haitian National Police board "to ensure professional standards were met" (ibid., para. 20). Yet the board was never established and the materials were never approved.

In 2013, the UN-Haitian National Police initiative to vet national police officers continued, with 5,410 candidates awaiting review (Secretary-General 2013b, para. 30). Steps were taken by the judiciary to reduce political interference, a new strategic plan for prison reform was adopted, and the mentoring and co-location of MINUSTAH prison staff continued (ibid., paras. 34, 37). Nevertheless, "the continued presence of MINUSTAH in Haiti [was] increasingly called into question by a number of political and civil society stakeholders," with the Haitian Senate passing a nonbinding resolution calling for the withdrawal of MINUSTAH (ibid., para. 8). In October 2013, the Security Council extended the mission's mandate.

There has been little self-reflection by the UN over its lack of success in Haiti. Of course, such environments often consist of a disintegrated values system caused by conflict, chronic corruption, and, in the case of Haiti, political interference in the judiciary—circumstances that are not very conducive to absorbing or implementing capacity-building initiatives. The years of UN reports make little reference to supporting less state-centric institutions (e.g., human rights commissions), civil society, or local initiatives generally. Such a top-down approach may "stifle innovation and indigenous learning" (Desai, Isser, and Woolcock 2011, 254). The reports also say little about "enmeshment" with international processes, such as the UN Human Rights Council's Universal Periodic Review or its Special Procedures. Nor do they discuss the need for radical change in the UN's posture vis-à-vis the government and its rule of law institutions.

The central question is, to what degree does the UN have leverage to push for radical change? Certainly in Haiti, some international officials have concluded that the UN and major international donors have exhausted their "leverage reserves." That was the view shared by a senior UN official and a senior diplomat for a leading rule of law donor in Haiti.[20] When such leverage resources have been exhausted, what is the role (and authority) of the UN in these circumstances? With trenchant political opposition to institutional change, should the UN be present at all? Haiti might be a political imperative to other UN member states, which presumably explains the UN's continued presence—but at what cost to the integrity of the organization?

UN Peacekeeping Doctrine

In 2008, with the publication of *United Nations Peacekeeping Operations: Principles and Guidelines* (known as the Capstone Doctrine), DPKO developed doctrinal guidance for peacekeeping. According to these principles, the core function of multidimensional UN peacekeeping operations is to "create a secure and stable environment while strengthening the State's ability to provide security, with full respect for the rule of law and human rights" (Department of Peacekeeping Operations 2008, 23).

The principles recognize that peacekeeping is increasingly mandated to perform a catalytic role, particularly around the restoration and extension of state authority with regard to law and order (ibid., 26). They identify the core components of multidimensional peacekeeping operations as stabilization, peace consolidation, and long-term recovery and development (ibid., 23).

The Capstone Doctrine defines rule of law in the context of postconflict settings as comprising "transitional justice; strengthening of national justice systems and institutions, including police and law enforcement agencies and prisons; and other priority areas such as victim and witness protection and assistance, anti-corruption, organized crime, trans-national crime, and trafficking and drugs" (ibid., 42, internal citations omitted).

In 2010, at the invitation of DPKO's Office of Rule of Law and Security Institutions, and in preparation for the development of DPKO's "early peacebuilding strategy," a research paper published by a nongovernmental organization proposed a framework that the office could use "for identification, sequencing and enhanced delivery of critical early peacebuilding tasks related to the provision of safety and security" (Ziai 2010, para. 1). One of the five areas that the paper focuses on is the area of police, corrections, and the judicial system. According to the paper, although "field missions have been tempted into the entire spectrum of peacebuilding activities," they are often not "necessarily staffed or resourced to address this wide and ever-changing array of need effectively" (ibid., para. 2)

As the research paper points out, a key premise of any strategy is the recognition that peacekeeping is political, not technical, and that it requires a strategic, not task-orientated, approach (ibid., para 4). Given the great degree of insecurity and volatility in these missions, "rather than launching straight into reform, the mission's first priority should be to ensure . . . that temporary safety and security are provided for the country's citizens" (ibid., para. 6). Moreover, "rather than hurriedly assessing institutional reform needs and rushing into implementation in the early months, the peacekeeping operation should engage in in-depth assessment aimed at understanding the country's conflict, history, culture, internal dynamics and the hopes and aspirations of the population" (ibid.). The key role for a peacekeeping operation is to "catalyz[e] or prepar[e] the ground for longer term reform, by helping national counterparts define the early peacebuilding security 'end state' and identify the activities required to get the country there" (ibid., para. 7).

The research paper states that "institutional reform is a complex, politically-fraught process and, despite the billions of dollars the international community has poured into these efforts over the years, it has been difficult to achieve major successes" (ibid.). The tendency of the international community has been to "underestimate challenges and substitute enthusiasm, hope and its own aspirations for realism" (ibid.). Police and prison reforms led by the UN have "often been pushed through without a coherent strategy across sectors . . . and in the absence of real political commitment by national authorities" (ibid.).

It concludes that peacekeeping operations have focused largely on providing basic safety and security, conducting in-depth assessments, and taking advantage of the UN's comparative advantages—such as the provision of strategic advice to national authorities, its authority to facilitate inclusive consultations that guide reform, and its ability to coordinate international donors. There has been little emphasis on capacity building, unless it relates to "some limited capacity building activities to ensure that existing institutions that are critical to security and stability function to a minimally acceptable level" (ibid., para. 10). The paper also highlights the need for greater strategic coherence across the UN's peacekeeping work, because headquarters and staff in the field "work largely in isolation" (ibid., para. 11).

The key recommendations of this paper were generally rejected. In 2011, DPKO issued *The Contribution of United Nations Peacekeeping to Early Peacebuilding: A DPKO/DFS Strategy for Peacekeepers* (Department of Peacekeeping Operations 2011a). This strategy "provides guidance to UN peacekeepers on prioritizing, sequencing and planning critical early peacebuilding tasks. Priority initiatives are those that advance the peace process or political objectives of a mission and ensure security and/or lay the foundation for longer-term institution building" (ibid., 1). The priority areas for early peacebuilding tasks are "basic security, including in protection of civilians, mine action, disarmament, demobilization and reintegration, strengthening of policing, justice and corrections systems, human rights, the initiation of security sector reform; support political processes; and restore and extend state authority" (ibid., 4).

The strategy outlines two tracks for undertaking this work. The first track consists of activities in "early priority" areas that aim to ensure security and thus advance the peace process or political objectives. These activities include, remarkably, "the immediate functioning of the criminal justice system,"[21] as well as

> the establishment of special chambers to adjudicate serious crimes; the deployment of emergency mobile courts to areas where justice institutions are absent; standardization of basic procedures and practices (for example, for recording arrest: serving court documents; and executing judicial decisions). Subject to the agreement of the host country, international judges, prosecutors and lawyers may be called upon to perform line functions for a limited period of time. (Department of Peacekeeping Operations 2011a, 16)

These activities will help lay the ground for the second track of activities, which are focused on longer-term institution-building.

The 2011 early peacebuilding strategy appears to have missed a major opportunity to ensure that peacekeeping is more strategic during the early phase of UN field operations. It also fails to consider radically limiting the UN's capacity-building activities or, at a minimum, taking stock of how these activities relate to the broader strategy of judicial-sector reform. The strategy does not exhibit any reflection on a decade's worth of capacity-building endeavors in Haiti and elsewhere. Nor does it attempt to ensure greater coherence across UN field operations in order to strengthen the organization's "knowledge" or strategic thinking in general. To date, the UN has made no attempt to ensure peer-to-peer discussion across various field operations working on similar, chronic problems, such as arbitrary or prolonged detention.

Perhaps most profound is the almost total absence of the potential role of international human rights law and its machinery in the development of a rule of law strategy in UN field operations. Though the document makes a token reference to a normative framework for UN peacekeeping (which includes the Charter of the United Nations, international human rights and humanitarian law, and Security Council resolutions), it does not mention the potential role of the Human Rights Council's Universal Periodic Review mechanism or Special Procedures, or the UN Working Group on Arbitrary Detention. Reports issued through the Universal Periodic Review process and through the Special Procedures often highlight the causes of injustice in a particular country, with recommendations for improving the situation.

Knowledge Management

In 2000, a highly influential UN report examining peacekeeping practice (known as the Brahimi Report) stated that many agreed with "the need to exploit cumulating field experience but not enough ha[d] been done to improve the system's ability to tap that experience or to feed it back into the development of operational doctrine, plans, procedures or mandates" (General Assembly and Security Council 2000, para. 229). Since peacekeeping was "generating new experience—new lessons—on a daily basis," the UN had to develop "sharper tools to gather and analyse relevant information . . . [relating to] peace and security issues" (ibid., paras. 65, 229).[22]

That same year, the Secretary-General voiced his support for the Brahimi Report's proposed creation of an Information and Strategic Analysis Secretariat. The secretariat, which was to report to the heads of the Department of Political Affairs and DPKO, would serve as a "catalyst and focal point for the formulation . . . of medium to long-term strategies of a cross-cutting nature that require a multidisciplinary approach, blending the political, military, development, socio-economic, humanitarian, human rights and gender perspectives into a coherent whole" (Secretary-General 2000, para. 4[b]).

In addition, it would serve as an "in-house centre of knowledge . . . by researching and analyzing issues which are fundamental to the successful implementation of mandates for peace and security activities" (ibid., para. 43[c]). A multidisciplinary approach would help "achiev[e] a better understanding of the root causes of particular conflicts" (ibid.). The idea for the secretariat was welcomed by the Security Council (Security Council 2000, annex III). However, for reasons not explained, the secretariat was never established.

In 2002, the Secretary-General stated that in order to make the UN "more effective, cohesive and dynamic," it "must deepen its knowledge, sharpen its focus and act more effectively" (Secretary-General 2002b, paras. 25, 36). In his *Uniting Our Strengths* report on the rule of law, issued in 2006, the Secretary-General again touched on the issue of knowledge and institutional memory:

> Our internal mapping has shown that the Organization is weak in institutionalizing and retaining best practice, expertise and staff. Despite the vast range of peacebuilding activities and the practical [rule of law] experience our staff have gained in the field, the ability of the Organization to reliably draw upon or improve our knowledge base has been insufficient. (Secretary-General 2006c, para. 20)

In 2006, DPKO launched its Policy and Practices Database, an online library of official peacekeeping guidance and good practices.[23] The database is managed by a knowledge management guidance team and "contains over 2,500 guidance and best practices documents" (iSeek 2013b). And in 2008, DPKO reported that it had developed

> "lessons learned" materials, as well as policy, guidance and training materials in the area of strengthening legal and judicial systems, prison systems and law enforcement institutions, for the benefit of judges, prosecutors, rule of law officers, the judicial system, prison officers, law enforcement officials, member states, and the senior managers of peace-keeping operations. (Secretary-General 2008b, para. 457)

DPKO also launched the Rule of Law Community of Practice, "an Inter-net-based networking and resource tool for rule of law practitioners serving in Department-led field missions, and headquarters counterparts within the United Nations system . . . including over 1,100 rule of law documents" (ibid., para. 459). However, that same year, the Secretary-General concluded that the "collective knowledge base remain[ed] thin" with regard to the inter-national rule of law of community (Secretary-General 2008c, para. 68).

In 2014, the situation remains generally the same. Other than an enormous amount of "guidance material," there is little coherence to gathering and pub-lishing what the organization is doing and learning, and no scholarship. This is not the case at the World Bank, the other major intergovernmental rule of law player. Through its Justice and Development Working Paper Series, the World Bank publishes "rigorous scholarship and topics about innovative approaches to law, justice, and development generally" (World Bank n.d.). These papers serve "as a platform for innovative thinking on justice and devel-opment that features work from World Bank and external authors" and cover a broad justice perspective well beyond the criminal justice system (ibid.).[24]

The UN has missed major learning opportunities from its peacekeeping and peacebuilding work. Possibly the greatest missed opportunity stems from the UN's engagement in Kosovo, which lasted from 1999 through 2008 (Security Council 1999). During this period, the United Nations Interim Administration Mission in Kosovo (UNMIK), described as an "international civil presence," was mandated to "organize and oversee the development of provisional institutions for democratic and autonomous self-government pending a political settlement" (ibid., para. 11), though UNMIK itself was not structured according to democratic principles. It held executive author-ity over the small province in Serbia, controlling the judiciary, police, prisons, and the legislature. The mission played a significant role in lawmaking, training legal actors, and mentoring judges and prosecutors. UNMIK also supported the establishment of an ombudsperson's office (United Nations Mission in Kosovo 2000, para. 3.1), a judicial training center,[25] and a legal research institute.[26]

In 2009, DPKO, joined by OHCHR and the United States Institute of Peace, launched a lessons-learned exercise to explore the successes and failures of the mission's work on rule of law assistance.[27] The preliminary findings were discussed at a meeting hosted by the United States Institute of Peace in July 2009 (see United States Institute of Peace 2009). Though set for publication in the fall of 2009, for reasons not explained, the report was never finalized.

Presumably, it was because the findings would have been highly embarrassing to DPKO—though the lack of accountability for UNMIK and the failure to investigate hundreds of interethnic murders was already well known, including by the UN Human Rights Committee (see Human Rights Committee 2006; see also Amnesty International 2013b).[28] Perhaps less known was that under the auspices of UNMIK, in addition to the mission's own full immunity, there was no legal remedy for "state" abuse committed by local public authorities that UNMIK had established. Although the UNMIK-drafted constitutional framework had provided for the creation of a judicial organ to review challenges to "state" authority, this judicial review body was never established (see United Nations Mission in Kosovo 2001, ch. 9.4.11).

The consequence was a UN mission that was established by the Security Council to promote and protect human rights and yet had "no existing legal framework to guarantee to every person whose rights ha[d] been violated by public authorities the possibility to hold the state liable and to obtain an adequate compensation" (Ombudsperson Institution in Kosovo 2004, 10). This was despite the fact that, at least on paper, all major international and regional human rights treaties were directly applicable in the province (see United Nations Mission in Kosovo 1999). The UNMIK-created ombudsperson's office described Kosovo under UNMIK authority as the "human rights black hole" of Europe (Ombudsperson Institution in Kosovo 2004, 18), where the "situation in general creates a paradox, whereby those entities that are in Kosovo to help preserve human rights and the rule of law are themselves not answerable to the very persons they are obliged to protect" (ibid., 16).[29] This state of affairs persisted for eight years. In 2008, UNMIK transferred authority for the justice system to the European Union.[30]

With regard to the UN's ability to assess and plan, a recent external review of the UN's rule of law work states that while the conflict analysis section of the UN's planning process focuses on conflict drivers, it does not focus on politics, power structures, leadership, legal structure, socioeconomic issues, or regional influences (see Kavanagh and Jones 2011, 63–64). The study concludes that "a lack of sound analytical tools and capacity . . . as well as consistent monitoring and assessment by the UN and its partners [have left] the UN unable to reach any conclusions about results" regarding its rule of law endeavors (ibid., 66–67).

In 2013, the Secretary-General approved a new policy on integrated assessment and planning in conflict and postconflict settings "where a multidimensional peacekeeping operation or field-based Special Political Mission is deployed alongside a UN country team" (United Nations 2013, para. 7). The new policy is "intended to maximize the individual and collective impact of the context-specific peace consolidation activities of the UN system," so that, at a minimum, "the political, peacekeeping, humanitarian, human rights and development entities . . . share a common analysis and agree on a set of common strategic objectives for peace consolidation" (ibid., para. 2). This approach seeks to, among other things, "improve the quality of the situational analysis; design interventions that are tailored to the requirements of each situation . . . [and] avoid gaps and overlaps between different UN activities" (ibid., para. 3). Importantly, such integrated, strategic assessments, which include risk analyses, will take place throughout the life cycle of the integrated UN presence.[31] Though not explicitly referenced in the new policy, past experience will presumably form part of any situational analysis.

Rapid Deployment

"Rapid deployment" in the context of rule of law assistance has been a mainstay of UN reports for more than a decade. The Brahimi Report is inundated with text regarding the need for rapid deployment, including in the rule of law sector (General Assembly and Security Council 2000, para. 84). This approach has also been welcomed by the Security Council (2000). But it is unclear what the purpose of rapid deployment in the context of rule of law reform is—after all, rule of law experts are not firefighters or emergency-room doctors. As indicated by the UN's experience in South Sudan, it was easy to deploy "rapidly" but then impossible to "rapidly" understand the dynamics at play on the ground, including the surrounding cultural, economic, political, and legal circumstances.

From my personal experience as the first head of the UN's rapidly deployable justice and corrections capacity that deployed to South Sudan, I believe that it is unclear what can be achieved "rapidly" in circumstances often found in postconflict and fragile states.[32] "Rapidly deploying" into a new UN field operation requires Herculean multitasking, particularly when the country is the size of France and Belgium combined and has almost no paved roads outside the capital.

Investing in meaningful outreach, public education, and dissemination of the principles of justice are long-term endeavors, as is drawing on the wealth of knowledge present in local civil society. Key stakeholders must be identified and their priorities understood; the international donor presence must be identified, along with its knowledge, budgets, and plans; staff, both local and international, need to be recruited; and vehicles and computers must be procured.

In South Sudan, our first-year tasks from headquarters included developing "a methodology for a baseline assessment of the justice sector, conducting assessments in all ten states, [and] establish[ing] a database for all existing courts, including their current staffing and equipment, as well as future needs at the national, state and county levels" (Department of Peacekeeping Operations 2011b). The instructions did not take account of the fact that the informal justice system is the main provider of justice for the South Sudanese (see United States Institute of Peace and Rift Valley Institute 2010). Language deficits would prove a major hurdle: the vast majority of the public, including "justice" actors, are illiterate. It soon emerged that tribal languages were the main means of communication. Moreover, the primary language used in the courts, prisons, and police stations was a form of Arabic, something that the rapidly deploying team had not been apprised of.

When rapidly deploying, one wants to know what knowledge has been generated from previous rule of law assistance. Only then can one rationally begin to plan and to ensure that "stakeholders" are meaningfully engaged, and in a language they understand. Then, at the magical three-month mark, which is generally the maximum period for temporary UN deployments, one departs the country, leaving behind a mystified constituency; few, if any, achievements; and, with it, all the goodwill that has been built.

It goes without saying that "knowledge" is best gathered well in advance of rapid deployment—but often, it is not. And even when one does possess such knowledge, it is questionable how deep one's understanding is going to be of the relationship between law, legal institutions, and the

> broader milieu that includes history, tradition, and culture of a society; its political and economic system; the distribution of wealth and power; the degree of industrialization; the ethnic, language, and religious make-up of society (the presence of group tension); the level of education of the populace; the extent of urbanization; and the geo-political surroundings (hostile or unstable neighbors). (Tamanaha, 2011, 214)

In this line of work, it is axiomatic that identifying, and then gaining the trust of, national counterparts is of paramount importance. Identifying and supporting local expertise that can help one better understand the relationship between justice, law, and society, and that can help one craft solutions should not be undertaken with a sense of urgency.

Capacity Conundrum

As the Security Council has devoted increasing attention to delivering rule of law assistance in postconflict and fragile states, there has been great uncertainty regarding the UN's actual capacity to undertake this work.

In 2002, at the request of the Secretary-General, an internal task force developed a strategic plan for strengthening the UN's rule of law capacities. The Executive Committee on Peace and Security Task Force for the Development of Comprehensive Rule of Law Strategies for Peace Operations considered how the UN could "best mobilize and apply existing expertise/resources within the UN system . . . to provide the necessary support to peace operations on rule of law issues" (ECPS Task Force for the Development of Comprehensive Rule of Law Strategies for Peace Operations 2002, para. 1). It identified gaps in rule of law expertise, as well as areas of strength. All told, it identified eight UN entities as able to provide rule of law expertise (ibid., annex B).

In an effort to "sustain an integrated approach and comprehensive strategy for dealing with [rule of law] issues in peace operations," the task force recommended the establishment of a network of rule of law "focal points" within relevant UN departments and agencies to respond to specific requests from DPKO "for advice and support on substantive/operational [rule of law] issues" (ibid., para. 15). This network would assist in identifying rule of law specialists for recruitment and rapid deployment to peace operations, and it would undertake rule of law assessments. The task force also recommended that a rule of law working group be established for the planning of peace operations. The working group would assist in mission planning, in-theatre assessment, mandate formulation, budgeting, recruitment, and deployment. Although it is not clear why, this recommendation was never implemented.

In 2004, in a seminal report on the rule of law and transitional justice, the Secretary-General outlined the scope of rule of law "services" provided by the UN, which was breathtaking. It included efforts to

> strengthen domestic law enforcement and justice institutions, facilitate national consultations on justice reform, coordinate international rule of

law assistance, monitor and report on court proceedings, train national justice sector officials, support local judicial reform bodies and advise host country rule of law institutions . . . help[] national actors vet and select national police, judges and prosecutors, draft new constitutions, revise legislation, inform and educate the public, develop ombudsman institutions and human rights commissions, strengthen associations of criminal defence lawyers, establish legal aid, set up legal training institutes and build the capacity of civil society to monitor the justice sector. (Secretary-General 2004b, para. 12)

The report recognized that this "range of activities would be demanding in any circumstances," and that "with limited staff devoted to rule of law and transitional justice, the United Nations [was] stretched" (ibid., para. 13). The Secretary-General stated that he would submit proposals to member states asking them to contribute both human and financial resources. He also recommended "a serious review" of some twenty years of UN experience in civilian policing, since such policing is "central to the restoration of the rule of law and worthy of better support and resources" (ibid., para. 29). This review, which was undertaken in 2011, stated that UN police personnel "are often located with their host State counterparts," which helps ensure "effective knowledge and skills transfer through targeted pairing" (Secretary-General 2011b, para. 23).[33] There was no analysis regarding whether such knowledge and skills transfer were actually taking place.

By 2006, the deficit in rule of law capacities continued. That year, the Secretary-General issued a report on the rule of law, in which he acknowledged the "limited staff and resources" for this work and promised that the organization would "deepen and rationalize its rule of law work, strengthen its capacities, enhance its institutional memory and coordinate more effectively within the United Nations and with outside actors" (Secretary-General 2006c, 2). The Secretary-General acknowledged the modesty of the UN's rule of law expertise, describing its capacity deficit as "striking, especially at Headquarters" (ibid., para. 19).

To address this deficit, the Secretary-General established a division of labor among key UN entities, whereby each entity would be designated as a "global lead" for a specific theme. This group of UN entities would form the Rule of Law Coordination and Resource Group (ibid., para. 48).[34] Being a global lead meant that the entity had to work toward ensuring deeper capacities on which the UN system could draw, a greater coordination of effort, and coherence in policy development. This new approach was intended to ensure a higher degree of predictability and accountability in the delivery of rule of law assistance to member states. DPKO was appointed the global lead for strengthening national justice systems and institutions in peace-keeping contexts, as well as for supporting national prison institutions and civilian policing.[35]

Shortly after this new division of labor was established, DPKO consolidated its rule of law work within a new structure (United Nations Peacekeeping 2014). The Office of Rule of Law and Security Institutions brought together various divisions and functions under one roof: police; judicial; legal; correctional units; mines; disarmament, demobilization, and reintegration; and security sector reform. In due course, this headquarters model would be replicated in UN field missions, including in South Sudan and Somalia.[36]

In 2008, member states began exploring alternatives to UN in-house capacities with regard to the rule of law. The Security Council asked the Secretary-General to consider how the UN could better support national efforts to secure peace more rapidly and effectively, including through civilian deployment. In response, the Secretary-General launched a review process that included the appointment of a senior advisory group, which carried out a review of the UN's civilian expertise in supporting the immediate capacity-building needs of countries emerging from conflict. The advisory group published its findings in 2011, concluding that "the United Nations is weighed down by its own conceptual baggage—conflict prevention, peacemaking, peacekeeping, early peacebuilding, peacebuilding, early recovery, recovery, and transition" (General Assembly and Security Council 2011, 8). The report stresses the need to access a wider range of civilian expertise and ensure that the UN becomes more agile and responsive to changing national needs.

Of particular interest to member states is the report's striking conclusion that of the five "critical capacity gaps," two relate to the UN's rule of law capacities: basic safety and security (policing) and justice (prisons, criminal justice, and legal and judicial reform) (ibid., para. 34). The UN has "unfilled capacity gaps that jeopardize the United Nations ability to support conflict-affected States" in these areas (ibid., 7). In addition to critical capacity gaps, the report also notes that the "United Nations struggles . . . to transfer skills and knowledge to national actors" (ibid., 5).

These capacity deficits might strike an outsider as peculiar in light of the bevy of previous reports and an exhaustive inventory highlighting the breadth and depth of UN rule of law expertise.[37] The advisory group's report appears to address this apparent conundrum when it notes that there "is evidence of many actors making aspirational claims of capacity, perhaps in the hope of generating resources" (ibid., para. 35[e]).

In response to the advisory group's report, the Secretary-General (2011a) published *Civilian Capacity in the Aftermath of Conflict*. This report provides a vision for how the UN can better partner and collectively strengthen the quality and effectiveness of support to postconflict institution-building, relying less on short-term consultants from Western countries and focusing more on the need for greater sensitivity to local culture and needs. An internal infrastructure—the CivCap initiative—has been developed to cover this work (United Nations 2014).

This initiative focuses in particular on the role that the global South can play in building capacity and sharing knowledge. One model that CivCap has been examining is a "coaching and mentoring" endeavor in South Sudan, implemented by the Intergovernmental Authority on Development's (IGAD) Regional Capacity Enhancement Initiative, a collaboration between Ethiopia, Kenya, South Sudan, and Uganda (see United Nations Development Programme 2014).

In 2011, 199 civil servants from Kenya, Uganda, and Ethiopia were sent to South Sudan for a period of two years. Participants were placed within national, state, and local government ministries, primarily within the health sector, and were "twinned" with a local counterpart, who sat in the same office and had the same job description. Conceptually, the idea of the initiative is to determine the extent to which skills and knowledge can be more effectively transferred among "peers" who are more likely to share a cultural affinity. Moreover, by employing joint recruitment—whereby all countries, including South Sudan, work together to develop the vacancy announcement and review and interview candidates—the endeavor aims to achieve more local "ownership" and thus a more effective and sustainable project. According to research reports, there has been some success despite an incredibly challenging context (da Costa et al. 2013b; see also da Costa et al. 2013a).

The IGAD initiative is an important capacity-building experiment in statebuilding. Given the increasing level of interest within the Security Council in rule of law mandates, and the seemingly limited rule of law capacity within the UN as a whole, exploring regional approaches like this one is a worthy effort. Although it is unclear to what extent such an initiative might translate to, say, the judiciary, one might see important benefits in developing and strengthening the "machinery" of justice institutions, such as their strategic planning and administrative functions.

Rule of Law Trajectory and the Intergovernmental Response

In terms of addressing conceptual and operational questions concerning the rule of law, there have been two processes in play—one within the General Assembly and the other within the Security Council.

General Assembly

The center of gravity for the rule of law has generally been found in the General Assembly—with the implementing entity being the UN Centre for Human Rights (which in 1993 became OHCHR)—and in the Secretary-General, who reports regularly to the General Assembly on rule of law activities.

In a 1955 resolution, the General Assembly asked the Secretary-General to consolidate all technical-assistance programs already underway (e.g., women's rights, discrimination, and freedom of information) with the broad program of assistance in the field of human rights. These programs would then be referred to as "advisory services in the field of human rights" and would be coordinated by the UN Centre for Human Rights. The resolution authorized the "advisory services of experts; fellowships and scholarships; and, seminars" (General Assembly 1955, para. 2[a]).[38]

With most international standard- and norm-setting related to the rule of law settled in the 1980s (see, e.g., General Assembly 1979, 1988, 1990; Economic and Social Council 1977), the international community moved to strengthening the rule of law "infrastructure." In 1993, the World Conference on Human Rights, held in Vienna, issued a final declaration in which it recommended that priority be given to national and international action to promote democracy, development, and human rights, with a special emphasis on strengthening the rule of law.[39] The declaration also recommended that the Centre for Human Rights coordinate the support given to national structures in strengthening the rule of law from a human rights perspective.[40]

The declaration further called for strengthening the Centre for Human Rights and establishing the High Commissioner for Human Rights. It urged member states "to increase considerably the resources allocated to programmes aiming at the establishment and strengthening of national legislation, national institutions and related infrastructures which uphold the rule of law."[41] In 1994, the General Assembly endorsed many of the Vienna Conference recommendations, including the creation of the Office of the High Commissioner for Human Rights, which would coordinate the UN's human rights promotion and protection activities and supervise the activities of the Centre for Human Rights (General Assembly 1994).

According to the Secretary-General's first report to the General Assembly on the strengthening of the rule of law, issued in 1994, the focus of many of these activities was to provide assistance in developing national plans of action, redrafting constitutions, holding elections, undertaking institutional and law reform, and training legal actors (Secretary-General 1994, para. 17). The Secretary-General stated that the focal point for UN efforts to assist states in strengthening the rule of law was the Centre for Human Rights and

OHCHR (ibid., para. 105). To carry out much of this work, the Centre for Human Rights opened small field presences in Burundi, Cambodia, Guatemala, Malawi, and Romania (ibid., para. 91). However, the enthusiasm for the provision of technical cooperation was not accompanied by sufficient financial resources. Between 1995 and 2003, the General Assembly expressed its dismay with the lack of financial support to the Centre for Human Rights and OHCHR.[42]

In 2002, the Secretary-General issued a "strengthening of the rule of law" report to the Third Committee,[43] which described OHCHR as responsible for coordinating the UN's rule of law activities (Secretary-General 2002a). The report highlighted the various types of rule of law assistance being provided to requesting member states; this assistance focused mainly on human rights training with regard to policing and elections and on technical support to national human rights institutions. In addition, the report noted that OHCHR was providing rule of law-related support to UN peace operations in Afghanistan, Bosnia and Herzegovina, Liberia, and Timor-Leste. The General Assembly welcomed the report, reaffirming that OHCHR remained "the focal point for coordinating system-wide attention for human rights, democracy and the rule of law" and would provide advice to human rights components of UN peace operations "in the field of the rule of law" (General Assembly 2003, paras. 8, 9).

This 2002 report would turn out to be the last report on "strengthening of the rule of law" presented to the Third Committee. For unknown reasons, this thematic issue, and the operational reporting from OHCHR, would vanish from the de facto human rights committee of the General Assembly. It would emerge four years later, at the request of Liechtenstein and Mexico, as an agenda item in the Sixth Committee (2014), the General Assembly's committee that addresses legal questions. The agenda item was renamed "the rule of law at the national and international levels" (General Assembly 2006b). As a follow-up to this agenda item, the Secretary-General was asked to present a number of reports in the coming years, including an inventory of rule of law activities of UN entities (which would be presented in 2008; see Secretary-General 2008b) and a report on ways and means for strengthening and coordinating UN rule of law activities (which would be presented in 2008 and annually since). In addition, the Secretary-General was asked to present a report on the views of member states on matters pertaining to the agenda item, which he did in 2007 (Sixth Committee of the General Assembly 2014; see Secretary-General 2007b).

In essence, with little explanation, the Third Committee (and OHCHR) lost authority over how the rule of law would be generally considered within the UN. The activities of UN entities doing this work would no longer be seen through a "social, humanitarian and human rights lens" but rather through the lens of public international law.

Security Council

Up until 2003, the Security Council had seldom used the term "rule of law" in its deliberations.[44] This changed following the Secretary-General's seminal 2004 report on the rule of law and transitional justice in conflict and postconflict societies, in which, for the first time, the Secretary-General defined the term "rule of law" (Secretary-General 2004b).[45]

The response from the Security Council was to hold an "open debate" under the agenda item "justice and the rule of law."[46] The debate, held at the request of the UK, began with the Secretary-General introducing his 2004 report, emphasizing that the "approach to justice must be comprehensive. We must address the police, courts, prisons, defence lawyers and prosecutors" (Security Council 2004a, 3). The debate took note of the fact that recently adopted Security Council mandates included, for the first time, rule of law and justice components in missions (such as in Liberia and Haiti), and that, for some members, these "should become a permanent priority" (ibid., 13, 15).

The Brahimi Report's assertions regarding the need to address "rule of law vacuums" and to develop global model legal codes were also discussed and welcomed by some members (ibid., 11, 16). France urged the Security Council to benefit from the knowledge and expertise at the national level and within nongovernmental organizations and the private sector (ibid., 20). China noted that addressing justice and rule of law issues were "closely bound up with political, economic and social issues," while Angola emphasized that "strategies for the implementation of an effective rule of law must stem from the grassroots level" (ibid., 21, 22). The need for rule of law to address economic or social issues through grassroots initiatives did not form any meaningful part of future Security Council debates.

Since 2004, the Security Council has held additional "open debates" on the rule of law in postconflict states—in 2006, 2010, 2012, and 2014 (see Security Council 2006, 2010a, 2010b, 2012a, 2012b, 2014). Three key issues have generally been discussed during these "debates": the promotion of the rule of law in conflict and postconflict situations, international justice, and the efficiency and credibility of sanctions.

The discussion during the 2006 debate was framed by the concept paper offered by Denmark, which held the Security Council presidency. The paper posed questions such as "How should the Council approach developing a policy on what United Nations peacekeeping missions could do in cases of rule-of-law vacuums, including the need for United Nations forces to take on detention powers?" (Security Council 2006, 3). In the discussion that followed, the UK, a major rule of law donor, stated that the UN must "consider post-conflict situations that were left with a 'security vacuum'" and voiced its support for the establishment of a "standing police capacity" (Department of Public Information 2006).

The 2010 debate also illustrated the importance of comprehensive support to "state institutions" in need of capacity building—particularly institutions in the areas of "law and order" and criminal justice (Security Council 2010a, 11, 13, 25). Following the 2014 debate, the president of the Security Council issued a statement that seemed to envelop the rule of law within a broader security sector, focusing on "the importance of a sector-wide approach for security sector reform, which enhances the rule of law, including through the establishment of independent justice and correction systems, and reaffirms that effective security sector reform requires developing a professional, effective and accountable security sector" (Security Council 2014, 2).

Security Council resolutions similarly illustrate this "law and order" focus. For example, in 2013, in the general context of peacekeeping and peacebuilding operations, the council welcomed a "comprehensive strategy for durable peace and security" that included assisting national authorities in the development of "critical rule of law priorities and strategies to address the needs of police, judicial institutions and corrections systems" (Security Council 2013a, paras. 1, 8[c]).

However, the "open debates" and resolutions do not take account of the decades' worth of experiences and lessons from UN field operations authorized and overseen by the Security Council. There is no reflection on whether such "comprehensive approaches" are working. Rarely is there any reference to the importance of informal justice processes or addressing injustices beyond the criminal justice system. There appears to be no room for possible innovations, such as concentrating efforts on empowering the disadvantaged through a focus on civil society, an approach that the World Bank (2014) has been taking in its "justice for the poor" work.

Recently, member states and UN entities have indicated a desire to improve rule of law engagements. There is greater attention to improving performance.[47] The UN Police Division is developing a "strategic guidance framework" that identifies the core principles of the UN's policing work, with "an emphasis on recording and sharing good practices" and placing "human rights and accountability at the centre of what UN Police officers do" (iSeek 2013a). And the UN Secretariat has issued a guidance note on using and developing national capacities to strengthen justice systems (Inter-Agency Team on National Capacity Development 2013). In addition, as discussed above, it is taking steps to deepen its general understanding of how UN field operations can strengthen assessments and planning.

However, the experience of the UN over the past decade demands deeper reflection and insight into questions about purpose. Decades of research and literature have provided insights into the history and experiences of the international rule of law movement, highlighting failures of planning, technique, and execution,[48] as well as why this billion-dollar industry has had such little impact in strengthening the rule of law. While law and legal institutions are potential parts of the solution to conflict and fragility, "this is not matched by a correspondingly clear sense of what should be done, how it should be done, by whom, in what order, or how success may be determined" (Desai, Isser, and Woolcock 2011, 241).

A growing body of research has been exploring conceptual and operational questions related to this assistance and the reasons for its lack of meaningful success. This literature has pointed to the lack of coherent, rigorous, and systematic evaluation of rule of law assistance ("aid organisations have proven themselves to be ill-adept at the task of generating and accumulating the sort of knowledge that would help fill the gap" [Carothers 2003, 13]) and to a misguided desire for whole-system approaches ("large donors have tended to move into comprehensive, integrated, or 'holistic' programs, but this often means little more than the pursuit of multiple objectives[;] . . . the strategic linkages among goals, components, and activities remain weak" [Hammergren, quoted in Jensen and Heller 2003, ch. 9]).

Further, as much of the literature highlights, a major flaw of international rule of law assistance is its failure to provide for a well-grounded rationale for this work; indeed, much of the assistance is based on a lack of understanding of the essential problem (see Carothers 1998, 2006; Tamanaha 2011), something addressed in greater detail in the chapter by Louis-Alexandre Berg, Deborah Isser, and Doug Porter. As the UN has increased its engagement in rule of law assistance, it has not equally invested in enhancing its understanding of the theory of rule of law reform. What is required of the organization is the development of an "enabling theory to inform practice, and practice to refine theory" (Asia Pacific Judicial Reform Forum 2009, 11).

Recent literature stresses the need to understand that "power" and "culture," not laws and institutions, form the roots of a rule of law state (Kleinfeld 2012). Checks and balances among the *structures* of power and culture, and of norms and habits, will define how a state treats its citizens (ibid., 20). The roots of the rule of law are a deeply cultural and societal product, rather than a universal notion imposed from above and detached from local context.

As the UN reports from Haiti indicate, the organization rarely engages with informal processes or civil society, nor does it undertake legal education efforts or potential innovations relating to pro-poor programs (e.g., legal aid programs, legal literacy programs, and alternative dispute resolution mechanisms). It could learn from the efforts of others, such as the Open Society Foundations (2014), which have invested heavily in such initiatives, with a major project to address pretrial justice deficits, particularly lengthy pretrial detention; or Namati (2014; see also Maru, this volume), a recently established international nongovernmental organization that supports grassroots efforts to develop legal empowerment strategies, with a focus on what it describes as five urgent global challenges, including community land rights and quality legal aid services.

The UN Human Rights Machinery

From a human rights perspective, seemingly little has been gained after years of rule of law assistance to postconflict and fragile states. What are the policy tools that the public and international community could bring to bear on governments that abuse or neglect their people's rights? There appears to be a considerable "human rights machinery" at the disposal of the UN. And if the UN has any leverage with member states to address justice deficits, what is it and how is it best utilized?

One tool that the UN could use more effectively is treaties and their monitoring bodies. Most countries where the UN has field operations have ratified the major international human rights treaties and have engaged with the bodies (known as committees) tasked with monitoring states' compliance with these treaties. The various committees regularly engage in dialogue with states that are party to the treaties, including by addressing individual complaints, reviewing the regular reports on compliance submitted by state parties, and issuing "general comments" interpreting the content of treaty provisions.

Other potential "tools of leverage" are also available. However, to date, they have generally been underused. In 2006, the General Assembly established the UN Human Rights Council, which replaced the oft-criticized Commission on Human Rights (General Assembly 2006a). A major function of the Human Rights Council is the Universal Periodic Review, a mechanism by which states present a report highlighting how they have been complying with their human rights obligations.

The primary objective of the Universal Periodic Review is the "improvement of the human rights situation on the ground" through a state's fulfillment of its human rights obligations (Human Rights Council 2007, para. 4[a]). The review of a particular state's human rights situation is based on the submission of three documents: a report from the member state under review; a compilation prepared by the OHCHR containing information from the reports of treaty bodies, Special Procedures, and other UN bodies; and "additional, credible and reliable information provided by other relevant stakeholders," including civil society (ibid., para. 15). The outcome of this process is "conclusions and/or recommendations, and the voluntary commitments of the State concerned" (ibid., para. 26). The member state explicitly identifies which recommendations it will adopt and which ones it will refuse, with explanation (ibid., para. 32). The process also includes a "subsequent review" of implementation of the agreed-on recommendations (ibid., para. 34).

The government of Haiti was reviewed in 2011 (Human Rights Council 2011). The Human Rights Council's list of recommendations to the state, generally organized around specific themes (e.g., justice, children's rights, women's rights), were vast and often sweeping.[49] In 2012, Haiti, in cooperation with the human rights section of the UN mission, organized a public consultation on the report, which included the participation of governmental human rights agencies and civil society (Human Rights Council 2012). Following this meeting, the Haitian government accepted 122 of the recommendations, including those relating to strengthening the rule of law.[50]

In addition to the treaty-body system and the Universal Periodic Review, fifty-one UN Special Procedures deal with country-specific and thematic human rights issues (High Commissioner for Human Rights 2013, para. 94).[51] In 2012 alone, Special Procedures mandate-holders conducted eighty country visits, including to all UN peacekeeping and peacebuilding missions.

Recent research suggests that states' ratification of international treaties may have a positive impact on domestic human rights practice. Beth Simmons (2009, 12) demonstrates how treaties have influenced domestic politics and practices, highlighting the "conditions under which such traction is possible." Such formal commitments may provide funding and galvanize social mobilization, "providing a crucial tangible resource for nascent groups and by increasing the size of the coalition with stakes in compliance" (ibid., 15). Simmons argues that in countries faced with political instability, international human rights treaties have the most significant effect when there is a degree of political participation and "a modicum of democratic governance" (ibid., 17).

With this context in mind, the strongest compliance with treaty obligations occurs "where domestic groups have both the motive and the means to
make civil rights demands on their government" (ibid., 161). Most important,
according to her research, is whether "the right in question is centrally violated and relatively easy to detect and monitor," such as the right to a fair trial
(ibid., 161). She concludes that even "marginal gains . . . under circumstances
in which the international community's arsenal of tools is quite limited are
important gains indeed" (ibid., 21).

Of course, evidence of states' willingness to abide by international law is not
measured by the simple signature and ratification of core human rights treaties.
It is demonstrated through other actions as well, such as states' acceptance of
individual complaint procedures, their reservations and declarations upon signing a treaty, and their willingness to undergo periodic reviews by the relevant
treaty bodies in Geneva (but see Open Society Justice Initiative 2010).

Many, if not all, postconflict and fragile states are emerging from decades
of strife and conflict, which has often been fueled by a lack of accountability
for mass crimes. A major priority for many within the international community is a transitional justice process that addresses the causes of conflict
and leads to some criminal accountability.[52] Prosecutions for human rights
violations constitute an important plank of meaningful transitional justice
processes. Recent empirical research, based on data from domestic, foreign,
and international prosecutions, has suggested that "through a combination
of deterrence and socialisation" (Sikkink 2011, 231), there is a strong link
between human rights prosecutions and improvement in human rights in
transitional countries.[53]

This trend, described as the "justice cascade," results in "a shift in the
legitimacy of the norm of individual criminal accountability for human rights
violations and in increase in criminal prosecutions on behalf of that norm"
(ibid., 5). Actors will change their behavior because "prosecutions help dra-
matize and communicate new norms," which become embedded within local
law and institutions and, in turn, impose "new costs" on violators (ibid., 5).
Kathryn Sikkink (2011, 16) states that this new norm is part of the larger
human rights revolution, including a global movement for accountability for
past human rights violations.

Though the Universal Periodic Review process and Special Procedures
are clearly relevant for the effective operation of UN field presences in implementing aspects of their rule of law mandates, UN mission reports rarely
mention them in their rule of law reporting. Of course, advances in human

rights promotion and protection are often due to multiple causes, including social and cultural change, that go above and beyond international legal obligations and the pressure to respond to advocacy, reports, and the recommendations of UN human rights bodies. Nevertheless, the potential of the UN "human rights machinery" appears great.

Conclusion

Unrealistic mandates, misplaced doctrinal approaches, insufficient expertise, poor planning and execution, and a lack of deep contextual knowledge have hampered good-faith efforts by the UN to assist postconflict and fragile states in rule of law reform. To ensure that the organization remains an indispensable instrument for the maintenance of peace and security, radical reforms—including innovations relating to the UN's analytical capacities that can make sense of complex, fractured settings—will be required.

The UN has undertaken an enormous amount of effort to improve its performance, as evidenced in the Secretary-General's numerous reports to the General Assembly and the Security Council. The Security Council, General Assembly, and Secretariat must take stock of what they have learned and identify the UN's comparative advantages in a field of many. The legitimacy and global character of the UN brings with it a particular responsibility in fragile states to provide "basic safety and security" that will reduce the threat of armed violence.

With regard to its rule of law agenda, the Security Council needs to recognize that good can be done, but on a smaller scale. The broad goals set by the council may be politically appealing, but, as the evidence suggests, they have proved impossible to meet. Member states must alleviate the burden placed on the Secretariat by reducing the scope of rule of law mandates, allowing the Secretariat to unmoor itself from the provision of capacity-building support during the early peacebuilding phase and to instead focus on narrow and solvable solutions, as well as exploring and supporting regional approaches such as the IGAD initiative in South Sudan. The organization will perform better with fewer, not more, objectives, and with rule of law work that is modest, focused, and incremental.

Although the need for capacity-building will remain present, it could be addressed by international development organizations and regional actors or through efforts such as the IGAD initiative. By offering strategic support only, and by preparing the ground for the United Nations Development Programme and regional actors to do long-term work, the UN will be more "informed" in its rule of law work, and its knowledge will be more likely to be home-grown, grounded in a broad range of local voices that help identify problems and solutions. The UN's role in the early window will be not to impose solutions but to nurture them from below, supporting others in building legitimacy around respect for law and its values.

In its field operations containing a rule of law element, the UN needs a common vision for its primary objectives. It needs to identify the core rationale for this work. Much of the UN's work appears to see beneficiaries as the people working *in* institutions rather than individuals who need a strengthened quality of justice. Rule of law reform should be centered on the person, not the institution, to ensure justice (or to end injustice), whether political and civil or economic, social, and cultural. Ensuring justice means embracing fundamental notions of fairness and equality in the treatment of individuals, whose rights are at the core of a democracy. Notions of fairness and equality are universal, common in both international and national law.

With this in mind, the General Assembly should consider moving the rule of law's center of gravity away from the General Assembly's legal committee, where the notion sits slightly off-center, and back to its original home—the social, humanitarian, and human rights committee. This will ensure that considerations of the issue have a greater breadth and depth that go beyond criminal justice. In UN field operations, rule of law and human rights components should be combined.

In addition to adopting fewer objectives and a shared vision, the UN must ensure that its rule of law assistance is informed by a deeper knowledge of context and problems. The UN has produced a vast number of guidance materials on the rule of law, but in more than a decade of work, there is little, if any, empirical knowledge being generated, and no scholarship. The organization must be more serious about learning from what it is doing.

The organization will perform better when it has more information on history, culture, language, geography, societal norms, and the actual needs of stakeholders. Prior to any planning, the UN must truly understand the situation in which it is considering intervention. A new approach to learning should embrace a decentralization of the gathering, analyzing, and implementation of knowledge, with the establishment of "knowledge centers" closer to the field. It should also decentralize its core staff. There is no rationale for continuing to keep such numerous staff in headquarters.

Specialized staff in the field, unmoored from a capacity-building role and a "law and order" approach, and with a deeper contextual knowledge, would be able to provide *strategic* advice to key national interlocutors and UN leadership regarding how priorities for rule of law reform can be established and how progress can be measured and assessed.

An approach that is modest, focused, and incremental should not be engaged in rapid assessments and deployments. "Rapidness"—and, for that matter, "comprehensive" or "holistic" approaches and "quick wins"—are counterproductive in efforts to reform the rule of law in fragile states, as is supporting the "*immediate* effectiveness" of justice systems (Department of Peacekeeping Operations 2013, 154). It is not possible to do everything at once and to remake an entire system within a couple of years. The UN should focus on a slower, trial-and-error experimentation rather than the rapid creation of institutions or laws that are likely to result in no local buy-in and weak(er) institutions. Fragile states are overburdened with international planning activities, proposing too much too soon, while raising expectations and constraining innovations that may emerge.

Moreover, the early stages of UN field operations are not an appropriate context for comprehensive approaches, since these situations are often defined by fragility, extremely politicized divisions, internal tensions among elites, and limited capacity. They are not conducive environments for broad, sweeping change, particularly when there is no agreed-on vision for rule of law reform. Large, comprehensive programs have resulted in large, comprehensive failures.

UN field operations also need to strengthen their "convening power" role. This could be pivotal in helping improve working relations among key actors, between formal and informal processes, and between the general public and the police.

Additionally, field operations need to ensure greater enmeshment with international human right processes, including the UN treaty bodies, the Universal Periodic Review, and the Special Procedures. Recommendations relating to the rule of law issued by these entities can have considerable leverage, and they should inform and strengthen the activities (and authority) of the UN's field presence.

In 2000, the Brahimi Report called on member states to acknowledge that the UN "is the sum of its parts and [to] accept that the primary responsibility for reform lies with them" (General Assembly and Security Council 2000, para. 266). It made recommendations aimed at "remedy[ing] a serious problem in strategic direction, decision-making, rapid deployment, operational planning and support" (ibid., viii). Unquestionably, we have reached a similar crisis whereby rule of law mandates in postconflict and fragile states are expensive and overly ambitious. Moreover, for more than a decade, the Security Council has expressed the desire to see UN field operations adopt "clear, credible and achievable mandates" (Security Council 2000, annex I; 2014, 2). The UN must now reflect honestly on its record of performance and not be fearful of exploring real, deep, and meaningful change. Only by acknowledging the inadequacies of our approaches can we have any chance of improving them. Rights-holders (and donors' taxpayers) deserve nothing less.

References

American Bar Association. 2008. "Proposals to Strengthen the Rule of Law Incubated at World Justice Forum; Funding for Projects Announced." Press release, July 7. http://apps.americanbar.org/abanet/media/release/news_release.cfm?releaseid=410.

Amnesty International. 2013a. "Amnesty International to Publish Report Exposing the UN Failure to Investigate Kosovo Missing." August 21. http://www.amnesty.org/en/library/asset/EUR70/012/2013/en/db677239-8bd0-40e7-b550-240446cc559a/eur700122013en.html.

———. 2013b. *Kosovo: UNMIK's Legacy: The Failure to Deliver Justice and Reparation to the Relatives of the Abducted.*

Asia Pacific Judicial Reform Forum. 2009. *Searching for Success in Judicial Reform: Voices from the Asia Pacific Experience.* New Delhi: Oxford University Press.

Autesserre, Séverine. 2010. *The Trouble with the Congo: Local Violence and the Failure of International Peacebuilding.* New York: Cambridge University Press.

Berg, Louis-Alexandre. 2013. "All Judicial Politics Are Local: The Political Trajectory of Judicial Reform in Haiti." *Inter-American Law Review* 45:1–32.

Carothers, Thomas. 1998. "The Rule of Law Revival." *Foreign Affairs*, March 1. http://www.foreignaffairs.com/articles/53809/thomas-carothers/the-rule-of-law-revival.

———. 2003. "Promoting the Rule of Law Abroad: The Problem of Knowledge." Working Paper 34. Carnegie Endowment for International Peace Rule of Law Series.

———, ed. 2006. *Promoting the Rule of Law Abroad: In Search of Knowledge.* Washington, DC: Carnegie Endowment for International Peace.

Commission on Legal Empowerment of the Poor. 2008. *Making the Law Work for Everyone Vol. I.* New York: Commission on Legal Empowerment of the Poor.

da Costa, Felix Diana, Søren Vester Haldrup, John Karlsrud, Frederik Rosén, and Kristoffer Nilaus Tarp. 2013a. "Civilian Capacity in the Aftermath of Conflict: A Case Study of OPEN." *DIIS Policy Brief*, May.

———. 2013b. "Friends in Need Are Friends Indeed: Triangular Co-operation and Twinning for Capacity Development in South Sudan." Oslo: Norwegian Peacebuilding Resource Center.

Department of Peacekeeping Operations. 2008. *United Nations Peacekeeping Operations: Principles and Guidelines.* New York: Department of Peacekeeping Operations.

———. 2011a. "The Contribution of United Nations Peacekeeping to Early Peacebuilding: a DPKO/DFS Strategy for Peacekeepers." http://www.operationspaix.net/DATA/DOCUMENT/6797~v~The_Contribution_of_United_Nations_

Peacekeeping_to_Early_Peacebuilding___a_DPKO_DFS_Strategy_for_Peace-keepers.pdf.

———. 2011b. "Multi-year Plan and Staffing Requirements for South Sudan UNMISS Justice Component." Draft, June 14. On file with the author.

———. 2013. *Handbook for Judicial Affairs Officers in United Nations Peacekeeping Operations*. New York: Department of Peacekeeping Operations.

———. 2014a. "Justice and Corrections Standing Capacity." *JCSC News*, January. On file with the author.

———. 2014b. *Justice and Corrections Update*. New York: Department of Peacekeeping Operations.

Department of Public Information. 2006. "Security Council, Following Day-Long Debate, Underscores Critical Role of International Law in Fostering Global Stability, Order." Press Release, June 22. http://www.un.org/News/Press/docs/2006/sc8762.doc.htm.

Desai, Deval, Deborah Isser, and Michael Woolcock. 2011. "Rethinking Justice Reform in Fragile and Conflict-Affected States: The Capacity of Development Agencies and Lessons from Liberia and Afghanistan." *World Bank Legal Review: International Financial Institutions and Global Legal Governance* 3:241–61.

Dobbins, James, and Laurel Miller. 2013. "Overcoming Obstacles to Peace." *Survival: Global Politics and Strategy* 55:103–120.

Durch, William J., Madeline L. England, and Fiona B. Mangan, with Michelle Ker. 2012. *Understanding Impact of Police, Justice and Corrections Components in UN Peace Operations*. Washington, DC: Stimson Center.

Economic and Social Council. 1977. Resolution 2076 (LXII): UN Standard Minimum Rules for the Treatment of Prisoners, adopted by the First United Nations Congress on the Prevention of Crime and the Treatment of Offenders. UN doc. E/5988.

ECPS Task Force for the Development of Comprehensive Rule of Law Strategies for Peace Operations. 2002. "Final Report." August 15.

EULEX Kosovo. 2012. "Rule of Law Remains Key Challenge for Kosovo." May 15. http://www.eulex-kosovo.eu/en/news/000360.php.

———. 2014. "What is EULEX?" Accessed February 6. http://www.eulex-kosovo.eu/en/info/whatisEulex.php.

Forst, Michael. 2012. Report of the Independent Expert on the Situation of Human Rights in Haiti. UN doc. A/HRC/20/35.

Fund for Peace. 2013. "The 9th Failed States Index: 2013." Accessed March 16, 2014. http://ffp.statesindex.org/rankings.

General Assembly. 1955. Resolution 926 (X): Advisory Services in the Field of Human Rights. UN doc. A/RES/926 (X).

———. 1965. Resolution 2006 (XIX): Comprehensive Review of the Whole Question of Peace-Keeping Operations in All Their Aspects. UN doc. A/RES/2006 (XIX).

———. 1979. Resolution 34/169: Code of Conduct for Law Enforcement Officials. UN doc. A/RES/34/169.

———. 1988. Resolution 43/173: Body of Principles for the Protection of All Persons under Any Form of Detention and Imprisonment. UN doc. A/RES/43/173.

———. 1990. Resolution 45/111: Basic Principles for the Treatment of Prisoners. UN doc. A/RES/45/111.

———. 1994. Resolution 48/141: High Commissioner for the Promotion and Protection of All Human Rights. UN doc. A/RES/48/141.

———. 2003. Resolution 57/221: Strengthening of the Rule of Law. UN doc. A/RES/57/221.

———. 2006a. Resolution 60/251: Human Rights Council. UN doc. A/RES/60/251.

———. 2006b. Resolution 61/39: The Rule of Law at the National and International Levels. UN doc. A/RES/61/39.

———. 2012. Declaration of the High-Level Meeting of the General Assembly on the Rule of Law at the National and International Levels. UN doc. A/RES/67/1.

General Assembly. 2014. "Fifth Committee Resolutions and Decisions of the 67th Session." Accessed February 18. http://www.un.org/en/ga/fifth/67/resdec67.shtml.

General Assembly and Security Council. 2000. Identical Letters Dated 21 August 2000 from the Secretary-General to the President of the General Assembly and the President of the Security Council. UN docs. A/55/305–S/2000/809.

———. 2011. Identical Letters Dated 18 February 2011 from the Secretary-General Addressed to the President of the General Assembly and the President of the Security Council. UN docs. A/65/747–S/2011/85.

Granderson, Colin. 1997. "Field Missions and Human Rights Monitoring." Presentation at International Journalists Roundtable on Human Rights, New York, Dec. 8–9.

"Haiti, Unfinished and Forsaken." 2014. *New York Times*, January 10.

High Commissioner for Human Rights. 2013. Annual Report. UN doc. A/HRC/25/19.

Human Rights Committee. 2006. Concluding Observations: Serbia. UN doc. CCPR/C/UNK/CO/1.

Human Rights Council. 2007. Resolution 5/1: Institution-Building of the United Nations Human Rights Council. UN doc. A/HRC/RES/5/1.

———. 2011. Report of the Working Group on the Universal Periodic Review: Haiti. UN doc. A/HRC/19/19.

———. 2012. Report of the Working Group on the Universal Periodic Review: Haiti; Addendum. UN doc. A/HRC/19/19/Add.1.

Human Rights Watch. 2012. "South Sudan: Arbitrary Detentions, Dire Prison Conditions." Press release, June 21.

———. 2014. "South Sudan: Ethnic Targeting, Widespread Killings." Press release, January 16.

Humphreys, Stephen. 2010. *Theatre of the Rule of Law: Transnational Legal Intervention in Theory and Practice*. Cambridge: Cambridge University Press.

Index Mundi. 2013. "Haiti Demographics Profile 2013." Last modified February 21. http://www.indexmundi.com/haiti/demographics_profile.html

Inter-Agency Team on National Capacity Development. 2013. "United Nations Guidance Note for Effective Use and Development of National Capacity in Post-Conflict Contexts." July 29.

"International Civilian Mission in Haiti." 1995. *MICIVIH News*, August 1. http://www.un.org/rights/micivih/rapports/news.htm

iSeek. 2013a. "From Many, One: The Basics of International Peacekeeping." November 21. www.un.int/wcm/content/site/portal/lang/en/home/pid/35803.

———. 2013b. "What's New in Peacekeeping Knowledge Management and Guidance." July 9. On file with the author.

Jensen, Erik, and Thomas Heller, eds. 2003. *Beyond Common Knowledge: Empirical Approaches to the Rule of Law*. Redwood City: Stanford University Press.

Kavanagh, Camino, and Bruce Jones. 2011. *Shaky Foundations: An Assessment of the UN's Rule of Law Support Agenda*. New York: Center on International Cooperation.

Kleinfeld, Rachel. 2012. 2012. *Advancing the Rule of Law Abroad: Next Generation Reform*. Washington, DC: Carnegie Endowment for International Peace.

Mulet, Edmond. 2010. "Speech to the Group of Friends of Haiti on the Rule of Law." New York, October 26. On file with the author.

Namati. 2014. "Namati." Accessed March 28. http://www.namati.org.

Office of Internal Oversight Services. 2012. *Audit Report: The Haitian National Police Development Programme in MINUSTAH*. New York: Office of Internal Oversight Services.

Office of the High Commissioner for Human Rights. 2014. "'We Must Not Fail on Protection for South Sudan's IDPs'—UN Expert Warns Amid Ongoing Crisis." Press release, January 31. http://www.ohchr.org/EN/NewsEvents/Pages/DisplayNews.aspx?NewsID=14209&LangID=E.

Ombudsperson Institution in Kosovo. 2004. *Fourth Annual Report: 2003–2004*. Pristina: Ombudsperson Institution in Kosovo.

Open Society Foundations. 2014. "Global Campaign for Pretrial Justice." Last modified March 6. http://www.opensocietyfoundations.org/projects/global-campaign-pretrial-justice.

Open Society Justice Initiative. 2010. *From Judgment to Justice: Implementing International and Regional Human Rights Decisions*. New York: Open Society Foundations.

Samuels, Kirsti. 2006. "Rule of Law Reform in Post-Conflict Countries: Operational Initiatives and Lessons Learnt." Social Development Paper 37.

Secretary-General. 1994. Human Rights Questions: Human Rights Questions, Including Alternative Approaches for Improving the Effective Enjoyment of Human Rights and Fundamental Freedoms; Strengthening the Rule of Law. UN doc. A/49/512.

———. 1995. Human Rights Questions: Human Rights Questions, Including Alternative Approaches for Improving the Effective Enjoyment of Human Rights and Fundamental Freedoms; Strengthening the Rule of Law. UN doc. A/50/653.

———. 2000. Report of the Secretary-General on the Implementation of the Report of the Panel on United Nations Peace Operations. UN doc. S/2000/1081.

———. 2002a. Strengthening of the Rule of Law. UN doc. A/57/275.

———. 2002b. Strengthening of the United Nations: An Agenda for Further Change. UN doc. A/57/387.

———. 2004a. Report of the Secretary-General on Haiti. UN doc. S/2004/300.

———. 2004b. The Rule of Law and Transitional Justice in Conflict and Post-conflict Societies. UN doc. S/2004/616 .

———. 2005. Report of the Secretary-General on the United Nations Stabilization Mission in Haiti. UN doc. S/2005/631.

———. 2006a. Report of the Secretary-General on the United Nations Stabilization Mission in Haiti. UN doc. S/2006/60.

———. 2006b. Report of the Secretary-General on the United Nations Stabilization Mission in Haiti. UN doc. S/2006/592.

———. 2006c. Uniting Our Strengths: Enhancing United Nations Support for the Rule of Law. UN doc. A/61/636.

———. 2007a. Report of the Secretary-General on the United Nations Stabilization Mission in Haiti. UN doc. S/2007/503.

———. 2007b. The Rule of Law at the National and International Levels: Comments and Information Received from Governments. UN doc. A/62/121.

———. 2008a. Report of the Secretary-General on the United Nations Interim Administration Mission in Kosovo. UN doc. S/2008/692.

———. 2008b. The Rule of Law at the National and International Levels. UN doc. A/63/64.

———. 2008c. Strengthening and Coordinating United Nations Rule of Law Activities. UN doc. A/63/226.

———. 2009a. Report of the Secretary-General on the United Nations Stabilization Mission in Haiti. UN doc. S/2009/129.

———. 2009b. Report of the Secretary-General on the United Nations Stabilization Mission in Haiti. UN doc. S/2009/439.

———. 2011a. Civilian Capacity in the Aftermath of Conflict. UN docs. A/66/311–S/2011/527.

———. 2011b. United Nations Police. UN doc. A/66/615.

———. 2012. Report of the Secretary-General on the United Nations Stabilization Mission in Haiti. UN doc. S/2012/128.

———. 2013a. Overall Policy Matters pertaining to Special Political Missions. UN doc. A/68/223.

———. 2013b. Report of the Secretary-General on the United Nations Stabilization Mission in Haiti. UN doc. S/2013/493.

Security Council. 1993a. Resolution 814. UN doc. S/RES/814.

———. 1993b. Resolution 867. UN doc. S/RES/867.

———. 1999. Resolution 1244. UN doc. S/RES/1244.

———. 2000. Resolution 1327. UN doc. S/RES/1327.

———. 2004a. 5052nd Meeting: Justice and the Rule of Law; The United Nations Role. UN doc. S/PV.5052.

———. 2004b. Resolution 1542. UN doc. S/RES/1542.

———. 2005. Resolution 1590. UN doc. S/RES/1590.

————. 2006. Letter Dated 7 June 2006 from the Permanent Representative of Denmark to the United Nations Addressed to the Secretary-General. UN doc. S/2006/367.

————. 2010a. 6347th Meeting: The Promotion and Strengthening of the Rule of Law in the Maintenance of International Peace and Security. UN doc. S/PV.6347.

————. 2010b. Letter Dated 18 June 2010 from the Permanent Representative of Mexico to the United Nations Addressed to the Secretary-General. UN doc. S/2010/322.

————. 2011a. *Cross-Cutting Report on the Rule of Law.* October 28. New York: Security Council.

————. 2011b. Resolution 1996. UN doc. S/RES/1996.

————. 2012a. Statement by the President of the Council. UN doc. S/PRST/2012/1.

————. 2012b. Statement by the President of the Council. UN doc. S/PRST/2012/29.

————. 2013a. Resolution 2086. UN doc. S/RES/2086.

————. 2013b. Resolution 2100. UN doc. S/RES/2100.

————. 2013c. Resolution 2102. UN doc. S/RES/2102.

————. 2014. Statement by the President of the Council. UN doc. S/PRST/2014/5.

Sikkink, Kathryn. 2011. *The Justice Cascade: How Human Rights Prosecutions are Changing World Politics.* New York: W.W. Norton.

Simmons, Beth A. 2009. *Mobilizing for Human Rights: International Law in Domestic Politics.* New York: Cambridge University Press.

Sixth Committee of the General Assembly. 2014. "Sixty-Second Session: The Rule of Law at the National and International Levels (Agenda Item 86)." Accessed March 28. http://www.un.org/en/ga/sixth/62/RuleofLaw.shtml.

Special Inspector General for Afghanistan Reconstruction. 2014. *Quarterly Report to the United States Congress.* Arlington: Special Inspector General for Afghanistan Reconstruction.

Tamanaha, Brian Z. 2011. "The Primacy of Society and the Failures of Law and Development." *Cornell International Law Journal* 44:209–47.

Teitel, Ruti G. 2002. *Transitional Justice.* New York: Oxford University Press.

United Nations. 2010. *Report of the United Nations in Haiti 2010, Situation, Challenges and Outlook.* New York: United Nations.

————. 2013. "Policy on Integrated Assessment and Planning." April 9.

————. 2014. "Civilian Capacities: Building National Institutions in the Aftermath of Conflict." Accessed February 5. http://civcapreview.org.

United Nations Assistance Mission in Somalia. 2014. "Rule of Law and Security Institutions." Accessed March 28. http://www.unsom.unmissions.org/Default. aspx?tabid=6268&language=en-US.

United Nations Development Programme. 2014. "IGAD Regional Capacity Enhancement Initiative." Accessed March 28. http://www.undp.org/content/south_ sudan/en/home/operations/projects/closed-projects/democratic-governance/ igad_regional_capacity.html.

United Nations Mission in Kosovo. 1999. Regulation No. 1999/24: On the Rule of Law Applicable in Kosovo. UN doc. UNMIK/REG/1999/24.
———. 2000. Regulation 200/38: On the Establishment of the Ombudsperson Institution in Kosovo. UN doc. UNMIK/REG/200/38.
———. 2001. Regulation 2001/9: On a Constitutional Framework for Provisional Self-Government in Kosovo. UN doc. UNMIK/REG/2001/9.
United Nations Mission in South Sudan. 2014. "Rule of Law and Security Institutions Support." Accessed March 28. http://unmiss.unmissions.org/Default.aspx?tabid=5442&language=en-US.
United Nations Peacekeeping. 2014. "Department of Peacekeeping Operations." Accessed March 28. http://www.un.org/en/peacekeeping/about/dpko.
United Nations Peacekeeping and United Nations Development Programme. 2012. "Fact Sheet: Global Focal Point for Police, Justice and Corrections." http://www.undp.org/content/dam/undp/library/crisis%20prevention/2012_12_07_The_Fact_Sheet_for_Global_Focal_Point_Dec_2012.pdf.
United Nations Rule of Law. 2014a. "UN Engagement." Accessed February 18. http://www.unrol.org/article.aspx?article_id=4.
———. 2014b. "United Nations Development Programme." Accessed February 18. http://www.unrol.org/article.aspx?n=undp.
United States Institute of Peace. 2009. "INPROL Second Annual Meeting." Accessed February 2, 2014. http://www.usip.org/events/inprol-second-annual-meeting.
United States Institute of Peace and Rift Valley Institute. 2010. *Local Justice in Southern Sudan*. Washington, DC: United States Institute of Peace.
Vera Institute of Justice. 2012. "Final Report: Review of Impact Achieved by UN Rule of Law Activities at the National Level." November 9. On file with the author.
World Bank. n.d. *Justice and Development Working Paper Series Brochure*. http://siteresources.worldbank.org/INTLAWJUSTINST/Resources/J&D_Flyer_2013.pdf.
———. 2014. "Justice and Development Working Paper Series." Accessed March 14. http://go.worldbank.org/SHG7QP4I30.
Ziai Fatemeh. 2010. "Developing a Strategy for Early Peacebuilding: Priorities, Sequencing and Delivery of Rule of Law and Security-Related Activities by UN Peacekeeping Operations." Background paper.

Notes

1. This was most profoundly the case in South Sudan. See United States Institute of Peace and Rift Valley Institute (2010).

2. Specialized agencies are autonomous organizations working with the United Nations. They include, among others, the World Bank Group and the World Health Organization.

3.   The World Trade Organization.

4.   Charter of the United Nations, 1 UNTS XVI, entered into force October 24, 1943, art. 7(1).

5.   Ibid., art. 24(1), authorizing the Security Council to maintain international peace and security.

6.   In addition to receiving mandates from the Security Council, DPKO is overseen by the Special Committee on Peacekeeping Operations, established in February 1965 "to undertake . . . a comprehensive review of the whole question of peace-keeping operations in all their aspects" (General Assembly 1965, para. 3).

7.   The costs of UN field operations vary depending on the scale of operations. The annual budgets for UN field operations in 2012–2013 ranged between US$500 million and $1 billion. See General Assembly (2014).

8.   The United Nations Development Programme has a presence in 166 countries. With regard to rule of law assistance in postconflict and fragile states, it has a presence in twenty countries. See United Nations Rule of Law (2014b).

9.   With regard to the rule of law, the breadth of UN's global rule of law assistance is impressive—it provides such assistance to over 150 countries, a significant rise from when the Secretary-General first reported on the UN's rule of law footprint in 2008. See United Nations Rule of Law (2014a). See also Secretary-General (2008c).

10.   No previous peacekeeping mission had undertaken such a task, and the UN had—certainly in 2011—no dedicated capacity in this field.

11.   For example, in UNMISS, the Security Council asked the Secretary-General to "utilize to the greatest extent possible opportunities for co-location of appropri-ate mission components with the Republic of South Sudan counterparts in the interest of building national capacity" (Security Council 2011b, para. 22).

12.   In addition to the 14,000 police officers mentioned above, according to DPKO, in 2014, there were 69 justice and 343 corrections government-provided person-nel working in UN field operations (Department of Peacekeeping Operations 2014b, 16).

13.   The DPKO *Justice and Corrections Update* states that such deployment is "a learn-ing experience through which [government-provided personnel] are acquiring news skills and expertise they can apply when returning to their home countries" (Department of Peacekeeping Operations 2014b, 16).

14. According to the Special Inspector General for Afghanistan Reconstruction (2014, 79), the United States' twelve-year effort in Afghanistan, "the most expensive reconstruction effort ever undertaken in a single country," has cost more than US$100 billion, of which over $4 billion has been allocated to rule of law programs.

15. For an overview of the international community's experiences in the Democratic Republic of Congo, see Autesserre (2010).

16. For an alternative approach, see the Failed States Index (Fund for Peace 2013), which ranks states according to their levels of demographic pressures, refugees or displaced persons, aggrieved groups seeking revenge, uneven economic development, poverty, economic decline, public services, security apparatuses, and rule of law. Afghanistan ranked the seventh-worst, trailing Somalia, the Democratic Republic of Congo, Sudan, South Sudan, Chad, and Yemen.

17. For a historical overview of the international judicial reform effort in Haiti, see Berg (2013).

18. The budget for the UN Police Division in 2010/11 was US$156 million (Office of Internal Oversight Services 2012, para. 5).

19. The vetting was to have been completed by 2007. By the end of 2011, 35% of registered national police officers (12,678) had been vetted (Office of Internal Oversight Services 2012, para. 22).

20. Senior MINUSTAH official and senior diplomat, interview conducted by the author, Port au Prince, December 5, 2012.

21. DPKO's *Handbook for Judicial Affairs Officers in United Nations Peacekeeping Operations* also suggests, in the chapter entitled "Immediate Effectiveness of the Justice System," activities that UN staff can undertake to "help national actors implement immediate measures to enhance the justice system's capacity to meet demand" (Department of Peacekeeping Operations 2013, 154).

22. The Brahimi Report recommended the creation of an Information and Strategic Analysis Secretariat that would "fine tune its analysis with regard to particular places and circumstances" (General Assembly and Security Council 2000, paras. 73, 75).

23. The database includes "guidance" (policies, guidelines, manuals, standard operating procedures, mission guidance, and templates for drafting policies and standard operating procedures); "best practices" (after-action reviews, end-of-assign-

ment reports, lessons learned, practice notes, mission projects and tools, and templates for drafting the above); and "additional references" (training materials, strategic peacekeeping reports, planning documents, and progress reports).

24. Recent research includes work on paralegals in the Philippines, legal empowerment, and alleviating poverty and case flow management. See World Bank (2014).

25. The Kosovo Judicial Institute.

26. The Kosovo Law Centre.

27. I participated in this exercise as a representative of OHCHR.

28. According to Amnesty International (2013a):

> Amnesty International slams the UN administration in Kosovo for failing to investigate the abduction and murders of Kosovo Serbs in the aftermath of the 1998-1999 conflict, where they had the responsibility for police and justice until December 2008. . . . The report calls for the legacies of the Kosovo conflict to be resolved—this includes resolving the fate of missing persons from all communities in Kosovo, bringing to account those responsible for war crimes and crimes against humanity, and providing reparation.

29. The *Fourth Annual Report: 2003–2004* of the Ombudsperson Institution in Kosovo (2004) should be mandatory reading for those considering establishing international presences with the breadth and depth of authority provided UNMIK by the Security Council.

30. In late 2008, the European Union took over responsibility for rule of law reform in Kosovo (see Secretary-General 2008a, para. 23; see also EULEX Kosovo 2014). Four years later, "The rule of law remain[ed] the biggest challenge that Kosovo faces in getting onto the European track" (EULEX Kosovo 2012, internal citations omitted).

31. The World Bank was provided a standing invitation to join the strategic assessment.

32. The Justice and Corrections Standing Capacity was established in 2010 by the General Assembly and sits within DPKO. See Department of Peacekeeping Operations (2014a).

33. The report highlighted the extensive use of seconded personnel—of UN police officers deployed to UN field operations, 14,333 were seconded from member states, and 94 were UN staff members (Secretary-General 2011b, annex I).

34. The Rule of Law Coordination and Resource Group consisted of the Office of

Legal Affairs, DPKO, OHCHR, the United Nations Office on Drugs and Crime, the United Nations Development Programme, the United Nations Development Fund for Women, and the United Nations High Commissioner for Refugees.

35. Some six years after the creation of the Rule of Law Coordination and Resource Group to ensure greater coherence, coordination, and capacities, it became clear that the mechanism was not meeting its obligations. Following several external and internal assessments, it was concluded that the group and the system of global leads would be replaced by a new architecture, the Global Focal Point for Police, Justice and Corrections, with DPKO and the United Nations Development Programme as joint leads (see United Nations Peacekeeping and United Nations Development Programme 2012; for the reviews, see Kavanagh and Jones 2011; Vera Institute of Justice 2012; Durch et al.).

36. In the South Sudan mission, the section undertaking rule of law work is entitled "Rule of Law and Security Institutions Support Office" (United Nations Mission in South Sudan 2014). In the Somalia mission, this section is entitled "the Rule of Law and Security Institutions Group (United Nations Assistance Mission in Somalia 2014).

37. In 2008, the inventory was published, with forty entities providing information on the UN's capacity to promote the rule of law at the national and international levels (Secretary-General 2008b).

38. There is little documentation of these activities prior to the 1990s.

39. Vienna Declaration and Programme of Action, World Conference on Human Rights, Vienna, Austria, UN doc. A/CONF.157/23 (1993), paras. 66, 67.

40. Ibid., para. 69.

41. Ibid., para. 34.

42. In 1995, the Secretary-General reported that the General Assembly had "expressed its deep concern at the scarcity of means at the disposal of the Centre for the fulfilment of its tasks" (Secretary-General 1995, para. 1; see also General Assembly 2003, para. 5).

43. The Third Committee has jurisdiction over a range of social, humanitarian affairs, and human rights issues.

44. For an overview, see Security Council (2011a).

45. Rule of law
refers to a principle of governance in which all persons, institutions and entities,

public and private, including the State itself, are accountable to laws that are publicly promulgated, equally enforced and independently adjudicated, and which are
consistent with international human rights norms and standards. It requires, as well,
measures to ensure adherence to the principles of supremacy of law, equality before
the law, accountability to the law, fairness in the application of the law, separation of
powers, participation in decision-making, legal certainty, avoidance of arbitrariness
and procedural and legal transparency. (United Nations Secretary-General 2004b,
para. 6)

The Charter of the United Nations Charter makes no mention of the rule of
law. The 1948 Universal Declaration of Human Rights mentions it briefly mentioned in its preamble but does not define it. It is important to note that in 2012,
the Declaration on the Rule of Law at the National and International Levels,
adopted by the General Assembly, revealed deep splits among member states
regarding the content of the rule of law. The declaration makes no reference to
the principles of the supremacy of law, separation of powers, participation in
decision making, or procedural and legal transparency.

46. "Open debates" are not actual debates but meetings in which statements are read
aloud by members of the Security Council and by senior UN officials.

47. In 2012, the Security Council requested that the Secretary-General report on
the effectiveness of the UN's support to the promotion of the rule of law in
conflict and postconflict situations (Security Council 2012a; see also Security
Council, 2012b).

48. For a concise overview of the "waves" of rule of law reform efforts, see Jensen
and Heller (2003) and Tamanaha (2011). See also Carothers (1998, 2006).

49. Haiti was asked to "increase efforts to strengthen the rule of law" (Human Rights
Council 2011, para. 88.44). Haiti received a total of 136 recommendations.

50. The government appointed a "commission that will formulate proposals for a
reform of the country's justice system" (Human Rights Council 2012, para. 8).

51. A number of thematic mandates are relevant to the UN's "rule of law" work
in fragile states. These include the Working Group on Arbitrary Detention; the
Special Rapporteur on Adequate Housing; the Working Group on Enforced
Disappearances; the Special Rapporteur on extrajudicial, summary or arbitrary
executions; the Special Rapporteur on extreme poverty and human rights; the
Special Rapporteur on freedom of peaceful assembly and of association; the
Special Rapporteur on the independence of judges and lawyers; the Special Rapporteur on torture and other, cruel, inhuman or degrading treatment or punishment; and the Special Rapporteur on violence against women, its causes and
consequences.

52. For an overview of transitional justice, see Teitel (2002).

53. Transitional countries were defined as "countries moving from an undemocratic to a more democratic regime" (Sikkink 2011, 21).

Abstract

By and large, in the study of the rule of law and in programmatic efforts in the field to develop it, sufficient heed has not been paid to the central lesson that legal pluralism has laid bare, which is that in any social field, there is more than one legal system in operation. Thus, state law invariably operates together with other legal systems in the same social field, each of which is "semi-autonomous" in its workings and none of which enjoys a monopoly on the maintenance of order. Indeed, there is much evidence that the role of the state as a global matter is evolving in a fashion that might very well decrease its influence in this complex system. Until and unless rule of law reformers grow acculturated to these realities, efforts to institute the rule of law are likely to fall well short of expectations.

This involves more than merely understanding how different legal systems operate in the broader social matrix. It even involves more than making the obvious concession to reality that any rule of law program operating in the developing world must, and often does, make—namely, that there are functioning nonstate systems, that they tend to dominate the legal landscape, and that they must therefore be a matter of premier concern. More centrally, it requires a form of decolonization of the mind. Specifically, rule of law policies and programs must come to realize that legal systems that are autonomous of state law will invariably exist, irrespective of what type of rule of law society ultimately emerges.

This chapter explores the deficiencies associated with the legal centralist assumption in the context of rule of law efforts, and the means by which rule of law as an operational matter could be better deployed once we deacculturate ourselves from that unjustified assumption. While the lessons are intended to be universal, the reference used to illustrate the point is the Islamic world, particularly Shi'i-dominated central and southern Iraq.

4 Decolonizing the Centralist Mind: Legal Pluralism and the Rule of Law

Haider Ala Hamoudi

Introduction

By and large, in the study of the rule of law and in programmatic efforts in the field to develop it, sufficient heed has not been paid to the lessons that legal pluralism has laid bare. These are that in *any* social field, there is more than one legal system in operation (Griffiths 1986, 38), and that state law by no means reigns supreme over all.[1] Of course, state law often plays a role, and in some cases that role is quite significant. Yet invariably it operates together—in coordination or competition, as the case may be—with other legal systems in the same social field, each of which is "semi-autonomous" in its workings and none of which enjoys a monopoly on the maintenance of order.[2] Indeed, there is evidence that the state's influence in this complex system of multiple sources of order is actually decreasing as a global matter (Patterson and Afialo 2008, 13–14). Until and unless rule of law reformers grow acculturated to these realities, internalize them, and incorporate them into their operations, efforts to institute the rule of law are likely to fall far short of expectations.

I would like to thank all of the participants from the Harvard Human Rights Program "International Rule of Law Movement" workshop held in November 2013 for their generous comments and support, with particular thanks extended to Gerald Neuman, David Marshall, Rachel Kleinfeld, and Erik Jensen. Any errors are mine alone.

This involves more than merely understanding how different legal systems, including the state system, operate in the broader social matrix, a point that has been made eloquently by Erik Jensen (2003, 362–63), among others. It even involves more than making the obvious concession to reality that any rule of law program operating in the developing world must, and often does, make[3]—namely, that there are functioning nonstate systems, that they tend to dominate the legal landscape, and that they must therefore be a matter of premier concern.

More centrally, it requires a "decolonization of the mind," to adopt a helpful phrase that Rachel Kleinfeld proposed during Harvard Law School's 2013 workshop on the international rule of law movement. Specifically, rule of law policies and programs must come to realize that legal systems that are autonomous of state law will invariably exist, *irrespective of what type of rule of law society ultimately emerges. That is, if the rule of law is supposed to represent a system where all law is state law—or at least where all legal systems operate in harmony in accordance with rules set forth in a foundational state law document, constitution or otherwise—then the rule of law is a fantasy.* It knows no existence on this earth, and if it did exist in such a pristine fashion, I surmise few would find it salutary. To quote Marc Galanter (1981, 4), one of the premier legal pluralist scholars of our era, "We know enough about the work of courts to suspect that such a condition would be monstrous in its own way."

Indeed, the very suggestion that law should ultimately derive from or be delegated by the state is so contrary to the reality of any social field that to advance it in the developing world is often a thinly disguised form of legal orientalism.[4] To take one example, three prominent scholars have indicated that not all societies share a commitment to the rule of law as it is found in the United States, and to illustrate, they offer a story, "perhaps apocryphal," of Arab camel herders whom a government sought to domesticate by building specially furnished homes for them. The camel herders took the homes, but instead of living in them, they let the camels roam through the homes while the herders remained in the desert tents to which they were so accustomed. After a short time, the camels had ruined the homes, and the nomads resumed roaming the desert. This "baffled" and "irritated" government officials, who had been trying, among other things, to provide the nomads with clean water, good education, and decent health care (Stromseth, Wippman, and Brooks 2006, 76–77). In this rendition, state law is analogous to modern health care, while informal adjudication beyond state control is akin to the hysterical and incoherent ranting of a medicine man in a drug-induced hallucinatory state.

Extending the analogy to modern rule of law operations as they often end up working in the field, a medical professional might argue that, in some circumstances, she must find a way to deal with the drug-crazed medicine man if there is no other way to penetrate the relevant social field. Through her interactions with him, she might be able to convince him to use slightly better medical techniques. Most modern competent medical professionals would certainly regard this as an improvement over the existing situation. Yet there can be no doubt about the ultimate goal of any medical program of Western origin committed to the improvement of health care in the developing world—the marginalization and ultimate disappearance of witches and medicine men, and their replacement with modern medical professionals working in well-appointed facilities. Whether such a position is justified or justifiable in the context of medicine is not a question explored in this chapter. Yet it is apparent that for rule of law operators to regard nonstate tribal and religiously based forms of adjudication in the same manner that modern medical professionals regard medicine men has been and continues to be a tragic mistake.[5]

Indeed, the selfsame analysis respecting the necessary central and near exclusive role of the state in managing legal disputes would appear deeply unsatisfactory when extended into the society the three authors above describe as culturally committed to the rule of law: the United States. In the private high school I attended years ago in Columbus, Ohio, the mother of a twelve-year-old child chose to address a serious physical injury done to her son by another boy by calling the school's principal and the other boy's mother. The matter was settled with a suspension, prolonged detention during which the boy did chores for his victim's family, school-ordered community service, a much-desired apology, and a school assembly on the problems associated with school violence. No money—the one remedy the victim's mother might have been able to obtain in state court—changed hands. She recoiled at the notion of filing a lawsuit against the boy and his parents, finding such an approach dramatically inappropriate and instead preferring the private resolution that was actually reached. I dare to presume that few would describe her refusal to seek redress in the court system as in any way similar to refusing her child a good education, clean water, or reliable health care. Fewer still worry about the state of the rule of law in Columbus upon hearing this story. Indeed, the suggestion that our Columbus mother should have been *required* to pursue a remedy in state court or to point to a state law permitting alternative means of resolution sounds, to use Galanter's phrasing again, positively "monstrous."

So, then, it is important to avoid the orientalist trap wherein one group's decision to resolve matters outside the court system and without reference to state law is a judicious deference to collaborative and customary forms of dispute resolution, while another group's decision to do so is demonstrative of their broadly uncivilized condition. And to avoid that trap, we must do away with the preposterous assumption that in a properly functioning society there is a natural legal gravity that pulls human beings toward the state as the supreme source of order in all contexts as moths to a flame.

This chapter explores the deficiencies associated with the legal central-ist assumption in the context of rule of law efforts, and the means by which the rule of law as an operational matter could be better deployed once we deacculturate ourselves from that unjustified assumption. While the lessons are intended to be universal, the reference used to illustrate the point is the Islamic world, particularly Shi'i-dominated central and southern Iraq.

The next section examines the depth of the legal centralist assumptions that dominate rule of law discourse as a matter of both theory and practice. The section after that discusses three plural sources of legal order in Iraq—the state, the *shari'a*, and the tribe—and describes the extent to which each is used in particular contexts. Finally, the last section illustrates the need to decolo-nize the legal mind away from legal centralism and reacculturate the rule of law community to the realities of legal pluralism. It also explains why such a decolonization and reacculturation process is salient in light of the weakening role of the state in the international order.

Before proceeding, however, it is necessary to make two clarifications. First, I do not wish to romanticize indigenous forms of ordering, whether reli-gious or tribal in origin. Common criticisms of indigenous law are generally sound and correct, even if the advantages of indigenous law are not praised as often as they should be. Hence, rule of law authors are not wrong when they point out that access to justice is often denied to women and minori-ties in customary tribunals (Stromseth, Wippman, and Brooks 2006, 336). Nor are these tribunals necessarily free of corruption and capture by elites, as some excellent fieldwork has demonstrated (Jensen 2003, 363). To this may be added other ills. Indigenous law tends to preserve existing structural inequali-ties (McMillan and Woodruff 2000, 2423), privilege members of certain sub-communities, and impose costs on broader society (Ellickson 1991, 249–50). If its means of resolving disputes tend to be quicker and less formal (Galanter 1981, 25), punishments exacted and forms of compensation demanded can be brutal and arbitrary (Stromseth, Wippman, and Brooks 2006, 336).

Still, while pointing this out, it is helpful to balance the picture, for the advantages of local tribunals extend far beyond the fact that they "command substantial loyalty and may offer useful models for more formal institutions" (ibid.). They command substantial loyalty for a reason. Indigenous law is familiar and accessible to its participants. Indigenous tribunals generally do not require one who wishes to make use of them to enter intimidating and strange courtrooms far from one's home. There are no lawyer-intermediaries speaking a language that participants can barely understand (Galanter 1981, 25). This is nearly impossible to achieve in any state tribunal that resorts to the use of "modern and effective legal institutions and codes" (Stromseth, Wippman, and Brooks 2006, 78). The costs of doing away with the informal processes are not insignificant.

The point, in any event, is not to engage in a preposterous mission of finding an "authentic" local, communal law that operates on an ideal plane and in contrast to alternative sources of order that would be disrupting and intrusive.[6] This merely replaces the fantastical claims of legal centralism with equally fantastical ones relating to cultural essentialism. The point, instead, is simply that indigenous law *does* exist and that it will not disappear into irrelevance if the mechanisms of state law manage to improve through extensive rule of law reform.

Second, I am not interested in engaging in the debate that has obsessed legal pluralists for decades respecting what forms of normative order other than those of the state can truly be considered "law."[7] The fact that the participants in these alternative systems think they are involved in a legal system is good enough to render it law in my view.[8] Yet to the extent that a critic seeks to describe alternative systems of order based on *shari'a* or tribal rules as not being "legal" but rather "normative," this will suit just fine.

Whatever these systems might be called, their existence is no less real, and their effects on state legal order no less felt. Nor can these alternative systems be wished away, even if many times and in many states, the state law actors themselves (from judges to lawmakers) tend to articulate such a desire, casually dismissing nonstate law as the backwaters province of the ignorant. The fact is that millions make use of such systems, and millions will continue to make use of them. Their interaction with state law in the social matrix is likely to be complex and multifaceted, and we cannot expect state law to reign supreme. In fact, if anything, state law is losing its relative force in the contemporary world, in developing and developed states alike. If any rule of law effort is to succeed, it cannot ignore this.

The Fallacy of the Dominant Approaches to Nonstate Law

The social fact of pluralism, first described decades ago by scholars such as John Griffiths (1986), Sally Falk Moore (1972), Marc Galanter (1981), and Sally Engle Merry (1988), has been demonstrated time and again in a variety of social fields. Whether the subject is land ownership in Tanzania (Moore

1972, 729–42), housing communes in England (Henry 1985), blood feuds in Egypt (Ben Nefissa 1999, 145–57), or even the maintenance of security in modern-day Japan (Milhaupt and West 2000), the ability of actors to circumvent state law—indeed, to operate in contravention of it—has been extensively researched and documented. The research demonstrates that in none of these instances was state law an irrelevancy, and yet in all of them it was not the only normative system in operation. This limited the ability of state law to control outcomes, though in most cases state law certainly influenced outcomes. Such rich lessons of legal pluralism have helped spawn an entire literature in the American legal academy known as "private ordering," which highlights instances where commercial actors in particular choose to adopt an alternative legal system that appears to meet their needs more effectively than state law does. Such actors regard state law as "destructively adversarial" and for this reason shun it (Feldman 2006, 315).[9] Similar lessons have also led some scholars to conclude that a great deal of economic development can be obtained without state-directed or state-controlled dispute-resolution mechanisms.[10]

Hence, in the world as it exists, the vast majority of disputes that are capable of reaching court, even in a developed society such as the United States, are not resolved by a court, and a sizable number of them are handled by institutions unaffiliated with the state according to norms that are different from state law (Galanter 1981, 19–21). Parties often prefer this. Rather than base their contracts or property rights on state law, social actors in many circumstances deliberately avoid doing so, with the hope of minimizing the possibility of ever having to litigate these rights in court.[11]

Yet much rule of law work—in both theory and practice—clings to the unjustified assumptions of legal centralism. Hence, it is often stated as axiom, disputes are settled in accordance with "universally applicable rules." This in turn necessitates the existence of "modern and effective legal institutions and codes"—created, of course, by the state (Stromseth, Wippman, and Brooks 2006, 78). Property and contract rights are too often assumed to be "founded on the law" (Carothers 2006, 5); indeed, the very notion of such a right existing independently of the state does not exist in this shackled conception of law and social order. This is so contrary to fact that it is better described as ideology rather than descriptive reality (Griffiths 1986, 4).

So enamored are rule of law theorists with the primacy of state law that they often do not seem to recognize the extent to which their models fail to address nonstate law in a satisfactory fashion. One might consider, for example, Kleinfeld, whose work on defining the rule of law has been praised, with much justification. I should therefore stress that I do not focus on Kleinfeld's work because it is particularly deficient in considering nonstate law. On the contrary, it is the best I have been able to find. Too many others are quick to castigate customary tribunals for their faults (as if the state's processes have none of their own), and concede, seemingly grudgingly, the need to work with them because they are the only justice mechanism available (Stromseth, Wippman, and Brooks 2006, 336–37). In the end, such scholars offer three alternatives regarding the future of customary tribunals: the state, as the supreme source of legal order, must restrict them, absorb them (by incorporating some of their practices into the state system), or abolish them (ibid., 337). Any other solution, it seems, would not accord with the rule of law.

Kleinfeld, by contrast, engages customary law in much greater depth and nuance. It is the fact that she does this and yet is still unable to incorporate customary law into a broader rule of law theory that makes her work such a compelling demonstration of the discipline's problems in addressing nonstate law. For example, in one section, Kleinfeld points out that a village elder might dispense justice sitting under the shade of a palm tree just as well as an elaborate court with Internet access and oak panels. Elsewhere, she indicates that the notion that contracts require effective judicial enforcement might be overstated. In a third section, she describes a rule of law idyll in British Columbia that seems to operate well without a court or police force in sight (Kleinfeld 2012, 33, 53, 80).

Yet, curiously, despite these and other instances, the considerations of nonstate law never seem to penetrate her definitional parameters, which are plainly directed at the state's role in the normative order. In this respect, the mind remains colonized, and the presumptions of legal centralism unmoved. Hence, precisely at the point where she insists that a trusted village elder might dispense justice efficiently, she turns to define the rule of law as having something to do with a relationship between a *state* and its society (ibid., 33). It is not clear why the state would need to be involved in adjudication by a village elder at all. The village surely knows its trusted elders better than the distant state could. Requiring that such a system be incorporated into the state's adjudicatory system could be costly, for it would require that elders be appointed as judges, appeals processes be organized, and formal rules of evidence be introduced. It could also prove perverse, both in limiting access to justice and leading to the creation of rules that destroy more effective informal systems that exist.[12] This is not necessarily so, and I do not deny that there may be sound reasons to involve the state in such adjudications. Yet it is not clear that the state must be involved—and if it is not, then either the nonstate law has nothing to do with the rule of law, or the rule of law involves considerably more than a relationship between a society and a state. Kleinfeld's definitions appear to anticipate neither of these possibilities.

The confusion deepens when Kleinfeld describes the "idyllic rule of law" as it exists on Salt Spring Island in British Vancouver. Nobody guards the boxes where the money from purchases is collected and stored over the course of the day. A buyer who likes an item simply takes it and leaves the appropriate amount in the unguarded cash box before walking out. The buyer could just as easily fail to pay, or even take money out of the cash box on her way out of the door. Yet when the possibility of theft is raised to islanders, they meet it with gentle derision (Kleinfeld 2012, 80).

To find a relationship between this social state of affairs and the state requires us to presume that the only reason citizens do not steal from one another is because the state has told them it is a crime to do so. More likely, the residents of Salt Spring Island are only vaguely familiar with the state's laws on larceny, but they all know that stealing is wrong. Also likely is the fact that they manage, in many cases, to effect this system through the enforcement of nonstate norms rather than the application of state law. It is possible that a sixteen-year-old resident of Salt Spring Island who steals finds himself in court because the police are called; it is more likely, however, that the offender is taken to his parents and that his family is sufficiently shamed to prevent a recurrence. After all, if the state were the effective deterrent and source of order, one would expect considerably more theft to occur when the police are not around. Plainly, there is much work to do concerning the role of nonstate law in maintaining order in a rule of law society.

In rule of law operation as opposed to theory, the matter is even worse. By and large, efforts to deal with nonstate law seem to consist of attempts to tame it and subject it to state restriction and control. Amnesty International is the most explicit in this regard. Distressed by the manner in which courts appear to haphazardly decline jurisdiction and in which nonstate tribunals engage in frequent and abusive violations of human rights, Amnesty concludes that an important component of the solution is to "regulate the informal justice system." Specifically:

> The competence of informal justice systems must be clearly set out in the law in order to remove any ambiguity regarding the role of Afghan informal justice mechanisms. The relationship between informal systems and the formal judicial system must be set out by law. In order to fulfil its obligation to exercise due diligence in protecting human rights, the [Afghan government] must ensure that *jirgas* and *shuras*, if they are allowed to continue to function, fully conform to international human

rights law. If this cannot be ensured then these informal justice mechanisms must be abolished. All cases in which there are indications that a *jirga* or *shura* has perpetrated human rights abuses must be thoroughly investigated and all those participating in them must be brought to justice. (Amnesty International 2003, 62)

Amnesty's obsessions with legal centralism are clear from the above passage. We may all share Amnesty's distaste in the human rights abuses committed by customary tribunals in Afghanistan, and we may all seek to put an end to such abuses, without embracing the state and state courts as a panacea. Surely Amnesty is aware that the greatest killing institution in the history of humanity is the state. When it comes to the adjudication of death, even the most brutal and arbitrary customary tribunals are not in the same league as courts administered, operated, and directed by regimes, from Nazi Germany to Ba'ath Iraq. It takes a mind colonized in the assumptions of legal centralism to presume that customary tribunals are so incorrigible, and state courts so capable of massive reform, that the only possible solution to abuses by the former is the exercise of control by the latter.

This rigid adherence to legal centralism is hardly limited to one (large and influential) human rights organization. Even the United Nations Human Rights Committee—the body responsible for monitoring states' compliance with the International Covenant on Civil and Political Rights—has expressed the same view. In its General Comment 32, which interprets article 14 of the covenant, the committee states:

> Article 14 is also relevant where a State, in its legal order, recognizes courts based on customary law, or religious courts, to carry out or entrusts them with judicial tasks. It must be ensured that such courts cannot hand down binding judgments recognized by the State, unless the following requirements are met: proceedings before such courts are limited to minor civil and criminal matters, meet the basic requirements of fair trial and other relevant guarantees of the Covenant, and their judgments are validated by State courts in light of the guarantees set out in the Covenant and can be challenged by the parties concerned in a procedure meeting the requirements of article 14 of the Covenant. These principles are notwithstanding the general obligation of the State to protect the rights under the Covenant of any persons affected by the operation of customary and religious courts.[13]

The distrust of and contempt for nonstate tribunals is unmistakable. Not only must state courts oversee the customary tribunals, and not only must they delegate to these tribunals only the most menial of matters—but even with regard to those minor matters, there must be a mechanism allowing parties to challenge their merits in a state court. The model is hardly one of cooperative pluralism. Instead, it is one of direct subjugation, with the tribal court playing the role of magistrate judge to a supervising court rather than exercising any meaningful authority of its own.

More measured, and more mature in its analyses and observations, is the United States Institute of Peace (USIP), which has an entire program focused on incorporating nonstate law into rule of law activities in postconflict states. In describing its efforts, USIP indicates that it intends "to provide guidance to . . . policymakers on the potential role of customary justice systems in postconflict states." This includes the following measures:

> [E]xamining such issues as the potential allocation of jurisdiction between formal and customary systems of justice, approaches to adapting customary practices that may contravene international human rights standards, possible limits and problems in the use of customary justice mechanisms, ramifications for the distribution of political and economic power, and the facilitation of dialogue and information-sharing between formal and informal systems. (United States Institute of Peace 2013)

There is much to like in this formulation, and yet there are also some points to question. Surely helping policy makers "understand the role of customary justice systems" is useful, and there is nothing wrong with considering approaches that might ameliorate the brazen assaults on international human rights that occur in any tribunals, whether state or nonstate. Yet USIP also lists the "allocation of jurisdiction," as well as "facilitation of dialogue and information-sharing." The two taken together suggest a particular formality to the division between state and nonstate adjudicative mechanisms that assumes state supremacy and legal centralism, for it is hard to see who or what could "allocate jurisdiction" between the tribunals save a legal rule of the state, memorialized perhaps in its foundational document. "Allocation of jurisdiction" is a phrase deeply imbued with a legalist hue. It requires the use of lawyer-intermediaries to convey its meaning to laypeople. State supremacy is presumed when "jurisdiction" is "allocated."

The same is true when USIP proposes "dialogue" between formal and informal systems. It is no secret that legal centralism permeates the mentality of local state actors at virtually all levels and in all jurisdictions. As a result, dialogue between state and nonstate systems is possible only to the extent that the customary adjudicatory systems are subservient to the broader state structure, proceeding where jurisdiction has been "allocated" to them by the state. It is difficult to believe that a state judge anywhere would make it a practice to share information with a tribunal that was not recognized by the state, or that state rules would make the judge do this. Hence, subtly but unmistakably, the broad demand is one of legal centralism, where the only law is that made by the state or specifically allocated to others by the state. That USIP (2013) has this in mind is betrayed amply in its more detailed description of the organization's work in Afghanistan, where it insists that Afghan state courts "retain an important role in ensuring that cases [adjudicated under customary law] are resolved equitably and in accordance with the law." The state tribunal, in other words, sits in review of the customary one.

I will not discuss at length the less than pragmatic assumptions that appear to attend to such formulations. It is difficult to believe that state legal systems broadly described within and beyond the rule of law community as effectively nonfunctioning will be able not only to establish themselves but to entrench themselves with such vigor that they can control, and abolish if necessary, any alternative legal systems that do not comply with their demands. Particularly incredible is the idea that such poorly functioning systems will be able to sensibly allocate jurisdiction by legal rule and then meaningfully adjudicate that necessarily elusive jurisdictional border with the type of complexity and nuance that is characteristic, for example, of courts in the United States administering the "minimum contacts" rules of *International Shoe* and its progeny.[14] Jurisdictional chaos and a broad disregard for whatever claims of jurisdictional exclusivity the state makes are far more likely results than any clarification of proper authority. But let us assume these problems away and imagine what such a world might look like if these legal centralist aims could be achieved—not in Afghanistan but rather in Shasta County, California, with specific reference to a seminal gem of private ordering literature, the work of Robert Ellickson (1991).

According to Ellickson, farmers and ranchers in Shasta County rarely litigate their disputes, at least not with regard to damage caused by trespassing animals and responsibility for building and repairing fences. In fact, most of the time, they do not even know the underlying law particularly well, and state officials seem to know it even less (Ellickson 1991, 49–50, 69–70). The community has instead developed its own norms and forms of policing, used with restraint in order to avoid feuding (ibid., 57–59). At times, the community pays heed to state legal rules—motor vehicle accidents, for example, are routinely addressed under state law. However, in their "workaday" affairs, residents manage their disputes without involving state legal processes or even invoking state legal rules about which they know so little (ibid., 69).

For example, if trespassing cattle cause damage to a landowner's fence, the landowner asks for help in rebuilding the fence. If this does not work, the landowner gossips, relying on reputational sanctions. In extreme cases, the landowner may threaten to kill or maim trespassing cattle that are deliberately left uncontrolled and for which the cattle owner does not offer to bear some responsibility (ibid., 58). Ellickson even reports that one landowner threatened to castrate a menacing bull that had repeatedly caused trouble, and that a law enforcement officer had informed the landowner that he would ignore the offense given the circumstances. Thus, though the castration would, if carried out, surely constitute a crime under state law, the actual state prosecution of such a matter seems highly improbable in light of the stated position of law enforcement on it.

This state of affairs appears to run almost directly contrary to that which Amnesty and the Human Rights Committee demand, and USIP suggests, should be the objective of rule of law efforts in Afghanistan. After all, in Shasta County, there is no "allocation of jurisdiction," at least not in any explicit sense. The law does not "clearly set out" the "competence of the informal justice systems." Rather, the decision regarding when state tribunals are used and when they yield to informal justice systems is left to custom and localized practice, presumably as it is in Afghanistan.

Moreover, in Shasta County, the informal justice system is not making its decisions "in accordance with the law"; in fact, no attempt is made to comply with the law given that nobody appears to know what it is. Not only does the state fail to "bring to justice" purported criminals for their participation in informal schemes that lead to the potential castration, kidnapping, or killing of cattle; it even implicitly endorses the scheme at times by turning a blind eye. Again, we might fairly assume that something similar occurs in Afghanistan.

In the legal centralist's world, none of this would occur. A rancher whose livestock trampled a neighbor's fence would not receive a friendly call and an offer to handle the matter using norms that have nothing to do with state law. Instead, he would be faced with a subpoena, or at least a call that initiated "bargaining in the shadow of"[15] established legal rules of which the participants would be made aware through lawyers. If the rancher refused to compromise, the next step would not be to initiate the informal reputational sanctions to which Ellickson refers, beginning with negative gossip. Rather, it would be to file a lawsuit, resulting in an even greater reliance on the lawyer-intermediary. Failing success at this stage, there would no threatened killing or castration of livestock but a lengthy court proceeding over the costs of mending a broken fence.

One could debate whether the realization of this legal centralist fantasy would be preferable to the reality that exists. The broader point, however, relates not to its *desirability* but to its *plausibility*. *This scenario has no actual existence on this earth.* It fails to describe accurately the internal order of Shasta County, California. It also fails to properly account for the maintenance of order in the private school of Columbus, Ohio, referred to in this chapter's introduction.

Perhaps the sweetest irony of all is that it does not even fully account for the manner in which order is maintained in the most prestigious universities of the United States, *including its law schools, where the state law is taught to aspiring students who then expect to enter the world to practice it.* Ellickson points out that academics, including legal academics, routinely flout copyright law by copying large portions of their colleagues' works for students to read in seminars and other limited-enrollment classes. Those who manage copy rooms within universities and law schools, and commercial copy centers nearby, do little to prevent this practice. And as with the farmers and ranchers in Shasta County, those engaged in the practice rarely seem to understand the law. Ellickson (1991, 260) points to one example where a commercial copy center refused—out of supposed compliance with copyright law—to copy more than 10% of a book, but permitted the patron requesting the service to use the center's equipment to make the copy himself. Suffice it to say, a commercial photocopy center does not avoid a claim of infringement by delegating the task of performing the copying to a willing volunteer.

It would be a mistake to describe the system at universities (including the one where this work is being published) as lawless with respect to copyright. Rules do exist—just rules that bear no resemblance to the actual state law. Copying an entire chemistry textbook and distributing it to the five hundred students enrolled in the class would be regarded by all as a copyright violation and a breach of academic norms (ibid., 262). However, copying journal articles or portions of books is widely practiced, and even encouraged by the authors themselves. For my own part, I know that large portions of my law review articles are routinely distributed by my colleagues to their students in Islamic law seminars around the country without advance permission having been sought either from me or from the publisher, in plain violation of copyright law. Yet, as an academic, I am flattered rather than offended by the violation—and I suspect many of my own colleagues feel similarly. Surely the publisher is aware that many of its articles are being copied illegally, and yet it makes no effort to find the violators and seek compensation from them. This, to reemphasize the point, is the manner in which America's leading universities, and its leading law schools, administer order within their ranks.

This is not to compare Afghanistan's *shuras* to Shasta County's resolution mechanisms, or to suggest that nothing is amiss in Afghanistan merely because the actual rules regarding copying at Harvard seem to work reasonably well while bearing no resemblance to state law. Obviously, there is a difference between a landowner castrating another person's bull, a professor copying a colleague's article for distribution, and a tribal leader offering young girls to rival tribes as compensation for an injury done to them by his tribe. My point is instead a more modest one: there must be better ways of addressing the severe justice deficits in Afghanistan, or Iraq, than demanding the establishment of a form of order that is entirely dependent on state law, in a manner that knows no existence on this earth.

State and Nonstate Legal Order in Iraq

Bringing the experiences of the Islamic world into sharper focus demonstrates the extent to which the assumptions of legal centralism are problematic not only generally, as described above, but in particular in regions where much rule of law work takes place. Of course, the region often described as "the Islamic world" is vast and varied, with as many differences as similarities among its many states. Generalizations are a mistake, and the notion that each Islamic state fits within an irreducible Islamic essence equally applicable to other Islamic states is preposterous (Abu Odeh 2004, 790). Yet even if this is so, it can be said with some justification that a number of Islamic states—and in particular those that are operational targets for rule of law programs—share similar characteristics that prove salient for the purposes of this chapter.

The first of these is a commitment to *shari'a* as a form of legal order, whether operating within the state or outside of it. This is hardly a surprise, as in virtually every Islamic state the *shari'a* plays some role, even if in some states that role is a highly reduced one. The history of the *shari'a* as the supreme source of legal order in Islamic states for centuries, as well as the religious commitments of countless Muslim citizens, renders the *shari'a* impossible to ignore entirely (Hamoudi 2008, 86–87). This is broadly recognized, and if there is a problem with regard to the way that outsiders tend to approach *shari'a*, it is not in granting it too little importance but in granting it too much. Just as state law does not govern in each instance where it may be applicable, the same might be said of *shari'a*, which is obsolete in any number of areas (Hamoudi 2010, 311).

A second, and less frequently discussed, source of legal order in many Islamic states is the tribe. There often seems to be a presumption that tribes apply *shari'a*, at least at times (Amnesty International 2003, 46). Much scholarship, however, points to a substantial divergence in fact between the rules

148

of the Pashtun tribes, known as *pashtunwali*, and the *shari'a*, even if the tribes claim adherence to both.[16] Certainly, my own extensive work with Iraqi tribes does not reveal any real connection between their resolution mechanisms and the *shari'a*, despite rhetorical insistence otherwise.[17]

The final, and in many ways most obvious, form of legal order is the state, whose legal system, like the *shari'a*, plays a greater or lesser role in virtually any Islamic society, depending on the state in question. State law tends to betray more vestiges of *shari'a* than tribal rules do. However, the influence often appears only at the margins, at least beyond the area of personal status (which comprises family law and inheritance). In the overwhelming majority of Islamic states, state law mostly derives either from a European transplant or, in cases such as Malaysia and Pakistan, from the adoption of the common law (Weiss 1998, 188; Abu Odeh 2004, 790–91).

While these are not the only sources of order that exist in an Islamic state, it is fair to say that in a considerable number of Muslim majority states, there are semi-autonomous social fields within the state where these three sources of order—the state, the *shari'a*, and the tribe—play a primary role. This is the case in much of the Shi'i-dominated areas of Iraq, where tribal affiliations run deep, where fealty to the *shari'a* as pronounced by the Najaf jurists is widely proclaimed, and where the state is hardly an irrelevancy, even if its role is reduced in particular contexts.[18] The rest of this section draws on the context of southern Iraq to explore these three sources of order and the complementary manner in which they interact.

Shari'a and Personal Status

Application of the *shari'a* proves most salient to Iraqis with regard to matters of personal status. The Personal Status Code takes advantage of the fact that the *shari'a* is not itself a uniform legal code. Rather, it is a broad corpus of overlapping and oft-conflicting norms and rules derived by medieval and modern jurists from Islam's sacred foundational texts—the Qur'an, the received book of God; and the Sunna, or the actions and utterances of the Prophet Muhammad (Hamoudi 2012, 431–32).[19] The code is therefore largely an enacted amalgam of rules from the Ja'fari (Shi'i) school of thought and the four classical Sunni schools, with the rules generally having been selected for enactment by the code drafters on the basis of how progressive they happened to be. Hence, for example, the code adopts the Shi'i rules respecting the inheritance rights of a daughter without brothers, which are more favorable than those of the Sunni schools.[20] At the same time, it adopts the Sunni Maliki rules respecting a woman's right to obtain a court-ordered marital dissolution, which are more favorable than those of the Shi'a and the other Sunni schools.[21]

For this reason, the code has long been resented by the Shi'a, and the Shi'i juristic classes, who view it as an imposition on the prerogative of the jurists to determine the rules of personal status (Stilt 2004, 751–52). Even more traditionalist Sunnis balk at the notion of state judges administering such fundamental religious rules as those of personal status. In light of this, it is not unusual for marriages in Iraq to be concluded by clerics instead of by judges in state courts. Technically, a husband who marries outside the personal status courts is committing a crime under the Personal Status Code,[22] though that fact seems to have done little to limit the prevalence of the practice. While urban elites tend to quickly follow religious marriages with legal ones concluded in court, the urban poor and rural populations usually do not bother to do so, often for a period of years.

Much the same can be said of marital dissolution. A man is obligated to register his divorce in court—unless it is infeasible to do so, in which case he must register it in court at a later date—and the legal effects of the divorce are attained only upon registration.[23] However, this requirement does not seem to concern many Iraqis, particularly the urban poor and rural populations, who rarely register their divorces in court until and unless there is some specific need to do so.

It should be emphasized that resort to religious mechanisms is not because of imperfections in the formal justice system, imperfect as it may be. As mentioned above, Iraqi couples *do* end up conducting formal marriages in a court eventually, in many cases long after their religious marriages have been concluded. Moreover, litigants in urban areas use the personal status courts often enough that a substantial body of jurisprudence has developed concerning the administration of marriage, divorce, alimony, child custody, inheritance, and other matters. The courts are thus sufficiently reliable and predictable to be used at times.

The problem, instead, is one of *legitimacy*. While the judiciary is not deemed illegitimate in all instances, it is deemed illegitimate with regard to matters of marriage and divorce, where Iraqis overwhelmingly vest their trust in religious authorities.

Tribal Resolution of Private Wrongs

Concerning matters of tort, the *shari'a* has long slipped into obsolescence. High jurists such as Sistani (2008, II:226–51) continue to pronounce extensive rules for such matters as the historic Islamic tort of *ghasb*, which involves "the hostile taking of the property of another, or a right therein." Yet, in reality, few among the laity even know what the Islamic rules are, much less show any interest in applying them. Commitment to the *shari'a* in this area is more rhetorical than real.

State courts, on the other hand, issue many decisions in tort disputes each year, as is the case with personal status.[24] Yet, at the same time, again similarly to the personal status courts, few Iraqis outside of the cities use the state courts. My own fieldwork suggests that this is because tribal members regard tribal resolution as a system that works well enough for its members. The process involves a series of escalating steps not unlike those taken by the farmers and ranchers of Shasta County, California. A tribal member who feels that a member of a rival tribe has perpetrated a compensable wrong against him informs his tribal leader, who then issues a notification. The allegedly offending tribe can demand arbitration of the dispute, conducted by one of several recognized elders throughout Iraq, if there is some question about who is at fault for whatever injury is alleged. If the offending tribe does so, at this stage or any other, the matter is referred to arbitration, and all further tribal resolution processes are suspended pending a determination by the arbitrator.

If the offending tribe ignores the notification, then begins the confrontation, or the *guama*. In the confrontation, several members of the injured tribe go, in public view, to the offender's home to demand compensation. This visit serves both to initiate negative gossip against the offenders and to threaten more severe action.

Usually, the dispute is resolved at this stage. The tribes are what are described in the private ordering literature as "repeat players"—they deal with each other frequently, and they know that a failure to answer for a wrong in one case will redound to their detriment when one of their own needs to make a claim in the future (Richman 2004, 2339). Tribes therefore do not take lightly wrongs that a tribal member has committed. Still, in the event that the tribe does not respond to the confrontation, the injured tribe initiates a striking, or *degga*, wherein it sprays the offender's home with bullets at a time when either nobody is home or all are asleep and the risk of injury is assumed to be low. The striking, which can be repeated several times, serves not only as a threat but also as a source of negative gossip about the resident and his tribe.

Disputes are almost always resolved after one or perhaps two strikings, as no offending tribe wishes to suffer the reputational consequences of numerous strikings. Traditionally, in the rare cases where the dispute is not resolved by this point, members of offending tribes might be kidnapped and held pending resolution. However, as the Iraqi state has taken a more strident position against kidnapping, even handing down the death penalty to those who commit the crime,[25] this procedure has been reduced to near extinction. In a two-year span, I learned of only one case that involved a kidnapping; and in this case, state intervention brought the tribal process to a halt when the tribe of the kidnapped member went to the police to complain.

In any event, once the offending tribe agrees to recognize its responsibility to compensate for a particular harm, a small number of its members pay a visit to the victim and request a respite, or an *atwa*, to pay a more formal visit in the future involving larger numbers of individuals of higher prominence. This will include, most importantly, an outsider respected by both sides who acts as a mediator and who is a *sayyid*, or a direct descendant of the Prophet. The only matter left is the payment of the appropriate compensation, which is determined in the final formal meeting, known as the *fasl*.

The State as Criminal Enforcer and Source of Largesse

As noted earlier, it would be a mistake to describe the state as completely absent in this complex semi-autonomous social field. Leaving aside the fact that much of the urban elite and even middle classes can and do make use of state court processes to marry and resolve disputes, imperfect as those processes are, virtually everyone in Iraq feels some need to interact with the state. This is most often because state-provided benefits require official documentation, and in a rentier state such as Iraq, such benefits are not insignificant.

Hence, for example, clerics unaffiliated with the state routinely perform marriages out of court, in violation of the law, and sometimes, though not usually, involving the marriage of minors. Initially, this presents no particular problem for the couple themselves, who can live perfectly happily without the state knowing or even caring about their violation of the law. However, it begins to present a problem when they seek to register their children in free public schooling, claim the food rations the government distributes monthly, or take advantage of whatever other largesse the state might distribute from time to time, whether it be land, free gasoline, or another item.

Inevitably, virtually all Iraqis appear in court at one point or another to "marry," even if the vast majority have already been religiously married. And the state does not enforce its provisions regarding the obligation to marry only in state court, even under circumstances where the violation is obvious. A judge in the Kurdistan region of Iraq, for example, married three couples—each of whom had at least two children with them—before me in a single morning. When I asked her about the legal violation, she shrugged and asked what good I expected it might do if she referred these cases to the criminal courts to imprison the husbands for three to six months, as the law requires.

The state's propensity to distribute largesse has caused the state's legal mechanisms to become more significant in other contexts as well. In the Ba'ath era, the state had a national insurance scheme pursuant to which a state-owned company, the National Insurance Company, would generously compensate anyone injured in an automobile accident, irrespective of fault.[26] The state practice brought tribal resolutions over such accidents virtually to a halt, as injured parties pursued their claims using state processes. Rather than resist this, the tribes encouraged it, and for good reason. As repeat players, the tribes preferred not to claim against one another—thereby running the risk of being claimed against in the future—if they could be compensated from an external source in a manner that cost them nothing. Hence, for a long period, the state determined compensation for automobile injuries almost exclusively, until the insurance scheme floundered along with the rest of Iraq's economy after the First Gulf War. At that point, the tribal role in addressing such disputes resumed.[27]

The criminal-enforcement aspect of state order is also important to note. While tribes and individuals violate certain laws with impunity (a fact that can be said of individuals in the United States as well), there are crimes, among them kidnapping and honor killing, with which the state is comparatively more concerned. This is not to suggest that the state manages to eliminate all occurrences of such crimes—plainly, it does not. Yet the public airing of a particularly gruesome honor crime in 2007 did lead to state intervention (Clark 2007), and the problem of kidnapping, particularly for ransom, has led the state to amend its penal code to render the crime a capital offense.[28] Tribes prefer to avoid conflict with the state, and thus they take its criminal laws seriously enough to avoid major confrontations when they can.

Also important to note is that tribes *use* the state's criminal processes for their own purposes. In some cases, tribes manipulate the judicial process by, for example, inducing a young man to "confess" to slander and spend time in jail as recompense for an honor crime prior to marrying the young woman who is his paramour. At other times, however, they work with the state. When a tort involves a serious crime, such as murder, the injured tribe often does not find the compensation sufficient recompense. Killing the offender only invites state attention, for the police do not ignore dead bodies, even in Iraq. In such cases, then, the resolution often involves the payment of a sum of money *and* the perpetrator's confession in state court, which allows the state to determine the appropriate punishment.

In this respect, the state's legal machinery can be thought of as working alongside that of the tribes. At first glance, the dominant modality seems to be one of competition in that both systems have different rules for dealing with the same matters of compensation for private wrongs. However, in reality, the state largely and implicitly delegates to the tribes the ability to administer an entire tort system on their own, without significant state interference, even when the torts committed also constitute criminal offenses. This benefits the state by relieving it of the duty to investigate such wrongs and address them in an underfunded and overburdened court system. It also permits the state to avoid intervening in affairs that social actors might regard as none of the state's business. At the same time, the tribes benefit from a broader state criminal-law system that not only can be used as a source of punishment for egregious wrongdoings but also prevents feuds from jeopardizing the public order. While negative gossip and reputational sanctions are remarkably effective tools for limiting public violence, they are imperfect ones. The willingness of the state to intervene and use criminal sanctions when feuds escalate uncontrollably enables the tribal system to function more smoothly.

The Withering of State Power and the Decolonization of the Legal Centralist Mind

The state is thus not supreme in Iraq, nor Afghanistan, nor even the most developed of societies. But equally importantly, the global trend concerning adjudication has broadly been *away* from state control—and even away from meaningful state monitoring of nonstate adjudication—primarily through the mechanism of arbitration. States have endorsed this trend. Thus, rather than increasing the level of judicial monitoring of arbitral tribunals as such tribunals proliferate, states have been acting to decrease it. Most telling in this regard is the ratification of the Convention on the Recognition and Enforcement of Foreign Arbitral Awards by the vast majority of the world's nations.[29]

Under the rules of the convention, courts of member states are required to honor arbitral awards obtained abroad. Courts may set aside foreign arbitral awards only on narrow enumerated grounds. Among these are that the arbitral agreement was invalid under the law that the parties chose to govern their agreement,[30] that one or more of the parties lacked the legal capacity to contract,[31] that the arbitral procedure did not afford one party a meaningful opportunity to present a case,[32] or that the award violated public policy in the state in question.[33] However, most saliently for the purposes of this chapter, courts may not overturn an arbitral award because of legal or factual error—in other words, because a ruling was not "in accordance with the law." This is precisely the basis on which USIP claims that Afghan courts have an important role to play vis-à-vis customary adjudication. The convention also does not require that only "minor" disputes be subject to arbitration. In fact, arbitral awards in the billions are not uncommon.[34]

Bolstering this legal regime is the model law on international commercial arbitration developed by the United Nations Commission on International Trade Law in 1985 and revised in 2006 (United Nations Commission on International Trade Law 2008). The model law prohibits courts from hearing international commercial disputes where the parties to the dispute have agreed to arbitrate it by contract (ibid., art. 8[1]). Instead, it requires such courts to stay the proceedings and refer the parties to arbitration (ibid.).[35] Courts are also obligated to enforce the substantive award, again without looking to the merits of the dispute and with exceptions on only the narrowest of grounds (ibid., sec. 4). The result of these developments has been the acceptance of arbitration as the preferred method of resolving international commercial disputes (Strong 2013, 502–3).

Nor is this trend of adjudication away from state courts limited to the international commercial context. Much domestic law has developed in the same direction. Under prevailing US Supreme Court precedent, for example, the United States' Federal Arbitration Act *obligates* an employee to use arbitration for disputes concerning the violation of antidiscrimination laws so long as the employment agreement contains an arbitration clause.[36] As in the international context, the grounds for overturning an arbitral award are narrow and do not include ordinary legal error, as opposed to such matters as fraud or corruption.[37]

The weakening of nation-state sovereignty extends far beyond the narrow confines of adjudication. In fact, many theorists have argued that the traditional Westphalian state is not likely to last much longer. Evidence for this includes the increased power of multistate alliances such as the European Union, the international use of force to prevent domestic human rights violations under the theory of a "responsibility to protect," and the loss of effective control over trade-related matters to transnational organizations such as the World Trade Organization (Patterson and Afilalo 2008, 13). Regardless of whether this means that the state is dying, is undergoing a fundamental paradigm shift, or is merely readjusting to a new international order, what is obviously occurring is a significant transfer of power away from the state.

It is striking to contrast this evolving set of facts with the rigid adherence of groups such as Amnesty International and the United Nations Human Rights Committee to legal centralism and classical models of state supremacy. Within these prominent members of the rule of law community, neither the state's diminishing power nor its limited ability to effectively manage adjudications seems to have penetrated the legal consciousness. The mind remains thoroughly colonized in the legal centralist mold. Under this framework, the state is considered the supreme adjudicator over all competitors. Religious and customary tribunals must be thoroughly subjugated, the jurisdiction delegated to them must concern only "minor" civil or criminal matters, and the ultimate judgment by the nonstate tribunal of that "minor" matter must be subject to challenge and review in state court. Anything else would be a violation of the right to a fair trial as guaranteed by article 14 of the International Covenant on Civil and Political Rights.[38] To say that this is not the rule regarding arbitration is to understate the matter considerably. A different approach is adopted, it seems, when a person with a suit, as opposed to one with a turban, happens to be the nonstate official doing the adjudicating.[39] This is hardly a surprise—the colonized mind might well be expected to be orientalist in its biases and presuppositions. Still, it is problematic.

Moreover, it is profoundly unhelpful. If we unshackle ourselves from this colonized conception of state centrality that has permeated our legal consciousness, in the rule of law field more than any other, we might be able to imagine a different and more salutary set of solutions to address problems related to the rule of law. Those solutions, to be clear, would be no more tolerant of human rights violations than any other. Nobody, including me, expects or wants state courts to enforce orders of nonstate tribunals—be they arbitral, tribal, religious, or any other—that result in human rights violations. The question, rather, is whether the solution to brazen human rights violations in any semi-autonomous social field is to limit our imagination to an increasingly ridiculous and patently counterfactual scenario where it is the *state* that will necessarily bring about the change we seek.

Instead, beginning with Kleinfeld's estimable wisdom that the rule of law is the pursuit of particular ends rather than the means deployed to reach them (Kleinfeld 2012, 13–15), we might ask what "end" we seek concerning the operation of personal status rules and norms in Iraq. If it relates to the eradication of forced marriage or child marriage, then that is not a reason to ban all nonstate marriage, as the Personal Status Code currently does, complete with jail terms for the husbands who engage in them. Not only does that lead to the law being largely disregarded by state officials themselves, but it also presumes that state judges will be more effective than tribal or religious authorities at policing forced marriage. This is a suspect position given that the populace does not trust the state to officiate marriages in the first place. In fact, precisely because of this lack of trust, the state judiciary is probably the worst possible institution to use to address this justice deficit regarding forced marriage and child marriage.

Naturally, the legal centralist mind might conceive of other solutions that are less dramatic than prohibition and imprisonment. Many might involve education initiatives whereby rule of law experts are sent into the field to convince recalcitrant Iraqis that state-court marriages are better for them. There is no *a priori* basis on which to conclude that such an initiative would be successful, much less beneficial to individuals preferring nonstate adjudications. After all, multinational international commercial actors across the globe have broadly and dramatically rejected state adjudication as less than ideal, and states have accepted diminutions of their own adjudicatory powers as a result. It is hard to understand why ordinary citizens cannot be trusted to reach similar conclusions regarding the benefits and detriments of state adjudication in particular circumstances.

Thus, in the place of these state-centric solutions, we could decolonize our minds and start to take religious and customary tribunals more seriously. We could conceive of them as the primary mechanisms for justice delivery. We could then work with them not to coordinate their functioning with the state, as USIP has suggested, nor subject them to strict state oversight, as Amnesty International and the Human Rights Committee have suggested, but rather to improve them on their own account, *without regard to the role of the state.* We might even seek a diminution of state authority in the area of marriage, a result no more problematic than the diminution of authority of state courts in the presence of arbitral agreements. The end, after all, is a reduction in the numbers of children forced into marriage—not the strengthening of a particular adjudicatory mechanism at the expense of another.

The same might be said regarding tribal dispute resolution. And in working with these institutions, we might even identify trends within the tribal networks (perhaps even transnationally) that could be expanded on or limited. If, as a purely hypothetical situation, the Jordanian wing of the Rabi'a tribe does not engage in the trading of women to compensate for injury, and the Iraqi wing does, this information might be put to good use in Iraq in particular. That there is no formal legal relationship between the state judiciaries of Jordan or Iraq, or the states of Jordan or Iraq for that matter, is of no moment.

This is not to say that the state should always be absent from rule of law considerations, for clearly it has a role to play. Although problems related to marriage formation might be addressed without considering state courts, surely we need to at least consider the use of state resources if the problem is one of the systemic commission of honor crimes across the national spectrum. And although a goat herder may be able to get a loan using nonstate mechanisms, no Arab entrepreneur in need of financing to develop a new globally desired piece of software is likely to be able to succeed without some state legal infrastructure in place.

The matter is admittedly complex and requires a great deal of contextual study. Yet we must dispense with the fantasy that at the center of order in any social field is, or should be, the state. Instead, we should view the state as one of many players in a multifaceted and multidimensional system. Legal centralism is not the reality in our world, and it is becoming increasingly less so. Until or unless we free ourselves from this conceptual prison and acculturate ourselves to a broader global reality, efforts to expand the rule of law are likely to fail.

References

Abu Odeh, Lama. 2004. "The Politics of (Mis)recognition: Islamic Law Pedagogy in American Academia." *American Journal of Comparative Law* 52:789–824.

al-Ujayli, Judge Lefta Hamil, ed. 2011. *A Selection, from the Rulings of the Federal Court of Cassation, Private (Law) Section*, vol. 1. Baghdad: Legal Books.

Amnesty International. 2003. *Afghanistan: Re-establishing the Rule of Law*. London: Amnesty International.

Ben Nefissa, Sarah. 1999. "The *Haqq al-'Arab*: Conflict Resolution and Distinctive Features of Legal Pluralism in Contemporary Egypt." In *Legal Pluralism in the Arab World*, edited by Baudouin Dupret, Maurits Berger, and Laila al-Zwaini, 145–57. The Hague: Kluwer Law International.

Carothers, Thomas. 2006. "The-Rule-of-Law Revival." In *Promoting the Rule of Law Abroad: In Search of Knowledge*, edited by Thomas Carothers, 3–14. Washington, DC: Carnegie Endowment for International Peace.

Clark, Natalie. 2007. "The Girl Who Was Stoned to Death for Falling in Love." *Daily Mail*, May 17.

Dupret, Baudouin. 2004. "What is Plural in the Law: A Praxiological Answer." *Egypte/Monde Arabe* 7:147–71.

Ellickson, Robert C. 1991. *Order Without Law: How Neighbors Settle Disputes*. Cambridge, MA: Harvard University Press.

Emon, Anver M. 2012. *Religious Pluralism and Islamic Law: Dhimmis and Others in the Empire of Law*. Oxford: Oxford University Press.

Feldman, Eric A. 2006. "The Tuna Court: Law and Norms in the World's Premier Fish Market." *California Law Review* 94:313–69.

Ferrié, Joel-Noël. 1999. "Norms, Law and Practices: The Practical Obstacles That Make It Impossible to Separate Them." In *Legal Pluralism in the Arab World,* edited by Baudouin Dupret, Maurits Berger, and Laila al-Zwaini, 21–28. The Hague: Kluwer Law International.

Galanter, Marc. 1981. "Justice in Many Rooms: Courts, Private Ordering and Indigenous Law." *Journal of Legal Pluralism* 19:1–47.

Griffiths, John. 1986. "What Is Legal Pluralism?" *Journal of Legal Pluralism* 24:1–55.

Hamoudi, Haider Ala. 2008. "Baghdad Booksellers, Basra Carpet Merchants and the Law of God and Man." *Berkeley Journal of Islamic and Middle Eastern Law* 1:83–126.

———. 2010. "The Death of Islamic Law." *Georgia Journal of International and Comparative Law* 28:293–337.

———. 2012. "Repugnancy in the Arab World." *Willamette Law Review* 48:427–50.

Henry, Stuart. 1985. "Communal Justice, Capitalist Society, and Human Agency: The Dialectics of Collective Law in the Cooperative." *Law and Society Review* 19:303–27.

Jensen, Erik. 2003. "The Rule of Law and Judicial Reform." In *Beyond Common Knowledge: Empirical Approaches to the Rule of Law,* edited by Erik G. Jensen and Thomas C. Heller, 336–81. Redwood City: Stanford University Press.

Kleinfeld, Rachel. 2012. *Advancing the Rule of Law Abroad: Next Generation Reform.* Washington, DC: Carnegie Endowment for International Peace.

Kranton, Rachel E., and Anand M. Swamy. 1999. "The Hazards of Piecemeal Reform: British Civil Courts and the Credit Market in Colonial India." *Journal of Development Economics* 58:1–24.

McMillan, John, and Christopher Woodruff. 2000. "Private Order under Dysfunctional Public Order." *Michigan Law Review* 98:2421–58.

Merry, Sally Engle. 1988. "Legal Pluralism." *Law and Society Review* 22:869–96.

Milhaupt, Curtis J., and Mark D. West. 2000. "The Dark Side of Private Ordering: An Institutional and Empirical Analysis of Organized Crime." *University of Chicago Law Review* 67:41–98.

Mnookin, Robert H., and Lewis Kornhauser. 1979. "Bargaining in the Shadow of the Law: The Case of Divorce." *Yale Law Journal* 88:950–97.

Moore, Sally Falk. 1972. "Law and Social Change: The Semi-Autonomous Social Field as an Appropriate Subject of Study." *Law and Society Review* 7:719–46.

Patterson, Dennis, and Ari Afilalo. 2008. *The New Global Trading Order: The Evolving State and the Future of Trade.* New York: Cambridge University Press.

Quraishi, Asifa. 2011. "What If Sharia Weren't the Enemy? Rethinking International Women's Rights Advocacy on Islamic Law." *Columbia Journal of Gender and Law* 22:173–249.

Rashid, Ahmed. 2000. *Taliban.* New Haven: Yale University Press.

Richman, Barak D. 2004. "Firms, Courts, and Reputation Mechanisms: Towards A Positive Theory of Private Ordering." *Columbia Law Review* 104:2328–67.

Ruskola, Teemu. 2013. *Legal Orientalism: China, The United States and Modern Law.* Cambridge: Harvard University Press.

Sistani, Ali. 2008. *Minhaj al-Saliheen,* vol. 2. Beirut: Arab Editing House.

Stephenson, Matthew. 2006. "A Trojan Horse in China?" In *Promoting the Rule of Law Abroad: In Search of Knowledge*, edited by Thomas Carothers, 191–215. Washington, DC: Carnegie Endowment for International Peace.

Stilt, Kristen. 2004. "Islamic Law and the Making and Remaking of the Iraqi Legal System." *George Washington International Law Review* 36:695–756.

Stromseth, Jane, David Wippman, and Rosa Brooks. 2006. *Can Might Make Rights? Building the Rule of Law After Military Interventions.* Cambridge: Cambridge University Press.

Strong, S. I. 2013. "Beyond the Self-Execution Analysis: Rationalizing Constitutional, Treaty, and Statutory Interpretation in International Commercial Arbitration." *Virginia Journal of International Law* 53:499–573.

Stynes, Tess. 2013. "Arbitrator Awards Mendelez $2.23 Billion in Damages in Starbucks Dispute." *The Wall Street Journal*, November 12.

Tamanaha, Brian Z. 2008. "Understanding Legal Pluralism: Past to Present, Local to Global." *Sydney Law Review* 30:375–411.

Tarasewicz, Yasmine, and Niki Borofsky. 2013. "International Labor and Employment Arbitration: A French and European Perspective." *ABA Journal of Labor and Employment Law* 28:349–66.

United Nations Commission on International Trade Law. 2008. *UNCITRAL Model Law on International Commercial Arbitration: 1985; With Amendments as Adopted in 2006.* Vienna: United Nations.

United States Institute of Peace. 2013. "The Role of Non-State Justice Systems in Fostering the Rule of Law in Post-Conflict Societies." Accessed December 10. http://www.usip.org/publications/the-role-non-state-justice-systems-in-fostering-the-rule-law-in-post-conflict-societies.

Upham, Frank. 2006. "Mythmaking in Rule of Law Orthodoxy." In *Promoting the Rule of Law Abroad: In Search of Knowledge*, edited by Thomas Carothers, 75–104. Washington, DC: Carnegie Endowment for International Peace.

Vogel, Frank E., and Samuel L. Hayes III. 1998. *Islamic Law and Finance: Religion, Risk and Return.* New York: Springer.

Weiss, Bernard G. 1998. *The Spirit of Islamic Law.* Athens: University of Georgia Press

Notes

1. For example, Galanter (1981, 1) quotes Griffiths to the effect that "the state has no more empirical claim to being the center of the universe of legal phenomena than any other element of that whole system does."

2. The phrase "semi-autonomous social field" was coined by Moore in a highly influential 1972 article wherein she maintains that the appropriate subject of study for the interaction of law and other normative ordering is a "semi-autonomous social field" capable of making its own rules but also set in a larger social matrix that affects its operation (Moore 1972, 720).

3. An excellent example of such work is provided by the United States Institute of Peace, which has an entire program dedicated to working with nonstate adjudicatory tribunals, as discussed in the next section.

4. In his pathbreaking work on the subject, Ruskola (2013) describes the phenomenon of "legal orientalism," wherein the decision of what is and is not considered law is often the subject of narratives, Western in origin, to distinguish the West (particularly the United States, presumed to enjoy the rule of law) from the Orient (particularly China, where the rule of law is deemed absent). The matter is not altogether different from the example provided in the main text.

5. Even in more nuanced treatments of nonstate adjudicatory mechanisms, the conception that dominates is one where the state is central to the maintenance of order in the relevant social field, with alternative systems occupying a secondary, inferior role at best. In such a conception, the analogy might be not to a medicine man but to an imperfectly trained nurse-practitioner—legitimate in the conducting of her activities but not to be trusted with anything terribly consequential if it can be avoided. In either case, and as explored below, legal centralism dominates the collective imagination of the rule of law community.

6. Dupret (2004, 158) notes this regrettable trend in some legal pluralist literature.

7. The central problem with which legal pluralists have grappled is how to define "law" once it has been determined that law is not limited to state institutions (Tamanaha 2008, 391). Merry's (1988, 878–79) indication that "the literature in this field has not yet clearly demarcated a boundary between normative orders that can and cannot be called law" is as true today as it was when she wrote it in 1988. Some have argued that even attempting such a distinction is impossible (Ferrié 1999, 21).

8. I am not the first to develop indicia of this sort to distinguish between law and nonlaw. Tamanaha (2008, 396) offers a definition of law in the context of nonstate systems wherein law is that which is socially recognized as such. In an interesting article on legal pluralism in Egypt, Dupret (2004, 160–61) elaborates on (and to some extent criticizes) Tamanaha's rather straightforward idea by giving more robust recognition to the practical and temporal context in which social actors may choose to deploy the term "law" to refer to a particular normative system.

9. Feldman (2006, 316 n.8) later (rightly) castigates the literature for what he describes as "norm centralism," in which the state is described as an inefficient and bumbling monstrosity, and private means of ordering are seen as necessarily superior. It certainly is not my position that the state is inherently incapable of resolving disputes efficiently in any context. I merely posit that the state is not, and has never been, the sole referent to which parties turn to administer disputes,

and it is not, and has never been, the sole source of rules. In making this claim, which in many circles would be modest and uncontroversial, I find myself at odds with significant parts of the rule of law community.

10. Upham (2006, 94–98), for example, demonstrates the extent to which Japan managed economic development by avoiding extensive use of the formal legal system, instead resolving disputes informally.

11. This is a point wisely made by Kleinfeld (2012, 53), among others.

12. Kranton and Swamy (1999) provide an excellent example of how the introduction of state law disrupted credit markets in colonial India. Concerned about the fact that lenders were exercising monopoly power over borrowers with whom they had long-term relationships, the state introduced formal contract rules, which created competition among lenders and a market among borrowers, thereby driving down interest rates, as was expected. However, it also severed the long-term relationships between lenders and borrowers, making lenders less willing to extend a borrower's repayment period given that the borrower might not return to the lender for future business. This resulted in economic shocks and widespread rioting when borrowers proved unable to pay in times of hardship (ibid.; Stephenson 2006, 208–9). Though Kranton and Swamy attribute the problem at least partially to a failure to develop a proper insurance market, one wonders whether this attribution is yet another example of the colonization of the mind in favor of legal centralism. Perhaps the problem is instead excessive faith in the state's ability to organize order. After all, the analogy of the Indian story to modern home financings in the legally mature United States is not hard to make. Mortgage securitization in the United States both lowered interest rates and rendered banks far more willing to foreclose rather than renegotiate mortgages when conditions turned sour.

13. United Nations Human Rights Committee, General Comment 32, UN doc. CCPR/C/GC/32 (2007), para. 24.

14. In the United States, courts in a given state generally have personal matter jurisdiction over a defendant only to the extent that the defendant has "minimum contacts" in the state in question. See *Int'l Shoe Co. v. State of Wash., Office of Unemployment Comp. & Placement*, 326 U.S. 310, 316, 66 S. Ct. 154, 158, 90 L. Ed. 95 (1945). The test for determining whether such minimum contacts exist has evolved and been refined over the course of decades. See *Corpus Juris Secundum (Courts)* 21 (updated December 2013), secs. 53–70. To describe court systems in most of the developing world as incapable of policing a jurisdictional line in this manner would be a serious understatement.

15. The term "bargaining in the shadow of the law" was coined by Mnookin and Kornhauser (1979) in the context of divorce disputes. According to the authors,

much bargaining takes place outside of courtrooms. However, the bargain ultimately struck is affected by the background law, which would of course apply should negotiations fail. While this is true in many instances, it is not true of the actors of Shasta County, who are not even aware of what the background law is.

16. As Rashid (2000, 112) notes, "The line between Pashtunwali and Sharia law has always been blurred for the Pashtuns. Taliban punishments were in fact drawn largely from Pashtunwali rather than the Sharia."

17. A notable example is in the respite offered to a tribe when it admits fault for an injury and plans for a resolution. Tribal leaders I interviewed insisted that the origins of the respite are from the Prophet Muhammad's ceasefire with the non-Muslim tribes in Mecca. The analogy is strained and difficult to support. The Prophet's ceasefire was between warring parties who saw mutual advantage in a break from fighting that both intended to continue at a later time (Emon 2012, 88 n. 24). The respite in this context is one that effectively acknowledges a surrender of sorts, as the main text makes clear below. The difference between the two can be demonstrated by the period of time set for the ceasefire alone. The Prophet's ceasefire expired after ten years (ibid.). This is unthinkably long in the context of an injured tribe offering a respite to an offending tribe prior to a final resolution. This is not the only tendentious reference to Islamic history in support of the almost unsustainable claim that the tribal compensation system is based largely on *shari'a*.

18. In the spring of 2013, I spent a great deal of time in Iraq interviewing tribal leaders and observing tribal resolution processes with two professors from Basra University School of Law, Wasfi al-Sharaa and Aqeel al-Dahan. Most of my time was spent among Shi'i tribes located in Baghdad, particularly Sadr City, though inevitably members of those tribes had relocated from elsewhere. The fruit of our research will appear in a chapter of a book entitled *Negotiating State and Non-State Law: Challenges of Global and Local Pluralism*, edited by Michael Helfand of Pepperdine University School of Law and to be published by Cambridge University Press. The three of us hope to expand our research into a book-length study in the future.

19. The more technically correct term for this corpus is probably *fiqh*, which refers to human understandings of divine law, with the term *shari'a* being reserved exclusively to the unknowable divine law itself (Vogel and Hayes 1998, 23–24). Yet both in the West and among Arab lawyers, the broad use of the term *shari'a* to refer to the corpus rather than to an unknowable divine will has become deeply ingrained. Hence, I use it here to avoid extensive exposition on a matter tangential to the thesis of this chapter. Quraishi (2011, 203) offers a more nuanced and detailed explanation of the terminology.

20. Personal Status Code of Iraq, art. 91(2).

21. Ibid., art. 43.

22. Ibid., art. 10(5) ("Every man who concludes a marriage contract outside of a court shall be punished by prison of not less than six months and not more than one year, or by a fine of not less than 300 dinars, and not more than 1000 dinars. The punishment shall be jail for a period of not less than three years, and not more than five years, if he concludes a marriage contract outside of court while already married.")

23. Ibid., art. 39.

24. Iraqi court cases are not systematically collected and organized as they are in the United States. Nevertheless, each year, a number of cases, particularly those of the highest appellate court, the Court of Cassation, are assembled and published in books widely available in Baghdad bookstores. Al-Ujayli (2011) provides a recent illustrative compilation.

25. Penal Code of Iraq, No. 111 of 1969, art. 421.

26. Law for the Mandatory Insurance for Car Accidents, No. 52 of 1980, as amended, art. 2.

27. Formally, the national insurance scheme remains in effect, but as a matter of practice, it does not exist. The payments made under its aegis dwindled during the hyperinflation of the 1990s brought about by United Nations sanctions. Eventually, the relevant offices and institutions were shuttered, rendering the law one of many Iraqi laws whose existence extended no further than the paper it was printed on.

28. Penal Code of Iraq, No. 111 of 1969, art. 421.

29. According to the convention's website, www.newyorkconvention.org, nearly 150 states were signatory to it at the end of 2013.

30. Convention on the Recognition and Enforcement of Foreign Arbitral Awards (1958), art. V(1)(a).

31. Ibid.

32. Ibid, art. V(1)(b).

33. Ibid., art. V(2)(a).

34. To take an example, in November of 2013, an arbitrator awarded Mondelēz International, Inc., US$2.23 billion in damages against Starbucks Corporation for the latter's termination of a distribution agreement (Stynes 2013). Under no reasonable conception can a dispute of this magnitude be deemed "minor."

35. Naturally, exceptions exist when there are challenges to the validity, enforceability, or practicability of the arbitration agreement. Therefore, a party could maintain in court that it never in fact signed the arbitration agreement in question or that its signature was procured under false pretenses.

36. See *Gilmer v. Interstate/Johnson Lane Corp.*, 500 U.S. 20, 26.

37. 9 United States Code sec. 10. The ability to arbitrate employment disputes is more controversial in Europe than it is in the United States, Canada, or Australia, where it is more widely practiced (Tarasewicz and Borofsky 2013, 349).

38. International Covenant on Civil and Political Rights, G.A. Res. 2200A (XXI), 21 UN GAOR Supp. (No. 16) at 52, UN doc. A/6316 (1966).

39. The natural argument might be that arbitration is consented to while religious or customary tribunals are not. Yet such a position fails upon the slightest introspection. An employee in the United States desperate for work has not "consented" to an arbitration clause in her employment agreement; or, perhaps better stated, her consent is no more meaningful than the consent of a wealthy wife of a tribal leader to have her marriage governed by Islamic law, administered by an out-of-state tribunal. In any event, General Comment 32 nowhere suggests that the concerns respecting customary or religious tribunals relate to the possibility that parties appearing before them are under duress. If this were the concern, there would surely exist better ways of dealing with it than demanding the full subjugation of these tribunals and their decisions to the monitoring and control of state courts.

Abstract

Two notions of governance—both attractive to their respective supporters—meet in this chapter: the rule of law and the dream of an Azande kingdom. Using the movement to reinstall the Azande king in South Sudan's Western Equatoria as a case study, the chapter highlights the challenges faced by the rule of law field when grappling with the notion of "context." Rule of law programs in South Sudan have focused primarily on providing access to legal services and on harmonizing customary and common law. Both approaches operate with the assumption that the rule of law can be improved by streamlining different justice providers and by providing capacity building to allow better navigation of the streamlined system.

Rule of law programs are now frequently expected to consider context in their programming, yet such a perspective often presumes that "context" is a stable entity. Using the notions of governance, justice, laws, and democracy expressed by supporters of reinstating the Azande king, this case study shows that context is a performative dynamic interplay between changing, symbolic, and imagined realities and histories. Any external rule of law program, including its own symbolic certainty about working in a context-specific manner, becomes part of this internal process. This means that constructing a singular "context" out of a history that is lived and re-narrated by those whose very context rule of law reformers are trying to understand is a more complex task than the movement to be context specific suggests.

5 Policy of Government and Policy of Culture: Understanding the Rules of Law in the "Context" of South Sudan's Western Equatoria State

Mareike Schomerus

Introduction

On July 9, 2011, people danced all over the newly created country of South Sudan as independence celebrations were held. In the capital of Juba, elated citizens gathered near the mausoleum of John Garang de Mabior, South Sudan's undisputed martyr father figure. He had been the leader of the Sudan People's Liberation Army, the rebel movement that fought against the government in northern Sudan and that had, after signing the Comprehensive Peace Agreement (CPA) in 2005, morphed into the government of southern Sudan through a power-sharing deal. Having died in a helicopter crash at the time of greatest hope for southern Sudan—just after the signing of the peace deal and before disillusionment and internal violence set in—Garang is enshrined as South Sudan's leading authority.

Many thanks to Naomi Pendle and Anouk Rigterink, whose research contributed to this chapter, to Deval Desai for inspiration and improvements, and to Hakan Seckinelgin for fieldwork discussions that informed this chapter. The fieldwork for this chapter, which I conducted in 2012 and 2013, would not have been possible without the help of Charles Taban and James Mishkin.

In Yambio, the capital of Western Equatoria State in the southwest of the country, however, independence celebrations in Freedom Square did not start with an homage to Garang. Instead, crowds of dancing, ululating, and flag-waving people first paid their respects to another dead leader. The tomb of King Gbudue in Yambio is nowhere near as lavish as Garang's mausoleum in Juba; and the white grave—in the traditional style of the Azande people, who hail from this area—is not guarded by soldiers. Yet on the day of independence, residents of Yambio remembered King Gbudue as the first to lose his life in the struggle for South Sudan's independence—in 1905, when he was killed by a British patrol. King Gbudue, venerated as the last king of the Azande people, was acknowledged during Yambio's Independence Day celebrations as the most important authority to rule over this part of the country.

Today, King Gbudue—both as a person and as an embodiment of the institution of the Azande king—is remembered as a protector of his Azande subjects and as the creator and guardian of the conventions that shaped this society. He had the power to invent and change the rules, to judge, and to punish. While these memories amalgamate facts with an imagined history, King Gbudue's living legacy can teach us much about implementing the rule of law in South Sudan. When the British colonial administrators arrived in this part of the country, they brought their own set of regulations and laws, which they sought to implement in the area inhabited by the Azande, as in other parts of southern Sudan. Eventually, the British found a way to impose their rules in the Azande kingdom through existing structures, eradicating those they found particularly unsavory and ruling with a sense of having tamed the existing unpredictable and personality-driven rules of law.

One hundred years passed between the killing of Gbudue and the signing of the CPA, which received wide international support. Following the peace agreement, the international postconflict reconstruction machinery hit southern Sudan with remarkable speed. From the start, the United Nations Mission in Sudan (which later became the United Nations Mission in South Sudan) had an explicit mandate to advise on the rule of law. The Global Programme for Strengthening the Rule of Law in Crisis-Affected and Fragile Situations of the United Nations Development Programme was among the first to set up shop in the capital of Juba to assess and pave the way for reforming the war-torn country's legal system. International rule of law experts sought ways to establish a legal system that would harmonize a future formal justice system with existing "informal structures"—a goal that has also received a lot of thought and criticism (Leonardi et al. 2010). Yet even in Juba, the center of power, it was tremendously challenging to find the capacity and political will to put such a system in place. Away from the center, trust in the endeavor was even lower; indeed, in Sudan—a diverse country with a history of brutal governance by a distant elite—rules set by a remote central government caused suspicion.

Western Equatoria is itself a diverse state, though the Azande form its largest ethnic group. Since the signing of the CPA, and even more so since independence, the Azande people have sought to reposition themselves within the country. Azande culture and identity predominate, including when it comes to questions of law and justice. The strongest manifestation of this is the recent movement to crown a new Azande king, more than a century after King Gbudue's death.

Overview

Two notions of governance, both attractive to their respective supporters, meet in this chapter: the rule of law and the dream of an Azande kingdom. Using the movement to reinstall the Azande king as a case study, the chapter highlights the challenges faced by the rule of law field when grappling with the notion of "context." While calls to consider "context" are becoming increasingly frequent in donor rhetoric, "context" is a deep-rooted and complex concept—one that embodies "the very complicated social realities, the polyphonies, that make up contemporary Africa," as described by Jean and John Comaroff (1993, xiv) in their discussion on modernity and ritual. This case study shows that while rule of law programs may pay heed to the need to understand the reality of a local context, the pursued reality is in fact a performative dynamic interplay between changing, symbolic, and imagined realities and histories. Any outside programming, even when it comes with assuredness and sensitivity with regard to working in a context-specific manner, becomes part of this internal process. This means that constructing a singular "context" out of a history that is lived and re-narrated by those whose very context rule of law reformers are trying to understand is a more complex task than the movement to be context specific suggests.

This chapter implicitly juxtaposes the principles of the rule of law with the reality in a society that sees rules and laws very differently. The question of how rule of law programs might navigate the complex interplay of local and global ideals of rules and governance—here embodied in the Azande kingdom and rule of law reform efforts in South Sudan—is particularly pertinent for societies emerging from war. Engaging with local actors and realities means fundamentally questioning how the meaning of rules, laws, and accountability is understood locally. This is important in unstable contexts where power is being contested among local actors, each of whom seeks to determine the rules. Such contexts are characterized by a simultaneous search for stability and quest for change. This in itself creates a sharp and challenging contradiction between the emphasis of rule of law on legal certainty and local requirements for flexible interpretation.

The chapter illustrates how this tension between stability, change, contested authority, and local rules of law plays out in Western Equatoria. It reveals a significant difference between the focus of rule of law, on the one hand, and the Azande version of *rules* of law as a broad range of governance and cultural issues, on the other. Furthermore, the notion of an Azande kingdom displays flexibility within seemingly rigid hierarchies that stem from a unique idea of how leaders are held accountable. As the international debate on rule of law engages with the question of broader law reform and the reform of public administration, thus reaching beyond self-created boundaries, the Azande version effectively narrows issues of governance and public administration to one office: that of the Azande king. The chapter begins with an overview of the various incarnations of rule of law in Zandeland. It then outlines how a rules-based approach to regulating social relationships and life is understood. Examining notions of governance drawn from interviews conducted in 2012 and 2013, it outlines expectations of the king as a provider of rules, social coherence, and justice. The chapter concludes by outlining the challenges that the rule of law movement faces if it is to engage with local structures in a serious manner.

The Rule of Law—Old and New—in Zandeland

Today's Azande people populate an area that stretches across the southwestern corner of South Sudan into the far east of the Central African Republic and the northeast of the Democratic Republic of Congo. Anthropological studies of the early twentieth century misleadingly portrayed the Azande as a homogeneous group, drawing on an assumption common at the time that saw tribal identities as an undeveloped stage of humanity fixed in its features and traditions (Seligman and Seligman 1932, xi). In reality, the Azande people were an amalgamation of several kingdoms, in which smaller groups were conquered and then governed by one of the kings. A crucial function of the tribal unit so governed was, in the eyes of E. E. Evans-Pritchard (1963), the most famous chronicler of the Azande, rule setting and governance.[1]

Understanding the dynamic nature of tribal belonging, traditions, and rule setting remains a challenge in international development debates. Taking local realities, local customs, and local authority seriously—an approach that has returned to the fore in recent years—is important. Yet, often, the notion of "the local" stressed in this approach comes surprisingly close to how nine-teenth-century anthropologists viewed traditional societies—as rooted in tra-ditions and largely unchangeable, including by the presence of those outsid-ers who came to record their customs. In addition, the notion of "context" and "the local" presupposes particular categories rooted in Western thinking. However, the Azande in particular have been the subject of a scholarly debate regarding the question whether they follow a unique logic (Jennings 1989). Evans-Pritchard has been criticized for his often simplistic accounts and judg-ments, as well as his tendency to present his perceptions as the only possible interpretation (Ivanov 2002, 454). It is true that Western Equatoria's Azande identify strongly with their tribal identities and that, as P. M. Holt and M. W. Daly (2000, 62) argue, the Azande historically "did not easily succumb to newcomers, but they were profoundly affected by them." Yet, broadly speak-ing, this means that they look to their tribal identity for cultural guidance, protection, and the provision of justice.

In paying deference only to the power of the major Azande kings and their kingdoms—with Gbudue the most prominent among them—reality and accepted wisdom become blurred. Before colonial rule, the Azande kingdom had many rulers, while during the Anglo-Egyptian Condominium Gbudue's power was severely curtailed, his reach limited to a small group of Azande. Other Azande kings at that time became government chiefs and were no lon-ger considered monarchs. Memories of Gbudue may be particularly strong because they appeared prominently in print two decades after he was killed, when Evans-Pritchard (1957, 61) conducted his fieldwork among loyal Gbu-due subjects.

When the Azande conquered other groups, the latter's governance struc-tures were maintained to deal with day-to-day tasks, although ultimately the local leaders were now answerable to the king. Surprising parallels emerge between the precolonial past of the Azande people, the experience of colo-nialism, and the present in independent South Sudan. In establishing native administration, the British colonial administrators used a similar tactic to that of the Azande conquerors, leaving local structures of those they conquered in place. However, they made sure that loyalties were adjusted to answer to the colonial administrators and that the sharpest edges were blunted of what the colonial rulers saw as unacceptable judicial procedures. In recent years, the debate on the provision of local justice in South Sudan has displayed a similar approach, utilizing local structures and adjusting them enough so that they fit with attempts to establish the rule of law.

In the past, the various Azande kings ruled over changing groups of people with an evolving and flexible set of rules. The kings' flexibility in establishing rules and administering punishment stemmed from the use of oracles (Evans-Pritchard 1957, 61). Since many of the cases brought before the king centered on alleged witchcraft, the king consulted a higher spiritual authority for appropriate guidance and punishment, thus also maintaining spiritual influence. British administrators, skeptical of spiritually driven justice but comfortable with what Douglas Johnson (2003, 12) describes as the Azande's "executive hierarchy ready to hand" were of the opinion that southern Sudan lacked obvious administrative structures—an issue they abbreviated as the "southern problem" ("Summary of the British Southern Policies" 1958, 5399). To address this, in 1922, Britain established the policy of indirect rule, which sought to synchronize local mechanisms with British government structures. The goal of indirect rule was to create stability through control, preferably by aligning customary justice systems with British notions. Yet the result was rather unstable. The next step was the Southern Policy, which came into effect in 1929 and decreed that southern Sudan would be administered separately from the north of the country. The Southern Policy was meant to strengthen—or, in reality, create—"a series of self contained racial or tribal units based upon indigenous customs, traditional usage and beliefs" in order to prevent Arabization (ibid.). On paper, chiefs remained separate entities, but in reality they were part of government—a setup that exists to this day (Leonardi 2013).

In Zandeland, although the number of chiefs proliferated as their tasks became more aligned with a British understanding of government, the narrative persisted that chiefs' authority was derived from their connection to the Azande royal lineage. This, in turn, reinforced the British self-perception that they were building on strong traditions and creating "an example of indirect rule in its purest form" ("Development of Local Government in Zande District, Yambio" 1948, 5439). A gradual retelling of the history shaped Azande memory of their kings as "chiefs," strengthening the notion that what was being built in Zandeland was of a pure tradition (ibid.; "Zande District Handbook" 1959). An added bonus was the understanding that outside intervention had improved society's well-being by enhancing the protection and representation of those who had, in British eyes, been exposed to an unjust and unpredictable system. That the colonial laws "must have seemed repressive," as Adam Jackson (2011, 52) argues, for they "did not include or relate to the values of the Azande people," was of limited interest. In practice, the way laws were implemented by colonial administrators meant that chiefs could rule in whatever manner they wanted, as long as it did not grossly offend British ideals.

One thing, however, sat uncomfortably with the British: rules and a penal code drawn from oracles. The colonial administrators thus introduced rules designed to curtail the judicial power of spiritual leaders, stressing that anything considered to be a "damaging practice" was in reality not rooted in tribal tradition. Colonial British intervention in the Azande justice system was strongly driven by the idea that Britain could offer a more just alternative to the Azande kings' cruel punitive practices (Wyld 1949, 51; Maurice 1930, 227). The British thought they could provide protection against such practices and against the possible arbitrariness with which they were administered by improving the set of rules used by kings in their judgments.

What the administrators overlooked was the Azande kings' broader function as the backbone of society, and the cultural importance of traditional practices. The district commissioners tabulated traditional Azande law, with the aim of checking its content and softening its most unsavory aspects. They also separated responsibilities, with civil issues to be dealt with by the demoted chiefs and criminal cases to be handled by British administrators ("Zande District Handbook" 1959). The principle of a strict division between criminal and civil cases highlighted that the British administrators did not view the chiefs' performance of all judicial functions as crucial to holding together the social fabric. A letter written in 1924 by the British governor of Mongalla outlined his understanding of the parallel structures:

> I take it that it is now clearly realised that the policy of the Government is to get the administration of affairs which are purely native back onto a Tribal basis and that the function of Government is to supervise, guide and mould tribal organization, rather than to destroy such systems of customary law, discipline and culture as the natives already possesses and to endeavor to replace these with an alien system little suited to his mentality which we will assimilate very slowly if at all. (Governor of Mongalla 1924)

Although he rejected the notion of introducing an alien system, the governor also wrote about "the establishment of the Native Courts," emphasizing that what was being established was a new system that, to a certain extent, had been interpreted through the lens of what were seen as existing structures (ibid.).

In the lead-up to Sudan's independence from British rule in 1956, a new debate flourished regarding whether local government across the country should be standardized. The issue at hand was how tribal authorities could be unified and codified. The system of appointment that existed in most tribal authorities sat uncomfortably with the British idea of Sudan as a democratic and federal nation (Robertson 1953, 5243). How to "merge tribal powers and functions either with the Central Government or Local Government," as imagined in the Traditional Authorities Bill, became a great challenge (ibid.). In British minds, as Marshall had written in a report in the late 1940s, the "warp of Tribalism and the woof of Local Government could not be woven together in a clear pattern until they could first be clearly distinguished one from the other" (ibid.). As a result, tribal authorities were clearly separated from local government and local councils; elected members tasked with delivering modern technical services were to coexist with tribal chiefs. In reality, the local councils were often populated by tribal chiefs, invited to join the councils as guardians of tribal traditions—which, in turn, meant that their presence on the unofficial council payroll increased the councils' control over traditional practices, including how tribal judicial functions were carried out. What was established under the cloak of Sudanization—and later became Sudanese government discourse as the start of "modern Local Government" among the Azande—set the stage for the uncomfortable parallel structures of modern government alongside tribal government, and of chiefs' or the king's rules of law alongside the movement to establish modern rule of law ("Zande District Handbook" 1959).

Today, there is an understanding in Zandeland that, with the central government being in Juba, laws and rules are made from afar. Many interview respondents argued that these laws are often in need of cultural adjustment to fit local circumstances. One chief stated that

> it is a group of lawyers who get this law out of the Constitution. [The] Constitution is made from all the counties and tribes. [The] Constitution is a perfect law with articles . . . . There should be traditional authorities with customary law. Customary law is not far from civil law, but we need to strengthen our customs and law.[2]

When asked to discuss the differences and tensions between the rule of law and Azande culture, the chief explained that the rule of law had already negated some customs, such as managing access to land. He argued that part of the Azande culture had been destroyed by the government's pursuit of the rule of law, such as through South Sudan's Land Act. In Azande culture, he stated, "we want to control access to land and how the Land Act is implemented because the land may be given to someone who is a problem." Rule of law meant that "if somebody needs land, they go to government," he said, citing a case of land leased to a mango-juice company that was suspected of having a hidden agenda to exploit the land for mineral extraction.[3]

The enthusiasm for the Azande king expressed by respondents also stems from negative experiences with central government rules, in addition to the desire to reinstate an imagined past. Yet the movement to reinstate the Azande monarch seems to be merely the latest chapter in Azande governance—a governance in which the Azande have experienced several swings between "royal" rule and Western models. In the past, British administrators had operated on the assumption that a natural overlap existed between what they saw as a monarchy and the colonial administration. It was easy to utilize the notion of the king, replacing him with a district commissioner (Evans-Pritchard [1937] 1963, 134) and prohibiting the further leadership of smaller groups that might threaten British authority. And less popular government policies—such as tax collection—were portrayed by British administrators as a continuation of the relationship between government and the governed. Thus, the British had taken what they found agreeable in Azande society and modified it to fit a modern model that upheld British engagement; however, the Azande rulers who benefited had drastically changed roles, and the society they governed shared no similarity with the Azande kingdom. The problematic idea that modernization can obtain legitimacy simply by adopting the *forms* of tradition is prevalent today, both in international development in general and in attempts to codify customary law so that it better fits with efforts to introduce the rule of law in particular.

Many respondents described the Azande king as allowing the people to be united, to revive and maintain their culture, and to focus on a single authority. "Every tribe, everybody, has their leaders. The Zande also. It is not a new system," explained one respondent.

> The system was there but we have to revive it. We have to build our culture to make sure the culture of Zande comes into effect. . . . It will help us to recall what our ancestors were doing in terms of systems of authority. How it has been. And somebody to direct it and under which umbrella.[4]

The authority projected onto the king thus stems from two sources: unquestioning acceptance of the king as the guardian of Azande culture, and higher powers. "It is God who made the king to judge people. That king will rule over his people. If he says to me [do something], I will do it if it is not against the Bible."[5]

Self-Determination and the Rule of Law

The CPA established the southerners' right to self-determination, which included being allowed to govern themselves in traditional ways. Customary governance is one of many manifestations of South Sudan's diversity. The landscape of what is accepted behavior, which rules and rulers to follow, and whom to turn to for justice and judgment is complicated. The rules of social interaction are not clear-cut and canonized, but flexible and negotiable. Crucially, in many communities in South Sudan, including Zandeland, social order is based on relationships and the ever-fluctuating acceptance of authority, rather than on the rule-based provision of justice. The right to self-determination, as evident in customary governance systems, might be at odds with the overall idea of the rule of law.

Yet, confusingly, particularly regarding the rule of law and judicial institution-building, donors have worked under the assumption that they are starting from scratch in South Sudan; they see themselves as having to build a basic understanding of what governance and the rule of law means. Summarizing successes in South Sudan, a judicial affairs officer from the United Nations Mission in South Sudan noted that "traditional authorities . . . had begun to understand rule of law and how it should be applied in their work" (United Nations Mission in South Sudan 2013). The underlying view of the state of South Sudan's justice system sees it as chaotic and lacking clarity and rules—and thus inhospitable to the rule of law.

The widely held assumption that local authorities first need to be taught what governance according to rules and law *is* has created a reliance on mostly off-the-peg solutions that see the provision of justice as requiring, first and foremost, a clear set of rules, institutions, and authorities. These readily deployed templates tend to involve institutional stopgaps aimed at bridging the transition to what is presumed to be the modern institutional future of the justice system, as well as capacity building aimed at shaping at how customary leaders deploy customary law and, by extension, imagine their communities. Funding priorities have been skewed in this direction, seeking to address the paucity of lawyers and judges by training paralegals, supporting legal aid clinics, and providing mobile courts. Others misinterpret the very nature of customary law by attempting to codify and professionalize it, supporting an underlying notion that the rule of law requires a written code and a hierarchical administration. Success tends to be measured in numbers—paralegals trained, cases mediated, and so on.

However, rule of law programming tends to overlook the fact that customary law might be the very opposite of a codified set of rules. Rather than shaping community behavior according to a preexisting code, it uses disputes and procedures to establish and reflect the *current* state of acceptable behavior, acknowledging "the ability of such customs to adapt and change" (Jackson 2011, 53). Customary law is distinct from common law in that the form and formalization of relevant institutions is underpinned by different notions of what creates legitimacy and authority. Thus, while punishment is very much a part of customary law—as is the ability of power relationships to determine who is allowed access to justice and of what kind—it is more useful to think of customary law as the expression of social order instead of the application of a strict penal code. This is particularly so because customary-law cases are often not clear-cut legal or moral questions but rather a mixture of criminal and cultural offenses.

Azande communities tend to see the provision of justice as a social contract between authorities at different levels and the community, who expect authorities to work in their favor; in this way, their vision is distinct from that promoted by rule of law programming. Thus, instead of seeing South Sudan as a messy reality of justice provision and many rules of law that must be transitioned toward a pristine rule of law, rule of law programmers should start by accepting that it is a unique society with mutable and negotiable behavioral and moral boundaries.

"Customary law is a manifestation of our customs, social norms, beliefs and practices," wrote southern Sudan's first chief justice, Ambrose Riiny Thiuk. "It embodies much of what we have fought for these past twenty years. It is self-evident that customary law will underpin our society, its legal institutions and laws for the future" (Jok et al. 2004, 54). The emphasis on customary law as part of South Sudan's legal order has thus also been, from the outset, a way to empower local traditions and actors in a country where a formal centralized justice system is unlikely to be fully established in coming decades—or ever. Attempts to regulate customary law as part of a broader rule of law intervention have a motivation reminiscent of British indirect rule—a proxy control of the judicial system through the top-down regulation of what is conceptualized as a bottom-up system. Rule of law programs seeking to ascertain the customary law of tribes such as the Azande run the risk of undermining the very basis of customary law—its flexibility and its emphasis on negotiating relationships through an accepted authority.

Such approaches ignore how authority in Zandeland is understood and how the authority to make judgments about behavior and wrongdoing is at the very heart of communities' self-definition. The bigger question of how justice is perceived and who can set the rules to battle injustice is treated only cursorily in the rule of law debate. While the principles of engaging with local actors, working with sensitivity to conflict, and honoring deeply ingrained traditions are prominent in rule of law reform rhetoric, how these principles are meant to play out in practice is less clear, often leading to reliance on generic and overly prescriptive approaches reflecting Western ideals.

Sticking to the Rules: The Azande King

Since the signing of the CPA, the South Sudanese have gone through a sometimes traumatic process of implementing internationally imposed measures aimed at achieving a modern democracy. It is fair to say that these efforts have been misguided and largely unsuccessful. The magnitude of the failure of democratic processes in South Sudan can be seen in how the selection of the Azande king is foreseen. The grueling conflict-ridden experience of the 2010 general elections—which were fought bitterly in Western Equatoria—feeds into the inherent distrust of democratic decision-making processes, in particular their volatility. In a group meeting, one respondent expressed the precariousness that democratization had brought: "The issue is, today the governor is there. Tomorrow is another governor. The king will always be there. Since the CPA, we had four governors."[6]

Conversely, the reinstatement of the king is linked strongly to idealized notions of governance, which are often nonparticipatory and elitist. Limited importance is placed on the public's participation in choosing the king. When asked who would elect the king, one respondent at a community meeting explained, "It has already happened. People met and discussed 'this is the right person' and then they contributed. . . . The name of the person elected is in Yambio. The information only came to us, but we don't know the name."[7] Another stated, "There will be no elections: this is the part of our culture we want to keep. Part of the government is saying this king should be elected, so this is where conflict comes."[8]

Most respondents said that to avoid conflict of the kind seen in the 2010 elections, the king should be appointed. The minority who thought the king would be chosen through free and fair elections also argued that the rules the king would implement would be decreed not by higher authority but by the grass roots: "The guiding principles will come from the community. It is the community to select him and give them to the king."[9] The notion of the king's laws is thus finely intertwined with a specific concept of democracy. South Sudan's peace agreement with the north provided for elections and ultimately a successful referendum on independence. While it might seem as if these two events created a positive experience of democracy, the debate about the king shows that this was not so—that, in fact, democracy is perceived as inferior. One respondent explained that reinstating the king means

178

giving freedom for the Zande. If we got a king, he can give us the word of the king. He can give Zande freedom. We've got freedom now, but we can get the word from our king. Before we [had] nobody ruling us. The governor was elected but . . . the king will be chosen by the people. . . . The kings, they've got people's respect since the world was created. But the government is new to us. But the king can order us to do that, not by words of the government [or] law of the government. The king can do that.[10]

What the respondent expressed was a view of democracy as constituting the need for antidemocratic governance; the image that emerges is one not of simple antagonism but of complex adoption, adaptation, and negotiation of the articulations of governance.

An older man in a community meeting explained that the king would work with the national government—which, in South Sudan, implies the lawmaking body—and would have a status higher than the elected state governor.[11] In another meeting, a group of young men agreed that the king is expected to be a worthy representative, unlike the elected representatives. "The person we voted for is getting his money from the government," explained one of them. "He bought a truck and he is using the truck in [our village]. . . . One hundred percent the king will represent us better than the person we elected to represent us."[12]

Romanticized notions of local authorities and customary law depict these as giving people a voice to live according to their tradition. The reality is often quite different, with local structures driven by elites. The movement to reinstall the king might at first look like a grassroots effort to return to or claim a particular culture. Yet, as many respondents noted, it is already becoming clear that citizens are expected simply to watch from the sidelines—to pay their dues (as they did in the presidential elections) but not to have a voice. "We don't actually have power," said one local chief:

> So we don't know when he will be inaugurated. Subchiefs and elders will elect, it's not the common man to vote because we don't want politics to enter. We shall be the one to tell the community, "This is your chief." . . . Because if you put this common man in, they can give some money to say "let me be the king." That is why it's only elders.[13]

The lack of clarity about the king's selection is a challenge that is not lost on potential candidates. "What are the criteria for the Zande king? On the ground most people are not informed, so it will take time, otherwise it will split the peaceful community into pieces," explained the paramount chief of Tambura, seen by many as a legitimate successor to the throne.[14] However, another respondent was not so sure: "There is a lot of pulling rope of who will be king, creating a lot of friction within."[15]

The rule of law movement aims for sustainable structural change, but one concern is that when outside support diminishes, artificially imposed systems will weaken and disappear. Such a perspective suggests an understanding of the rule of law movement as a fresh approach rather than as history repeating itself. Generally speaking, the sustainability of a political system is attained through accountability, which is ultimately achieved through democratic processes. In a twist on sustainability and accountability, respondents at a community meeting stated that they did not consider themselves able to hold their elected member of parliament (MP) to account. Instead, they expected the unelected king to take on this battle for them. One respondent voiced the group's sentiment:

> The difference between the Zande king and the MP is that when the MP was given money to build schools, he built instead his lodge in Yambio and Tambura. And he has four cars. If something like that happens with [a king in power], [the] king could call on him and even change him there for the community.[16]

The king is appointed potentially for life, and his authority is believed to stem, in part, from his distance from what is perceived as a volatile system of choices: "The kings are not to be changed like governors. That person is there for life. Unless he becomes weak, which is when he needs to get changed."[17]

The King Rules

When explaining the need for an Azande king, a majority of respondents argued for the need to reestablish moral boundaries that have disappeared in Zandeland. The king is viewed as a cultural savior who will reclaim a way of life and interaction. He is expected to revive a way of seeing the world that has been lost—first to time itself, then to colonial rule and war, and now to a central government that rules by being both overpowering and neglectful. Crucially, when questioned on the king's judicial function, respondents revealed a complex understanding of what justice and injustice are in Zandeland, and what rules and legal boundaries need to be set by the king. When asked to define "justice" during empirical fieldwork conducted in early 2013, most respondents described rules of personal behavior, portraying "injustice" as a failure to behave in the right way according to Azande culture.

180

Asked what cultural aspects in particular had been lost, respondents mentioned "respect among the Azande," "obedience," "marriage culture" (because an adjusted dowry system had commercialized marriage), conservative dress, and contributions to palace life (e.g., bringing harvest produce and hunted animals to the king).[18] One of the cultural concerns that people think need the king's "legal" enforcement is the revival of locally made pots in place of Chinese-manufactured cooking utensils. "These days we don't cook in pots, we cook in saucepans. These things should be brought back by the king," said one respondent.[19] Other cultural practices that respondents wanted to revive include group cultivation; behavioral rules, particularly ones intended to control the way that girls and young women dress and to curb their involvement in drinking and casual relationships; and the need to show respect for the king, including rules requiring that visitors to the king "don't just go to greet the king, [they] kneel down far away and approach."[20]

The less savory aspects of Azande culture—for example, practices mandating that the king be buried with living young children or that adultery be punished by cutting off a man's penis—were not part of the imagined cultural revival. Respondents were quick to separate good parts of culture from bad, although it was also clear that there was no agreement on what constituted each category. In the past, the king's power was drawn from what was perceived as his spiritual power. In light of the strong influence of the church in this part of the country, as well as a long history of British rule outlawing "magical" practices destructive to the community, public approval of witchcraft has declined—although that does not mean that it is not practiced. However, a significant change is that rather than wishing to see the king reclaim magical practices as part of his authority, people now want his power to come from his ability to oppose "bad" witchcraft. Despite the official outlawing of witchcraft in Zandeland, it is unclear what would happen if Azande interpretations of cultural law clashed with government laws. In this debate, contradictions between rules and culture are foregrounded: "We cannot say we don't want any law from Juba—that is not our culture. We must respect them. Any law that can be passed from Juba, we agree, including our chiefs. We do respect the policy of the government and the policy of our culture."[21]

When asked to provide negative examples of Azande culture, a group of fifteen women listed early marriage. One of them suggested that rather than leaving lawmaking to the king,

> the women themselves will make the rules. If government imposes law
> on us, we will decide what is a good law and what is bad. If it is bad,

we will just leave it out. We . . . look at that law and discuss. Is it good for women? If not, we will send somebody to the government to tell them it's not a good law. To some extent the government listens, to some extent it denies.[22]

As these women discussed some of the "government laws" they considered negative, it became clear that these were also cultural laws—for example, the law mandating that when a girl becomes pregnant, she must leave school. The women in this particular town had then lobbied against the practice and convinced the commissioner to put pressure on the director of the school to abandon the practice.[23]

A question underpinning not only rule of law programming but also development in general is who or what the driving forces of change are. The rule of law movement works under the assumption that the government and its elected officials are necessary to implement change. In Zandeland, the perception of change is different—the government and the changes it brings are seen as volatile, whereas the king is perceived as a steady authority who simultaneously helps maintain the status quo, reverse development in some areas, and push for change in others. The Azande king is expected to strike the right balance between cultural revival and modernization, between the rules of law and the rule of law. He is expected to be the direct link between the people and the government, and he is seen as a direct link to the president: "Because he is the king, if the government does not listen to him, it can be taken to the president. That's simple."[24]

The Azande King as Justice Provider

The historical punitive measures of Azande kings included spearing, mutilation, ordering payment in women, and the death sentence (Reining 1966, 14). The envisaged future king is also widely perceived to be the ultimate provider of rules and justice. He is imagined as bridging the divide between "official" justice and the "local justice" provided by the chief's courts by being the ultimate authority to which both types of justice providers would defer. According to one respondent, "The big king will have a palace and the paramount chiefs will come there to look into their problems. He will not have a court like the paramount chief, but a chiefs' forum to discuss issues."[25] A member of a women's group said, "Before, when we were having a king, there was unity and information was passing. When we have the king the flow of information, the culture will improve. Unity will be there."[26]

Although South Sudan's 2009 Local Government Act stresses the importance of integrating traditional authorities into the country's governance structure, it fails to outline how this is to work in practice. In Zandeland, where the current discourse is focused on providing an alternative yet equally powerful and somewhat centralized government through the king, this tension is coming to a head. One respondent explained that, according to his understanding of how the government was expected to run, "the governor and chiefs work together. Laws are made by [the] state, and chiefs will implement [them] unless they have to carry customary law."[27] Another respondent in a church youth group argued that if a law is not in line with local cultural understanding, "even the government of the state . . . cannot impose [it]."[28] The principle of being able to reject national laws on the basis of local cultural understanding is strongly held. Narratives of how such power was exerted by the king in the past inform people's ideas about current relationships between government laws and local rules: "Before, if you want to bring the law, the government can call the chiefs and say this is the law we want to implement. And the chiefs can say this law is not good for us," explained a chief in Ezo County.[29]

A woman reiterated, "The community can decline. These things come first to the community. If it is legal for that community and the elders, it can be implemented. If the community declines, it cannot be implemented."[30] A young man explained his understanding of how government laws would work in Zandeland:

> When a decision of law is given by the government, it is given to the state. And then it's the responsibility of the minister of local government to look into it and if it is something to do with culture, it needs to be arranged. If a law is imposed directly by government, it needs to look at culture. After a discussion with the chiefs, the law then comes through the community if it is approved.[31]

When asked how a distinction would be made between laws that connect to culture and those that do not, another respondent stated firmly, "Every law is related back to culture."[32]

This is a crucial point for the rule of law movement, and it highlights why implementing the rule of law is a complex endeavor. As the importance of engaging with local structures and realities returns to the fore of international development approaches, programming that aims to engage local justice structures in a constructive way faces a range of challenges. Rule of law programs will need to explore how to develop approaches that navigate some of the flexibilities, understandings, and contradictions presented in this chapter. Fundamentally, that requires negotiating the idea that law is rooted in culture, but that culture is a permanently evolving and reimagined manifestation of social realities. Further, law and culture are not locked in an unchangeable relationship; they can be utilized according to particular interests and realities. A crucial insight is that rule of law actors are endogenous to this process of renegotiation—they introduce concepts and reject norms that become benchmarks of acceptance or rejection for those targeted by the program.

The notion of the Azande Kingdom is a compelling one that seems to have overwhelming popular support. Thus, any externally imposed reform that ignores it might appear neocolonial. Yet support for the king's reestablishment might pit the elders—who are seen as pillars of the community and necessary for development—against a younger population seeking a governance system that allows for stability and modernization at the same time. "The elders want to see that this kingdom is restored," explained a county executive director (the deputy of the county commissioner). "But the youth . . . think about their education. They are not interested. . . . Back then, Gbudue, when he walked, people had to bend. Maybe the youth today, they are educated. They will not bow."[33] Two young men in the market in one of Gbudue's hometowns had an even stronger opinion on the matter. As one of them stated:

> When king coughs, the people cough. When king cries, the people cry. It used to be like that. It cannot be like that anymore. The government cannot agree with [the Azande elders] on the king. Today the position of the king is represented by president. No one can take the king again.[34]

At times, public skepticism toward the king is an extension of a general skepticism of government and authority in South Sudan. As the two young men elaborated, the government in South Sudan did not always work for the people; rather, it sometimes controlled the people, often with intimidation and weapons. They worried that a future king might gather groups of armed men around him, ostensibly for protection, but that these forces could then be used against the people. They predicted that these forces might even be used against the government army, because the government will not allow the king to claim a position of authority higher than the state governor, and possibly even equal to the president. "The king has no good plan for the rest of the country," one of them explained. "The king used force. That is now against human rights."[35]

Local Notions of Rules of Law

While the authority assigned to the Azande king might be romanticized and all-powerful, trust in the king's voice as the representative of the people brings into sharp focus one of the many challenges in establishing the rule of law in South Sudan. How the different authorities—those of the "official" government and the so-called traditional authorities—can truly work in parallel and under one system is unclear, as is how a commitment to honoring local customs can sit with the rule of law.

"What is the kingdom going to be?" asked a state minister. "How will the kingdom operate within government? Will our government be skilled enough to maintain a relationship between monarch and government? The definition of that relationship has to be very clear; the boundaries . . . need to be clearly defined."[36] One government administrator wondered, "Where will the minister sit with the king? When the last king was in power, Western Equatoria was not a state."[37] Some see the king as advising the state governor on matters of concern to Western Equatoria. As a Catholic sister explained, "The governor is also a representative of the king."[38] A former MP went even further, declaring, "The king's order is more respected than the president's."[39]

One religious leader, however, believed that framing the debate as modern structures versus traditional ones revealed a fundamental misunderstanding of the meaning of the Azande kingdom. "People who are saying the Zande king is like government are misleading the idea. . . . Whether the Zande king engages in politics will depend on the constitution of the Zande kingdom. The Zande intellectuals will write it."[40] Thus, he did not see any tension:

> For me, the system is not harmful. It will help even the government. If the Zande elect their king, he will be like a president. People have to listen. And the king will link the Zande people to the government. It really will make life between government and Zande community very simple.[41]

One of the goals of rule of law programming is a well-functioning justice system, and current wisdom on international development, particularly in postconflict situations, dictates engagement with existing realities and local structures. In Zandeland, respondents often described their rules of law as deeply ingrained in their culture and traditions. However, Azande culture and traditions have also grown out of previous interventions to establish the rule of law. As one respondent explained:

> Local government in South Sudan is taking the shape of what the British left. There are some changes but half of the plans and laws are what the British left for us. . . . If you look into past laws, it's still upheld, there's no difference. In regard to the social laws, it remains as it is. An example could be the taxes, introduced in those days, like a social service tax, it is still in our budget. Another example, very simple and common, the local brew/alcohol was prohibited [by the British] and up to now it is still not allowed in the market. . . . If one goes really

deep one finds that not much has changed. Since then up to now the criminal law is the same. Now there is human rights, which was not our case because in Sudan human rights was not there. For the community human rights might be better, for the government it's more difficult. Now if somebody kills a person he is not guilty until proven by law. If children throw stones against this window, the police can come but what can they do?"[42]

Conclusion: Rule of Law and Rules of Law

The image of the Azande king as a rule setter and justice provider shows how Azande notions of democracy, the rule of law, and justice systems are profoundly different from those in the rule of law discourse. This case study has highlighted that advancing the understanding of how a context-specific approach to the rule of law might actually look requires an in-depth understanding of local interpretations of rule of law concepts. One conclusion might be that rule of law approaches are not appropriate in specific contexts and could end up alienating society from the very values they seek to implement.

What crystallizes in the notions of the Azande king is that the coexistence of multiple belief systems is a crucial characteristic of the Azande community—an appointed king can be seen as a better representative of democracy than an elected government official, and what might be seen by outsiders as a nothing more than a cultural faux pas is interpreted by the Azande as breaking a cultural law. When it comes to spirituality, the understanding that several belief systems can peacefully coexist within one person or community is well established. Religious beliefs, however amalgamated, are usually perceived as located in the private sphere, where their fluidity is less complicated. The provision of justice, on the other hand, is assumed to require clarity and codification as something that happens in the public sphere. However, the case of the Azande king illustrates a perspective that understands that rules of law can be similarly fluid and shifting, located in neither the private nor the public sphere but instead a community one. Such an understanding might hold the key to adjusting rule of law programming; however, operationalizing a flexible understanding of rule of law is a challenge that has yet to be met.

The profound sense of loss of community cohesion expressed by respondents when debating their romanticized notions of governance highlights another challenge of rule of law and access to justice programs. Legal aid clinics or paralegals might be able to deal with, for example, cases of rape or domestic violence in a manner that is fairer to women; however, if the community loses cohesion because judgment over cultural appropriateness is no longer part of the traditional authority's remit, other problems might arise. Furthermore, judicial proceedings are often the moment when citizens connect most directly with authority, and, as such, they can be an important component of nation-building. Yet if the nature of the state is unclear, as is the case in South Sudan, such a connection might not even be a worthwhile ambition. It is also unclear how South Sudan will exert control over its citizens, considering that the state has limited capacity to rule and could easily be challenged.

An answer—as shown by British native administration and the debate over the importance of local structures for governance—is that the state needs to rely on pluralist mechanisms that function more or less without explicit state influence. Yet the central state is, at least theoretically, built on the notion that the principles of governance within it must be diverse, and that the essence of the state lies not in one principle—or one rule of law—but in finding a way in which contradictions can coexist.

A further question emerges from this case study. How will the international community engage with a local authority figure who is not democratically elected, does not need to follow a set of rules, and is imbued with seemingly unlimited power and a somewhat vague, although apparently effective, accountability structure? Here, again, the answer may lie in local solutions. In Zandeland, the answer is clear: by turning demand and supply on its head. Rule of law experts might usually consider the rule of law movement as the supplier of laws and justice. But Azande respondents, when interpreting how the Azande king and international notions of justice and rules can work together, described their own culture as the supply side of justice. In their view, integrating local authority and rules with the broader international framework is achieved not by adjusting to outside demands but by inviting the outside in to observe. "For the crowning we will invite [the United Nations and the] international community," said one man in a community meeting, "so that the government cannot say we don't recognize your king, because UN was also a witness and signatory."[43] The Azande community envisages contextualizing its own imagined and perhaps eventual rules of law with the presence of the international community by asking the international representatives to observe, to protect the Azande community against a South Sudan government vision that goes against Azande culture, and, generally, not to interfere.

References

Comaroff, Jean, and John Comaroff. 1993. "Introduction." In *Modernity and its Malcontents: Ritual and Power in Postcolonial Africa*, edited by Jean Comaroff and John Comaroff. Chicago: Chicago University Press.

"Development of Local Government in Zande District, Yambio." 1948. July 8.

Evans-Pritchard, E. E. (1937) 1963. *Witchcraft, Oracles and Magic among the Azande*. London: Clarendon Press.

———. 1957. "Zande Warfare." *Anthropos* 52:239–62.

Governor of Mongalla. 1924. "Reply." Sudan Archive, March 12.

Holt, P. M., and M. W. Daly. 2000. *A History of the Sudan: From the Coming of Islam to the Present Day*. Harlo: Longman.

Ivanov, Paola. 2002. "Cannibals, Warriors, Conquerors and Colonizers: Western Perceptions and Azande Historiography." *History in Africa* 29:89–217.

Jackson, Adam. 2011. "The Influence of European Colonialism on Zande Customary Law." *Totem: The University of Western Ontario Journal of Anthropology* 11:51–58.

Jennings, R. C. 1989. "Zande Logic and Western Logic." *The British Journal for the Philosophy of Science* 40:275–85.

Johnson, Douglas. 2003. *The Root Causes of Sudan's Civil Wars*. Oxford: James Currey.

Jok, Aleu Akechak, Robert A. Leitch, and Carrie Vanderwint. 2004. *A Study of Customary Law in Contemporary Southern Sudan*. Middlesex: World Vision International.

Leonardi, Cherry. 2013. *Dealing with Government in South Sudan: Histories of Chiefship, Community and State*. Oxford: James Currey.

Leonardi, Cherry, Leben Nelson Moro, Martina Santschi, and Deborah H. Isser. 2010. *Local Justice in Southern Sudan*. Washington, DC: United States Institute of Peace.

Maurice, G. K. 1930. "The History of Sleeping Sickness in the Sudan." *Journal of the Royal Army Medical Corps* 55:161–241.

Reining, C. 1966. *The Zande Scheme: An Anthropological Case Study of Economic Development in Africa*. Evanston: Northwestern University Press.

Robertson, J. W. 1953. "Traditional Authorities Bill." Edited by Civil Secretary, March 4.

Seligman, C. G., and B. Z. Seligman. 1932. *Pagan Tribes of the Nilotic Sudan*. London: Routledge.

"Summary of the British Southern Policies." 1958. In JD/SCR/1.A.3, edited by Assistant Governor of Equatoria.

United Nations Mission in South Sudan. 2013. "Local Government Act Must Be Implemented, Judge Says." *ReliefWeb*, May 18. http://reliefweb.int/report/south-sudan-republic/local-government-act-must-be-implemented-judge-says.

Wyld, J. W. G. 1949. "Sudan Notes and Records." University of Khartoum 30(1):47–57.

"Zande District Handbook." 1959.

Notes

1. Evans-Pritchard's work also reflects a static notion of tribes and their traditions.

2. Azande chief, interview with the author, Ezo Town, May 1, 2013.

3. Ibid.

4. Two junior county officials, interview with the author, Tambura Town, May 10, 2013.

5. Azande trader, interview with the author, Ezo Town, May 5, 2013.

6. Azande chief, interview with the author, Ezo Town, May 1, 2013.

7. Community meeting conducted by the author, Degere boma, May 6, 2013.

8. Azande chief, interview with the author, Ezo Town, May 1, 2013.

9. Ibid.

10. Government inspector, interview with the author, Ezo Town, May 5, 2013.

11. Community meeting with Azande elders conducted by the author, Mabenge boma, May 20, 2013.

12. Community meeting with a group of young Azande men conducted by the author, Nyasi boma, May 23, 2013.

13. Chief in Ezo County, interview with the author, May 22, 2013.

14. Mboribamu Renzi Tomburo, interview with the author, Tambura Town, May 13, 2013.

15. High-level state government official, interview with the author, Yambio, December 19, 2012.

16. Community meeting conducted by the author, Mabenge boma, May 20, 2013.

17. Community meeting conducted by the author, Degere boma, May 6, 2013.

18. Ibid.

19. Former MP, interview with the author, Ezo Town, May 4, 2013.

20. Ibid.

21. Community meeting conducted by the author, Mangdangau boma, May 3, 2013.

22. Community meeting with women's association conducted by the author, Tambura Town May 13, 2013.

23. Ibid.

24. Community meeting conducted by the author, Degere boma, May 6, 2013.

25. Ibid.

26. Community meeting with women's association conducted by the author, Tambura Town May 13, 2013.

27. Community meeting conducted by the author, Degere boma, May 6, 2013.

28. Community with Catholic youth group conducted by the author, Ezo Town, May 2, 2013.

29. Chief in Ezo County, interview with the author, May 22, 2013.

30. Community meeting with Catholic youth group conducted by the author, Ezo Town, May 2, 2013.

31. Ibid.

32. Ibid.

33. Executive director, interview with the author, Tambura Town, May 10, 2013.

34. Fieldnotes, Tambura Town, May 10, 2013.

35. Ibid.

36. State minister, interview with the author, Yambio, December 19, 2012.

37. Executive director, interview with the author, Tambura Town, May 10, 2013.

38. Catholic sister, interview with the author, Mopoi, May 11, 2013.

39. Former MP, interview with the author, Ezo Town, May 4, 2013.

40. Religious leader, interview with the author, Ezo Town, May 1, 2013.

41. Ibid.

42. Executive director, interview with the author, Tambura Town, May 10, 2013.

43. Community meeting conducted by the author, Mabenge boma, May 20, 2013.

Abstract

This chapter focuses on community rights to land and natural resources, arguably the greatest rule of law challenge of our time. It explores three struggles in particular: communities in Liberia, Uganda, and Mozambique documenting customary land claims; rural land owners in Sierra Leone renegotiating an inequitable agreement with a large agribusiness project; and coastal communities in Kutch, India, seeking the enforcement of environmental law against a massive coal plant and port. From these experiences, the chapter draws insights into how people pursue the rule of law. It addresses, in turn, the way that communities in each of these stories confront power imbalances, the way they interact with the administrative state, and the way they grapple with internal rule of law problems. It concludes with a reflection on the relationship between the rule of law and social movements.

6 Legal Empowerment and the Land Rush: Three Struggles

Vivek Maru

Introduction

If international "rule of law promotion" is only about assisting state elites, then it is a narrow, technical concern. Imagine if "democracy promotion" was only about helping officials hold elections or run parliaments. If, on the other hand, "rule of law promotion" is to have moral force and global significance, it needs to be in support of a broader social movement, something akin to the movement for democracy.

What does that movement look like? This chapter will focus on the issue of community rights to land and natural resources, arguably the greatest rule of law challenge of our time. A combination of two things—increased investment interest in land and natural resources, and insecure tenure for the people who live and depend on those resources—is leading to exploitation, conflict, and decisions that favor short-term profit over long-term stewardship.

I will describe three struggles: communities in Liberia, Uganda, and Mozambique documenting customary land claims and strengthening local

Thank you to my teammates at Namati and the communities with whom we work, without whom I would know nothing about these subjects. Thank you to Rachael Kleinfeld, Erik Jensen, Rachael Knight, Tania James, Sonkita Conteh, and the other authors in this volume for very helpful comments on a first draft. Thank you David Marshall for making me write this. Thank you Morgan Stoffregen for thoughtful, careful editorial assistance. I dedicate this chapter to a fallen soldier for justice, Achmed Dean Sesay. Achmed worked on the case from Sierra Leone described here, and on many others. He could squeeze justice out of a broken system. In honor of his memory, we are fighting on.

land governance; communities in Sierra Leone renegotiating an inequitable and fraudulent agreement with a large agribusiness project; and coastal communities in Kutch, India, seeking the enforcement of environmental law against a massive coal plant and port.

I will draw from these experiences insights into how people pursue the rule of law. I will address, in turn, the way that communities in each of these stories confront asymmetries of power, the way they interact with the administrative state, and the way they grapple with internal rule of law challenges. I will conclude with a reflection on the relationship between the rule of law and social movements.

The Rush for Land and the Rule of Law

For billions of people, land is their greatest asset: the source of food and water, and the site of history and culture. More than ever, that land is in demand. The pace of large-scale land sales surged when food prices spiked in 2007–2008. And while food prices have slowed, the land rush has continued. Estimates of the size of the phenomenon vary, with one World Bank study finding that 56.6 million hectares of land were leased or sold in one year—an area equivalent to roughly the entire landmass of Spain and Portugal, and more than thirteen times the average amount of land opened to cultivation annually between 1961 and 2007 (Deininger et al. 2011).

In principle, these transactions have the potential to create jobs and stimulate economic growth. But approximately three billion people in the developing world live without secure legal rights to their lands, forests, and pastures (Rights and Resources 2014). Colonial powers centralized authority over much of the land they conquered, diminishing the ownership rights of rural communities into more fragile use rights, or in some cases no rights at all. Some postcolonial states have sustained those regimes of appropriation to this day. Others have made *de jure* changes to restore customary rights or decentralize land governance—India's 2006 Forest Rights Act, for example, and Mozambique's 1997 Lei de Terras—but those laws have gone largely unimplemented (Cotula 2013, 15–26; Alden-Wiley 2012).

It is this historical legacy that makes the current rush for land and natural resources arguably the greatest rule of law challenge of our time. When the rights of existing owners are insecure, there is great risk of fraud, conflict, and irresponsible land-use decisions. Indeed, recent evidence suggests a race to the bottom: large-scale acquisitions and concessions are disproportionately concentrated in countries where land rights are weakest (Arezki, Klaus, and Harris 2012, 49).

Three Struggles

This section explores three grassroots efforts to protect community rights to natural resources in the context of increased investment interest. I work with a group, Namati, that, along with local partner organizations, is supporting communities in each of these cases.

These stories illustrate three key moments in the arc of interaction between rural communities and large-scale firms: securing customary rights before industrialization arrives, negotiating the terms under which industrialization will take place, and seeking compliance with contractual and legal requirements once industrialization has begun.

Securing Tenure in Liberia, Uganda, and Mozambique

In Liberia, Uganda, and Mozambique, Namati and national partner organizations are pursuing a proactive, preventive approach to the land crisis: we are helping rural communities document their customary land claims and strengthen local governance over those lands. In Mozambique and Uganda, we are working to bring to life provisions in existing laws—the Lei de Terras in Mozambique and the Land Act in Uganda—that have gone largely unimplemented. In Liberia, we are working under the auspices of a memorandum of understanding with the Liberian Land Commission.

Most efforts to strengthen land rights involve the titling of individual household plots. Our work instead focuses on community claims. By starting with the outer boundary of the community, it is possible to protect more land faster and at a lower cost per hectare. Community land claims also include common resources—like forests, grazing lands, rivers, and lakes—that are particularly vulnerable to exploitation, and yet are left out if individual holdings are the only rights protected.

This work grows out of a two-year experiment with our three partners—the Sustainable Development Institute in Liberia, the Land and Equity Movement of Uganda, and Centro Terra Viva in Mozambique—and the International Development Law Organization (Knight et al. 2012).[1] The most significant finding from that study is that in order for community land protection efforts to be effective, they should combine the technical work of mapping and titling with two thornier, more political tasks: the resolution of border disputes and the strengthening of local systems for land governance.

When those efforts were joined, they produced remarkable changes. Communities wrote down their rules for land use, revised those rules to ensure compliance with their national constitutions, and developed plans for managing their natural resources. In the process, communities established new mechanisms for holding their leaders accountable and protecting the rights of women. They revived old conservation rules that had lapsed—restrictions on felling trees in reserve forests, for example—and created new ones.

In October 2013, I attended a public gathering under a tree in Mata, a small coastal town in Inhambane Province, Mozambique. The people of Mata had recently completed the documentation process laid out in the Lei de Terras, and the provincial land administration had granted them a land delimitation certificate. Community members put up a celebratory arch of coconut fronds and magenta-colored flowers for the occasion.

Antonio Augusto, the elected mayor of Mata, dressed in suit and tie, explained that the journey had not begun easily. When Nelson Alfredo, a staff member of Centro Terra Viva, first visited the area speaking about maps and deeds, many people suspected he was angling to purchase land, as investors had been doing along the coast. But Alfredo, Augusto said, had patience and a good sense of humor, and he persisted.

As people in Mata learned from Alfredo about the Lei de Terras, and as they heard stories from neighboring communities about exploitation by investors, their interest in securing land rights grew. The community began following the steps in the documentation process—first electing an interim committee, then mapping their lands. Mata had been having a longstanding boundary dispute with a neighboring town. Motivated by the prospect of formalizing ownership, leaders from the two towns managed to resolve the conflict after extensive negotiation.

In a series of meetings, some consisting of men and women separately and some open to all, Mata residents documented their existing rules for land use and debated potential revisions. According to Augusto, Mata's traditional rules dictated that ownership over individual plots be vested in the male head of household. A lawyer from Centro Terra Viva, however, pointed out that this was inconsistent with the Mozambican Constitution.

"After much discussion," said Augusto, "we accepted." Mata's by-laws now state explicitly that women can own land and that if a husband dies, family property goes to his widow. When we walked out to the beach that day in October, after the public discussion had concluded, several women repeated this to us: we now have equal claims.

A South African businessman attended the same celebratory gathering in October 2013. He had moved to Mata and set up a small facility to extract and bottle coconut oil. Augusto and other elders emphasized that they wanted to attract more investors of this kind. Now that Mata had formal land rights, clear rules, and an elected management committee, Augusto said, the town would be in a position to negotiate fair terms.

196

The two-year experiment by Rachel Knight et al. (2012) tested three models for facilitating community land protection: a full legal-services approach, in which communities received direct assistance from lawyers; a pared-down education approach, where information, and little else, was provided; and a middle-path paralegal model, in which a community representative was trained and supported to drive the process forward.

Knight and her colleagues found that of these three, the community paralegal model was most effective. Communities receiving full legal services tended to rely heavily on the outside professionals, while communities with paralegals took greater ownership over the process. Paralegals also proved most capable of mediating contentious border disputes, which can otherwise sideline protection efforts (ibid., 191–95).

Namati is currently working to scale up community land protection activities in all three countries. We train and support paralegals in communities that request it, and we work with land administration departments to make the documentation process easier to complete. We are also conducting a cross-country longitudinal study to determine the long-term impacts of this approach.

Renegotiating with an Investor in Sierra Leone

In recent years, about a million hectares—one-seventh of Sierra Leone's land mass—has been leased out for mining and large-scale agriculture projects (Oakland Institute 2012). As in many other parts of Africa, the vast majority of land in Sierra Leone is held under customary tenure, with no formal documentation and no clear governance arrangements for making land-use decisions.

Since Sierra Leone, unlike Mozambique and Uganda, does not yet have a law that allows communities to formalize their customary land claims, Namati has instead focused further down the stream of interaction between communities and firms, on the point at which the two sides negotiate the terms by which industrialization takes place. In one project that we are involved in, the people of forty-eight villages in the Northern Province are attempting to renegotiate an agreement with the Sierra Leonean subsidiary of the Swiss energy firm Addax and Oryx Group.

In 2009, newspapers reported that Addax would be exploring a €200 million investment project in Sierra Leone—the company proposed growing sugarcane and producing ethanol for export to Europe. In 2010, the firm signed fifty-year lease agreements with three chiefdom councils in the Northern Province—Makari Gbanti, Bombali Sebora, and Malal Mara—acquiring

23,000 hectares of land. The firm agreed to pay US$3.60 per acre per year; half of this would go to landowning families and the other half would be divided between the chiefdom and district councils.

Over the following year, the company signed "acknowledgement agreements" with individual landowning families, under which the firm committed to paying an additional US$1.40 per acre per year. However, landowners from one village, Masethle, refused to sign the acknowledgment agreement. They had learned that although Addax had said that it intended to use one-fourth to one-third of the village's land, the lease actually covered all of it: all farmland, all common areas (such as forests, swamps, and streams), and even the land where people had their homes. We became involved in the case when a native of Masethle living in Freetown contacted Namati's Sierra Leone director, Sonkita Conteh. Ultimately, we were engaged by the landholding families of all forty-eight affected villages.

When we explained the scope of the lease to other landowners who had already signed the acknowledgement agreement, they were shocked. "Ah staful lie," said the chief of Lungi Acre village—roughly translated, "that's a preposterous lie." He and most of the landowners were illiterate. They had placed their thumbprints on the acknowledgment lease without understanding the terms.

There is a tradition in Sierra Leone whereby a "stranger" comes to a village and asks for land, perhaps because he has married someone there or because he has migrated south from Guinea. A chief can grant available land to use and farm; a small rental payment at harvest time serves as an acknowledgment that the land does not belong to the newcomer. But no stranger can lease the entire village, including the common areas and the settlements.

The chief's response was an eerie echo of the way some Native Americans responded upon learning the terms of treaties to which they had supposedly assented: not only "I didn't agree to that" but "that is not possible."[2]

In principle, denizens of the forty-eight affected villages were provided with lawyers, but those lawyers were paid for by Addax, and the villagers said they hardly had any contact with them. Contrary to the written agreement, local political leaders indicated that Addax would use only a portion of their land. Sierra Leonean president Ernest Bai Koroma, meanwhile, repeatedly championed the project in public speeches (see, e.g., Sierra Leone State House 2010). In the end, our clients saw this not as a negotiation but as a fait accompli.

Chiefdom authorities, district councilors, and local parliamentarians repeatedly told villagers "dis go pull you 'pon povaty" (the project would lift them from poverty) and "den go tek you pikin dem" (they will hire your children). Two years into the project's operations, however, most landowning families are disappointed. The company promised jobs, new borewells, schools, and clinics. But according to our clients, there are very few jobs, the infrastructure remains largely unbuilt, and Addax has not communicated plans for completion (see, e.g., Action Aid 2013).

Landholding families are also very concerned about damage to their environment. They claim that Addax is depleting water supply and contaminating water sources with chemical waste; that the company is permanently destroying swamps and bolilands, which our clients had understood would not be touched under the project; that the companies' trucks and tillers have caused severe dust pollution; and that speeding company vehicles have caused several fatal road accidents.

We asked our clients whether they would like to see the company leave. Unanimously, they said no; rather, they would like to change the terms under which the company operates.

When we presented these findings to Addax in 2013, to our surprise, company representatives agreed to renegotiate the terms of the lease. There had been a change in staff at the company's Sierra Leone office. The new officials acknowledged that at least some of our claims were valid and that in a fifty-year project, the company could not afford to have hostile relations with its hosts.

Addax asks—reasonably, perhaps—that the three paramount chiefs who signed the original agreement take part in any renegotiation. All three chiefs admit that there are serious problems with the lease and that their constituents are dissatisfied. But there are obvious reasons why a public figure might not want to tamper with an arrangement backed by the president of the country, even when the company is willing. Initially, two of the chiefs agreed to renegotiate, while one, who lives in the president's hometown, did not. Conteh began to consider a somewhat creative legal action against this chief, for breach of his fiduciary duty to the residents of his chiefdom. But as of this writing, that third chief has said that if Addax and the others go forward, he will not stand in the way.

Although Conteh is the lawyer representing the landowners, he is not handling this case alone. Organizers from the Sierra Leone Network on the Right to Food and Namati's own community paralegals have been crucial in serving as a bridge between Conteh and residents of the forty-eight villages. The organizers and paralegals have convened community meetings, explained the contents of the lease, and gathered information from farmers about their experience with the project thus far. They have sought in particular the views of women and less well-off residents, to make sure that we are representing the interests of the villages as a whole.

As the case has progressed, we have received requests from communities in several other parts of the country: regarding a sand-mining operation on the southern coast, two iron ore mines in the north, and a proposed palm-oil plantation in the southeast. All over, deals are being cut for the use of rural land. And all over, the Sierra Leoneans whose land it is want to be able to shape the terms.

Seeking the Enforcement of Environmental Regulation in Kutch, India

Kutch is a district in the western corner of India. Historically, Kutch's poverty, remoteness, and semi-arid landscape have rendered it of little interest to the rest of the country. Even the British Empire left it alone: Kutch was an independent princely state when it joined free India in 1947. In the late 1990s, however, the district began attracting industry. Land in Kutch is relatively cheap, and rich in minerals like limestone, lignite, and china clay. Kutch is also attractive for its harbor, and the Ahmedabad-based Adani Group chose the Kutchi town of Mundra to build what is now the largest private port in the country.

Unfortunately, the new port is located in the heart of what was Kutch's richest mangrove marine ecosystem. The mangrove is a special tree, a cornerstone species for the three traditional livelihoods: fishing, farming, and animal husbandry. The mangroves thrive in the estuaries, where fresh and sea water meet. Their root systems and falling leaves create a fertile breeding ground for fish, making the trees crucial for fisherpeople along the Kutchi coast. The trees also create a natural barrier against salinity ingress, protecting the purity of inland farmers' well water. Finally, mangroves provide a good source of fodder for cattle and camels (see, e.g., Kohli 2011).

In addition to building the port itself, the Adani Group built several industrial projects in its vicinity that provide the port with shipping contracts—including a coal power plant, a salt works, and an edible oil refinery. In the process, Adani and other companies destroyed hundreds of thousands of mangrove trees. Satellite data from the Indian Space Applications Centre show that mangrove cover on Navinal and Bocha, two of the major coastal mudflats, dropped from 590 hectares in April 1988 to 346 hectares in 2000.[3] Cutting down any tree without permission is illegal; and mangrove trees are further protected by India's Coastal Regulation Zone Notification.

Adani also closed off the ecosystem's lifelines by building dams across its creeks. Starved of water, the creeks became filled with silt. This dried out the fish breeding grounds and eventually transformed the mangrove habitat into barren land. Coastal Regulation Zone protection is dependent on the location of the high tide line; the dams physically forced that line further into the sea.

In 2000, I worked with a coalition of local organizations known as the Forum for Planned Industrialization of Kutch. As the careful name suggests, the forum sought not to oppose industrialization but rather to ensure that industrialization benefited the Kutchi people and was in harmony with the traditional livelihoods that sustain most Kutchis. The forum embraced the idea of a port in Kutch but argued that it should be located on the western coastline, between Mandvi and Jakhau, where the land is less ecologically productive and where outside employment was more needed.

I had never confronted so squarely the brute face of power. The Adani Group's destruction of the mangrove ecosystem was blatantly illegal, and yet all attempts at resistance were crushed in a hazy mixture of bribery and state complicity. Several lawsuits were dismissed in their final stages when one of the plaintiffs mysteriously withdrew.

In 1999, members of the Coastal Zone Management Authority, a body meant to enforce the Coastal Regulation Zone Notification, came to visit the port project and stayed in Adani's guest houses. The forum organized a rally of fisherpeople at the port's gates and delivered a petition documenting violations. But after its visit, the authority took no action. The state government, meanwhile, maintained its unambiguous support of the company. On January 23, 2000, at the port's dedication ceremony, Gujarat chief minister Keshubhai Patel stated that whoever opposed the Adani Port was antipatriotic and was opposing him personally.

I spent one morning with Muhammad Jaffar of Shakhadia village. He is a member of the Pagadia community, which still fishes by wading on foot rather than by boat. During the rainy season, when fish are most plentiful, Pagadia fisherpeople connect their nets and divide the catch equally. Jaffar used to be the person who connected the nets; now, he stays home and his sons go to fish. He said that his community had been practicing fishing in this way for as many generations as could be remembered. He told me that his people would not want boats even if they could afford them. Laughing, his wife said that if you give a Pagadia man a boat, he would sail away and never make it back to shore.

Members of Jaffar's village had a lawsuit pending against Adinath Salt Works, one of the earliest industrial projects in the area. The villagers were arguing that four kilometers of the land, which they had used for generations but which had now become Adinath property, should be left open for them to access the sea. Jaffar told me that his catch had decreased by 50% over the last five years, which he attributed mostly to industrial pollution. The lawsuit might prevent this livelihood from ending right away, he said, but even then he thought the fishing would end shortly. He was beginning to look for other work but felt qualified for nothing but fishing. He was considering buying an auto rickshaw. Did I have any suggestions?

That afternoon, I went to visit the port. There, I faced massive warehouses, roaring cranes, and a steady flow of trucks. I was most startled by the enormous piles of sulfur, sitting in the open, waiting to be transported for use as an ingredient for a chemical processing plant. Sulfur is neon yellow, and the piles were at least fifty feet high and one hundred feet wide. The world that makes use of this sulfur was a very different world from that which Jaffar lived in. At what table, I found myself asking, could Jaffar and the movers and users of this sulfur negotiate equally?

As industrialization continued over the following decade, no such table was made available. In 2006, the government designated 6,400 hectares around Mundra as a special economic zone, creating tax incentives for industry. Adani's coal plant now operates at 4,600 megawatts and is one of the biggest in the world. Adjacent to it, in 2012, Tata Power completed another mega-coal plant, which now operates at 4,000 megawatts.

Since 2012, Namati has worked with fishing and farming communities along the southern Kutch coast. This work is much further downstream than that in Mata, Mozambique, where communities are seeking to strengthen land governance in advance of major industrialization, and Northern Sierra Leone, where communities are aiming to negotiate fairer terms with an industrial project that has just begun.

In Kutch, the landscape has been transformed. Although the terms of industrialization had been set on paper—in mandatory conditions attached to the clearance of each project and in laws like the Coastal Regulation Zone Notification—many of those terms were violated. At this stage, communities in Kutch are seeking compliance with those broken commitments, as well as protection of what remains of the ecosystem on which their livelihoods depend.

Volunteer community paralegals began by researching the contents of the conditions to which Adani and other firms had committed when receiving their environmental clearances from government. The paralegals then used satellite maps, cell phone pictures, newspaper clippings, and government documents to compile extensive evidence on violations of three key conditions in Adani's clearance: that it should not cut mangroves, that it should not dam creeks, and that it should not block fisherpeople's access to the sea (Namati et al. 2013).

These paralegals have now formed a new group with perhaps a less diplomatic name than its predecessor—Mundra Hit Rakshak Manch, or Forum for the Protection of Rights in Mundra. Namati and the Manch, along with a women's association, Ujaas, and a fisherpeople's association, MASS, are seeking enforcement actions based on the evidence gathered by the paralegals. Together, we are also developing a proposal—based on extensive community consultations—to declare the remaining portion of untouched coastline, around the village of Bhadreswar, a "critically vulnerable coastal area" under the Coastal Regulation Zone Notification. If adopted, the proposal would prohibit heavy industry, make provisions for ecological restoration, and improve facilities for fisherpeople.

Confronting Power Imbalance

The basic difference between a Hobbesian state of nature and a social contract governed by law is that under the latter there are limits on private power. Law is meant to provide, in the words of the Fourteenth Amendment to the US Constitution, "equal protection." But in the three struggles described above, power imbalances render nominal legal protections hollow. The recognition of customary land rights under laws in Uganda and Mozambique is easy to bypass when communities have no maps and no deeds. Contract law has little meaning when villagers in Sierra Leone are pressured to accept an agreement without understanding its contents. Powerful companies in India ignore environmental regulations with impunity.

When people stand up to confront these imbalances of power, civil society organizations of various kinds—local membership-based groups like the fisherpeople's association in Kutch, and national mission-driven organizations like the Sustainable Development Institute in Liberia—can provide a source of countervailing power.

Lawyers working in the public interest are scarce and costly. In India, for example, with a population of over one billion, there are fewer than a dozen practicing lawyers focused on environmental protection.[4] As these three stories illustrate, "community paralegals" trained in law and in approaches such as mediation, organizing, education, and advocacy can form a larger front line.

There is a growing body of evidence suggesting that paralegals, with quality training and supervision, can succeed in surmounting power imbalances and achieving concrete remedies to injustice.[5] Paralegals' flexible set of tools, and their closeness to the communities they serve, makes them well placed not just to provide a technical service but to "empower"—to strengthen citizens' ability to understand and use the law.

Just as primary health workers are connected to doctors and hospitals, it is important for paralegals to be connected to a small corps of lawyers who can engage in litigation or high-level advocacy if frontline methods fail. Paralegals are more cost-effective than a purely lawyer-based model, but they are not free. Paralegals who work full time require a salary; and those who serve their own villages or membership associations as volunteers require support from "lead paralegals" or other advocates who earn salaries and work full time. There are also costs associated with training, office space, materials, transportation, and the few lawyers who support the front line.

Yet there is a persistent financing gap for legal aid efforts that support the least powerful. Addax in Sierra Leone recognized the need for affected communities to have representation, but it created an obvious conflict of interest by directly hiring a private law firm to fulfill that role. There are far better ways to narrow the financing gap.

Governments can provide resources through autonomous bodies such as ombudsman's offices or public legal aid boards if the bodies genuinely respect civil society independence. Investors like Addax could be asked to contribute funds to those institutions rather than hiring opposing counsel themselves. Namati and other groups have argued for such an arrangement in Sierra Leone, and have managed to incorporate that proposal into new voluntary guidelines for agricultural investment (Bioenergy and Food Security Working Group of Sierra Leone 2013, 10).

Client fees and contributions are also important for defraying costs and ensuring the accountability of legal aid providers to their constituents. In Sierra Leone, we intend to experiment with contingency-fee arrangements, through which communities would cover a portion of the cost of our representation by promising to pay us a small percentage of future rental revenue. We would compensate lawyers and paralegals on a salary basis, unrelated to revenue generation, in order to avoid an incentive to push communities to accept deals that are not in their best interest.

Legal empowerment, like public health and the environment, is arguably a public good. Legal empowerment efforts render governments more accountable to their citizens and make economic development more equitable. But unlike public health, there is a natural disincentive for states to finance such programs within their borders, because legal empowerment efforts constrain state power.

Moreover, the power imbalances that make legal aid necessary are often international, as in the case of multinational firms investing in natural resources belonging to poor rural communities. It makes sense, then, for there to be international collaboration in the attempt to address those power imbalances. We have therefore argued for a multilateral financing mechanism (Maru 2011; Hall and Maru 2013; Namati and Open Society Foundations 2014).

In our view, a "global fund for legal empowerment" should be reciprocal: countries should agree not only to contribute but also to receive investments, albeit in different proportions. There is no country where laws work perfectly for citizens. Legal empowerment efforts must adapt to social and legal context, but in some form they are useful everywhere. The distribution of funds across countries could be tacked to metrics of governance, such as the Rule of Law Index published by the World Justice Project.

Furthermore, coalitions of civil society organizations, such as the Rights and Resources Initiative and Namati's legal empowerment network, can facilitate collaboration among local groups across borders. Organizations can learn from one another about strategy and methodology; they can also work together to take on specific cases. Swiss and European law regulates Addax's operations abroad, for example, and so communities affected by the Addax project in Sierra Leone may find public interest lawyers in Switzerland helpful.

No number of community paralegals or public interest lawyers will eliminate the power disparities that characterize today's rush for land and natural resources. But if we take the rule of law seriously, our international regime should commit to narrowing those disparities as much as possible.

Engaging the Administrative State

Efforts to improve the rule of law often focus on judicial systems—including courts, prosecutors, and bar associations (Golub 2003, 8–9; World Bank 2012, 3–5). But for many people around the world, law touches life most directly through the administrative state. In each of the three stories described here, administrative institutions are meant to play a crucial role. Ruefully, they often fail.

In Uganda, communities have been unable to acquire certificates of incorporation for their newly formed land associations, despite having completed all of the steps in the legal process, because the government has yet to appoint a provincial official with the authority to issue the certificates. In India, research by Kanchi Kohli and Manju Menon (2009) found rates of noncompliance with environmental clearance conditions set by the Ministry of Environment and Forests to be as high as 60%.[6] In Sierra Leone, when we asked the Environmental Protection Agency to provide us with a copy of the environmental impact assessment for the Addax project—something that

205

should be a public document—the agency told us it had only a hard copy, which it could not locate.[7]

Disputes over land and natural resources are some of the most significant conflicts of our times, and yet the administrative agencies meant to deal with them are often neglected backwaters of government. There is a massive need to strengthen the effectiveness and fairness of those institutions.

But reforms should not set priorities based on idealized conceptions of what a legal system should look like—that approach is a major reason why prior generations of rule of law efforts have faltered.[8] Instead, reformers could take their cues from the lived experience of constituents, addressing institutional failures that form a "binding constraint" on attempts to obtain justice. The World Bank (2012, 9) suggests a similar approach in its latest strategy on justice reform:

> While taking into account the views of professionals in the system, such as judges, lawyers, and administrators, the diagnosis of problems should be anchored in the priorities of end users—citizens and firms. Rather than beginning with the question of how to modernize the court system, such efforts should begin by asking where failings of the justice system are a constraint to equitable development.[9]

The World Bank speaks of "end users" as a whole, perhaps anticipating aggregating the views of individuals through surveys. A variant of that approach, one that may be more politically realistic, is for reformers to respond to the demands of existing grassroots efforts.

In Liberia, for example, the Sustainable Development Institute, Namati, and other groups successfully advocated for Liberia's first national land policy to establish a process for formalizing customary rights. The policy, which was issued in 2013, embraces the model that we piloted in Rivercess County during the three-country, two-year experiment described above. The policy recommends that rural communities be allowed to demarcate boundaries, establish governance structures and by-laws, and register community land associations (Liberia Land Commission 2013, 15–20).

The Land Commission has agreed that the Sustainable Development Institute, Namati, and other civil society groups should support communities in following that legal process. We will aim, moreover, to incorporate feedback from the communities with whom we work into the design of the administrative body that will review land association applications.

Reformers of administrative institutions should pay particular attention to policies that hold back attempts to overcome imbalances of power. In India, for example, the Ministry of Environment and Forests has prohibited civil society organizations from participating in environmental public hearings on projects such as the Adani Port (Indian Ministry of Urban Development 2006). This kind of constraint hinders nongovernmental organizations' ability to counterbalance the power of private firms.

In Sierra Leone and many other countries, social and environmental commitments—for example, the number of jobs that will be created or the measures that will be taken to mitigate pollution—are framed as voluntary corporate social responsibility measures. Instead, governments should require that such commitments be included as binding provisions of land lease agreements. The conditions will then be the explicit subject of company-community negotiations, and host communities will have legal recourse in the event of a breach.

These are the kinds of priorities that emerge from a reform agenda grounded in the experience of grassroots efforts.

Strengthening the Law Within

Power can trump law at all levels. Defenders of individual liberties are rightfully cautious about action by communities, because community institutions can be captured by local elites. B. R. Ambedkar voiced this concern in response to Mahatma Gandhi's embrace of decentralization during debates about the Indian Constitution.[10] A recent review of participatory approaches to development emphasizes the same risk (Mansuri and Rao 2013).

The paramount chiefs who signed the original Addax agreement without prior consent from their constituents are a case in point. Unaccountable local elites also caused the early cases against the Adani Port to fall apart. And in Uganda, Mozambique, and Liberia, local elites often stall the process of community land protection when they realize that it may lead to constraints on their power.

Efforts to protect community rights to natural resources are not only about the fight outside. They also involve an internal struggle for fairness and equity. Four observations about that internal struggle stand out from the stories described here. First, decentralizing control over land and natural resources creates new opportunities for people to hold their local leaders accountable.

For example, in 2012, the *gram panchayat* (the most local level of government) election in Bhadreswar turned on the question of a third proposed coal plant on the Kutch coast. Voters rejected the existing *sarpanch* (village head), who had been in favor of the plant and had allegedly accepted money from the project proponent. In his place, they elected a vocal opponent of the project. That kind of election would not have been possible before the 73rd

Amendment to the Constitution and the 1993 Gujarat Panchayat Act, which grant *gram panchayats* the power to make rules and decisions regarding their natural resources.

But, second, decentralization should not be completely unfettered. Local rules must comply with the constitution and laws of the country. For this reason we advocate for administrative bodies to review community by-laws before registering land associations. Reviewing agencies can check to make sure that by-laws are constitutional—that they do not discriminate against women, for example. Agencies can also set minimum standards for downward accountability. Land associations might be required, say, to establish an elected land-use committee subject to term limits (Knight et al. 2012, 185–86).

Third, the presence of an external threat can create an opportunity to improve local governance. In Mozambique, Uganda, and Liberia, Knight et al. found that communities that perceived the immediate possibility of a land grab were the most motivated to establish governance structures and to write and revise rules (ibid., 204). In Sierra Leone, the villages that engaged Namati to represent them in the Addax matter are now working to strengthen local downward accountability, to ensure that future negotiations are conducted with genuine consent. A fight outside, it seems, can open space to grapple with inequities within.

Lastly, there is the question of civil society organizations themselves. These groups claim to support communities in the pursuit of justice, but what ensures that they are accountable to their constituents? In Indonesia and the Philippines, many paralegals are a part of membership organizations—such as farmers' and fisherpeople's associations—and therefore must answer to their members. In Sierra Leone, paralegal organizations have adopted the model of the organization Timap for Justice, which includes community oversight boards in every chiefdom where paralegals operate. The boards are charged with ensuring that the paralegals are serving the constituent community effectively.[11] Such structures are crucial for ensuring civil society legitimacy.

Conclusion

The rule of law is a procedural rather than substantive ideal. It has a neutrality that is both a strength, in that it can attract diverse allies, and a weakness, in that it lacks teleological content and can therefore fail to inspire. Rule of law, many people naturally ask, to what end? But grassroots efforts to secure the rule of law are seldom neutral. They are almost always in pursuit of a thicker, substantive vision of society.

In the case of community rights to nature, the struggles described in this chapter are about more than the rule of law. They are about democracy: the ability of people to govern their resources and to undo a history of centralization of authority. The struggles are also about protecting the traditional livelihoods of farming, animal husbandry, and fishing in the midst of industrialization. Last, they are about stewardship of our most precious resources. Research shows that giving communities the power to govern their natural resources leads to decisions that are more environmentally sound (Ostrum 2009; Persha et al. 2010).

The global movement for women's rights is similarly multidimensional. Many of the movement's goals involve the rule of law—the enforcement of nominal rights, for example, and protection from violence. But women are also seeking other kinds of changes, like new cultural norms for gender and family.

Perhaps the rule of law field will find its brightest future by following the lead of the great social movements of our time. If rule of law efforts take their priorities from those movements, the practical significance and moral urgency of the rule of law may grow more clear. And comparative learning across social movements may yield new insights about what methods work under which circumstances. Out of that diversity might emerge a genuine, crosscutting social movement for the rule of law itself.

References

Action Aid. 2013. *Broken Promises: The Impacts of Addax Bioenergy in Sierra Leone on Hunger and Livelihoods.* Johannesburg: Action Aid.

Alden-Wiley, Liz. 2012 "Looking Back to See Forward: The Legal Niceties of Land Theft in Land Rushes." *Journal of Peasant Studies* 39:751–76.

Arezki, Rabah, Klaus Deininger, and Harris Selod. 2012. "Global Land Rush." *Finance and Development* 49:46–49.

Bioenergy and Food Security Working Group of Sierra Leone. 2013. *Guidelines for Sustainable Agricultural and Bioenergy Investment: Sierra Leone.* Freetown: Food and Agriculture Organization of the United Nations.

Carothers, Thomas, ed. 2006. *Promoting the Rule of Law Abroad: In Search of Knowledge.* Washington, DC: Carnegie Endowment for International Peace.

Cotula, Lorenzo. 2013. *The Great African Land Grab? Agricultural Investments and the Global Food System.* London: Zed Books.

Dale, Pamela. 2009. *Delivering Justice to Sierra Leone's Poor: An Analysis of the Work of Timap for Justice.* Washington, DC: World Bank.

Daniels, Ronald, and Michael Trebilcock. 2008. *Rule of Law Reform and Development: Charting the Fragile Path of Progress.* Cheltenham: Edward Elgar.

Deininger, K., and D. Byerlee, with J. Lindsay, A. Norton, H. Selod, and M. Stickler. 2011. *Rising Global Interest in Farmland: Can It Yield Sustainable and Equitable Benefits?* Washington, DC: World Bank.

Golub, Stephen. 2003 "Beyond Rule of Law Orthodoxy: The Legal Empowerment Alternative." Working Paper 41. Carnegie Endowment for International Peace Rule of Law Series.

Goodwin, Laura, and Vivek Maru. Forthcoming. *What Do We Know about Legal Empowerment?* On file with the author.

Hall, Margaux, and Vivek Maru. 2012. "From Bribery to Empowerment." *Project Syndicate*, November 2.

Hammergren, Linn. 2007. *Envisioning Reform: Improving Judicial Performance in Latin America.* University Park, PA: Penn State University Press.

Hawk, Black. 1999. *Black Hawk's Autobiography.* Edited by Roger L. Nichols. Ames: Iowa State University Press.

Hinsdale, W. B. 1927. *The Indians of Washtenaw County, Michigan.* Ann Arbor: G. Wahr.

Indian Ministry of Urban Development. 2006. *Gazette of India Extraordinary.* Pt. II, sec. 3(ii).

Jacobs, Krista, Meredith Saggers, and Sophie Namy. 2011. *How Do Community-Based Legal Programs Work? Understanding the Process and Benefits of a Pilot Program to Advance Women's Property Rights in Uganda.* Washington, DC: International Center for Research on Women.

Jayal, Niraja Gopal. 2013 *Citizenship and Its Discontents: An Indian History.* Cambridge, MA: Harvard University Press.

Jensen, Eric, and Thomas Heller, eds. 2003. *Beyond Common Knowledge: Empirical Approaches to the Rule of Law.* Redwood City: Stanford University Press.

Knight, Rachael, Judy Adoko, Teresa Auma, Ali Kaba, Alda Salomao, Ailas Siakor, and Issufo Tankar. 2012. *Protecting Community Lands and Resources: Evidence from Liberia, Mozambique, and Uganda.* Rome: International Development Law Organization and Namati.

Kohli, Kanchi. 2011. "The Cost of the Coast." *India Together*, August 30.

Kohli, Kanchi, and Manju Menon. 2009. *Calling the Bluff: Revealing the State of Monitoring and Compliance of Environmental Clearance Conditions.* New Delhi: Kalpavriksah.

Koroma, Simeon. 2008. "Paralegals and the Experience of Community Oversight Boards in Sierra Leone." In *Legal Empowerment in Practice: Using Legal Tools to Secure Land Rights in Africa*, edited by Lorenzo Cotula and Paul Mathieu, 77–82. Rome: International Institute for Environment and Development and Food and Agriculture Organization of the United Nations.

Kumar, M. Sunil. 2013. "A Systems Approach for Providing Legal Aid for Land." Paper presented at the World Bank Conference on Land and Poverty, Washington, DC, April 8–11.

Liberia Land Commission. 2013. *Land Rights Policy.* Monrovia: Liberia Land Commission.

Mansuri, Ghazala, and Vijayendra Rao. 2013. *Localizing Development: Does Participation Work?* Washington, DC: World Bank.

Maru, Vivek. 2011. "Legal Power to the People." *Project Syndicate*, November 9.

Namati, Centre for Policy Research, Mundra Hitrakshak Manch, Machimar Adhikar Sangharsh Sangathan, and Ujjas Mahila Sangathan. 2013. *Closing the Enforcement Gap: Findings of a Community-Led Ground Truthing of Environmental Violations in Mundra, Kutch.* New Delhi: Namati-CPR Environment Justice Program.

Namati and Open Society Foundations. 2014. *Appeal to the Member States of the United Nations: Justice Should Be Included in the Post-2015 Development Goals.* Washington, DC, and New York: Namati and Open Society Foundations.

Oakland Institute. 2012. *Farmers Make their Voices Heard on Large Land Investments in Sierra Leone.* Oakland: Oakland Institute.

Ostrum, Elinor. 2009. "A General Framework for Analyzing Sustainability of Social-Ecological Systems." *Science* 325:419–22.

Persha, Lauren, Harry Fischer, Ashwini Chhatre, Arun Agrawal, and Catherine Benson. 2010. "Biodiversity Conservation and Livelihoods in Human-Dominated Landscapes: Forest Commons in South Asia," *Biological Conservation* 143:2918–25.

Ramanathan, Soundaram. 2013. "Rs. 200 Crore Fine on Adanis for Mundra Misdeeds." *Down to Earth*, September 3.

Rights and Resources. 2014. "RRI's Rationale for Engagement." Accessed March 24. http://www.rightsandresources.org/pages.php?id=92.

Sandefur, Justin, Bilal Siddiqi, and Alaina Varvaloucas. 2012. *Timap for Justice: Impact Evaluation Report.* Oxford: Centre for the Study of African Economies.

Sierra Leone State House. 2010. "President Koroma Hails Addax Group's Multi-Million Dollar Biofuel Investment in Sierra Leone." Press Release, February 11. http://www.statehouse.gov.sl/index.php/component/content/article/34-news-articles/142-president-koroma-hails-addax-groups-multi-million-dollar-biofuel-investment-in-sierra-leone-.

Trubek, David, and Marc Galanter. 1974. "Scholars in Self-Estrangement: Some Reflections on the Crisis in Law and Development Studies in the United States." *Wisconsin Law Review* 4:1062–102.

World Bank. 2012. *The World Bank: New Directions in Justice Reform; A Companion Piece to the Updated Strategy and Implementation Plan on Strengthening Governance, Tackling Corruption.* Washington, DC: World Bank.

Notes

1. Rachael Knight initiated this effort while working with the International Development Law Organization; she joined Namati as a program director in 2011.

2. See, for example, *The Indians of Washtenaw County*:

> [L]ack of entire comprehension as to land titles is what led to the misunderstanding of . . . treaties. The most of [Native Americans from what is now Michigan], if not all, supposed when they acceded to treaty bargains that they were simply granting the other party the same and only the same opportunities as they gave one another—that is, a place for a temporary home, rights to hunt in the woods, to navigate the streams and lakes, to breathe the air and to "enjoy" whatever other

211

benefits might occur from this situation, without molestation upon their part. They could not grasp the idea of land title and probably little pains were taken to explain it to them. (Hinsdale 1927)

See also Black Hawk's (1999, 41) autobiographical account regarding nineteenth-century treaties between the United States and Native Americans.

3. I obtained this data from the Bhuj-based organization Sahjeevan. See also, e.g., Ramanathan (2013).

4. Rigorous data are not available. This estimate is based on conversations with Manju Menon, Kanchi Kohli, and Ritwick Dutta, each of whom has worked on environmental justice in India for over fifteen years.

5. This is one of the key findings of a forthcoming book, edited by Varun Gauri and me, that includes empirical studies of paralegals in Indonesia, the Philippines, Kenya, South Africa, Liberia, and Sierra Leone. See also, e.g., Dale (2009, iv, 33); Jacobs, Saggers, and Namy (2011); Kumar (2013); Sandefur, Siddiqi, and Varvaloucas (2012). A forthcoming review of evidence on legal empowerment found a total of forty-five studies of community paralegals (Goodwin and Maru, forthcoming).

6. Kohli and Menon (2009) analyzed government "monitoring reports," which are often derived from self-reported data submitted by firms without any form of verification. Independent review would likely reveal even higher rates of non-compliance.

7. Sonkita Conteh, phone interview with the author, December 2013.

8. See, e.g., Carothers (2006); Daniels and Trebilcock (2008); Hammergren (2007); Jensen and Heller (2003); Trubek and Galanter (1974).

9. I should disclose that I was one of the authors of this document.

10. In contrast to Gandhi's embrace of village-level democracy, Ambedkar described villages as "a sink of localism, a den of ignorance, narrow-mindedness and communalism" (Jayal 2013, 309).

11. Timap cofounder Simeon Koroma elaborates on the experience of community oversight boards in Koroma (2008).

Abstract

This chapter describes how Adeola Ipaye, the attorney general in Lagos State, Nigeria, changed the practice of filing "legal advice"—the process by which prosecutors decide whether to charge a suspect being investigated by the police for a grave criminal offense. It also describes the contribution to that change made by the use of "indicators" of the pace of prosecution that were designed in collaboration with the Program in Criminal Justice Policy and Management at the Harvard Kennedy School of Government. The chapter investigates the operating principles of these indicators, focusing on their dependence on the collective identity of "state counselors" in the Directorate of Public Prosecution and the organizational authority of its leaders. It then offers reflections on the relationship between mundane improvements in the administration of criminal justice and big ideas about the rule of law. It concludes with suggestions about how to cure the current despair in the global effort to promote the rule of law.

7 The Rule of Law in Ordinary Action: Filing Legal Advice in Lagos State

Todd Foglesong

Introduction

This chapter describes how Adeola Ipaye, the attorney general in Lagos State, Nigeria, changed the practice of filing "legal advice" upon the completion of an investigation of a homicide, armed robbery, fatal motor vehicle accident, or other grave offense.[1] It also describes the contribution to that change made by the design and use of "indicators" of the pace of prosecution. The indicators were the result of an extended collaboration between the Lagos State Attorney General's Office and the Program in Criminal Justice Policy and Management at the Harvard Kennedy School of Government, where I currently work. The change in practice, I believe, was the result of the careful cultivation of new relationships—first, between line staff and supervisors at the Lagos State Ministry of Justice and then between prosecutors, police, and the courts.

The work to produce the indicators of the pace of prosecution described in this chapter was led by a team that included Innocent Chukwuma, former director of the CLEEN Foundation in Lagos and now representative of the Ford Foundation's office in West Africa; Raphael Mbaegbu, researcher at the CLEEN Foundation; and Julien Savoye, research fellow and colleague at the Harvard Kennedy School Program in Criminal Justice. None of this work would have been possible without the agreeable collaboration of the attorney general of Lagos State, Adeola Ipaye; his senior special adviser, Akingbolahan Adeniran; the director of public prosecution, Bisi Ogungbesan; and many of their colleagues in the Lagos State Ministry of Justice.

It is not clear why or even whether a story along these lines belongs in a volume about the promotion of the rule of law. The attorney general in Lagos never uttered the phrase "rule of law" in the course of our collaboration; nor did the director of public prosecution or state counselors within that agency ever describe their work, ideas, or goals in these or other exalted terms. The Program in Criminal Justice, for its part, generally eschews the pursuit of grand schemes in public policy: instead, it works with government agencies both in the United States and elsewhere on projects of modest scale and ambition, helping officials resolve problems that get redefined in the course of pedestrian research. It also may be counterproductive to portray an accomplishment in criminal justice in Nigeria as an example or vindication of a big idea about law and the organization of political power that originates elsewhere. Evangelical writing about justice reform abroad can move attention and credit away from the people most responsible for improvements in government and the lives of ordinary people. It can also obscure local sources of inspiration and the manifold motivations for justice.

Nevertheless, there are two good reasons to regard ordinary changes in the practice of public prosecution in Lagos in terms of the advancement of the "rule of law." One is to focus attention on the relationship between banal acts in public administration, on the one hand, and big ideas about law and the power of governments, on the other. If the rule of law is not a set of rules about law and the making of rules but rather something ethereal and intangible—the metaphorical soul, mind, or conscience of a nation—then how do the actions of individuals in ordinary life contribute to it? Do specific decisions in a justice system somehow incarnate the rule of law? Do good practices accumulate over time and accrete into something spectacular, a whole that is greater than the sum of its parts? Do certain processes or procedures make the rule of law more likely?

A second reason is to scrutinize the normative bases of the Program in Criminal Justice's work on indicators: Is the effort to build measures for management purposes in the justice agencies of foreign governments a good thing? Does it prop up or make more reputable systems of justice that are corrupt, unaccountable, or otherwise disagreeable? Does the introduction of foreign-born tools of governance supplant native systems of authority, replacing them with alien implements of power? Does the effort to govern justice through indicators favor the pursuit of efficiency and effectiveness over values in law and justice that are less easily measured and protected? In short, if indicators are not neutral instruments of exchange in the growing global commerce in public policy, then by what moral and ethical criteria should we evaluate their effects around the world?

For this story to fit in this volume, I need to present and defend an unconventional notion of the rule of law. I also have to propose a more stringent definition of "indicators" than one generally finds in the work of international development agencies. I will do so at the end of the chapter. The chapter starts, though, by describing the relationship between the Program in Criminal Justice at Harvard and the attorney general of Lagos, as well as the new understanding of the justice system that came from studying and then trying to expedite the filing of legal advice. It then analyzes the "governance work" of justice indicators—changes in the relationships of authority within government, and changes in the nature of knowledge about systems. The chapter ends with reflections on a potential cure for the despair in the rule of law field.

Building Relationships over Baselines

Adeola was appointed attorney general of Lagos State in the fall of 2011. He had served as a special adviser on taxation and revenue for the governor between 2007 and 2011. When he became attorney general, he inherited a relationship with Harvard's Program in Criminal Justice that his predecessor, Olasupo Sasore, had begun in earnest in the fall of 2009. That relationship may have seemed natural by the time Adeola assumed his position. It all started when Yemi Osinbajo, Lagos State's attorney general from 1999 to 2007, shared the results of his research on delay and corruption in the civil courts at a Harvard workshop funded by the UK Department for International Development, and pledged his agency's interest in a collaboration on "indicators."[2]

I wrote to Olasupo Sasore in June 2009, shortly after Yemi Osinbajo had left office, asking whether the new attorney general would like to work with the program, too. Sasore agreed, and he suggested that we start by working together on pretrial detention. I was thrilled. I fancied myself an expert on the subject, having ran an experiment to reduce overcrowding in a pretrial detention facility in Russia a decade earlier. I also believed that there was a good opportunity to improve on the indicator of detention most commonly used in the world—the proportion of prison inmates on any given day who await sentencing. In fact, I was convinced that Sasore and his staff could generate a much more discerning and actionable indicator—the average duration of detention—by sampling the files of people leaving prison each month. I also knew that we could work with the CLEEN Foundation, a well-regarded human rights organization in Lagos that had steadily built a working rapport with the federal and state police, the commissioner of state prisons, and the former attorney general.[3]

There were plenty of reasons to focus on pretrial detention in 2009. A national initiative to "decongest" prisons, announced by the president in 2006, was yielding uneven effects across the country and was having a limited impact in Lagos, the state with the greatest number of inmates.[4] Every lawyer, public servant, and casual reader of the Nigerian press knew that Lagos's prisons were severely overcrowded—primarily with suspects and defendants awaiting trial. Judges occasionally released inmates they considered to have spent too much time in detention.[5] Scholars, prosecutors, and police acknowledged that there was a deep, structural problem in the justice system, even if they disagreed on its sources and solutions. Sasore convened an interagency justice forum in May of that year to encourage joint efforts to mitigate the problem. All that was needed, I thought, were more precise, reliable, and valid measures.

I spent a few weeks in the summer of 2009 with a researcher from CLEEN and Akeem Bello, the attorney general's senior special adviser, trying to generate a shared understanding of the problem. We visited the Ikoyi Prison, the most overcrowded facility in the state; rummaged through files in the office of the director of public prosecution (DPP); chatted with the director of police investigations; and canvassed a new "case tracking system" that a private software company had set up with funding from the Department for International Development to facilitate the "monitoring and evaluation" of defendants' criminal proceedings. But none of these sources yielded a measure of the detention problem that was reliable, believable across government departments, and able to inspire individual agencies to take action on their own.

Over the next eighteen months, with help from students on summer internships and the assistance of my colleagues during breaks in their calendar, I worked fitfully with senior staff from the Attorney General's Office and researchers from CLEEN to build a new system-level understanding of the dynamics of pretrial detention, along with a baseline from which to chart improvements. One reason for the fitfulness was that the attorney general and his staff were often busy solving more urgent problems—crumbling cases, staffing crises, fuel shortages, and the drafting and defending of new legislation. Their day job—running a government ministry—left little time to pursue the public interest outside the normal channels of public administration. Another reason was that neither the Program in Criminal Justice nor CLEEN wanted to develop this understanding without the Attorney General. We knew that the sense of obligation or duty that can come from new knowledge stems primarily from its production. Real ownership is not received.

We agreed with Sasore's staff that we should measure two things: the duration of custody for remanded defendants and the length of proceedings before and after the completion of police investigations. The attorney general some-how persuaded the warden of Ikoyi Prison, home to one-third of the state's inmates, to permit us to conduct an "exit sample" of those leaving the prison each month. Using the remand warrants that accompanied every inmate to and from prison, we learned that more than half of all inmates spent less than a month in detention. Only a tiny fraction of all prisoners—fewer than 5%—remained in detention for a year or more. But as figure 7.1 shows, the small group of inmates who stayed more than a year accounted for almost half of the prison spaces occupied by pretrial detainees.[6]

To us, the findings were exhilarating. They upset the conventional wisdom about delay as a source of prison crowding. In addition, the bimodal distribu-tion of "length of stay" implied two clear organizational conclusions: first, that the courts responsible for the hundreds of remand prisoners spending short periods in detention should reduce the number of individuals detained in the first place and, second, that the courts responsible for the small number of remand prisoners still in detention after a year should focus on complet-ing those cases soon. But justice systems are rarely so purposive and single-

Figure 7.1 Detainees and prison space used by length of stay in detention, Ikoyi Prison, Lagos, 2011

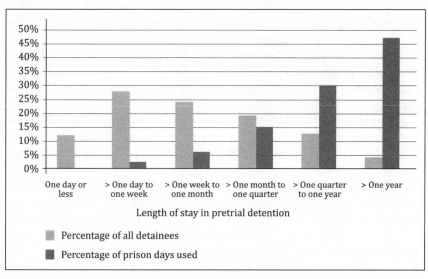

Source: CLEEN Foundation and Harvard Kennedy School of Government, prison exit samples from January, March, and June 2011

minded. Judges are also not teleological: like other legal actors, they face multiple demands and often struggle to reconcile competing obligations.[7] In order for this insight to affect the operation of the justice system, the attorney general would have to persuade the courts not only that reducing the amount and duration of detention was the right thing to do but also that it was more important than other things.

The portrait of detention that we developed, in other words, was diagnostically powerful but politically impotent. To put it another way, the data on the duration of detention lacked the kind of independent and comprehensive political power that most indicators seek. This should not have been a surprise. Data become an agent of change only when they find a genuine principal, and a system of pretrial detention lacks a single governor. A broken system of pretrial detention, moreover, is overdetermined—the result of decisions and actions taken by individuals who are motivated by different and often conflicting ideas, impulses, incentives, and imperatives. This state of affairs has a powerful and insidious political logic, like the "tragedy of the commons." A good system of pretrial detention, conversely, is a bit like a collective good, a minor miracle in constant need of a benevolent invisible hand. In this respect, it may even resemble the rule of law.

There was, we learned, little the attorney general could do on his own to fix the problem with pretrial detention. There was nothing he could do directly about the large number of defendants placed in detention for short periods of time, for most of these cases were prosecuted by the police. His monopoly over prosecution was limited to a tiny fraction of the cases involving detention. Nor could he single-handedly expedite the trials of inmates who had been remanded into custody by the courts. In other words, without the cooperation of other agencies, the attorney general's ability to reduce crowding was minimal.

Fortunately, our inquiry had a parallel track. In September 2009 and again in March 2010, we spent a lot of time trying to understand two practices that were under the control of the DPP, who reported to the attorney general: making a decision about the charge ("filing legal advice") and preparing cases for trial ("filing information"). Our research was flimsy. We were unable to develop a random sample of cases from which to measure the duration and outcomes of prosecution. An archive of completed cases was inaccessible, we were told, and the registry could not generate a list of cases that had come to the DPP from the Criminal Investigations Division (CID) of the state police for any finite period of time. I still do not understand why it was impossible to apply a tourniquet to the flow of cases coming into the office of the DPP. There were two dedicated couriers from CID.

One day, though, Akeem corralled the files of fifty cases that had been tried in 2009. Using a simple tracking sheet that he had devised for measuring the number of days that elapse between key events (such as arrest and arraignment and receipt of the file by the DPP), we calculated that it took an average of 128 days for prosecutors to file legal advice and another 261 days to file information. The combined time exceeded a year. And yet that was still a small fraction of the total time it took for a case to move from arrest to verdict: the trials in these cases alone took, on average, 1,043 days.

If the goal of the attorney general was to reduce prison crowding, it would make little sense to focus on prosecution. As figure 7.2 shows, filing legal advice took only 7% of the total time to complete a case by trial; and filing information took another 16%. Even a dramatic acceleration of these two processes would have only marginal effects on prison population dynamics. But both Akeem and the attorney general were shocked by the delay in prosecution and decided to do something about it.

Over the summer and fall of 2010, Akeem used this tracking sheet to remind state counselors of the attorney general's concern regarding delays in prosecution. The attorney general circulated a "recommendation" to file advice within a month of a case's receipt from CID. At a seminar at Harvard in October, Akeem reported that the time used to file legal advice had decreased to forty-four days, a contraction of nearly 300%. It was a remarkable accomplishment. But I was distracted by the effort to routinize the pro-

Figure 7.2. Proportion of days consumed at each stage of criminal proceedings, Lagos, 2009

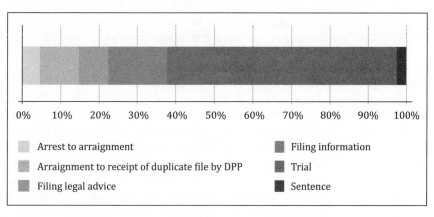

Source: Lagos State attorney general's sample of fifty completed cases, April 2010

duction of the prison exit samples, which I thought were the only reliable source of knowledge about the justice system as a whole. I spent more time working with CLEEN on prison exit samples than the staff of the attorney general on filing legal advice. As a result, the effort to measure and expedite the process of charging defendants was never institutionalized. By the time Akeem returned to teaching at the University of Lagos in the summer of 2011, the effects of the campaign to expedite legal advice had waned.

Better Legal Advice? Measure Speed and Quality

Soon after Adeola was appointed attorney general, I sent him a memo outlining three strategies by which he might continue the work of his predecessor and "demonstrate leadership" of the justice sector as a whole. I recommended that he renew the effort to quicken the pace of prosecution. I also advised that he find a way to supervise police charging practices (many defendants left prison months after their arrival when their cases were "struck out" by a court). Finally, I suggested that he work with the courts to change the practice of calendaring bail hearings at three-week intervals, which, according to our research, was contributing substantially to prison crowding.

But Adeola came to the office with a different set of concerns. He was particularly interested in improving the treatment of victims and witnesses. He also did not want the preoccupation with speed and efficiency in the filing of legal advice to compromise other important objectives. Accelerating the process of filing legal advice was a fine idea, he said, but it was "not the only goal." At a meeting at Harvard in November 2011, he commented:

> I dare say that once we have achieved that shortening of the period of time it takes [to file legal advice], the question that would need to be asked again is about the quality of the advice, to be sure that in trying to speed it up we haven't compromised on quality.[8]

I was moved by this statement. With two colleagues, I spent a week in Lagos in March 2012 working with the attorney general's senior advisers and a fleet of interns and junior staff to develop a method for measuring victims' experiences with justice. Together, we designed an interview protocol that the interns could use to solicit the views and experiences of victims at pretrial conferences, court hearings, and immediately after the trial. The process of developing the instrument and selecting a sampling frame was riveting. And the exercise yielded a better understanding of victims' experiences, which the attorney general then used to design a new "witness support unit." But since we were unable to schedule enough interviews to generate a reliable indicator on a routine basis, we turned our attention back to pretrial detention.

The following week, I joined a meeting of the leaders of most justice agencies in Lagos to discuss how pretrial detention might be redressed jointly by the police, prosecutors, and courts. No agency wanted to reduce the number of defendants remanded into detention, so I proposed a simple indicator at the margins of the problem that my colleagues and I thought would upset no one's sense of safety or justice and could be shared by all agencies: the number of inmates who had already spent more than twelve months in detention in the state's two main prisons. On the day of our meeting, that particular measure was small—twenty-three defendants. The number was generated by the Crime Data Registrar, an information system shared between agencies and which we accessed that day during a break in the meeting. The value of reducing this number was undisputed. But as participants started discussing potential solutions for individual cases, disagreements about specific facts grew into ideological debates about the law and then insinuations of incompetence and interagency meddling. The indicator was shelved.

Instead of waiting for the emergence of better conditions for interagency cooperation, the attorney general redirected his attention to the pace of prosecution. He knew from our research with his predecessor that the number of days it took prosecutors to file legal advice constituted a small fraction of the total time it took to investigate, prosecute, and try defendants. But he also knew that the amount of time it took prosecutors to file legal advice was unnecessarily long. More importantly, he knew that it could be improved. He assigned Akingbolahan Adeniran, Akeem's successor as the senior special adviser to the attorney general, to work with us to generate a way to measure the speed and quality of legal advice.

Akingbolahan, who told us to call him Boye, and his colleague Yinka Ademuyiwa struggled to find the kind of information with which to measure the speed and quality of legal advice. They were both new in their roles and had no formal authority over the forty-two state counselors who filed legal advice. Indeed, they had few direct relationships with the counselors, all of whom were civil servants rather than political appointees. Some of the counselors treated the files in a proprietary manner, which made them difficult to review. The DPP actively cooperated in the enterprise, but her registry still recorded only the date that cases arrived from police investigators—not what happened afterwards. Boye and Yinka had to improvise, hunting down the files from individual prosecutors who were often in court or other locations with their files in hand. Sometimes, the files simply could not be found.

For another three months, we struggled to help Boye and Yinka generate a measure of the duration of this phase of prosecution, even for a small sample of completed cases. The registry was, in our view, in disarray; the files meandered across the office between counselors who charged and counselors who prosecuted cases in court. There were multiple layers of internal review and vetting for each decision. The dates of draft decisions and other events in the life of a case were irregularly recorded on the inside leaf of file covers. Only after several intra-office circulars and personal reminders from the attorney general was it possible for Boye and Yinka to devise a rudimentary yet reliable method for measuring the number of days that elapsed between the arrival of a case from the CID of the police and a final decision on legal advice by a state counselor. Nevertheless, by June 2012, they were reporting this figure to the attorney general on a monthly basis, along with an analysis of the proportion of cases in which advice was filed within one month of the receipt of a completed investigation from the police—a target the attorney general wished to meet.

The initial trend, as figure 7.3 shows, was confusing. On the one hand, the proportion of cases in which counselors were meeting the recommended deadline (thirty days) increased from 0% in March, when we began counting,

Figure 7.3. Time required to file legal advice, Lagos State Ministry of Justice, 2012

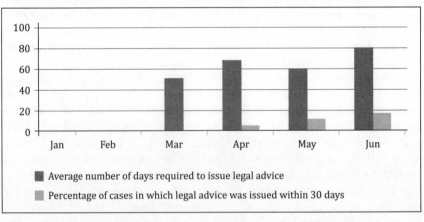

Average number of days required to issue legal advice

Percentage of cases in which legal advice was issued within 30 days

Source: Lagos State Ministry of Justice

to 17% in June. On the other hand, the average number of days required to file advice also increased, from fifty to eighty days. The explanation, we later discovered, lay in the fact that some counselors were focusing on old cases, clearing out the "backlog" in response to the attorney general's instructions, while others attended to new cases, achieving, in some instances, a swift turn-around time.

We advised the attorney general to focus on only one indicator in order to eliminate ambiguity about whether progress was being made and to send a single message to his staff. But the reduction of backlog also mattered greatly to him. It was more than just a symbol of the malaise in prosecution; it was an injustice by itself—a kind of "double jeopardy" for victims, he said. Thus, against our advice, he insisted on both measures. Later, he added a third: an indicator of the "productivity" of prosecutors.

Organization and Authority

In June 2012, the attorney general reorganized the Directorate of Public Prosecutions, dividing its staff into two separate groups of state counselors. One group, the Legal Advisory Unit, would now focus exclusively on filing legal advice. The other, the Court Group, would prosecute cases in court. The attorney general hoped that the creation of the Legal Advisory Unit would improve both the speed and consistency of decisions. It might also allow the Court Group, which assumed responsibility for the subsequent management of all cases that were charged, to improve the quality of prosecution at trial, as well as the attentiveness of state counselors to the complex needs of victims and witnesses.

The reorganization was not intended solely to facilitate the work of the indicators, but it was an essential condition for the indicators to have a positive effect on performance. In order to align their efforts toward a common goal, prosecutors had to see themselves as having a specific and shared objective: swift prosecution. By themselves, the indicators could not cause such an effect. Indeed, indicators that aggregate the results of individual outcomes (such as the average amount of time it takes prosecutors to file legal advice) require a prior collective conscience in order to take effect. But there was another consideration and motive for the reorganization. The attorney general wanted to avoid an ugly trade-off between speed and quality, recognizing that counselors might focus more attention on the objective for which there was a clear indicator and neglect others. He hoped that separating the Legal Advisory Unit from the Court Group would mitigate that potential bind.

Organization, of course, is not the only way to produce collective identity, and the performance effects of the indicators were not immediate, as described below. But the combination of the indicators and organizational innovation conspired to produce two effects on knowledge and governance that facilitated the exercise of authority in a discrete and transparent manner. First, it triggered a cycle of adjustment and innovation. Second, it spawned new forms of accountability in the justice system.

Knowledge and Governance Effects[9]

The first formal use of the indicators took place in October 2012, nearly four months after a method for generating the measure was established. The attorney general convened a meeting with all of the counselors in the Legal Advisory Unit and discussed the charts (reproduced in figure 7.4) depicting the two measures of speed that Boye and Yinka had circulated in advance. There was some anxiety about the likely effects of the indicators, in light of lingering doubts about the accuracy of the data ("What if the measures turn out to be wrong?" Boye kept asking). There was also some concern that counselors might take offense at having their work represented in such an instrumental manner. The results, finally, were mixed. The average number of days to file legal advice had increased from eighty in June to ninety-two in September

Figure 7.4. Time required to file legal advice, Lagos State Ministry of Justice, 2012

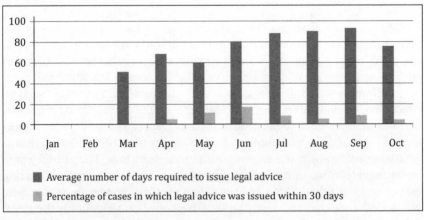

Source: Lagos State Ministry of Justice

226

before falling to seventy-five in October. The proportion of cases filed within thirty days of receipt from the police had fallen from 8.5% to 4.5%.

Nevertheless, the confrontation with the indicators sparked a lively conversation between the attorney general and counselors in the Legal Advisory Unit and yielded an agreement about three things: (i) the strategic significance of issuing timely legal advice; (ii) possible solutions to the obstacles to that goal; and (iii) the need for better reporting practices. Counselors, for their part, acknowledged shortcomings in their performance alongside frailties in the data. They then offered to help improve the reliability of the information by promptly and consistently reporting the status of their cases. Counselors also noticed that it was in their interest to better document their productivity so that it could be reflected in charts. In the end, counselors agreed on a set of steps by which to increase the speed at which they issue legal advice. Their action created the first step in a cycle of feedback and accountability for performance.

The indicators did more than just force a discussion that illuminated organizational processes that required change. They helped diffuse knowledge and power about prosecution, making frontline experience equal to external advice. They also made the attorney general partly responsible for the success of the operation. For example, despite the establishment of a specialized unit for legal advice, which in theory had freed the counselors from an obligation to make court appearances, some prosecutors were still obliged to go to court: magistrate court cases were still assigned to them *personally*. These structural obstacles to desired outcomes could not be ignored if the attorney general wished to see progress. The attorney general, accordingly, had to use his authority to renegotiate the rules for assigning cases with the magistrates' courts. He also had to make available new resources to his staff. Specifically, he decided to transfer these cases to the Court Group and to dedicate two counselors to the caseload, pushing a little further the functional specialization of responsibility he had initiated in June of that year.

A second governance effect resulted from the disaggregation of data by type of offense. As figures 7.5 and 7.6 show, productivity—the third indicator of interest to the attorney general—was particularly low for the group filing legal advice in homicide cases. In comparison, the group filing legal advice in robbery cases was filing more than double the number of cases each month, despite a higher caseload and equal number of counselors. It was unclear why this variation persisted. Its discussion prompted a conversation about the reasons for shortcomings and involved staff in the hunt for solutions, some of which were simple. For example, asked why legal advice had been issued in only a few cases over the past months, the head of the homicide group said that many drafts of advice were still on her desk, awaiting action. She then apologized to counselors in her group who were upset that the charts had failed to capture their good work.

The use of the productivity indicator in disaggregated form exposed different management practices in each department within the Legal Advisory Unit, as well as the need for improvements in counselors' skill sets. The head of the robbery unit had been vigilantly monitoring conduct, and some prosecutors had developed more efficient ways to analyze case files and draft legal advice in complex cases. Taking note of this, the attorney general instructed the heads of each group in the Legal Advisory Unit to emulate the practices of the robbery unit—closely monitoring performance and discussing cases in pairs. He advised them of his intention to follow the work of each individual counselor in the future. The attorney general also organized trainings in which he, Boye, and experienced prosecutors created guidance for cases with multiple defendants. The attorney general eliminated layers of internal review that he deemed superfluous, including the DPP's review of most advice to prosecute. These changes appear to have had a large effect: the number of homicide cases in which legal advice is filed each month now exceeds the number of new cases from the police.

Accountability Effects: Internal and External

The use of indicators to drive performance has changed the structure of accountability within the Lagos State Ministry of Justice. The constituent groups of the Legal Advisory Unit are now expected to achieve progress and contribute to the overall goal of a swift and nimble prosecution service. Prosecutors are also now held individually responsible for results: each counselor writes his or her name on every instance of legal advice drafted. This new accountability has come with additional authority. Not only do line prosecutors now play a central role in the collection of the data underlying the indicators by which they are evaluated, but they are also expected to propose solutions to problems revealed by the indicators. In short, the use of the indicators has done more than simply increase communication between line counselors and senior management—it has created a system of reciprocal responsibility.

The use of these indicators has also begun to make prosecution more publicly accountable, although this particular effect lies at some distance from its originating cause. In response to a request made by the governor of Lagos State to some of his ministers in late 2012, the attorney general started reporting on his activities during monthly press conferences, even sharing the

Figures 7.5 and 7.6. Measures of productivity in the filing of legal advice, Lagos, 2012

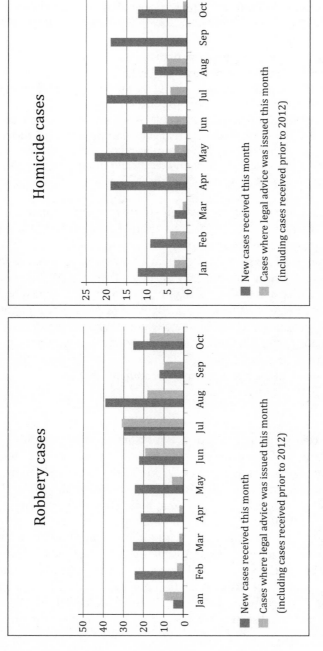

Source: Lagos State Ministry of Justice

monthly figure on productivity. This unexpected "off license" use of the productivity indicator has made the attorney general more accountable to actors outside the justice system, who are now able to scrutinize at least one aspect of the ministry's work.

In late 2012, the press began to report the monthly figures on productivity in prosecution, quoting promises of better performance from the attorney general. An article in *Vanguard*, for example, quoted the attorney general as saying:

> [A] lot of cases are prosecuted daily by the Police at the Magistrate courts. 753 reports of various investigations reached us for legal advice in 2012 and we exceeded the 70 percent mark in dealing with them. In 2013, we shall be stepping up our prosecution to ensure Lagosians that criminals will not go unpunished. (Abdulah 2013)[10]

Such media coverage of prosecution efforts may end up broadening the accountability structure for the administration of criminal justice as a whole. The media may become accustomed to receiving corroborated claims of improved results on a regular basis. It may also ratchet up pressure for continuous progress. During the attorney general's February 2013 press conference, one journalist asked whether the Legal Advisory Unit would be able to sustain its pace of improvement, especially if more cases were brought to the attention of prosecutors by police investigators. While it is too early to tell how durable the demand is for continuous improvements within the ministry, other justice agencies in Lagos have taken notice of the possibility of and pressure around making small-scale yet meaningful change.

Side Effects

One unexpected yet beneficial side effect of the attorney general's effort to accelerate the pace of prosecution is that the judiciary appears more measured in its own approach to resolving delays in pretrial detention. In March 2013, in advance of scheduled visits to the Kirikiri Medium Prison and Kirikiri Female Prison, the chief judge of the Lagos State Judiciary sent the attorney general a list of the 573 inmates who had been awaiting trial in these two prisons for more than three months. The chief judge informed the attorney general that she was considering releasing those prisoners whose cases had not been issued legal advice by the Directorate of Public Prosecutions and whose continued detainment could not be justified.[11] This time, the judge also communicated her intention at a meeting of the Criminal Justice Sector Reform Committee, a forum recently established to discuss and resolve problems common to several agencies, including the Ministry of Justice, the judiciary, the police force, and the prison system.

The judiciary's announcement was unsettling to the attorney general, especially since the profile of the charges for defendants who might be released indicated that prosecutors in the Ministry of Justice were responsible for 423 (87%) of the defendants held in Kirikiri Medium for more than three months. The other 150 had been charged with offenses that are prosecuted independently by the police. A deeper inspection of the list by the attorney general's staff, however, revealed a more complicated and disturbing picture of the relationships between police, prosecutors, and courts. In approximately 200 of the cases on the list, prosecutors had not yet offered legal advice to police investigators, lending credence to the suspicion that prosecution was a source of prison crowding. But in another 200 cases, the DPP had not yet received the case file from the police. This meant that the police had not submitted the file to the DPP even after a magistrate had authorized the suspect's remand.[12]

Instead of accusing the police of the unlawful practice of deliberate delay, the attorney general simply forwarded to the police the list of 200 prisoners awaiting trial whose cases had never been brought to the DPP, inquiring about the status of these cases. The police promptly forwarded 115 of these cases, soliciting legal advice. The influx of cases was inconvenient for the DPP, for it taxed staff resources and compromised forward movement on the indicators regarding the speed of prosecution. Nevertheless, as figure 7.7 shows, a temporary mobilization of a task force on backlog combined with persistent attention to deadlines helped the Legal Advisory Unit sustain progress. From May to July 2013, prosecutors took an average of sixty-six days to file legal advice. Between August and December, this average dropped to fewer than sixty days.

Boye and his colleagues were pleased and also surprised by the resilient manner in which the justice system in Lagos responded to the judiciary's destabilizing initiative. For them, the prospect of a rupture in relationships across the sector seemed considerable. After all, the possibility of an arbitrary release of inmates charged with serious offenses could have been perceived as a threat to public safety, for which the attorney general feels personally responsible—and is sometimes treated so by the governor. But instead of responding antagonistically to the judiciary, the attorney general used the opportunity to strengthen the system of interagency governance. He dropped charges in the cases of those inmates who had been released by the chief judge, thereby demonstrating respect for the judiciary's initiative and also reinforcing the message that swift prosecution matters. Boye then asked the prisons to share, on a monthly basis, the figures on prisoners awaiting trial; this would allow the attorney general to indirectly keep tabs on the incidence of remand, one of the drivers of prison crowding. The attorney general also requested that, in the future, he be involved sooner in the judiciary's review of the list. He then convened a joint training with judges concerning section 264 of the Administration of Criminal Justice Law of Lagos State, which enjoins magistrates to release defendants after sixty days of remand and yet is rarely applied. That training not only reiterated an important formal norm in criminal justice but also suggested that prosecutors and courts must agree on what the law really requires and seeks to achieve.

Indicators in Development

It is easy to exaggerate the role of the indicators in these developments. Without the attorney general's savoir faire, no amount of knowledge and measurement in such circumstances would have made the delays in prosecution susceptible to intervention and improvement. The indicators themselves,

Figure 7.7. Time required to file legal advice, Lagos State Ministry of Justice, 2012–2013

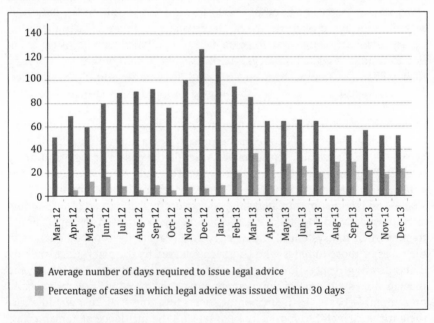

Source: Lagos State Ministry of Justice

232

moreover, did not moderate the relationships within the Directorate of Public Prosecution or between the leaders of different agencies. The attorney general did. Prudent leadership by a gifted individual may explain most of the movement in this story.

But it is also easy to underestimate the role of indicators. In this case, both the indicators themselves and the process of their generation made possible the kind of *understanding* and *politics* required for a leader to exercise influence on a system that is, by design, difficult—if not impossible—to govern.

Understanding and Politics in Justice

Justice and safety are intangible and ineffable concepts. Only the crudest materialist would reduce justice and safety to the bureaucratic operations that agency leaders measure and manipulate on a daily basis. Justice systems are also sprawling and unruly, even in developing countries where the number of victims and offenders, suspects and inmates, police officers and prison guards—not to mention judges, prosecutors, and defense attorneys—seems small when compared to countries such as the UK and United States. One needs conceptual aids to imagine justice as a system, to see the whole behind the sum of the parts, and to see the lasting value of a simple act taken today.

Indicators are, above all, conceptual aids. By counting and connecting the results of organizationally and temporally dispersed decisions, they can help people notice the collective effects of individual action. Indicators can also help people whose actions are modest, whose perch is low, and whose sphere of influence seems small find a relationship between their work and the larger mission for which they labor. Of course, indicators do not do this work alone. Their interpretation—the effort to ascribe meaning to the measure—is what generates a governance effect. Interpretation requires a conversation in a collaborative setting, whether in a board room, a management meeting, or an international seminar. As the police inspector general in Bangladesh recently told me, the discussion of indicators in public can make you "conscious and cautious" in the exercise of political authority.[13]

Not all indicators have these properties and effects, and few are designed with a discursive purpose. Most indicators of justice and safety used in the world today are designed to expose shortcomings in the operation of someone else's system. Many convert complex problems of justice and its governance into a question of compliance with a new and alien norm. Some indicators abbreviate conversations about the purposes of justice rather than fostering deliberations about competing beliefs in society and facilitating choices about how to improve government operations in inauspicious conditions. Only some kinds of indicators help people solve a problem on their own terms at their own pace.

Indicators that are small and designed locally for idiosyncratic and even fleeting purposes may be ideally suited for justice reform. Justice systems all over the world are loosely coupled sets of practices and institutions with no single principal, or principle, in charge. In no country is there a minister with control over and responsibility for all operations and outcomes in justice and safety, nor is there a super-norm with which all behavior must comply. Any change within an individual agency has knock-on effects for others, upsetting not only the routines to which line officials are attached and reasonably expected to be devoted but also the appearance of control that often symbolizes the authority and power of their leaders. Big changes can be a political menace, especially in systems that are imbalanced in favor of one institution, such as the police. In other words, structural adjustments within this sector can be politically destabilizing: they tend to cause decoupling rather than recoupling.

Small Impact, Big Value

But what is the value of such modest changes in justice and an indicator that works on such a small scale? What good are new practices and institutional innovations that do not cause systemic change? What if improvements in justice remain small islands of excellence (or mediocrity) within a broken system of law, public safety, and governance? Why on earth would anyone support that kind of development?

The millenarian mood in law and development is thick these days. Every international organization appears to be in a hurry to cause "transformational" change across the globe, as if a day of judgment were fast approaching. The rush to influence the content of the United Nations' post-2015 development agenda may be adding to such haste. But the urgency may have deeper sources. Behind the fascination with "big data," the feverish focus on "delivery" and "results," and the ever-closer calibration of the "costs and benefits" of development assistance can be discerned a sense of despair about the state of the world and a nervous desire to see and experience transcendence *now*.

The impulse to telescope development—the desire to bring an attractive horizon closer to home—is understandable, especially for individuals and organizations spending money on problems that seem far away. Many of us feel responsibility for the welfare of others; some of us have a big dose of guilt. But raising the stakes and ratcheting up pressure to deliver now on some future promise rarely helps people manage their present challenges in careful ways. It can privilege the ends over the means in justice, which some scholars believe causes the neglect of individual rights (Easterly 2013). It may also confuse "global justice"—relief, repair, and other remedies for structural inequality between states—with "local justice," the search for solutions to conflicts between people and "unending arguments" about what is a good thing and what is the right way to be (Walzer 2011).

Still other considerations, I think, oblige development and justice reform in particular to start and stay local and small. The encouragement of modest adjustments in existing operations is simply a better bet in "fragile states" with "weak governments"—the terms conventionally used to depict the systems of order and rule in many developing countries. This is not just because the legitimacy of innovation within an individual institution is less likely to be contested when it builds on a current practice rather than new routines. It is because of the relatively small size of justice systems in developing countries, which is their greatest comparative advantage. In small systems, minor changes do not have to be "scaled up" before their effects become visible to others and start to inspire complementary or even countervailing action. System-level effects are inevitable in justice, even if they are difficult for outsiders to discern and not always the ones most desired. The value is in the movement, not the end result.

Friendly Help or Technical Assistance

What was the role of the Program in Criminal Justice at Harvard? And what kind of development practice did the project represent? It certainly was not any type of technical assistance. No one on our team knows how to run a government agency in a foreign country. Our default response to questions such as "Is vertical prosecution better than horizontal prosecution?" or "What should we do about witnesses?" was always "I don't know; what do you think?" Instead of offering advice, we shared our skills, which were fairly rudimentary—for example, how to populate a spreadsheet and compile a chart in excel, how to avoid jumping to conclusions when the data are unreliable and the findings are ambiguous, and how to scavenge files for insight about the operation of justice systems.

We provided help rather than assistance—and, like the help one receives from a friend, it sometimes involved unwelcome questions, such as "Why are you trying to do that right now?" and "Are you sure you want to focus on witnesses, even if they are not victims?" We were patient most of the time, and often pursued ideas that we suspected would be dead ends. Weeks elapsed between conversations. Data sometimes got lost. The project zigzagged. We abided by the changing interests and priorities, irregular work patterns, and different customs of collaboration in Lagos.

It probably mattered greatly that our help was subsidized by a third party, the UK Department for International Development. No money exchanged hands between Harvard and the government in Lagos. Not only, though, were there no financial transactions—there were no memorandums of understanding, no program documents, and no contracts. Our program was the party that really needed the relationship: we required results in order to demonstrate our value and acquit ourselves of an obligation to our funder. This general condition gave our colleagues in Lagos the freedom to reject our advice, follow their own intuitions, and determine the rhythm of the collaboration. True, working with an elite institution of higher learning in the United States may have been a draw, but there was no training, no certification, and no financial carrot or political stick.

It also may have mattered greatly that we were not alone. Although no one at the CLEEN Foundation had prior experience in prosecution or policing, the director had a strong public reputation and its researchers were known to be skilled. CLEEN's political credibility opened the door for the project in 2009, gave us confidence in times of doubt, and lent consistency to our communications coming from across the Atlantic. But it was personal rapport and professional respect that made the work continue. No one wishes to be judged or monitored and evaluated by their peers. But watching and learning together with friends is an attractive proposition, especially when it is a consensual threesome.

Indicators and Measures

There are many kinds of indicators in the world of justice and safety, and most serve a wide range of purposes—mobilizing resources, communicating success, denouncing failure, crediting accomplishments, or drawing attention to certain topics while pushing it away from others. The indicators that my program developed with the attorney general of Lagos State served a narrower and fairly immediate purpose in governance: helping a person with formal legal authority acquire influence over a range of loosely coordinated activities. The indicators, in this sense, were assertions of power, but not power itself.[14] They might be called indicators of achievement or performance or some other action. Their main function was to measure the relationship between two complex operations that someone sought to change. That is my definition of indicators.

236

The Rule of Law

What if despair about the state of the rule of law in the world today is mainly the result of what James Goldston suggests in this book—that we know only how to measure the absence of the rule of law rather than its presence? According to this view, there might be much more rule of law in the world today, or at least movement toward the rule of law, than we know and believe. Indeed, the sense of crisis and despair in the movement to promote the rule of law could be partly the result of its excessive attention to failure: we brood over grotesque distortions of the rule of law in some places and ignore the massive number of minor accomplishments in the rule of law that take place all over the world on a daily basis. Taken as a whole, these modest improvements might even outweigh the glaring deteriorations and amount to positive net gains. Perhaps, like the cosmologists of the last century, we are too focused on the luminous matter that comprises only a small fraction of the total energy and matter in the universe.

Another possibility, though, and one that has much less appeal, is that the problem with the rule of law in the world today is actually much, much worse than we realize, and far more grave than the authors in this volume are willing to contemplate. Under this view, the predicament with the movement to promote the rule of law is like that of global warming: there has been an irreversible increase in the global quantum of lawlessness and legal alienation (or whatever the opposite of the rule of law is). It is the cumulative result of the overproduction of tyranny and injustice, which is itself rooted in forces that are so powerful and uniformly appealing that no one really wishes to suppress them. In this scenario, the efforts of individuals and organizations to reinforce the rule of law around the world resemble the remedies for "climate change" recommended by middle-of-the-road environmental economists—a cap-and-trade system for impunity here, special tariffs for tyrants there.

My own view is sunny, but I think the movement to promote the rule of law may have painted itself into a corner by treating the rule of law as a specific set of constitutional arrangements found in just a few settings, or as a particular state of affairs that is rarely exemplified fully and consistently in any one place. The movement may be simply too literal about law and too fictive about justice, insisting on "universal and inalienable rights" that turn out to be eminently alienable and frequently abridged. Is the rule of law really a peaceful and stable state of affairs, an equilibrium of law and power made possible by an elite settlement and restored, when disturbed, by able and impartial courts? Is the rule of law really the degree to which governments are accountable to clear and just laws, fairly enacted, effectively enforced, and equitably applied by independent and demographically representative legal professionals?

There is a different view of the rule of law—one that treats it as a precarious "notion," an idea about the restraint on power that can come from law but which is more like a cultural belief than a commonly observed practice (see Thompson 1975). According to this view, the rule of law is rare, like grace, but it is not providential decision making at critical junctures in history. Instead, the rule of law can be found hidden in plain view: in the practice of political power in conditions of legal uncertainty, the circumspect exercise of public authority in novel conditions, and the prudential management of complex and conflict-ridden systems of justice.

To me, the *manner* in which justice officials in Lagos have gone about quickening the pace of prosecution, improving the quality of police investigations, and mitigating problems in pretrial detention exemplifies the rule of law. They have developed partial and temporary solutions to recurring and probably eternal conflicts between ideas about justice and safety and also between the individuals, institutions, and interests that revolve around them. They have reconciled conflicts between what *is* and what *should be* the norm without moving only in one direction. They have imposed constraints on their own power by developing and then regularly reviewing indicators that measure the pace of a routine operation in the justice system and that register change in painfully small increments. They do not panic when the results are inglorious. They simply try again.

References

Abdulah, Abdulwahab. 2013. "Lagos Has Zero Tolerance for Crimes and Criminals— Ipaye." *Vanguard*, February 14. http://www.vanguardngr.com/2013/02/lagos-has-zero-tolerance-for-crimes-and-criminals-ipaye.

Adesomoju, Ade. 2012. "Decongesting Lagos Prisons." *Bestnaira*, September 24. http://news.bestnaira.com/posts/view/decongesting-lagos-prisons.

Easterly, William. 2013. *The Tyranny of Experts: Economists, Dictators, and the Forgotten Rights of the Poor*. New York: Basic Books.

Foglesong, Todd, and Christopher E. Stone. 2011. "Prison Exit Samples as Tools of Development." *Harvard Kennedy School Indicators in Development: Safety and Justice*, April.

Harvard Kennedy School. 2008. "Indicators of Safety and Justice: Their Design, Implementation and Use in Developing Countries." Accessed March 14, 2014. http://www.hks.harvard.edu/programs/criminaljustice/research-publications/measuring-the-performance-of-criminal-justice-systems/indicators-in-development-safety-and-justice/annual-workshops/2008.

"Lagos Prosecuting 1,204 Cases in Court—Ipaye." 2013. *Naij*, February 11. http://news.naij.com/23530.html.

Merry, Sally Engle. 2011. "Measuring the World: Indicators, Human Rights, and Global Governance." *Current Anthropology* 52(S3):S83–S95.

Onanuga, Adebisi. 2012. "Lagos to Enforce Rule of Law, Says Ipaye." *The Nation*, December 11. http://thenationonlineng.net/new/law/lagos-to-enforce-rule-of-law-says-ipaye.

"Plight of Awaiting Trial Inmates." 2010. *Tribune*, October 16.

Posner, Richard. 2013. *Reflections on Judging*. Cambridge, MA: Harvard University Press.

Stone, Christopher. 2011. "Problems of Power in the Design of Indicators of Safety and Justice in the Global South." *Harvard Kennedy School Indicators in Development: Safety and Justice*, April.

Thompson, E. P. 1975. *Whigs and Hunters: The Origins of the Black Act*. New York: Pantheon Books.

Walzer, Michael. 2011. "Global and Local Justice." Strauss Institute Working Paper 8/11, New York University.

Notes

1. Although the Constitution of the Federal Republic of Nigeria gives the attorney general of each state the authority to "institute and undertake, take over and continue or discontinue criminal proceedings against any person before any court of law in Nigeria," article 23 of the Police Act of 1990 empowers the police to conduct "all prosecutions in any court." In practice, the police charge and prosecute the overwhelming majority of all offenses in the magistrates' courts. In Lagos, the attorney general decides whether to charge and prosecute in police investigations of murder, armed robbery, fatal motor vehicle accidents, serious fraud, and a few other infrequent offenses. The decision whether to charge and, if so, for what offense is called "filing legal advice."

2. See Harvard Kennedy School (2008) for an account of this research and the workshop at which the project on indicators began.

3. CLEEN was established in 1998 by Innocent Chukwuma and worked loyally but critically with successive governments in Nigeria. Its experience with foreign development organizations and capable research unit made it a particularly attractive partner for us and the attorney general.

4. In 2010, the federal Ministry of Justice estimated, through a one-day "survey" of all prisons, that there were approximately 45,000 inmates in Nigeria's prisons. In June of that year, the state controller of prisons for Lagos State told me that the facilities held 5,808 inmates—13% of the total. For press accounts of the number of inmates at the time, see "Plight of Awaiting Trial Inmates" (2010).

5. See, for example, Adesomoju (2012).

6. For a detailed account of the research methods and findings, see Foglesong and Stone (2011).

7. Richard Posner (2013), a judge for the United States Court of Appeals for the Seventh Circuit Court of Appeals of the United States, defends the opposite view.

8. Comments made at the annual workshop on indicators of justice and safety at the Harvard Kennedy School of Government, September 30, 2011 (transcript on file with the author).

9. See Merry (2011) for a description of the effects of global indicators in terms of knowledge and governance.

10. For other accounts of the attorney's general statements, see Onanuga (2012); "Lagos Prosecuting 1,204 Cases in Court" (2013).

11. Earlier, in August and September of 2012, the new chief judge of Lagos had publicly threatened to release from custody all inmates whose length of pretrial detention exceeded twelve months and whose further confinement could not be justified by specific circumstances. In October, the chief judge released 233 such inmates.

12. In another 123 cases, prosecutors had already filed legal advice but defendants were either awaiting the issuance of a formal indictment (a separate phase of criminal proceedings that takes place after legal advice to charge has been filed), the assignment of their case to a judge, or the commencement of a trial at three other postcharge stages of legal processing.

13. Comments made by Hassan Khandker, inspector general of the police, at the annual workshop on indicators of justice and safety at the Harvard Kennedy School of Government, October 2, 2013 (transcript on file with the author).

14. For an earlier statement of this view, see Stone (2011).

Abstract

For certain types of complex development interventions, such as those associated with most justice reform activities, we rarely know in advance what will work. This is so not because policy makers or development professionals are insufficiently bright or diligent, or because they lack the necessary resources or political support. It is because the complex and fluid nature of social systems means that outcomes in response to inputs are rarely knowable in advance with any reasonable confidence. One response to this inherent state of uncertainty is to adopt a more conscious stance of experimentalism. Under such an approach, decisions on what policies, practices, and procedures to apply are not based solely on "expert" opinion (known in the business world as HiPPOs—the "highest paid person's opinion"—or in development as "best practice"). Rather, practitioners begin with a candid admission of doubt about what is most likely to be successful. They then design projects that allow data to be collected in real time from an evolving set of activities, and use the most encouraging empirical findings to iterate toward locally legitimate, context-specific ("best fit") solutions. This chapter sets out an example of this experimentalist approach as tried by the World Bank's Justice for the Poor program in Sierra Leone. The program, which sought to improve justice and accountability outcomes in the delivery of health services, tested a range of intervention and measurement options with different cost implications and levels of implementation complexity. This was more than simply undertaking randomized controlled trials (increasingly popular in development work) on justice programming—it represents a broader approach of experimentalism. It offers one example of how justice programming can be a vehicle of greater humility, enhanced learning, and (we hope) increased development effectiveness.

8   From HiPPOs to "Best Fit" in Justice Reform: Experimentalism in Sierra Leone

Margaux Hall, Nicholas Menzies, and Michael Woolcock

Introduction

To find out what happens when you change something, it is necessary to change it.
    —Box, Hunter, and Hunter (1978), quoted in Gelman (2010, 1)

The inspiration for this chapter stems from an exhortation by the volume's editor, David Marshall, lamenting the absence of substantive learning in justice reform activities. We are not sufficiently pessimistic to conclude that there is a complete lack of learning across all justice practice, but we do concur with the general sentiment. Internationally supported justice reform[1] initiatives can do a much better job of promoting systems that are accessible, legitimate, and effective in the eyes of everyday citizens; and to do so, they must learn

Our heartfelt thanks go to Gibrill Jalloh, Lyttelton Braima, Felix Conteh, Isata Foray, Kadija Shaw, Frederick Kamara, and Alfred Conteh, on whose hard work much of this chapter's analysis and argument rest. We would also like to recognize Vivek Maru, formerly with the World Bank and now with Namati, who designed and led the initial stages of this work and who has remained a crucial partner in its implementation. We also appreciate the many helpful comments and suggestions we received during the authors' workshop at Harvard Law School. The work described herein was possible due to generous support from the World Bank's Nordic Trust Fund and the Trust Fund for Environmentally and Socially Sustainable Development. The views expressed in this chapter are ours alone and should not be attributed to the World Bank, its executive directors, or the countries they represent.

more effectively from their experiences. While there are many opportunities for improved learning from justice practice,[2] we offer a constructive response to Marshall's concern by focusing here on a development project in Sierra Leone.

In our view, justice practitioners would do well to adopt an approach that is ubiquitous in the web-based tech world (and elsewhere)—namely, continual testing and refinement of operational alternatives based on ongoing data gathering.[3] Most tech leaders are inherently skeptical about their ability to predict the way people will react to their products. Before Google makes any decisions about the way ads appear in users' search feeds, or Amazon decides how shopping results are displayed, or the Obama campaign finalizes the content of an email blast seeking donations, a myriad of alternatives are tested. Different versions of text, color, images, and the like are run before an unsuspecting subset of users to see how they react. Does one version lead to more clicks, purchases, or donations compared to others? It is on the basis of this data—not prior assumptions or perceptions about what will be most effective—that versions are scaled out to all users. This principle is so embedded within tech culture that employees at Google have noted that "experimentation is practically a mantra" (see Tang et al. 2010).

The types of changes one encounters in justice reform are much more complex (and arguably consequential) than those of most web outfits, yet we structure projects as though we are more certain about the links between our activities and desired outcomes.[4] We know that very different *forms* of justice systems (and their constituent institutions) have emerged in different places, serving broadly the same *functions*. Most obviously, common-law and civil-law systems involve different institutional structures and practices, yet it is hard to argue that one delivers demonstrably "better" justice. Similarly, each member country of the Organisation for Economic Co-operation and Development has discerned, over long periods of time, its own particular way of structuring relations between banks and the state, of conducting elections, of regulating businesses, and of administering property (rights). It is rare, however, for justice reform initiatives to begin by accepting that different (known or unknown) forms may be optimal in a particular space, let alone by testing two (or more) alternatives alongside each other to discern what might be most appropriate. Human rights advocates might argue that we *do* know how we want the justice system to look—it is set out in international conventions. Yet even if these conventions represent a level of agreement on the normative principles and values that we would like a system to imbue, we do not necessarily know the forms and processes that will best embody these principles in any one place.

The practice of justice reform could be improved by embedding in project architectures the uncertainty that most thoughtful legal reform practitioners experience—in other words, by adopting an explicit infrastructure of experimentalism.[5] Through experimentalism, project architects monitor projects in real time and use emerging information to refine the project design. Ultimately, this approach seeks "best fit" solutions for a particular context and set of problems. In short, the shift we propose might look something like table 8.1.

This chapter's case study of the World Bank's Justice for the Poor work in Sierra Leone illuminates some of what we mean by context-specific experimentalism in local justice reform and seeks to document the approach's virtues, challenges, and limits.

Learning in "Classic" Justice Projects Is Poor

Internationally supported justice reform work straddles a wide range of objectives, disciplines, and approaches—from transitional justice and human rights promotion to business climate reform and violence prevention. This makes it difficult to clearly define what justice reform "is" and to make claims about how and whether it "works." That said, much of the field[6] has focused on the justice-related institutions of the state (e.g., legislation, courts, and police) and on delivering resources (e.g., goods, technical assistance, and capacity building) to address gaps, deficits, and dysfunctions, whether real or perceived (see Berg, Isser, and Porter, this volume). It has generally done so by working toward what external experts deem to be "best practices" that accord with international norms.[7] In the business world, these "best practices" are often

Table 8.1. Shifting from classic justice projects to experimentalism and "best fit"

"Classic" justice projects ⟶ Experimentalism	
• Project design completed at the start; includes all activities and "success" indicators. • Purpose of monitoring is to ensure compliance.	• Project design ongoing; parallel testing of operational alternatives; space provided for new iterations to cascade in response. • Monitoring promotes intra-project learning and adaptation.
• Evaluation at project "midterm" and end, based on data collected by external expert evaluators.	• Evaluation constant, based on justice institution data, surveys, and qualitative work.
• Evaluation of singular effort based on inputs and outputs.	• Evaluation of impacts compared to alternative uses of funds (and no activities).

derided as HiPPOs—the highest paid person's opinion—as are the individuals who espouse them. According to one definition, HiPPOs are leaders so confident in their ability to identify the correct approach that they need neither empirical data nor the wisdom of others to validate, or challenge, their beliefs (see DeRose and Tichy 2013).

By its nature, this "classic" type of justice programming privileges certain types of evaluation and learning. Because it is known ex ante what kind of institutional forms should exist ("best practices" informed by international norms tell us) and it is presumed that form determines function (i.e., how those institutions should perform), there is little need to experiment with different approaches. As a result, much justice programming has constrained local experimentation by prescribing the forms and functions that should exist in a particular space, without any reference to the underlying needs or challenges (see Andrews, Pritchett, and Woolcock 2013). A look at design documents for standard justice projects illustrates this bias: such projects usually diagnose deficiencies within existing justice agencies and then propose a set of inputs to remedy those deficiencies. Once the inputs are proposed, a separate specialist is engaged to design a monitoring and evaluation framework, which includes indicators of "success" that will illustrate the progress that has been made toward delivering the predetermined inputs. As in much development work, implementation of the activities is commonly subcontracted to an entity separate from that which undertook the design, limiting the ability of implementation feedback to alter the design as the project progresses. Indeed, in an effort to hold the implementation team accountable for "results," there is usually little flexibility built into the design, and changes are both bureaucratically cumbersome and viewed with suspicion.[8] Within the implementing party, the "monitoring and evaluation" function is often further separated from the core implementation function. This separation of design, implementation, and evaluation means that projects are rarely structured in a way that maximizes learning.

More recently, the framing of justice programming has undertaken a rhetorical—and in some cases operational—shift, expanding the range of legitimate issues and interlocutors (see, e.g., World Bank 2011). The World Bank's Justice for the Poor program has been part of this process, contributing both to the way "justice in development" work is conceived and to how it is undertaken and assessed (see Sage, Menzies, and Woolcock 2010). The program seeks, first, to understand a population's most important sources of injustice and grievance and, then, to support the emergence of legitimate and effective justice institutions, through a more targeted focus on justice issues across sectors of development, and through deeper engagement with locally driven processes of social contestation. Given this recent shift in justice programming and the problems with "classic" projects, there is a need to modify approaches to measurement and iterative learning. Below, we explain one way in which the Justice for the Poor program has attempted to introduce new models.

Doing It Differently: Experimentalism in Sierra Leone

Since 2010, our experimentalism in Sierra Leone has proceeded along multiple lines of inquiry. Not only have we been interested in the impacts of specific justice interventions in improving health services and outcomes, but we have also explicitly tested interventions that vary in terms of implementation complexity and cost (to understand their sustainability and scalability). In addition, we have tested different methods of measurement, again with different complexity and cost implications.

Health Context

A small West African country with just under six million residents, Sierra Leone emerged from civil war in 2002 (see Zhou 2009), is still considered a fragile and conflict-affected state (see World Bank 2013), and remains near the bottom of the United Nations Human Development Index.[9] While the country has enjoyed relative peace and stability since 2002 and has recently experienced strong economic growth, more than half of its population lives below the poverty line.[10] The country's health statistics reflect similar deprivations: Sierra Leone has among the world's highest under-five and maternal mortality rates (see United Nations Children's Fund 2012, 87). One in six children dies before reaching the age of five.

In April 2010, President Ernest Bai Koroma launched the Free Health Care Initiative for pregnant and breast-feeding women and for children under five years of age. Even with the initiative, however, significant problems in care persist—improper fees, shuttered clinics, and murky lines of accountability (see, e.g., Amnesty International 2011). The government enacted the initiative without any supporting policy documents detailing entitlements and obligations, leaving considerable room for ambiguity, confusion, and extractive opportunism. For instance, one nurse in Moyamba District was reported as providing free immunizations to infants, but demanding payment for registration cards to document the immunizations and exacting cups of rice as gratitude for her "free" vaccinations (see Hall 2012). In a more sympathetic case reported in Tonkolili District, a nurse was erroneously deleted from the government's payroll but nonetheless continued to operate, on a voluntary basis, a clinic serving 3,000 residents. She asked patients for optional "contributions" to help support herself, which community members felt compelled to provide. Individuals who could not afford these "contributions" avoided the clinic, even if they qualified for free health care.[11]

Evolving Operational Alternatives

The scale and preventable nature of many of the maternal and under-five deaths in Sierra Leone are an undeniable injustice. However, one might reasonably conclude that such service-delivery-related problems[12]—even this entire domain of development policy—should be left for public health and other specialists, not justice practitioners. Yet our hypothesis was that ambiguity in law and policy, as well as in the means to enforce them, was contributing to the country's tragic health statistics. In other words, a child's ability to access immunizations depends not only on the formal "letter of the law" (i.e., the content of the Free Health Care Initiative) but also on the discretion of various frontline agents who interpret and give effect to that law. We predicted that legal and quasi-legal approaches—such as instituting community-clinic "compacts," improving administrative procedures, clarifying rights, creating grievance channels, and using paralegals—could remedy some of the underlying reasons for service breakdowns, complementing other approaches and leading to enhanced service delivery.[13]

The account that follows offers a linear narrative of an evolutionary process of experimentalism. It does so in an attempt to paint a clear picture of how a particular program actively measured its own outcomes and then adapted to emerging information. It illuminates with a level of self-consciousness some poor choices, missed opportunities, and misdiagnoses; and it also highlights the fortunate choices (whether deliberate or not) that led to demonstrable change. Table 8.2 summarizes the implementation and measurement mix, and the following narrative provides insight into how and when these elements emerged. As with any development project, the true, lived experience was more "messy" and complex than any retrospective account can likely capture.

Early steps

The work began in 2009 as a small pilot project under the World Bank–financed Decentralized Services Delivery Program.[14] This program included funding for a social accountability component that would help empower citizens to demand better services from local government officials.

248

Although our team had been conducting in-depth research on the local context, grievances, and areas of contestation for many years, we began our consideration of program alternatives by acknowledging that we did not know what would work best. As a result, we returned to the field to more deeply consider what sorts of justice-based interventions might best respond to grievances around service delivery at the community level.[15] We unearthed a range of gaps in the functioning of local service delivery—in health, education, water, and sanitation—and saw that overall local governance structures were fragmented. There was considerable demand for creative approaches to accountability in the health sector at the time. The country's poor health outcomes, which had become well known, were a centerpiece of the government's agenda for change. The government and civil society had observed gaps in monitoring and accountability in the form of improper user fees, absent nurses, and missing drugs, to name a few. The government's proposed solution was to employ citizens (who are closest to the point of service deliv-

Table 8.2. Summary of implementation and measurement options

	Randomized controlled trial		Cascading experimentation	
Intervention	Implementer	Measurement	Implementer	Measurement
Community-clinic compacts	International nongovernmental organizations (NGOs)	Household community and clinic surveys	Local paralegal organizations	Administrative records; observation; interviews
Nonfinancial awards	International NGOs	Household community and clinic surveys	N/A	N/A
Paralegal health cases	N/A	N/A	Local paralegal organizations	Case tracking; interviews; administrative records
Health management committees	N/A	N/A	Local health NGOs	Case tracking; interviews; administrative records

ery) to monitor service provision and press for change. At the same time, an encouraging research study had just emerged from Uganda that indicated dramatic results in reducing under-five mortality through community participation in local compacts (see Bjorkman and Svensson 2009). Our team thus decided to engage in the health sector and adapt the Uganda experiment to the Sierra Leonean context.

Community-clinic compacts

In the community-clinic compact intervention, representatives[16] from every village in a clinic catchment attended a meeting at which they viewed a scorecard documenting their clinic's performance compared to that of others in the district. Trained facilitators guided the discussion and shared information on healthy behaviors (e.g., increased hand washing and decreased open defecation) and on citizens' service entitlements and health workers' obligations. During the meeting, community members were encouraged to consider local actions that they could take to address health issues. Health clinic staff attended a separate meeting where they conducted the same exercise. Community members and clinic staff then attended a joint facilitated meeting where they discussed health challenges and made mutual commitments to one another to improve health care delivery.[17] These clinic-community commitments were drafted in the form of "social compacts"—or locally constructed contracts—drawing on conceptions of "soft law."[18]

Following these initial meetings, the community representatives and nurses for each clinic met on a quarterly basis to evaluate and score one another's compliance. This focus on mutual accountability in the compacts was a response to noted weaknesses in the principal-agent framing of much social accountability work—especially for fragile and clientelistic contexts such as Sierra Leone (see Booth 2012). The mutual-accountability framing also sought to address real risks to individuals and groups from "one-sided" action.[19]

In its initial conception and planning, the community-clinic compact intervention was to unfold as a small pilot. The team would test and refine the methodology for one year, transferring lessons to programming in the health sector and beyond. But as the planning unfolded, the team was contacted by a set of academic researchers from well-regarded universities, who suggested that the government utilize a randomized-controlled trial (RCT) to rigorously evaluate the impact of the intervention (as was done in the Uganda study). Our team found the promise of rigorous evaluation persuasive, and we agreed, without anticipating the impact that our decision would have on our flexibility to iteratively pursue a variety of evolving operational alternatives.

One constraint of the RCT was the need to implement at scale. The need for statistical power to measure impact meant that more clinics would have to be involved—and so the intervention grew in size to encompass (as either treatment or control) 254 health clinics across four of the country's thirteen districts. International nongovernmental organizations (NGOs) became the only actors with the capacity to conduct the interventions at this scale, as well as to navigate the complexities of government-run (World Bank–directed) procurement policies. Even then, the complexity of the contracting process delayed implementation for almost a year. With three international NGOs involved, the cost of the intervention ballooned.[20] Further, the RCT presupposed a "treatment" that was as static as possible to allow for the most robust measurement of impact. This increased supervision costs to ensure "uniformity" and was directly at odds with an approach of iteration within and across clinics. The real cost of limiting iteration became apparent when the compact process turned out to be much more complicated for facilitators and participants to implement than first imagined.

Nonfinancial awards

As the community-clinic compact intervention evolved, we worked with the academic researchers to plan another experimental component as part of the same RCT. This nonfinancial award intervention was intended to be less complex and costly to implement. It drew on a program in one of Sierra Leone's districts, wherein the district medical officer motivated clinics to compete against one another for recognition. The nonfinancial award intervention—named "Respect Pass Money" (Krio for "hard work trumps financial reward")—ranked all of the clinics within a single district on the basis of clinic utilization data and user feedback. The intervention presented a wall clock to the best-performing and the top quintile of most-improved clinics in each district, and a certificate to each individual working at those clinics. One goal of the intervention was to examine whether and how user feedback could be integrated into a national performance-based financing program in the health sector, which to date includes quality and utilization metrics but not user feedback. This intervention, like the compact intervention, engaged the same set of international NGOs as implementers. It did so for the same reasons—those NGOs were able to navigate procurement policies and implement the activity at a large scale.

Before the RCT experiments could begin, the researchers needed to collect baseline data to "match" similar clinics and randomly assign them to treatment or control groups. Implementation was delayed because, among other things, the research team embarked on this rigorous process of data collection during the country's rainy season. The contemplated "pilot" had become an enormous and costly research experiment; the stakes were now even higher. Our team was also beginning to recognize that the RCT interventions were expensive and incredibly complex—so much so that the government of Sierra Leone likely lacked the funding and capacity to scale them *even if* they were effective. In response to this realization, and even before we had started the experiments, we went back to the drawing board to contemplate what we dubbed "a lower-cost hybrid." We were eager to pursue alternatives that would allow for more active, iterative experimentation within and across components of the project.

Paralegal health cases

One way in which we aimed to improve the durability and affordability of our interventions was by engaging existing accountability structures, including local management committees and paralegals. We predicted that using local groups—rather than international NGOs—as the implementers could reduce costs (in light of local groups' lower overhead expenses); these groups could also serve as a permanent local infrastructure for improving accountability around service delivery. Further, early qualitative research alongside the RCT had cast doubt on how effectively community-clinic compacts could resolve more complex grievances. Many health injustices were emerging in the context of power imbalances (e.g., chiefs expropriating critical resources) and policy confusion (e.g., understanding whether registration cards or ambulatory care were included in the Free Health Care Initiative), which called for engagement with more traditional legal avenues—administrative redress mechanisms or, in extreme cases, the threat of litigation.[21] Our team therefore wanted to explore the role of paralegals in clarifying the law and resolving health problems.

In examining the existing systems for grievance resolution, we were struck by the power of paralegals in resolving disputes. Community paralegals (lay persons trained in the law) reside in approximately 40% of Sierra Leone's chiefdoms and represent an existing, cost-effective "institutional architecture" (see generally Maru 2006). Our intervention thus sought to train local paralegals, whom we identified through two local paralegal organizations, in health accountability and administration and in how to take up individual and community-level health cases.

Another response—an attempt to improve the sustainability of the community-clinic compacts—was to train a limited number of paralegals to test community-clinic compact processes in four clinic sites in two additional districts (outside of the four districts covered by the RCT). Our hypothesis was that since paralegals already engage in routine mediation, they may be particularly well suited to facilitate the community-clinic compact processes.

Health management committees

During the course of implementing the above activities, the then minister of health and sanitation launched citizen-based accountability committees to oversee health-care delivery at the clinic level.[22] Working with partners, we helped the ministry draft terms of reference for the committees. These new health management committees were constituted quickly and trained over a period of less than two weeks.

Having attended the trainings and observed the limited capacity of these committees to assume the tasks within their ambit, we initiated an additional training program for a select group of committees to see whether they could be made more effective. In particular, our program examined ways to link the committees with other accountability structures at the community and district levels, as well as to empower these committees to address collective community grievances. We also began to investigate ways in which the committees could work with paralegals, through a compact process or otherwise, to navigate grievance channels on behalf of communities or clinics.

In assessing the impact of the paralegal and health-management-committee activities described above, we adopted a different, smaller-scale method of evaluation than with the RCT. Our selection of the districts for the activities was driven largely by the location of willing paralegal organizations. Within these districts, three treatments (paralegals trained in health cases; paralegals facilitating compacts; and additional health committee support) and a control were assigned across eight comparable chiefdoms,[23] with matching on the basis of remoteness of the clinic and clinic utilization data for key maternal and under-five health services. Although the sample size was too small for any robust statistical comparison, our assignment of treatment (and control) activities in this way provided some confidence that the impacts (or lack thereof) could be attributable to the activities themselves rather than the underlying nature of the locations. To further reduce costs, we adopted simplified measurement techniques that relied on data collected from clinics by the Ministry of Health and Sanitation, as well as case tracking (which entails conducting interviews with parties to a health grievance) and key informant interviews. These data were collected prior to and during the interventions.

Policy support for the Ministry of Health and Sanitation

Through the implementation of the above activities, the impact of the policy gaps became evident. As noted earlier, Sierra Leone's Free Health Care Initiative was not accompanied by any policy documents, and it lacked guidance regarding the specific services covered. Confusion and opportunism were therefore rife. We documented this situation and engaged closely with the Ministry of Health and Sanitation to encourage the issuance of policy decisions and clarification, including the publication of a health "fact sheet" that was distributed to participants in the interventions and to individuals throughout the country. To date, we continue to work with the ministry to respond to emerging tensions around the Free Health Care Initiative. For instance, one tension relates to drug supply. While UNICEF has continued to support the Free Health Care Initiative, other donors (including the World Bank) have recently begun supporting a system of cost-recovery drugs for users who are not covered under the Free Health Care Initiative. As a result, clinics often receive two supplies of the same drug, which leads to staff confusion (and room for opportunism). For example, if Free Health Care paracetamol runs out, but cost-recovery paracetamol is available, should staff provide that drug free of charge to qualifying users of the Free Health Care Initiative? Together with the community paralegals and other local agents who report local grievances and confusion, we have helped clarify the policy landscape as it continually shifts.

Key Elements of the Experimentalist Approach
Iterative design, accounting for varying costs and complexity

The open nature of the "project" not only allowed us to test options in parallel, as is common in experiments, but also gave us the flexibility to iteratively design, refine, and test new alternatives. Such an approach enabled us to test the compacts against the nonfinancial awards, with the latter being an order of magnitude cheaper and much simpler to implement. Experimentalism allowed us to further iterate and use local paralegals to run compact processes more cheaply than international NGOs could. Paralegals could also test simpler compact processes that they predicted would work well in a particular setting, based on their past experiences in that community. Especially outside of the RCT, we allowed the frontline implementers to use discretionary behavior, which provided for a rich level of "subexperimentation." When the paralegals led their own set of compact interventions, for example, they each designed and tested their own scorecards and then graded themselves and one another on the clarity of their presentations.

254

Engaging accountability problems at many levels

Our interventions engaged different actors and sought to remedy injustices at different levels. Our experiments tested the following types of engagement at different levels: *refining existing government interventions* (health management committees and nonfinancial awards); *engaging existing accountability networks* (health management committees and paralegals); *clarifying underlying legal landscapes* (policy guidance to the Ministry of Health and Sanitation); and *developing new quasi-legal processes* for local health-related problem solving (community-clinic compacts). While the community-clinic compacts targeted possible improvements *absent* any broader structural changes to the health system, it quickly became clear that many local problems could not be resolved without inputs from higher up the line. For example, while local compacts seem to have been effective in reducing nurse absenteeism,[24] they have been incapable of resolving the challenge of nurses being omitted from government payroll. In this instance, agents such as paralegals have been particularly helpful in advocating on behalf of nurses. By embracing flexibility in design, we were able to target the same broad injustice (poor health-service delivery's contribution to dire health outcomes) through a range of approaches.

Multiple means of measuring impact

The experimentalist approach extended to *what* we measured. We measured a vast range of information, including the utilization of services and objective health outcomes,[25] levels of community participation and trust, and changes in general welfare and political engagement. The inclusion of outcomes beyond immediate justice-related measures was driven by the nature of our engagement on health issues; nevertheless, we would suggest that more justice practitioners consider this approach, for it helps demonstrate the impact of justice work to a broader development audience. Further, to determine "impact," nearly all justice reform work relies on experts' or evaluators' ex post observations of a singular project or program. In contrast, we set up counterfactuals ex ante to measure different means to achieve the same ends (as well as if nothing was done—i.e., control sites).

Experimentalism was also apparent in *how* we measured impact. The RCT surveys covered a raft of information, yet their nature as panel surveys limited their possibilities for evolution. In response, our qualitative research was sensitive to feedback from interlocutors regarding the changes they were observing (whether positive, negative, or nonexistent). The researchers were also able to seek out the views of people who were important to service-delivery outcomes but who were not covered by the large respondent surveys (e.g., chiefs, district health officials, and religious figures). When researchers returned from each field visit, the scope of measurement and the interlocutors engaged were refined to include evolving themes and dynamics of change.

RCT measurement was complicated and expensive, as was the underlying design, which evolved to test increasingly nuanced research questions. The RCT surveys involved tens of enumerators, took months to prepare and field, and required specific technology to collect and analyze the data. The design, in turn, was also incredibly complex—facilitators and even the international NGOs required significant technical support from the Justice for the Poor program in order to implement the intervention according to the design documents. The capacity to implement such programs and measure them through an RCT is limited in Sierra Leone.[26] In total, the cost of design, implementation, and measurement of both the compacts and nonfinancial awards far outweighs the government's current resources to introduce the programs at a broader scale across Sierra Leone's thirteen districts.[27] While the initial thinking was that compelling results would lead to more donor resources to support the government in expanding these programs, perhaps a greater constraint is the mismatch of methods to existing local implementation capacity, even if resources are available. Further, while RCT data have credibility in some circles in terms of providing confidence about causal relations,[28] in our experience the process was alienating for those tasked with implementing the activities and understanding the outcomes, potentially undermining the impact of the results. The alternative strategy of using an iterative approach allowed us to test less complex and possibly more sustainable designs and means of measurement, such as the use of case-tracking methodologies and ministry of health data. Clearly, with different means of measurement there are issues to be balanced with respect to data quality and scope, as well as the ability to collect it.

Suggestions for a More Experimentalist Justice Practice

Given the nature of justice reform activities and the difficulty (if not impossibility) of confidently predicting outcomes ex ante, programming could benefit from the adoption of a more experimentalist mindset. Adopting such a mindset would represent a radical shift from the status quo and would require cultivating an infrastructure to support experimentalist policy makers and practitioners. As our discussion above shows, *experimentalism* should be conceived of as a practice made up of many parts and as more than just the implementation of (randomized) *experiments*.[29] In our view, experimentalism has three defining features, the first two of which are relevant to experiments and the third of which goes a bit deeper. First, practitioners are deliberate about what they try, when they try it, and where they try it; ideally, they test operational alternatives against one another and a counterfactual. Second, practitioners engage in systematic data collection, ideally before, during, and after an intervention (Gelman 2010, 4). And third, practice is designed to allow space for iterative program design to flow from experience and for these options themselves to be subject to the first two features.

In light of these three defining features of experimentalism, what does it mean to adopt an experimentalist mindset in justice? It means moving from narrow "successful/unsuccessful" evaluations on a set of predetermined outcomes to evaluations that anticipate a cascading range of alternatives from the start. How to pick the initial alternatives then becomes an important art. It is of little use to test activities that have a minimal chance of being continued should they prove effective, including due to their cost, complexity, or political sensitivity. In picking the operational or policy alternatives to be tested, it is important to involve those actors with an interest in the results and the ability to influence institutional reform (e.g., managers, politicians, and unions). One challenge with our project was that even though we worked closely with the Ministry of Health and Sanitation, our activities were largely funded by another ministry—the Ministry of Local Government, which has little day-to-day operational oversight of the staff working in health clinics.[30] Finally, it is important to be mindful of tensions that may exist between, on the one hand, having researchers interested in questions and approaches with international or cross-country resonance and, on the other, having local relevance and feasibility. In our case, we started with the former (community compacts) and broadened to the latter (paralegals).

Certain areas of justice programming may be particularly amenable to an experimentalist approach.[31] One such area is the training of justice personnel—police, judges, lawyers, and paralegals. International donors and domestic taxpayers spend millions of dollars each year on the training of these personnel, with almost no robust data on the impacts, let alone comparative data on the effectiveness of different training curricula or delivery models.[32] Applying an experimentalist approach in this arena would be relatively straightforward. For instance, training programs could be structured so that recipients are split into three groups: the first group would receive intensive weeklong residential courses; the second would receive periodic lunchtime seminars; and the third would undertake peer-to-peer learning. The impact on the three groups could be measured according to metrics of interest (e.g., speed of decision making and adherence to rules). This would provide a more informed basis than currently exists for scaling up certain methods and dropping others. Another area in which experimentalism could be engaged is in efforts to improve efficiency in the issuing of judgments. One real-world example of an experimentalist approach in this area is a World Bank–supported effort to alert judges in Senegal about delays in issuing judgments (see Kondylis and Stein 2012). Finally, a third area is the use of management techniques **to** incentivize justice personnel to improve their performance. Techniques that mix supervision, sanctions, and rewards (both financial and nonfinancial) are almost wholly untested and ripe for experimentation.

Constraints and Limitations

Of course, the experimentalist approach has a number of constraints and limitations.[33] Getting an organization or agency to focus on properly implementing *one* policy or activity can be a challenge—getting it to do two (or more) things at once, or to respond to real-time feedback coherently and efficiently, increases the chances that projects are implemented poorly (or not at all). Testing operational or policy alternatives is also of little use if there is no consensus on the desired outcomes or the definition of "success." In justice, the targeted outcomes are notoriously contested: progress is not as easy to define as increased sales for Amazon or more donations for Obama. Further, experimentation relies heavily on the collection of data. In many countries, systems for gathering even basic national data collection are poor (see, e.g., Jerven 2013), and systems for collecting specific data on the workings of justice institutions can be practically nonexistent. There can also often be strong political interests against the collection and publication of sensitive data in some security and justice areas. That said, the bar is currently low regarding confidence in knowing what works and what does not. For these reasons, we flexibly define what "counts" as relevant data. We also believe that an experimentalist approach should use and improve existing agency data rather than creating bespoke surveys that may not be replicable once a particular experiment ends.[34]

A common critique is that the requirement for a counterfactual limits experimentation to "small reforms," directing attention away from potentially more dramatic changes. A similar argument contends that experiments often ignore the overarching political settlement and political economy that determines the scope of possible reform.[35] This claim about the "blinkering effects of incrementalism" is also made in the high-tech world and has some merit (see Christian 2012). One reason we support a broader approach of experimentalism is that it overcomes some of the conceptual and logistical constraints that frequently accompany the implementation of experiments. This includes being mindful of and responsive to broader political dynamics.[36]

Conclusion

Broad optimism and a belief in "quick wins" still dominate many areas of development work. However, the history of internationally supported justice activities suggests that we should be less confident in what we think we know, and certainly less confident in predicting that specific project activities will axiomatically lead to particular development outcomes. Uncertainty about the effects of our actions will not materially diminish with more ex ante knowledge—whether in the form of ethnographies, indicators, or political economy analyses. Given the nature of the systems and processes with which we work, there will always and inherently be significant levels of indeterminacy. The experience of our tech colleagues illustrates that there are far too many unobservable characteristics to confidently predict behavior—even in response to relatively simple inputs.

One way to live with this indeterminacy is to adopt an experimentalist approach to project design, implementation, and evaluation. To show how this can be done, we have offered an example of programming in Sierra Leone that illustrates how different implementation methods and ways of measurement can generate a range of data on impact, cost, and sustainability. We have also outlined some broad principles that might guide the development of such an approach, as well as constraints and limitations. Nevertheless, building a broader experimentalist mindset (and supporting infrastructure) in justice will require overcoming obstacles inherent to the field itself and countering the "results" culture of development more broadly—in other words, a culture that interprets project "accountability" as having an ex ante blueprint and "success" as implementing that blueprint. In contrast, embracing "best fit" solutions will require processes that generate responses to the problems that local agents identify and prioritize. A key role for external agents in promoting a culture of experimentalism is to use project structures that allow the details of reform to emerge through domestic political processes informed by data, thereby imbuing projects with the necessary contextual relevance to be legitimate, durable, and effective.

References

Abbott, Kenneth, and Duncan Snidal. 2000. "Hard and Soft Law in International Governance." *International Organization* 54:421–56.

Amnesty International. 2011. *Sierra Leone: At a Crossroads; Sierra Leone's Free Health Care Policy*. London: Amnesty International.

Andrews, Matt. 2013. "Do International Organizations Really Shape Government Solutions in Developing Countries?" CID Working Paper 264.

Andrews, Matt, Lant Pritchett, and Michael Woolcock. 2013. "Breaking Capability Traps through Problem-Driven Iterative Adaptation (PDIA)." *World Development* 51:234–44.

AusAID. 2012. *Building on Local Strengths: Evaluation of Australian Law and Justice Assistance*. Canberra: Australian Agency for International Development.

Basu, Kaushik. 2013. "The Method of Randomization, Economic Policy, and Reasoned Intuition." World Bank Policy Research Working Paper 6722.

Booth, David. 2012. *Development as a Collective Action Problem: Addressing the Real Challenges of African Governance*. London: Africa Power and Politics Programme.

Bjorkman, Martina, and Jakob Svensson. 2009. "Power to the People: Evidence from a Randomized Field Experiment on Community-Based Monitoring in Uganda." *Quarterly Journal of Economics* 124:735–69.

Christian, Brian. 2012. "The A/B Test: Inside the Technology That's Changing the Rules of Business." *Wired*, April 25. http://www.wired.com/business/2012/04/ff_abtesting.

DeRose, Chris, and Noel Tichy. 2013. "What Happens When a 'HiPPO' Runs Your Company?" *Forbes*, April 15.

Freedman, David H. 2010. "Lies, Damned Lies, and Medical Science." *The Atlantic*, October 4.

Garner, Bryan, ed. 2004. *Black's Law Dictionary*, 8th ed. St. Paul: West Group.

Gelman, Andrew. 2010. "Experimental Reasoning in Social Science." Memo, Columbia University, August 7. http://www.stat.columbia.edu/~gelman/research/published/yalecausal2.pdf.

Hall, Margaux. 2012. "Justice in Health Care Delivery: A Role for Sierra Leone's Paralegals." *World Bank: Investing in Health Blog*, March 30. http://blogs.worldbank.org/health/justice-in-health-care-delivery-a-role-for-sierra-leone-s-paralegals.

Jerven, Morten. 2013. *Poor Numbers: How We Are Misled by African Development Statistics and What to Do about It*. Ithaca: Cornell University Press.

Kondylis, Florence, and Mattea Stein. 2012. "The Speed of Justice: Dakar Regional Court, Senegal." Presentation at the Innovations in Investment Climate Reforms: An Impact Evaluation Workshop, Paris, November 12–16.

Levy, Brian, and Michael Walton. 2013. "Institutions, Incentives and Service Provision: Bringing Politics Back In." University of Manchester: Effective States and Inclusive Development Working Paper 18.

Maru, Vivek. 2006. "Between Law and Society: Paralegals and the Provision of Justice Services in Sierra Leone and Worldwide." *Yale Journal of International Law* 31:427–76.

————. 2010. "Allies Unknown: Social Accountability and Legal Empowerment." *Health and Human Rights: An International Journal* 12:83–93.

Menzies, Nicholas. 2013. "Are Impact Evaluations Useful for Justice Reforms in Developing Countries?" *Governance for Development Blog*, May 8. http://blogs. worldbank.org/governance/are-impact-evaluations-useful-justice-reforms-developing-countries.

Prichett, Lant, and Justin Sandefur. 2013. "Context Matters for Size: Why External Validity Claims and Development Practice Don't Mix." Center for Global Development Working Paper 336.

Sage, Caroline, Nicholas Menzies, and Michael Woolcock. 2010. "Taking the Rules of the Game Seriously: Mainstreaming Justice in Development in the World Bank's Justice for the Poor Program." In *Legal Empowerment: Practitioners' Perspectives*, edited by Stephen Golub, 19–37. Rome: International Development Law Organization.

Tang, Diane, Ashish Agarwal, Deirdre O'Brien, and Mike Meyer. 2010. "Overlapping Experiment Infrastructure: More, Better, Faster Experimentation." In *Proceedings of the 16th Conference on Knowledge Discovery and Data Mining*, 17–26. Washington, DC: ACM.

United Nations Children's Fund. 2012. *The State of the World's Children 2012: Children in an Urban World*. New York: United Nations Children's Fund.

United Nations Development Programme. 2013. *Human Development Report 2013: The Rise of the South* New York: United Nations Development Programme.

Woolcock, Michael. 2013. "Using Case Studies to Assess the External Validity of Complex Development Interventions." *Evaluation* 19:229–48.

World Bank. 2011. *World Development Report 2011: Conflict, Security and Development*. Washington, DC: World Bank.

————. 2013. "Twenty Fragile States Make Progress on Millennium Development Goals." Press release, May 1. http://www.worldbank.org/en/news/press-release/2013/05/01/twenty-fragile-states-make-progress-on-millennium-development-goals.

Zhou, Yongmei, ed. 2009. *Decentralization, Democracy, and Development: Recent Experience from Sierra Leone*. Washington, DC: World Bank

Notes

1. We use the term "justice reform" in this chapter because it is the most common term applied within the World Bank; however, broadly analogous terms, including "rule of law reform" and "legal and judicial reform," are also common.

2. Some common sites of learning include sector assessments, portfolio reviews, construction of indices, ethnographies, political economy analyses, and population and user surveys.

3. Often referred to as A/B testing.

4. The level of contestation about what constitutes a desired outcome is also much greater in justice reform, and the structuring of such contests is also arguably an inherent feature of well-functioning justice systems.

5. For an extensive discussion of this point, see Andrews, Pritchett, and Woolcock (2013).

6. See Desai (this volume) for a discussion about whether justice reform is in fact a "field."

7. This importation of justice norms and form is still prevalent, even after many years of critique—see, for example, AusAID (2012) and Andrews (2013).

8. Despite evaluations being conducted against ex ante stated objectives—which would seem to create an incentive to set less ambitious targets that make "success" more easily achievable—a common refrain from evaluators is that objectives are overly ambitious. Assessments of "failure" (against the original objectives) can thus be as much a product of expectation mismanagement as one of shortcomings in substantive design or implementation.

9. In 2013, the country ranked 177th out of 186 countries (United Nations Development Programme 2013).

10. See United Nations Development Programme (2013) for Sierra Leone's Human Development Index values and rank changes.

11. Field notes from visit to Tonkolili district, June 2013 (on file with the authors).

12. Ultimately, health outcomes are a product of much more than just government health service delivery. Other factors include diet, smoking, accidents, employment conditions, and environmental quality.

13. These other approaches include a performance-based financing project supported by the World Bank and drug procurement chains set up by the United Nations Children's Fund.

14. The work described in this chapter as "ours" was in fact the product of large team effort—in design, implementation, and measurement—going well beyond the efforts of the authors. For the RCT, the team included personnel from the Decentralization Secretariat in the Ministry of Local Government and Rural Development, the Ministry of Health and Sanitation, Namati, Innovations for Poverty Action (including primary investigators), Concern Worldwide, Plan, the International Rescue Committee, and the World Bank. For the activities outside

of the RCT, the team included the Ministry of Health and Sanitation, Namati, BRAC, Methodist Church Sierra Leone, and the World Bank.

15. Gibrill Jalloh, interview with the authors, Freetown, June 18–19, 2013.

16. Five representatives were meant to attend from each village—two men (one young and one older); two women (one young and one older); and the village's traditional birth attendant. In practice, participation varied over the course of the four facilitated meetings, and the payment of travel stipends skewed representation in some cases.

17. By way of example, in response to the challenge of having a clinic with irregular hours (contrary to government policy), one community committed to raising a vegetable garden for the nurse to ease her after-hours workload, and the nurse agreed to keep the clinic open during standard operating hours and to remain on call for emergencies. While the nurse's commitments fell within the ambit of her employment contract, in practice the government lacked the capacity to monitor her behavior or enforce this "hard law."

18. See Garner (2004, 426): "1. Collectively, rules that are neither strictly binding nor completely lacking in legal significance." See also Abbott and Snidal (2000).

19. In some cases, clinic staff have retaliated by refusing future service to individuals or villages that have complained about the lack or quality of service.

20. This was due, in part, to their overhead and supervision costs.

21. The potentially mutually complementary approaches of social accountability and legal empowerment have been set out in Maru (2010).

22. The committees are composed of local representatives and generally include a teacher, the mammy queen (female traditional leader), and traditional birth attendants.

23. Sierra Leone has a system of 149 chiefdoms. These chiefdoms, each headed by a paramount chief, have administrative, fiscal, and political powers.

24. At the time of publication, quantitative results from the RCT were not yet available. Findings reported here are based on qualitative research (which for the RCT covered only a limited number of catchments).

25. The RCT endline included height, weight, and upper-arm circumference measures for under-five children.

26. The process was designed and run by a US-based research firm and three international academics.

27. Implementation of the community-clinic compact and nonfinancial award experiments has cost more than US$1 million, with the endline measurement alone costing at least an additional $500,000.

28. For a recent critique of this claim to causal confidence, see Basu (2013).

29. See Menzies (2013) for a description of some of the small number of existing experiments of justice reform activities.

30. A further complication was that near the end of the community-clinic compact and nonfinancial award interventions, almost all of our contacts in the Ministry of Health and Sanitation were suspended on misappropriation charges unrelated to the interventions, in the country's largest series of Anti-Corruption Commission indictments to date. (Nearly all were subsequently acquitted.) Partly because of the nature of the suspensions, new staff were unwilling to fund even the small amount required for the nonfinancial award ceremonies. Government promises to frontline clinic staff, therefore, were in jeopardy, potentially undermining an important component of the nonfinancial award intervention—the notion that recognition from the government would follow hard work. Moreover, with the suspension of former staff, the ministry lost important institutional knowledge needed to facilitate the expansion of these activities.

31. Much of the following discussion is taken from Menzies (2013).

32. A likely reason for this is that international development agencies assume that low local "capacity" constrains effective implementation.

33. The issue of ethics frequently arises when testing alternatives, particularly when dealing with issues of great importance, such as someone's life or liberty. These are tough issues that cannot be resolved in the abstract and very well may, in a given case, lead to a decision *not* to experiment. While this chapter does not delve into these ethical questions in detail, it does raise several counterarguments. If the functioning of the justice system is as important as many of us believe, it could be unethical to *not* know with some confidence which reforms work best and whether scarce resources are being used effectively. Resource scarcity also offers a practical cover under which to experiment. For example, few jurisdictions have enough money to provide free legal counsel to all who need it, or to train all justice personnel at once. One way to deal with this scarcity is to use a lottery to select individuals for "treatment"—which gives each person an equal chance of being selected—and to use this experiment to test impact. As in many other fields, safeguards can be built in to guard against unfair gain or harm.

34. This is also one means to address questions regarding the external validity of outcomes achieved through experiments (see also Woolcock 2013; Prichett and Sandefur 2013). Indeed, questions about the replicability of experimental results have been raised in the "high church" of medical trials, where treatments are easier to standardize and where the context into which they are introduced—the human body—is more fully understood (see Freedman 2010). Theory and experience would suggest that changes over time in one place or between places in the broader socioeconomic and political landscape, as well as implementation capacity, would have a material impact on the outcomes of justice reform. This is one of the reasons we recommend using and strengthening agency data systems—new alternatives can be constantly tested in real time and the impacts determined.

35. As statistician Andrew Gelman (2010, 3) wryly notes, "It would be tempting to split the difference in the present debate and say something like the following: Randomized experiments give you accurate estimates of things you don't care about; observational studies give biased estimates of things that actually matter."

36. Levy and Walton (2013) suggest a framework for analyzing the political settlement and its manifestation in different service delivery areas.

Abstract

The limited impact of justice reform efforts stems in part from flawed assumptions that drive programming, a focus on an unduly narrow set of institutions, and a fixation with filling organizational deficits that have been defined in relation to international standards. This chapter proposes three questions aimed at reframing the challenge and pointing toward a new approach to addressing it, based on understanding how institutions actually function in local contexts. The first question examines the nature of the justice problem, in which justice is understood as a core function of public authority that cuts across state and nonstate institutions. The next question focuses on identifying the relevant institutions, and proposes three lenses—political-economic, organizational, and normative—through which to understand how these institutions are governed in practice and to identify potential pathways for change. The third question interrogates the role of external assistance in enabling just development. We suggest two ways that such assistance might be beneficial: by paving the way for reform trajectories through incremental changes and by enabling constructive forms of contestation around salient justice problems to facilitate new forms of authority and institutions. We illustrate the argument with reference to efforts to strengthen justice institutions in Solomon Islands.

9 Beyond Deficit and Dysfunction: Three Questions toward Just Development in Fragile and Conflict-Affected Settings

Louis-Alexandre Berg, Deborah Isser, and Doug Porter

Introduction

Global efforts to address chronic insecurity and injustice in fragile and conflict-affected settings appear to be in crisis. Creating durable institutions that deliver outcomes that are popularly perceived as just has once again been singled out as crucial for enabling successful transitions from fragility and conflict, broad-based growth, and equitable development.[1] Yet scholars remain hard pressed to find credible examples that support the claims and expectations that donors project about their interventions. Three decades of evidence from efforts to strengthen justice institutions warns against untested assumptions, the translation of best practices irrespective of contextual realities, preoccupation with legal and institutional forms rather than functions, the tendency to securitize justice, and the continual evasion by donors of the societal contests most crucial to achieving just development.[2]

This chapter draws from an ongoing work program at the World Bank under the Justice for the Poor program. We acknowledge the support of the Bank-Netherlands Partnership Program and the Justice for the Poor program, a partnership between the World Bank and the Australian government, which has made this work possible.

This chapter argues that progress, especially in fragile and conflicted settings, will require a reframing of the challenge. Our argument is prompted by several increasingly familiar realizations, including the need to eschew standard templates of capacity-building activities in favor of a problem-solving approach; the need to focus on justice outcomes achieved by politically dynamic and socially embedded institutions rather than inputs and linear pathways; and the need to look, in promoting justice outcomes, beyond the hallowed halls of courts and other justice-sector agencies toward the wide range of formal and informal institutions where contests occur over livelihoods, personal safety, and basic services.[3] Applying this awareness in practice has proven difficult, not least because it challenges the corporate structures and incentives of the donor community. More significantly, while there is a clear case for acting on these realizations by pursuing justice outcomes rather than inputs and engaging with a wider set of institutions in ways that are better attuned to politics, practitioners and scholars are not certain how to go about doing this in practice.

This chapter is an effort to deepen this conceptual shift and explore its implications for donor interventions.[4] To set the scene, in the first section, we recap the conventional approach—what we refer to as the "deficit and dysfunction approach"—by exploring its key features and assumptions, especially when practiced in fragile and conflicted settings. We then organize the rest of the chapter around three questions that summarize a diagnostic we use when appraising the likely efficacy of new engagements or when holding existing engagements up for serious review. Although we do not discuss the details of this diagnostic, it is apparent that we draw on a wide range of similar efforts.[5] Through reframing the analysis of justice challenges in terms of problems, processes, and outcomes, we aim to help development actors tailor engagements to context, to think politically as well as technically, to avoid the temptation of best practices, and to seek novel ways to engage. As we argue, a more promising role for development actors is to enable contestation around salient justice problems that emerge in spaces where a reordering of authority and institutional forms is occurring.

The first question—what is the justice problem?—takes us beyond an understanding of justice as a particular set of institutions and orients us to justice as an outcome across all engagements in what donors term "development sectors." In other words, justice is the outcome of contests over social, political, and economic goods in domains that are mediated by a broad range of state and nonstate authorities. Broadly, we classify these domains as social order, the regulation of economic assets, and the allocation and use of public resources. The second question—how is the justice problem being governed?—again takes us beyond a focus on justice-sector institutions and encourages us to regard justice outcomes as a core function of a wide range of public authorities. The institutional forms and behaviors that shape these outcomes respond to broader contextual factors that require deeper examination. We summarize three sets of lenses—the political, organizational, and normative—that we find useful in responding to this question. Finally, the instrumental tone in the third question—what is the appropriate role for external assistance?—is intended to push attention beyond the technical to recognize that engagements are always political. This question begins by recognizing that while experience and analysis can provide reasonable confidence regarding the domains where justice outcomes are most keenly contested and developmentally relevant, we lack ex ante predictive power to determine which contests are likely to trend toward outcomes that will be popularly perceived as just. This prompts us to ask, How can external actors constructively facilitate these contests rather than evading them or reproducing patterns of authority that constrain "just development"? And what kinds of donor instruments and modalities are likely to be the most constructive?

We illustrate this approach in reference to Solomon Islands, drawing from a body of research and operations conducted by the World Bank's Justice for the Poor program.[6] Ten years after the deployment of the fifteen-nation Regional Assistance Mission to Solomon Islands (RAMSI) in response to the 1998–2003 tension, several mostly peaceful political transitions have occurred, the basic security and functioning of many core state institutions have been restored, and incomes and service delivery are almost back to pre-tension levels. But the reach of services, including the police and judiciary, are confined largely to the capital city and province centers. Most Solomon Islanders say that their communities are unsafe and that neither local nor national public authorities would be able to cope if RAMSI's security cover were withdrawn. Locally, the structures of colonial authority (courts, police, ward councils, and administrative offices) that used to provide some degree of political authority and administrative outreach are no longer present. Nor have local authorities (chieftainships, religious authorities, customary authorities, and various kinds of business trusts) been able to fill the gap. The implicit fear is that the retreat of the state, coupled with the disintegration of local authorities, will create "ungoverned spaces" (Mallet 2010) that will eventually pose a risk to the country's order and stability.

The Deficit-and-Dysfunction Approach

The failure of justice programs in fragile and conflict-affected settings is rooted in part in the assumptions underpinning the conventional approach. Numerous critiques of development actors' justice and rule of law interventions have highlighted these failings (Kennedy 2006; Tamanaha 2004), but programming has not substantially changed on the ground. Although the reasons for this lack of progress are complex, the difficulty of overcoming the conventional approach can be traced in part to the ways that justice challenges and engagement are framed. Two sets of assumptions have been particularly detrimental to advancing justice programming.

First is the privileging of justice-sector institutions in efforts to understand how states and societies achieve justice outcomes. The justice sector is typically narrowly defined to include the police, judges, and prosecutors; while it sometimes includes corrections facilities, legal defenders, and human rights advocates, it is generally restricted to institutions deemed crucial for law and order. Donor preoccupation with law and order and the *form* of justice institutions tends to create blind spots around justice needs and challenges that affect people and that contribute to conflict and fragility. The form of justice institutions is defined narrowly around an overly securitized conception of justice that prioritizes criminal justice over other forms of dispute resolution or grievance redress, and that neglects a wide range of arenas—from land and property rights to access to basic services—in which grievances and disputes occur.

Even within this narrow conception, donor efforts have largely failed to bring about the desired outcomes. For instance, while peacekeepers often succeed in maintaining an end to major hostilities and reducing certain forms of violence (Fortna 2008; Doyle and Sambanis 2006), their engagements typically leave local agencies ill equipped to respond after the peacekeepers and advisers have left (Collier et al. 2003). In development actors' failure to address the types of injustice that affect most people, the grievances fueling conflict remain unresolved, and the new forms of violence, crime, and grievance that accompany the transitional reordering of society are neglected.

Conventional justice-sector interventions are also prone to a second assumption whereby improvements in the technical and organizational capacity of these institutions is expected to result in greater effectiveness and responsiveness to justice needs. Fixated with global norms, standards, and best practices, these efforts identify institutional deficits and fill gaps by revising constitutions, laws, and procedures; training judges and lawyers; rebuilding court infrastructure; and instituting case-management systems (Samuels 2006; Call 2007; Stromseth, Wippman, and Brooks 2006). The litany of consequences—from the premature overloading of local institutions to the creation of politically and fiscally unsustainable edifices—is well documented (Kennedy 2006; Tamanaha 2004; Desai, Isser, and Woolcock 2012; Pritchett, Woolcock, and Andrews 2010; Dinnen and Allen 2012). Over time, as these supply-side efforts run into difficulties, as formal justice institutions remain chronically incapable of assuming the roles mandated to them, or where these efforts simply cost more than countries can afford or donors are prepared to fund, donors turn to bottom-up approaches. In such cases, the mainstream repertoire typically includes links with customary or nonstate actors (Harper 2012; Isser 2011; Faundez 2011); legal empowerment and "demand side" activities that seek to build the capacity of legal aid and advocacy organizations (Golub 2010; Van Rooij 2009); and efforts to conjure up "local ownership" of interventions, generally by seeking out "local champions" and various forms of stakeholder consultation and participatory processes (Donais 2008; Scheye and Peake 2005; Narten 2008). These efforts, however, tend to reproduce the flaws of the overall paradigm by again focusing on forms, symptoms, and perceived deficits.

These two assumptions point to a fundamental problem of conventional efforts, which couple the lens of deficits and dysfunctions with a capacity-building approach: the idea that donors can bring peace, development, or justice merely by building organizations and installing trained and enlightened individuals capable of delivering a set of goods more effectively. The long history of institutional formation and development suggests otherwise: that institutions emerge as a result of particular forms of political and social contestation that sometimes coalesce into agreements to adopt institutional changes (Khan 2010). A country's laws, procedures, and organizational forms, and the ability to sustain them politically and financially, necessarily arise from political bargains and shared norms. In practice, donor-driven reform efforts tend to assume a reverse logic—namely, that irrespective of the nature of ongoing political contests and settlements, by installing or restoring institutional forms, it is possible to drive political settlements in particular directions or incentivize them to take on particular characteristics. Typically, interventions seek to create demonstration effects (e.g. via model courts, police-citizen liaison committees, or the hybridizing of customary and formal legal processes) that are coupled with a host of ritual events (e.g., stakeholder participatory roundtables), all enabled through the identification of champions and star performers in order to ensconce manufactured versions of local ownership and ventriloquize declarations of political will (Craig and Porter 2006).

271

Toward Just Development

As a way out of the conventional paradigm, we propose a method for reframing the justice challenge through a series of questions. We start with an "upside-down view" of justice, moving through an examination of the political, social, and organizational context to seek pathways through which credible justice institutions might emerge, and through which external assistance might play a useful role. As the Institute of Development Studies (2010) refreshingly argues with respect to governance, this entails examining the concept of justice unencumbered ex ante by normative claims or filtered by preferences for particular institutional forms and "rule of law" conventions. Three relatively high-level questions can help invert the conventions.

What is the Justice Problem?

Clarity about the nature of the problem, and for whom it may be an issue, is an obvious first step toward a context-tailored and open-minded strategy for engagement. Defining the justice problem can help shift attention away from institutional deficits and dysfunctions that are easy to identify but less relevant to justice outcomes. In other words, this approach will help focus on issues that seriously impinge on development and conflict and that affect popular perceptions of justice. One way to approach this is to first take note of where social contests typically occur in fragile and conflicted settings and where claims for justice (or complaints framed around injustice) are most pronounced as potential drivers of conflict. Scholars of comparative politics and economic history—their vast and important differences aside—tend to agree that such contests occur around "core societal governance questions."[7] Where settlements are reached around these questions, public authority is invested with trust and loyalty, and particular institutions are provided with sufficient skills and resources to manage these struggles. As contemporary Melanesia shows, where these arrangements are not regarded as "just" in outcome or process, or are perceived as incapable of adapting to the demands made upon them, people withdraw from these institutions the loyalties, trust, obligations, skills, and resources needed for them to operate effectively (Dinnen, Porter, and Sage 2010; Craig and Porter forthcoming). In such cases, people seek other means—including violence—by which to press their claims.

According to this view, justice is not necessarily the outcome of a particular set of justice-sector institutions—although that can certainly be the case—but an outcome of how public authority is exercised around social contests.[8] We identify three core domains in which these contests typically occur and which are defined as "justice problems" in fragile and conflict-affected situations. These domains correspond to the core societal governance questions—that is, the governance of social order, the regulation of economic assets, and the allocation and use of public wealth. Although not the exclusive domains in which relevant contests occur, they draw attention to the primary justice challenges in a given context.

Social-order contests encompass security, safety, public order, criminal justice, and, sometimes, family matters. Within this broad category, the types of problems and institutions that matter vary widely, and they include but are not limited to those typically within the purview of criminal justice. In Solomon Islands, a recent study of local justice found that the most common and corrosive social-order disputes centered on the illegal production and use of narcotics and the disintegration of long-standing norms around marriage, propriety, and intergenerational obligations and conduct (Allen et al. 2013).

Contests over the regulation of economic assets occur around the definition of rights to alienate and benefit from natural and manmade resources, along with the responsibility to deal with externalities. In fragile and conflict-affected settings, disputes and grievances typically occur around rights regarding property and labor, the right to accumulate rents from the commodification of natural assets (e.g., land, water, minerals, and forests), and the trade and transfer of assets across borders. In Solomon Islands, natural assets are largely governed in diverse village and customary domains, but rapid globalization, articulated through the resident ethnic Chinese business community, has intensified contest among Melanesian Solomon Islanders around the rights to commodify land, forests, and, increasingly, gold and nickel mineral resources. The capacity of state agencies to regulate and supervise natural-resource deals has been undermined and overwhelmed by a combination of clientage payments by investors, the pace of change, and the difficulties of the country's archipelagic geography. Citizens perceive the state to be "in retreat" and unable to credibly manage these ongoing social contests. At the same time, local governance and customary or traditional systems are also overwhelmed by the high stakes of these conflicts, by conflicts of interest, and by the fact that the conflicts involve actors far beyond their reach (Craig and Porter 2014).

Disputes around the collection and allocation of public wealth—through state spending on public services or otherwise—are often pronounced in countries beset by institutional fragility and conflict. These contests frequently escalate and contribute to violence in combination with ethnic or other identity-based grievances. In particular, economies that are dominated by volatile aid flows or by the proceeds of single commodities such as oil or agroforestry products—or by a combination of both—can undermine the state's capability to collect revenue, impose decisions, or distribute public goods and services (Chauvet and Collier 2006). Similarly, as Solomon Islands illustrates, contests are likely to be pronounced around the arrangements through which public wealth is allocated, whether through formally budgeted state services or through "off budget" patronage arrangements. Especially when they play out along identity lines, these contests foster perceptions of exclusion and injustice. In Solomon Islands, contests over access to public wealth (such as aid flows, expenditure on services, and payments through political constituency grants) are filtered through complex blends of notions of rights and entitlements—secular and religious, customary and modern—each infused with deeply held conceptions of justice.

As these contests play out, they fuel deeper disputes about how authority is achieved and reproduced, which, in turn, can fuel violence and conflict. In Solomon Islands, the inability of public institutions to successfully mediate and reach durable agreements in these three domains is exacerbated by ongoing disputes regarding where authority should be vested at different levels of territorial scale—from the village to provincial to national level—and how, at each level, nonstate institutions (such as chiefly, customary, and religious bodies) should share their authority with the state.

This upside-down view of justice immediately expands the fields of attention for would-be justice promoters. It entails looking beyond the confines of what is known as the justice sector. At the same time, the areas in which injustice is experienced, and the public authorities responsible for mediating that experience, are well within the ambit of development actors. The challenge at the outset is to identify which functional problems—of social order, economic regulation, or public wealth distribution—are of greatest significance in terms of their links with social justice; their effects on conflict, security, and prosperity; and how they are weighted by stakeholders. The next challenge is to identify the institutions that are managing the most salient problems, and to understand how these institutions are being governed.

How Are Justice Problems Being Governed?

The second question binds together two presumptions. First, as outlined above, it regards justice outcomes as a core function of a range of public authorities, including but not limited to justice-sector institutions. Second, it presumes that any domain of contest will already be governed, instead of being a void awaiting intervention. The task, then, is to analyze the dynamics that shape the way the problems are being managed, not in terms of deficit or dysfunction but in terms of the broader factors that determine institutional performance. Understanding the political, economic, and social conditions that have led elites and citizens to invest in particular institutions and ways of governing domains of social contest—whether concerning social order, economic regulation, or public wealth—is crucial to understanding the conditions under which they might choose to invest in doing things differently. This analysis also provides the basis for the third question, which considers the role of external actors in influencing those choices. Understanding these dynamics is not a hard science. Different observers will have different interpretations; different disciplines will emphasize different factors. Justice practitioners will never have the time, funds, or means to fully explore the underlying political, economic, and social conditions that determine how justice problems are governed. But we can certainly add rigor, purpose, and more systematic analytical engagement to our repertoire by drawing on scholarship that has animated development practice in other areas. Without being comprehensive by any means, we highlight three sets of lenses—political/economic, organizational, and normative—that are useful in addressing this question.

Political contest, pacts, and settlements

The institutions involved in governing social contests, and thus delivering justice outcomes, emerge through processes involving social and political contests, compromise, and bargaining among elites and citizens. These dynamics have been explored by scholars of political economy (e.g., Mushtaq Khan, Robert Bates, and Douglas North) and historical institutionalism (e.g., Kathleen Thelen), as well as through a rich set of comparative politics and sociolegal studies that examines the development of legal and justice institutions in particular.

It is important to distinguish our approach to politics from a contemporary genre of donor political engagements in institutional reform. Recognizing that institutions, including those in the justice sector, are shaped by these broader political dynamics, scholars and practitioners have advocated for a more politically oriented approach (Kleinfeld 2012; Carothers and de Gramont 2013). In a few cases, donors have sought to follow this advice by coupling diplomacy—"the use of carrots, sticks and rhetoric to affect the decisions of government leaders"—with support to local advocacy groups to "build local constituencies for reform" (Kleinfeld 2012, 177, 126). Significant changes have occurred in some of these cases, especially when development agencies, diplomats, peacekeepers, and other external actors are aligned and coordinated. More often, however, competing donor objectives and mixed incentives make aid conditionality incoherent. External actors—whether diplomats or donors—also tend to neglect whether local coalitions, interests, and incentives are sufficiently aligned to sustain reforms. In practice, therefore, attempts to apply a "political" approach have resulted in a host of unintended effects (Ahmad and Porter 2006), ranging from relatively benign institutional mimicry and "cut and paste" investments that lead to mere ephemeral changes, to complex rituals of signaling and ventriloquism aimed at satisfying donor conditions without any real change (Pritchett, Woolcock, and Andrews 2012). Less benign are the ways that ill-conceived external leverage can crowd out domestically driven initiatives as local actors become attuned more to external pressure than to domestic constituencies (Ginsburg 2011; Weinstein 2005).

In some ways, a rapidly growing literature on the role of "strong enough" or "inclusive enough" political settlements and pacts cautions against this genre of political engagement (Hickey 2013). Foremost, it argues that institutional changes that enable public authorities to effectively and durably handle social contests depend crucially on political compromises between powerful groups in society, particularly economic and political elites (Khan 2010, 1). The World Bank's 2011 *World Development Report* usefully highlights the role of bargains and pacts among elites and donors as the basis for exiting fragility and conflict. This chimes well with development professionals' alertness to the power of contextual diversity and historical contingency; more attention to these dynamics would benefit engagements in the justice sector. But three points of caution are useful. First, there is a lack of agreement in the literature about the meaning of core terms that describe these compromises, deals, and accommodations (political settlements, coalitions, pacts, and so on); how these compromises structure the possibilities for some, rather than other, institutions to emerge; and, in turn, how they are influenced by this process. Second, it is clear that political settlements, pacts, and coalitions are fundamentally dynamic, which runs counter to the linear mindsets and routines of development agencies. There is nothing remotely teleological about how settlements and pacts behave, nor is it clear in any programmable sense how they affect institutional change through time.

Third, institutions often evolve and change under circumstances that differ from idealized versions of "inclusive settlements." The focus on elite coalitions and bargains is a useful starting point for understanding how institutions emerge to promote or constrain developmental or justice outcomes. But as soon as these ideas are mapped to a particular country, institution, or development challenge, any narrative simplicity or predetermined sequencing disappears (Craig and Porter 2014; Roque et al. 2010). In most fragile and conflict-affected states, successful transitions are rare, and the processes of collective action and broad-based coalitions needed to underpin such changes are often elusive (Moore, Schmidt, and Unsworth 2009). Conversely, effective institutions often emerge from very different conditions.

A review of comparative research nonetheless points to a host of context-specific factors that shape political authority and competition, determine the scope and depth of possible political settlements, and, in turn, affect the trajectory of institutional change and the outcomes of justice-related contests. Scholarship on judicial reform, for example, suggests that effective and independent judiciaries have, in a few cases, developed under authoritarian regimes, which see these institutions as a way to deflect regime challenges (Hirschl 2008). In democratizing contexts, research has pointed not to inclusive or dominant coalitions but to the diffusion of power and competition among elites as the driver of judicial reform (Ramseyer 1994; Ginsburg 2003; Stephenson 2003; Dressel and Mietzner 2012). These conditions can create incentives for politicians to support independent judicial institutions to avoid being punished when they are out of power. Reforms also occur when important constituencies are sufficiently organized to exert pressure on their political leaders (Weingast 1997; Widner 2001a). In some cases, significant reforms have emerged from "critical junctures" in which interests among elites align with active support among key constituencies, a favorable normative context, and effective leadership by key individuals (Widner 2001b; Prado and Trebilcock 2009). In fragile and conflict-affected settings, however, short time horizons, weak political parties, and limited capacities to mobilize may undermine such incentives, suggesting that incremental change is more likely (Aydin 2013).

These challenges are no more apparent than in Solomon Islands, where the type of inclusive settlement seen as necessary to exiting fragility has so far been elusive.[9] A combination of factors—a population that is geographically scattered over ninety islands, an electoral gerrymander that favors rural constituencies over urban centers, and a complex ethnic cleavage between economic and political elites—has not been conducive to the formation of stable political parties, broad-based coalitions, or political agreement. Instead, these conditions favor a narrow, monetized form of clientage in which elected officials focus on negotiating temporary agreements with economic elites, providing access to logging concessions and other natural resources in their home districts in exchange for benefits to their narrow constituencies. While government decision making is centralized in the capital, Honiara, political momentum points toward the periphery and favors narrow, clientelist governance and distributions of resources over the consistent enforcement of rules or credible national budgets.

In this context, the state security and justice apparatus runs mostly parallel to and divorced from core political processes. According to one political economy analysis, local courts—which were established to enhance the accessibility of justice but have been crippled by backlogs and delay—rarely adjudicate issues relevant to local politics; instead, they remain largely irrelevant to political elites, who are unlikely to invest in significant improvements (Craig 2012). If anything, local elites appear to benefit by parking land-related disputes in the courts for years or forcing them to be resolved through mechanisms that more directly reflect their authority. Although the local courts are perceived as relatively credible and uncorrupted, political underinvestment is likely to undermine any attempts to improve management and resolve accessibility challenges.

These conclusions come with one proviso. Further analysis is likely to reveal that justice problems in two areas—urban security and mining enclaves—are closely linked to functional constraints on Solomon Islands' development and are significant drivers of violent conflict. Moreover, these justice problems are felt jointly by the public and economic elites, thus opening the door for political lobbying for the state to invest in their resolution. And while a range of executive agencies (e.g., municipal agencies, land administration, and the mines department) are important for managing these contests, the superior courts are largely responsible for handling them. Thus, it may prove to be the case that the conditions exist for a classic organizational change agenda to succeed.

Organizations, leadership, networks

Even where political opportunities open up, potential reformers must inevitably contend with organizational challenges in the form of vested interests, path dependencies, entrenched practices, and inherent complexity. From the perspective of scholars of organizational change, strengthening institutions that deliver justice is notoriously difficult.[10] Both within the justice system, where processing a single case involves the work of numerous agencies, and in other areas (such as land and natural-resource management) that involve multiple authorities, the organizational complexity is often stacked against efforts to improve the responsiveness of organizations.[11] Even if one organization improves its responsiveness, weakness in other entities may undermine impacts. The number of actors and the volume of transactions create numerous opportunities for internal opponents to veto reforms, while a high level of discretion among individual actors increases the difficulty of monitoring and changing behavior (Mahoney and Thelen 2010). Justice institutions must also contend with unique combinations of challenges, including the tension between presumed independence and accountability, the multiple lines of accountability, the complexity of tasks, and the autonomy of actors that undermine incentives for greater responsiveness.

Scholars of organizational change have offered insights into how to address such organizational challenges. Clearly, achieving desired outcomes requires aligning organizational and political incentives; and it is unwise to assume that this alignment can be engineered simply through the passage of new legislation. Neither adopting new laws nor building the technical capacity to implement them is sufficient without addressing the organizational relations in which actors are embedded and which govern the lines of authority, resource allocation, and potential beneficiaries. For instance, new regulations adopted in several West African countries in the late 1990s that aimed to redistribute the benefits of forestry to local communities by devolving decision making to local governments failed to achieve their objectives in the absence of complementary mechanisms to incentivize national and local government actors to respond to the demands of communities (Ribot 1999). Efforts to institute reforms must also stay attentive to the process through which organizational change occurs. When Sierra Leone's civil war ended in 2002, political incentives aligned to favor a comprehensive reform of the police, but political leaders still had to contend with an organization that functioned on the basis of clientelistic relationships and small-scale rent seeking. External advisers helped identify a group of internal leaders who became invested in the changes, although it is not clear how deeply these changes were embedded as donor assistance declined (Albrecht and Jackson 2009). Greater attention to the insights from organizational theory, behavioral economics, and social psychology could inform reform efforts in these domains.

In Solomon Islands, a close review of the lower courts has generated a list of measures to improve organizational performance (World Bank 2014). These measures include improving information management, budgeting, and planning capacities; undertaking a productivity review with the aim of establishing targets and measures to track performance; programming court circuits according to need; altering lower court jurisdictions; rationalizing procedures for assigning and tracking cases; and prioritizing expenditures. All are familiar and justified measures that also have the merit of offering a host of opportunities for donors to align around self-evident deficits.

A closer look at organizational incentives reveals the potential limits of some of these proposals and points toward other possible pathways. In Solomon Islands, the local courts—which occupy the lowest rung of the judicial system and are staffed by lay justices from the communities they serve —were originally established to integrate customary law and to remain close to citizens. But these courts have grown overly centralized and now depend heavily on the oversight of magistrates and the vagaries of budgets and management systems emanating from the capital. The failure to overcome the management challenges necessary to resolve even the small number of cases handled by these courts calls for attention not only to how budgets are set and managed but to the incentives of the magistrates and other central actors responsible for them. The performance of lower courts also depends on a range of other actors, from the police (whose decisions to bring cases determines access to criminal justice) to lawyers and litigants (who appear to benefit from indefinite delays of cases as they avoid the possibility that these cases might be decided against them). Even a narrow focus on lower courts thus requires deeper investigation into these actors, their organizational relations, and their lines of accountability. Such an investigation leads quickly back to the political context, which shapes actors' interests and determines how the desire to improve access or efficiency might stack up against interests to maintain the status quo. More fundamentally, it is by no means clear that a functioning system of subordinate courts in Solomon Islands would materially affect constraints that bind economic prosperity and equity or would dissuade acts of violence.

Normative frameworks

The normative frameworks in which institutions are embedded tend to be underexamined, or considered in partisan ways. This refers to more than the specific laws that govern judicial procedure, define criminal offenses, or adjudicate land claims; it includes the broader fabric of social perceptions and values in which these written laws must be embedded if they are to be authoritative. In contrast to the assumptions of many donor programs, which see norms as a fixed category to be converted or replaced, norms do not stand above or outside social contests. Rather, they are historically derivative. The dichotomies that donors frequently perceive between international and local, secular and religious, state and nonstate, are often manipulated by local actors who seek to frame widespread grievance as a conflict between competing norms—thereby undermining efforts to resolve them—or to promote particular conceptions of authority. At the same time, norms are not merely reflective of social contests—they are also constitutive (Moustafa 2013). They limit and enable particular ways of viewing injustice and structure the fields of possible action (Hilbink 2009). The most sustained institutional changes are those that are simultaneously rooted in local norms and customs and emerge from efforts to reinterpret and adapt these norms in response to new tensions or challenges (Englund 2012; Merry 2003).

The prevailing response of development actors to these tensions often produces adverse effects and undermines normative change. Efforts to "reform" or "harmonize" normative frameworks—which have become a popular part of external interventions, from Afghanistan (Gaston, Sarwari, and Strand 2013) to South Sudan (Leonardo et al. 2011)—tend to reify normative frameworks and dichotomies between them, and are often based on an incomplete understanding. This can have the unintended effect of solidifying fault lines between competing social groups that claim to represent one set of norms against another, while leaving the underlying grievances—and the power dynamics that drive them—unchanged. Instead, emerging normative tensions should be further investigated, both to understand the underlying drivers of conflict and to enable the search for constructive ways to express and grapple with social, political, and economic claims in ways that respond to local norms and allow space for crafting new responses (Isser 2011).

In Solomon Islands, the RAMSI intervention has, for the most part, stayed away from these normative tensions while reinforcing the dichotomies that undermine constructive contestation and institutional change. From the perspective of outsiders, the primary focus has been one of criminality, seen as a product of the failure of personal responsibility, to which the most effective response has been to prosecute individuals in a formal court. In practice, however, local conceptions have shaped how external interventions are perceived, undermining the ability of external actors to embed these approaches locally. For instance, violence and criminality are perceived by many as legitimate "weapons of the weak" and hence normatively acceptable (Dinnen et al. 2010). Meanwhile, a wide range of nonstate ways of dealing with disputes and achieving justice outcomes—notably public forms of reconciliation and compensation—have been neglected by external actors. As a result, the formal processes and decisions promoted by RAMSI may have succeeded in the short term—indeed, the justice delivered has been widely appreciated—but the institutional reforms and innovations have failed to embed or achieve the popular legitimacy needed for them to be sustained.

Yet the experience in the Solomon Islands also suggests that these normative frames are neither fixed nor exclusive. Instead, they evolve and adapt in concert as local actors seek to deal with social and political challenges. Politicians have adapted customary forms of compensation as a legitimate way to resolve disputes, while opportunistic elements have sought to manipulate *kastom* to claim money and power from the state for political or criminal purposes (Fraenkel 2004). Yet rather than engage with these sites of tensions and adaptation, external actors have merely reinforced a perceived dichotomy between international and local norms that stunts the potential for constructive innovation. This has been further reinforced as external actors have become aware of their inability to deliver justice in far-flung geographic areas and have sought to jump from one set of norms to another by engaging with "local" norms around "local" problems. Elsewhere in Melanesia, new actors have deliberately sought to navigate multiple normative frames to seek innovative solutions to social issues. In Solomon Islands, however, such efforts have been overshadowed by the emphasis on establishing state-based criminal processes as a basis for state-building while relegating *kastom* to a local solution to local problems beyond the scope of the state (Dinnen, Porter, and Sage 2010, 20).

As these brief examples from Solomon Islands illustrate, justice outcomes emerge through contestation in and around a range of development issues and institutions, in ways that are shaped by historical and contextual factors. Each of the lenses we describe—political, organizational, and normative—provides a partial and different perspective on the ways in which institutions evolve and the pressures to which they respond. Taken together, these lenses provide useful insights for analyzing and identifying constraints and opportunities around the promotion of just institutions. The question of whether and how to engage once such entry points are identified leads us to the next element in our analysis.

What Is the Appropriate Role for External Assistance?

The third question moves from an examination of local trajectories of change to understating how external actors might fit into them and eventually enable more just outcomes. The two questions above help steer attention from a predefined set of institutions toward the justice issues and institutions that matter, as well as the dynamics that shape them. We start by identifying justice problems, focusing on core governance questions linked to binding constraints to development, drivers of conflict, and widespread perceptions of injustice. Next, we seek to understand how those problems are being governed, focusing on political, economic, organizational, and normative pressures that shape the evolution of particular institutional forms. In framing the third question, about the appropriate role for donors, we look for possible pathways toward institutional change and justice outcomes. On the one hand, scholars are rightly skeptical that donors can themselves bring about large-scale reforms, or the broad-based, inclusive political settlements believed to generate them. On the other hand, donors have at times contributed to justice outcomes and to institutional change, but often in ways not typically conceived or expected. In most cases, the changes that are achieved remain incremental, at best generating further opportunities for new actors to emerge or for existing actors to more effectively shape the outcomes of ongoing contests. While donors cannot anticipate these trajectories, they can build on—and in some cases modify—their political, organizational, and normative foundations to increase the chances for more credible institutions and just outcomes to emerge.

In this approach, we draw both caution and inspiration from the history of donor approaches in fragile and conflict-affected settings. As several evaluations demonstrate, donor efforts (in justice and other areas) tend to have three effects, in rough order of frequency (Craig and Porter 2006). First, engagements bounce—or, at best, leave a few skid marks—and are largely irrelevant. Donor programs also fail to affect the "justice problem" due to the absence of broader social and political transformations, or due to these programs' tendency to neglect or evade the key contests and binding constraints. As a result, they leave behind organizations and practices that are quickly abandoned, or they preemptively "exit" at the slightest sign of resistance or corporate fatigue.

Second, also from bitter experience, interventions do harm. This can happen because they create new sites for contest around rights and entitlements at the wrong time or place, or via institutions that are not "fit for purpose." They reproduce patterns of privilege and power about which people have serious grievances. They may also do harm because the instruments that donors routinely have available fall short of what is needed; these instruments range from loans and country programs that focus on the national level—whereas the supranational or local level may be most appropriate—to short-term programs focusing on "returns" that skew incentives domestically.

Third, there is a possibility of positive engagement. Interventions can be successful in two ways. The first is relatively straightforward but often difficult to achieve: using aid to alleviate injustice through a legal or organizational fix. In addition to producing immediate relief, such fixes may also result in some incremental change, thus paving the way for a much longer trajectory. Ideally, such changes open space for new forms of contestation or spur further investment in institutional capability, leading to virtuous cycles of elite and citizen investment. Examples of this are readily at hand. Security engagements that restore confidence while enhancing the stability needed for development can, if accompanied by astute political engagement, open space for more systemic change. Development projects might also help correct marginalization derived from geographically inequitable public spending by introducing different formulas for fiscal transfers to local governments; they might create temporary employment opportunities for aggrieved youth while facilitating longer-term employment opportunities.

In the judicial arena, under the right conditions, development actors might promote measures to rationalize the jurisdiction of courts in order to alleviate backlogs of cases, with the effect of encouraging more attention by elites and citizens to strengthening the courts as a viable means of dispute resolution.

Engaging in this first approach requires understanding both the problems that matter and the factors that drive institutional performance. Success may be the result of serendipity, emerging from a deficit-and-dysfunction approach that happens to work due to the fortuitous alignment of underlying forces or effective pressure among highly coordinated external actors. But the odds are better when the approach is based on a deeper understanding of the contextual basis of change than is generally present in donor engagement. Achieving even incremental changes that improve institutional responsiveness therefore entails analyzing the constellation of forces that give rise to such practices, in order to identify means through which improved practices might emerge and pathways through which elites and citizens might invest sufficiently to sustain them. Interventions that appear conventional—such as modifying laws, building skills, and creating new procedures—might often be warranted, but the rationale for these interventions would be arrived at through a different route. Moreover, the design should account for a broader set of political, organizational, and normative factors than are generally considered.

The second type of success is trickier, for it seeks to promote pathways to better justice outcomes where there are no straightforward fixes or where institutional change appears blocked by political forces. Rather, it aims to promote the *spaces and processes of contestation* that lead to the reordering of power and politics and result in elites and citizens investing in effective and legitimate justice institutions. This requires donors to engage directly in the contests that matter, where authority is at stake and where perceptions and experience of justice are on the line. By engaging in these arenas, perhaps by favoring one direction or another or by enabling new means of contesting and resolving key grievances, donors might foster new pathways toward institutional change. This requires grappling with additional questions: Can we identify potential pathways of "socially generative contestation"—that is, particular sites of contest that, given the particular dynamics, are likely to promote positive adaptation, change, and reordering? And, if so, can we identify ways in which donor support can shift these pathways toward more just outcomes?

A dose of realism is warranted regarding donor structures, incentives, and limitations. As we have noted, it is often impossible to know what struggles and issues will prove socially generative, or to be specific about the interventions that will support this. We hope that looking beyond the usual set of institutions to the broader sets of problems and forces that shape them might provide some clues that lead to reasonable chances that investments might succeed. In addition, practitioners must be aware of their own institutional constraints and incentives that close off certain types of approaches and arrangements. Considerable ink has been spilled describing the short-term horizons, the mediocrity and perverse incentives, and other features of development agencies that inhibit the type of engagement necessary to respond to local contexts. On the other hand, even within such constraints, resourceful practitioners might find ways for their own organizational incentives to align in ways that enable long-term and flexible engagement, and to focus on specific and incremental changes that could prove transformative.

By way of illustration, we return to Solomon Islands.[12] The decade since the period known locally as the "tension" has been marked by two kinds of unforeseen institutional transformation. Each reflects, in different ways, competing elite efforts to occupy local spaces where social contests occur. In the first of these, injections of around US$1.2 billion in aid over the decade (equivalent to roughly 50% of Solomon Islands' gross national income) have been used to create a new layer of institutions in which core state functions are coproduced by the state and donor agencies. These arrangements are focused especially on social services, the police and judiciary, and monetary and fiscal governance. Among their range of consequences, two are relevant here. First, the standards and apparatus for service delivery created through these arrangements have generated fiscal obligations that exceed the state's revenue capability in the foreseeable future, thus reinforcing Solomon Islanders' dependence on a political settlement with Australia, the regional power. Second, by design, coproduction regimes aim to protect state functions from political interference in order to ensure that state agencies—and the lion's share of the national budget—work according to international norms and standards. Coproduction agreements allow a restricted kind of administrative politics to occur at the local level—for instance, around health-clinic management committees, school boards, or community-development committees mandated under agreements with donors—through which citizens are encouraged to participate in a selective menu of choices, rights, and obligations. But at the same time that they serve to block political elites from interfering, they also effectively relieve them of primary responsibility for funding or ensuring outcomes in these areas.

Parallel to these arrangements, constituency development funds (CDFs) have arisen as the primary instrument through which members of Parliament relate to citizens. CDFs, which are under the control and discretion of individual members of Parliament, now account for around 15% of national spending, and the thirteen individual funds amount to more than all spending on primary health and primary education. Given the government's limited reach into village life, and the blocking of political participation in areas of coproduced services, CDFs enable politicians to bolster their status not just as cultural "big men" but as effective, local pork-barreling politicians.

Together, coproduction and CDFs arguably constitute the most significant institutional reforms in Solomon Islands since independence. But at this point, it cannot be said that either transformation has dramatically affected the three kinds of justice problems noted above. Moreover, our analysis has pointed to the futility of conventional measures that seek to reform local courts by improving organizational performance. With the provisos mentioned (urban security and mining enclaves), the alignment of political and constituent interests appears elusive. The organizational incentives and normative tensions suggest that even successful reforms will have little impact without other sets of institutional change.

Within this apparently bleak picture, it is nonetheless possible to discern alternative spaces that lead to possible development trajectories. We conclude by pointing to one possible arena for action: community officers.[13] Rooted in the "area constables" of the colonial era that blended executive and judicial function as the lowest rung of indirect rule, the community officers were established by a RAMSI-supported police program to act in the manner of extension agents for the police at the local level. Since community officers combine horizontal functions (mediating local disputes) with vertical ones (providing a link to higher levels of the state), their potential as a credible and legitimate service appears intriguing. A recent evaluation of a pilot program found that community officers were often effective in addressing social-order issues and were appreciated locally (Dinnen and Haley 2012). The evaluation, along with an analysis of the court system, has also yielded lessons about the ways in which the organization of community officers might be altered (e.g., by shifting lines of reporting and oversight) to foster accountability between citizens and local and national governments. Additionally, it has been suggested how community officers might act with greater legitimacy by straddling and engaging with the normative tensions that define disputes at the local level.

Community officers also present a possible trajectory toward engaging in justice problems beyond social-order issues. Unsurprisingly, the evaluation showed that they were less effective in disputes related to the regulation of assets or the distribution of public wealth such as aid or constituency funds. These are areas where political elites are actively investing through CDF administrative procedures and other means in order to reinforce existing patterns of authority. Community officers' absence from these spaces can be seen as an advantage, at least initially. With regard to the World Bank's support for the community-officer process, it makes little tactical sense to encourage direct engagement by community officers in the most contentious contests around CDFs, mining, and concessions—if only because combinations of domestic and foreign elite and donor politics would become too difficult to manage. However, increasing the capability, local legitimacy, and organizational linkages of community officers will inevitably embroil them in these contests. The strategy, therefore, is to begin under the radar, investing in a "hybrid" institution that straddles national and local, as well as custom and colonial, legacies in ways that have a reasonable likelihood of becoming locally embedded, and thus support the creation of a new institution through which social contestation will likely occur. To reinforce dialogue around this new institution, monitor its trajectory, and prompt continual adaptation, support for this program should include the documentation of change processes across a range of "contests" (e.g., CDFs, logging, mining, and gender violence). Support for this community-officer project is just beginning; we owe readers an analysis of how it fares along the way.

Conclusion

We are aware that this approach is ambitious and greatly expands the scope of what has heretofore been considered the domain of justice reform. Our critiques of standard approaches are not new; they have been around for decades, and their articulation by several scholars and practitioners has generated an increasingly clear consensus on the problems with current approaches.[14] But efforts to address these shortcomings have succeeded only in achieving minor tweaks around the edges of the paradigm that drives these approaches. This chapter is premised on the notion that what is needed is nothing short of a new paradigm. While we do not claim to have achieved that, our hope is that the analytical framework laid out in this chapter has started to put some of the building blocks in place. By drawing attention to three fundamental questions that are too rarely considered, our aim is both to highlight the empirical and theoretical paucity of standard interventions and to reorient the way we understand justice and the role of donors in promoting it.

The first question leads us toward a clear identification of justice problems in fragile and conflict-affected settings: those directly linked to core functions of public authority, including the maintenance of social order, the regulation of economic assets, and the allocation of public wealth. Examining these domains can help identify the development challenges that are most linked to perceptions of justice and to conflict and fragility. The second question moves us from an immediate focus on the justice sector to ask which institutions matter for the problem at hand, and helps us uncover how these institutions reflect the conditions in a given society. By tracing the political, economic, organizational, and normative dynamics that have shaped the trajectory of institutions and outcomes, we can begin to discern possible pathways toward institutional change and alternative justice outcomes. The third question asks how development actors might engage with these dynamics in ways that enable such changes and outcomes. It points us to incremental changes that open the possibility for constructive contestation and longer-term trajectories of institutional change.

Our approach draws heavily on the cutting-edge scholarship and practice that seeks to embed development work—particularly governance work—within a broader understanding of sociopolitical trajectories. We recognize that much more efforts are needed in applying this knowledge base to the specific challenges of justice in fragile and conflict-affected settings, and in deepening and broadening our understanding of how donors interact with these trajectories. For too long, however, the practice of justice reform in fragile and conflict-affected settings has been detached from this emerging knowledge. The challenges of operating in unstable and often crisis-ridden environments, combined with the well-intentioned but narrow normative frameworks of many justice reform actors, may be partly to blame. Overcoming these challenges and achieving normatively derived goals ultimately requires a deeper engagement with the reality in which these processes unfold. We hope that our framework helps overcome this exceptionalism and contributes to engagement with the inevitably complex, nonlinear, and messy realities to enable practical—and ultimately effective—development strategies.

References

Ahmad, Raza, and Doug Porter. 2006. "Justice Sector Reforms and Policy Conditionality: Symbiosis, or Mutual Denial?" In *Searching for Success: Narrative Accounts of Legal Reform in Developing Transition Countries*, edited by T. McInemey, 69–90. Rome: International Law and Development Organization.

Albrecht, Peter, and Paul Jackson, eds. 2009. *Security Sector Reform in Sierra Leone 1997–2007: Views from the Front Line*. Geneva: Geneva Centre for the Democratic Control of Armed Forces.

Allen, Matthew, Sinclair Dinnen, Daniel Evans, and Rebecca Monson. 2013. *Justice Delivered Locally: Systems, Challenges and Innovations in Solomon Islands*. Washington, DC: World Bank.

Andrews, Matt. 2008. "Creating Space for Effective Political Engagement in Development." In *Governance Reform Under Real-World Conditions: Citizens, Stakeholders and Voice*, edited by Sina Odugbemi and Thomas Jacobson, 95–111. Washington, DC: World Bank.

———. 2013. *The Limits of Institutional Reform in Development: Changing Rules for Realistic Solutions*. Cambridge: Cambridge University Press.

Australian Government Department of Foreign Affairs and Trade. 2014. *Lessons from Australian Aid: 2013 Report on Independent Evaluation and Quality Assurance*. Canberra: Office of Development Effectiveness.

Aydin, Aylin. 2013. "Judicial Independence across Democratic Regimes: Understanding the Varying Impact of Political Competition." *Law and Society Review* 47:105–34.

Biddulph, Robin. 2010. "Geographies of Evasion: The Development Industry and Property Rights Interventions in Early 21st Century Cambodia." PhD dissertation, University of Gothenburg.

Call, Charles. 2007. *Constructing Justice and Security after War*. Washington, DC: United States Institute of Peace.

Carothers, Thomas. 2003. "Promoting the Rule of Law Abroad: The Problem of Knowledge." Working Paper 34. Carnegie Endowment for International Peace Rule of Law Series.

Carothers, Thomas, and Diane de Gramont. 2013. *Development Aid Confronts Politics: The Almost Revolution*. Washington, DC: Carnegie Endowment for International Peace.

Chauvet, Lisa, and Paul Collier. 2006. "Helping Hand? Aid to Failing States." DIAL Working Paper 14.

Collier, Paul, Lani Elliott, Havard Hegre, Anke Hoeffler, Marta Reynal-Querol, and Nicholas Sambanis. 2003. *Breaking the Conflict Trap: Civil War and Development Policy*. Washington, DC: World Bank.

Craig, David. 2012. "Security, Justice and Governance in Solomon Islands: Institutional Drivers, Institutional Prospects with an Extended Discussion of Programming Possibilities and Parameters for the World Bank." Unpublished notes, January 18 and March 23.

Craig, David, and Doug Porter. 2006. *Development Beyond Neo-liberalism? Governance, Poverty Reduction and Political Economy*. London: Routledge.

———. 2014. "Some Comparative and Institutional Perspectives on Post-Conflict Political Settlements and Transitions in Solomon Islands." Brooks World Poverty Institute Working Paper Series. (Under review.)

———. Forthcoming. *Layering Power: New Institutions and Regime Formation in Post-Conflict Cambodia*. (Monograph, under review for publication.)

Davis, Kevin E., and Michael J. Trebilcock. 2008. "The Relationship Between Law and Development: Optimists versus Skeptics." *The American Journal of Comparative Law* 56:895–946.

Department for International Development. 2013. "DFID Policy Approach to Rule of Law." London: Department for International Development.

Desai, Deval, Deborah Isser and Michael Woolcock. 2012. "Rethinking Justice Reform in Fragile and Conflict-Affected States: Lessons for Enhancing the Capacity of Development Agencies." *Hague Journal on the Rule of Law* 4:54–75.

Dinnen, Sinclair, and Matthew Allen. 2012. "Paradoxes of Postcolonial Police-Building: Solomon Islands." *Policing and Society* 23:222–42.
Dinnen, Sinclair, and Nicole Haley. 2012. *Evaluation of the Community Officer Project in Solomon Islands.* Washington, DC: World Bank
Dinnen, Sinclair, Doug Porter, and Caroline Sage. 2010. "Conflict in Melanesia: Themes and Lessons." Background paper for *World Development Report 2011: Conflict, Security and Development.*
Domingo, Pilar, and Lisa Denney. 2012. *The Politics of Practice: Security and Justice Programming in FCAS.* London: Overseas Development Institute.
Donais, Timothy, ed. 2008. *Local Ownership and Security Sector Reform.* Geneva: Centre for the Democratic Control of Armed Forces.
Doyle, Michael, and Nicholas Sambanis. 2006. *Making War and Building Peace: United Nations Peacekeeping Operations.* Princeton: Princeton University Press.
Dressel, Bjoern, and Marcus Mietzner. 2012. "A Tale of Two Courts: The Judicialization of Electoral Politics in Asia." *Governance* 25:391–414.
Englund, Harri. 2012. "Human Rights and Village Headmen in Malawi: Translation beyond Vernacularisation." In *Law against the State: Ethnographic Forays into Law's Transformations*, edited by Julia Eckert, Brian Donahoe, Christian Strümpell, and Zerrin Özlem Biner, 70–93. Cambridge: Cambridge University Press.
Faundez, Julio. 2011. "Legal Pluralism and International Development Agencies: State Building or Legal Reform?" *Hague Journal on the Rule of Law* 3:18–38.
Fortna, Virginia Page. 2008. *Does Peacekeeping Work? Shaping Belligerents Choices After War.* Princeton: Princeton University Press.
Fraenkel, Jon. 2004. *The Manipulation of Custom: From Uprising to Intervention in the Solomon Islands.* Wellington: Victoria University Press.
Fukuyama, Francis. 2004. *State Building: Governance and World Order in the Twenty First Century.* Ithaca: Cornell University Press
Gaston, Erica, Akbar Sarwari, and Arne Strand. 2013. *Lessons Learned on Traditional Dispute Resolution in Afghanistan.* Washington, DC: United States Institute of Peace.
Ginsburg, Tom. 2003. *Judicial Review in New Democracies.* Cambridge: Cambridge University Press.
———. 2011. "In Defense of Imperialism? The Rule of Law and the State-Building Project." In *Getting to the Rule of Law*, edited by James Fleming, 224–40. New York: New York University Press
Golub, Stephen, ed. 2010. *Legal Empowerment: Practitioners' Perspectives.* Rome: International Development Law Organization.
Grindle, Merilee S. 1997. "Divergent Cultures? When Public Organizations Perform Well in Developing Countries." *World Development* 25:481–95
Harper, Erica, ed. 2011. *Working with Customary Justice Systems: Post-Conflict and Fragile Systems.* Rome: International Development Law Organization.
Hickey, Sam. 2013. "Thinking about the Politics of Inclusive Development: Towards a Relational Approach." ESID Working Paper 1.
Hilbink, Lisa. 2009. "The Constituted Nature of Constituents' Interests Historical and Ideational Factors in Judicial Empowerment." *Political Research Quarterly* 62:781–97.

Hirschl, Ran. 2008. "The Judicialization of Mega-politics and the Rise of Political Courts." *Annual Review of Political Science* 11:93–118.

Institute of Development Studies. 2010. "An Upside Down View of Governance." Brighton: Institute of Development Studies.

Israel, Arturo. 1987. *Institutional Development: Incentives to Performance.* Baltimore: Johns Hopkins University Press.

Isser, Deborah, ed. 2011. *Customary Justice and the Rule of Law in War-Torn Societies.* Washington, DC: United States Institute of Peace.

Jensen, Erik. 2003. "The Rule of Law and Judicial Reform: The Political Economy of Diverse Institutional Patterns and Reformers' Responses." In *Beyond Common Knowledge: Empirical Approaches to the Rule of Law*, edited by Erik Jensen and Thomas Heller, 336–81. Redwood City: Stanford University Press.

Kennedy, David. 2006. "The 'Rule of Law,' Political Choices, and Development Common Sense." In *The New Law and Economic Development: A Critical Appraisal*, edited by D. M. Trubek and A. Santos, 95–173. Cambridge: Cambridge University Press.

Khan, Mushtaq. 2010. "Political Settlements and the Governance of Growth-Enhancing Institutions." Unpublished paper in research paper series on growth-enhancing governance. http://eprints.soas.ac.uk/id/eprint/9968.

Kleinfeld, Rachel. 2012. *Advancing the Rule of Law Abroad: Next Generation Reform.* Washington, DC: Carnegie Endowment for International Peace.

Leonardi, Cherry, Deborah Isser, Leben Moro, and Martina Santschi. 2011. "The Politics of Customary Law Ascertainment in South Sudan." *The Journal of Legal Pluralism and Unofficial Law* 63:111–42.

Mahoney, James, and Kathleen Thelen, eds. 2010. *Explaining Institutional Change: Ambiguity, Agency, and Power.* Cambridge: Cambridge University Press.

Mallet, Richard. 2010. "Beyond Failed States and Ungoverned Spaces: Hybrid Political Orders in the Post-Conflict Landscape." *eSharp* 15:65–91.

McAuslan, Patrick. 2004. "In the Beginning Was the Law . . . an Intellectual Odyssey." *The Practice of Law and Development: Socio-Legal Approaches.* Paper 2.

Merry, Sally Engle. 2003. "Rights Talk and the Experience of Law: Implementing Women's Human Rights to Protection from Violence." *Human Rights Quarterly* 25:343–81.

Moore, Barrington. 1978. *Injustice: The Social Bases of Obedience and Revolt.* White Plains: M.E. Sharpe.

Moore, Mick, Anna Schmidt, and Sue Unsworth. 2009. "Assuring Our Common Future in a Globalised World: The Global Context of Conflict and State Fragility." Background paper for the Department for International Development, April 28.

Moustafa, Tamir. 2013. "Liberal Rights versus Islamic Law? The Construction of a Binary in Malaysian Politics." *Law and Society Review* 47: 771–802.

Narten, Jens. 2008. "Post-Conflict Peacebuilding and Local Ownership: Dynamics of External-Local Interaction in Kosovo under United Nations Administration." *Journal of Intervention and Statebuilding* 2:369–90.

Netherlands Ministry of Foreign Affairs Evaluation Department. 2013. "Investing in Stability: Dutch Policy on Fragile States Reviewed." IOB evaluation 379.

Newton, Scott. 2006. "The Dialectics of Law and Development." In *The New Law and Economic Development: A Critical Appraisal*, edited by D. M. Trubek and A. Santos, 174–202. Cambridge: Cambridge University Press.

Organisation for Economic Co-operation and Development. 2012. *Rethinking Policy, Changing Practice: DAC Guidelines on Post-Conflict Transition*. DAC Guidelines and Reference Series, OECD Publishing. doi: 10.1787/9789264168336-en.

Porter, Doug, Deborah Isser, and Louis-Alexandre Berg. 2013. "The Justice-Security-Development Nexus: Theory and Practice in Fragile and Conflict-Affected States." *Hague Journal on the Rule of Law* 5:310–28.

Prado, Mariana, and Michael Trebilcock. 2009. "Path Dependence, Development and the Dynamics of Institutional Reform." *University of Toronto law Journal* 59:341–79.

Pritchett, Lant, Michael Woolcock, and Matt Andrews. 2010. "Capability Traps? The Mechanisms of Persistent Implementation Failure." Center for Global Development Working Paper 234.

———. 2012. "Looking like a State: Techniques of Persistent Failure in State Capability for Implementation." UNU-WIDER Working Paper 2012/63.

Rajagopal, Balakrishnan. 2007. "Invoking the Rule of Law in Post-Conflict Rebuilding: A Critical Examination." *William and Mary Law Review* 49:1347–76.

Ramseyer, J. Mark. 1994. "The Puzzling (In)Dependence of Courts." *The Journal of Legal Studies* 23:721–47.

Ribot, Jesse C. 1999. "Decentralization, Participation and Accountability in Sahelian Forestry: Legal Instruments of Political-Administrative control." *Africa* 69:23–65.

Roque, Paula, Judy Smith-Höhn, Paul-Simon Handy, Le Dang Doanh, David Craig, and Omar McDoom. 2010. "Exit Pathways: South Africa, Mozambique, Vietnam, Cambodia, Rwanda." Background paper for *World Development Report 2011: Conflict, Security and Development*.

Samuels, Kirsti. 2006. "Rule of Law Reform in Post-Conflict Countries: Operational Initiatives and Lessons Learnt." World Bank Social Development Paper 37.

Scheye, Eric, and Gordon Peake. 2005. "Unknotting Local Ownership." In *After Intervention: Public Security in Post-Conflict Societies: From Intervention to Sustainable Local Ownership*, edited by Anja Ebnöther and Philipp Fluri, 235–60. Geneva: Centre for the Democratic Control of Armed Forces.

Stephenson, Matthew C. 2003. "'When the Devil Turns...': The Political Foundations of Judicial Independent Judicial Review." *Journal of Legal Studies* 32:59–89.

Stromseth, Jane, David Wippman, and Rosa Brooks. 2006. *Can Might Make Rights? Building the Rule of Law After Military Interventions*. Cambridge: Cambridge University Press.

Tamanaha, Brian Z. 2004. *On the Rule of Law: Politics History, Theory*. Cambridge: Cambridge University Press.

Van Rooij, Benjamin. 2009. "Bringing Justice to the Poor, Bottom Up Legal Development Cooperation." *Hague Journal on the Rule of Law.* 4:286–318.

Weingast, Barry. 1997. "The Political Foundations of Democracy and the Rule of Law." *American Political Science Review* 91:245–63.

Weinstein, Jeremy. 2005. "Autonomous Recovery and International Intervention in Comparative Perspective." Center for Global Development Working Paper 57.

Widner, Jennifer. 2001a. *Building the Rule of Law.* New York: W.W. Norton.

———. 2001b. "Courts and Democracy in Postconflict Transitions: A Social Scientist's Perspective on the African Case." *American Journal of International Law* 95:64–75.

World Bank. 2011. *World Development Report 2011: Conflict, Security and Development.* Washington, DC: World Bank.

———. 2012. *The World Bank: New Directions in Justice Reform; A Companion Piece to the Updated Strategy and Implementation Plan on Strengthening Governance, Tackling Corruption.* Washington, DC: World Bank.

———. 2013. "World Bank Support to the Community Governance and Conflict Management Project in Solomon Islands: Concept Note." August. On file with the authors.

———. 2014. *Synthesis Report: Institutional and Fiscal Analysis: Lower courts, Solomon Islands.* (Under review.)

Notes

1. The importance of justice and security institutions in fragile and conflict-affected settings is central to several recent policy documents, including, inter alia, World Bank (2011) and Organisation for Economic Co-operation and Development (2012).

2. For critical perspectives on the historical evolution of these efforts, see McAuslan (2004); Jensen (2003, 336–81, 345–48); Newton (2006); Samuels (2006); Davis and Trebilcock (2008); Desai, Isser, and Woolcock (2012); Rajagopal (2007); Biddulph (2010).

3. These lessons are captured in several recent policy documents, including, inter alia, World Bank (2011, 2012); Department for International Development (2013); Australian Government Department of Foreign Affairs and Trade (2014); Netherlands Ministry of Foreign Affairs Evaluation Department (2013); and Domingo and Denney (2012).

4. This chapter builds on our exploration of these themes in Porter, Isser, and Berg (2013).

5. We draw inspiration from several recent efforts aimed at improving donor engagement in fragile and conflict-affected settings, notably a draft "Diagnostic Protocol for Public Sector Management" under development at the World Bank, as well as a review of justice and security programs in fragile and conflict-affect-

ed settings by the Organisation for Economic Co-operation and Development's DAC International Network on Conflict and Fragility, among other efforts. For an overview of some of the key concepts, see Andrews (2008, 2013).

6. The authors have worked in various capacities on this program, a partnership between the World Bank and the aid program within the Australian Department of Foreign Affairs and Trade.

7. Moore (1978, 9) conceptualized these as three questions: How should resources be distributed? How should production be organized? And who shall make decisions and rule on these matters? See also Hickey (2013).

8. We do not mean "public authority" as limited to state authority; it can also be exercised by other forms of political and social collectives (customary, religious, and so on) that carry out activities in the public interest.

9. Our remarks on Solomon Islands' political economy draw on Craig and Porter (2014).

10. These insights are explored in a vast literature on organizational change, although they are rarely applied directly to the justice sector. See Grindle (1997); Fukuyama (2004); Mahoney and Thelen (2010); Israel (1987).

11. Fukuyama (2004) examines features of organizational complexity, such as a high volume of transactions, numerous veto points, and low task specificity in undermining institutional reform.

12. These points are drawn from Craig and Porter (2014).

13. This approach is elaborated in World Bank (2013).

14. The most widely cited and accepted critique is likely Thomas Carothers' 2003 article "Promoting the Rule of Law Abroad: The Problem of Knowledge." See *supra* n. 1 for others.

Postscript: An Immodest Reflection

Erik G. Jensen

David Marshall is persistent. I was a reluctant participant in an authors' workshop at Harvard, and then eventually agreed to write an immodest reflection for this book. Ultimately, I agreed to both because the volume brings together a good collection of authors trying to vigorously bridge theory and practice. That most of the contributors are at least a half generation younger than I was an additional draw. And yet another draw was that David Marshall's restlessness, which I view as very constructive, if disruptive, was not unfamiliar to me.

This postscript is divided into three sections. The first is a brief personal account of my observations of and frustrations with the performance of the rule of law industry over nearly three decades. Somehow that unease connects me with the next-generation authors in this volume. In the second section, I deconstruct an example of received wisdom to illustrate the complexity of developing legal systems and the multitude of contingencies at play in doing so. The example should also serve as a caution to those who aspire to install legal institutions quickly. Finally, in the last section, I critically reflect on the contributions to this volume.

Background

I have enjoyed an existential relationship with the rule of law industry for nearly thirty years. I relish the numerous opportunities that I have had to engage with local collaborators in research and action. Through our work in the 1980s and early 1990s, we learned a great deal from one another as we tried to make a difference, exploring the relationship between law/legal institutions and social, political, and economic development. We were self-critical and keenly aware of moral dilemmas. But our research was good, and some of our actions were novel. We sensed modest progress (a topic to which I will return later). Still, my apprehension grew as the rule of law industry mushroomed in size in the mid-to-late 1990s—and even more so in this century—compared to its very humble scope in the 1980s.

By the end of the 1990s, I had developed what I hoped was a constructive and well-informed restlessness about the gap between theory and practice. The deficiencies in the industry were manifest: too much of the practice seemed uninformed by empirical knowledge, history, serious comparative work, interdisciplinary connections, an understanding of political economy, or even a general knowledge of the arc of economic development and the role or potential role of legal institutions in that development. By the way, let's not glorify theory: it is a horse race between practitioners and academics as to who has published more pabulum about law and development. As a friend once said, "Those who write don't know, and those who know don't write." Now it seems that many who *should know* either do not know or have too much self-interest in perpetuating ideas and donor interventions that do not work. One channeling of my restlessness was a book that my colleague Tom Heller and I assembled, entitled *Beyond Common Knowledge: Empirical Approaches to the Rule of Law* (2003).

Deconstructing an Assertion about the Role of Law and Legal Institutions in Economic Development

In the 1990s, when the World Bank and other multilateral development banks began to support "rule of law" projects, they asserted time and again that a well-functioning judiciary is necessary for economic growth and development. A corollary assumption underlying their support for such projects was that substitutes for a well-functioning judiciary entail high transaction costs.

These assertions were supported by neoclassical economic theory,[1] but not by a realist's historical assessment of current developing countries and the few countries that have transitioned from underdevelopment to OECD-level development within the last fifty years. How and, importantly, *when* do formal legal institutions become consequential to economic growth and development? Neoclassical economic theory stresses the importance of formal legal institutions for the enforcement of contracts and the protection of property. According to this view, the sequence is clear and the causal arrow goes in one direction: build strong legal institutions and economic growth, and development will follow. This view seems to be correlated with outcomes. After all, most OECD countries have relatively strong legal institutions. But those outcomes do not prove a causal story about how developed economies became developed or about when in that process legal institutions became more consequential to growth and development.

Indeed, even a cursory consideration of three of the most dramatic economic growth and development stories of the last fifty years confounds received wisdom.

Detailed accounts of the "East Asian miracle" (Hong Kong, Singapore, South Korea, and Taiwan) make virtually no reference to the role of legal institutions. India, under its economic reform program, achieved high growth rates for two decades with a court system that ranks at the very bottom in contract enforcement. And China achieved 9% growth over thirty years with a woefully underdeveloped legal system and an opaque property rights regime. China is responsible for nearly three-quarters of the reduction in poverty globally over that period of time.

Today, the East Asian Tigers all have reasonably strong legal institutions, China's legal institutions are improving (though very unevenly), and India's legal institutions, especially at the lower court level, continue to flounder (though, correspondingly, arbitration practice is booming). The point is that dramatic economic growth and development can ensue alongside poor legal institutions. And during these periods of growth, substitutes for well-functioning laws and legal institutions can proliferate and even flourish. Substitutes may be informal (e.g., relations, reputation, repeat dealing, and so forth), market-based, technological, or rudimentary (e.g., adjusting contracts depending on available institutions).

Collective demand and pressure from economic actors on judiciaries takes time to build as business actors use dysfunctional courts to their advantage. As an Indian banker once said, "If we have a strong case, we settle; if we have a weak case, we go to court." That strategy is often pursued until the complexity of economies reduces such advantages and obfuscates winners and losers. Thus, the need for effective legal institutions becomes pronounced at a later stage of development when economies become more complex.

I urge readers to compare this account of the historical evolution of legal institutions to the recommendations in the Brahimi Report. These recommendations, based on the finding that the "rule of law vacuum" is the greatest threat to states transitioning from conflict to peace, call for an almost SWAT-team-like installation of laws and legal institutions (United Nations Secretary-General 2000, analyzed in Marshall, this volume).

Critical Reflections on the Chapters in This Volume

Turning to the book in hand, we had an epiphanic moment at the authors' workshop when we took stock of the level of development in the countries under consideration in this volume. Many, though not all, of the countries are least-developed postconflict or conflict states. None of the least-developed states under consideration are in a position to allocate jurisdiction across secular, religious, and customary possibilities. Part of that stems from the fact that the some of them are juridical states but not empirical states.

Another reason is that legal pluralism endures over time, as Haider Hamoudi's chapter on Iraq nicely illustrates. So, even in more developed states such as Iraq, legal pluralism is a historical fact. Legal pluralism baffles and frustrates rule of law technocrats. Predictably, some of the donor experiments to centralize and coordinate that pluralism have been massive failures.

Doctrine, structuralism, and formalism continue to impede rule of law practice. For example, many rule of law promoters and consultants of my generation who were very critical of their own legal systems used to go to developing countries and advocate the US model as a pristine way to separate powers. Of course, as my colleague Gerhard Casper (1997) illustrates so well in his account of how power is separated in the United States, separating power is a negotiated, deeply contextualized, and highly contingent evolutionary process. Another example of doctrinal blinders from my generation is the way it pursued judicial independence as the *sine qua non* for the rule of law: if judiciaries were not independent, the rule of law could not exist. This binary approach to the rule of law belied the messiness and unevenness of the development of rule of law. The rule of law is not like pregnancy—you do not either have it or not. The reality is that rule of law has many gradations as it episodically develops across countries.

Many of the chapters in this volume capture important aspects of that complexity. Mareike Schomerus's account of the rule of law in the context of South Sudan's Western Equatoria State takes us about as far away from the doctrinalist camp as we can travel. She interrogates how power and authority are constructed in a traditional society and demonstrates how important that analysis is to understanding how institutions can or might evolve.

Louis-Alexandre Berg, Deborah Isser, and Doug Porter's chapter argues persuasively that technical and capacity-building solutions to institution-building may be necessary but are utterly insufficient unless they are situated within the political economy of contestation. The value of their chapter is in laying out the complexity of the field of contestation. This chapter should be read as a *caveat emptor* to any donor embarking on large rule of law projects that contemplate broad institutional reform. The likelihood of missing the mark on large-scale institutional reform projects with bloated expectations is significant. Contestation analysis is important, but it needs to feed into change analysis. How is the equilibrium going to change in favor of excluded populations? Arnold Toynbee once observed that some people think that history "is just one damned thing after another." I would argue that in developing countries with weak institutions, change does not happen with one damned contestation after another. The need to aggregate strands of contestation in collective action and political settlement is manifest.

Margaux Hall, Nicholas Menzies, and Michael Woolcock probe another dimension of what the political economy of donors in rule of law focuses on: "success." Indeed, one explanation for stunted results in rule of law programs is risk aversion. In the Silicon Valley, 90% of technology start-ups fail (see, e.g., Kelly 2013). In the rule-of-law industry, failure is unacceptable. In this risk-averse industry, somehow doing the same things that do not work well (but that can be financially accounted for) is preferable to experimenting with projects that may fail in the frame of donor results but may succeed in producing knowledge and advancing learning.

Deval Desai undertakes an analysis of human resources practices in four international agencies that deploy a range of "rule of law experts." Who are these people anyway, and what are they qualified to do? I have argued for well over a decade that it is insufficient to examine just the political economy of any given country; one also needs to understand the political economy of donor assistance. Desai's inquiry into donor hiring practices is an important part of coming to grips with where money goes in rule of law assistance and why.

I would urge Desai and others to continue this line of research into the organizational behavior of donors in rule of law industry. An area ripe for research is requests for proposal and proposal writing. Most requests for proposals (RFPs) in rule of law assistance (and democracy assistance for that matter) make normative assertions that may or may not be supported by empirical evidence.[2] Proposals in response to the RFPs, if they are to succeed, must reassert the normative conjecture that was framed by the prospective donor. My hypothesis is that through repeated cycles with RFPs framed in a risk-averse, must-succeed environment and proposals reinforcing normative assertions, practitioners start to believe the assertions made. The machine in the development industry perpetuates and reinforces received wisdom.

The RFP-proposal process also incentivizes overpromising what can be achieved in any given project. Bloated expectations are everywhere. A point that I made repeatedly during the authors' workshop is that modest expectations and success within the scope of those modest expectations should be valued. That was my reaction to chapters by James Goldston, Todd

Foglesong, and Vivek Maru. Todd Foglesong tells a wonderful story about reform in the public prosecutor's office in Lagos, Nigeria. A modest project achieved results.

As the commentator on an earlier draft of Maru's chapter, I had three sets of comments. First, Maru is right: if you put the needs and demands of the common citizen first, you will quickly understand the centrality of land to a host of primary and ancillary problems that people care about in transitional countries. You will also learn about the primacy of administrative decision making for the vast majority of citizens. Second, for those of us who entered the field of law and development inspired to reduce levels of economic deprivation, Maru's grassroots stories from Uganda, Sierra Leone, and India remind us that microsuccesses can be significant. The role that paralegals played in these stories was vital. Community organizers who are aware of the law, legal rights, and potential legal rights—and who work to connect community needs and demands with lawyers able to help—are worth their weight in gold as actors in grassroots legal development.[3] Third, an earlier draft of Maru's chapter outlined the possibility of going global. My advice was to delete that section. The pressure to scale-up project impacts and tell a much bigger story often detracts from the small but significant successes achieved.

My advice was born of experience. During the 1990s, the Asia Foundation and the Ford Foundation provided assistance to a group of high-quality legal resource nongovernmental organizations (NGOs) in the Philippines who represented various disadvantaged sectors: fisherfolk, farmers, women, upland communities, and the urban poor, among others. These legal resource NGOs received referrals from paralegals, and they represented these disadvantaged communities, often before administrative agencies, to assure that the communities received fair treatment. The legal resource NGOs achieved many microsuccesses. But the strategic plans of each of the NGOs sought "structural change" in society and governance as their overarching goal. These fabulously productive NGOs have never achieved their ultimate goal, but along the way, they have done a great deal of good for the communities they represent.

Returning to Foglesong's story from Nigeria, his narrative also underscores the central importance of relationships to the quality of development achieved. Foglesong's group developed a relationship with the public prosecutor's office that leveraged a reform in which no monetary assistance was exchanged. The development industry, ironically, assumes that we are functioning in a postmodern transactional world of impersonal exchange in which technocratic benchmarks are set and achieved. Yet, to state the obvious, we are not functioning in countries that are part of the postmodern world. And even if we were, both the value and extent of impersonal exchange is exaggerated in the literature and also in the behavior of agents in some donor institutions. The best development work that I have done over the last three decades is directly related to the depth and quality of relationships that I enjoyed with nationals of the countries in which I worked.

Beyond bloated goals and objectives, two related dynamics exacerbate the view that the rule of law industry is rife with failure. One is that critics fail to ask the question, compared to what? In other words, what is the experience in other areas of the development industry? In my more cynical moments, I see multilateral banks' gravitation toward rule of law assistance as motivated in part by the even greater failures they experienced with civil service reform. Judiciaries are viewed as a smaller, more contained subset of the civil service. Yet, most rule law academics and practitioners do not have experience in other so-called sectors of development.

Another related dynamic is that lawyers like to write. A disproportionate volume of scholarship critiques the rule of law industry. Far be it from me to excuse wasteful funding that neither achieves modest success nor advances learning. But reading critiques, one would think that the rule of law industry wastes more funding than any other. Indeed, David Trubek and Marc Galanter's (1974) brilliantly written critique convinced a generation of American law students who simply did not know better that "law and development" was a failed field. The authors' expansive critique was based on a measly US$5 million of US-based donor assistance to strengthen the rule of law in Latin America.[4] And if you asked the beneficiaries—legal academics from Latin America placed in elite US law schools for postgraduate studies, and US legal academics placed in ministries of government and universities in Latin America—you would get a substantially different assessment of the value of the donor assistance (see, e.g., Pérez-Perdomo 2006).

So, is David Marshall's critical reflection on the role of the United Nations an overreaction fueled by his love of the pen? I think not. Large institutions are subject to mission creep, and they often conflate their conferences, workshops, and proclamations with progress on the ground. In addition, these institutions, while often slow to change, are nimble in adjusting their objectives to fit the development jargon of the day. For example, a multilateral development bank project to computerize the courts may have been justified during an earlier era as improving the environment for foreign direct investment. Later, that same project would be justified as decongesting the courts. And, later still, that same project would be justified as improving access to justice for the poor or even as strengthening national security. The same project on the ground has nimble objectives that can shift depending on the *carte du jour*.

Marshall's chapter outlines many reasons for mission creep regarding the United Nations' rule of law programs. I single out only one reason. It relates to Marshall's close reading of a 2011 special advisory group report that identifies critical capacity gaps in policing and justice. Related to these capacity gaps, the report also notes "evidence of many actors making aspirational claims of capacity, perhaps in the hope of generating resources" (United Nations General Assembly and Security Council 2011, para. 35[e]). That observation gets to the heart of the political economy of donor institutions (not just the United Nations, but many development organizations): some are more influenced by market opportunity than others. By the way, the Secretary-General is to be applauded for initiating a review process that included this special advisory committee. Candid and considered reports are part of the baseline needed for thoughtful reform, and they are not very popular with internal constituencies within development institutions.

As I embarked on this exercise, one question was in the back of my mind throughout: what positive change has occurred in the rule of law industry over the last decade? One positive change is a growing body of empirical research on law and legal institutions in developing countries. The quality of that research varies wildly, but there is more good research—in other words, papers and books that I find useful—published with each succeeding year. With research that increasingly employs mixed methods, inquiries can get at issues that actually matter. And that research should translate to better and more effective programs on the ground. In this immodest essay, I have selectively highlighted issues that actually matter that were raised either directly or implicitly by the authors. Now the easy part: bridging theory and practices.

References

Casper, Gerhard. 1997. *Separating Power: Essays on the Founding Period.* Cambridge, MA: Harvard University Press.

Jensen, Erik, and Tom Heller. 2003. *Beyond Common Knowledge: Empirical Approaches to the Rule of Law.* Redwood City: Stanford University Press.

Kelly, Samantha Murphy. 2013. "Why 90% of Startups Fail." *Mashable*, February 4. http://mashable.com/2013/02/04/why-startups-fail.

North, Douglass C. 1991. *Institutions, Institutional Change and Economic Performance.* Cambridge: Cambridge University Press.

Pérez-Perdomo, Rogelio. 2006. *Latin American Lawyers: A Historical Introduction.* Redwood City: Stanford University Press.

Schuler, Marge. 1986. *Empowerment and the Law: Strategies of Third World Women.* Washington, DC: OEF.

Trubek, David, and Marc Galanter. 1974. "Scholars in Self-Estrangement: Some Reflections on the Crisis in Law and Development Studies in the United States." *Wisconsin Law Review* 4:1062–102.

United Nations General Assembly and Security Council. 2011. Identical Letters Dated 18 February 2011 from the Secretary-General Addressed to the President of the General Assembly and the President of the Security Council. UN docs. A/65/747–S/2011/85, para. 35(e).

United Nations Secretary-General. 2000. Report of the Secretary-General on the Implementation of the Report of the Panel on United Nations Peace Operations. UN doc. S/2000/1081.

Notes

1. Even Nobel laureate Douglass North, one of my all-time favorite economists who made Max Weber accessible to economists, thought that legal institutions and judicial enforcement were necessary to transition from a traditional economy to a developed economy: "Missing in the suq [bazaar economies engaged in regional trade] are the fundamental underpinnings of legal institutions and judicial enforcement that would make such voluntary organizations viable and profitable. *In their absence, there is no incentive to alter the system*" (1991, 124, emphasis added).

2. See the deconstruction above of one such assertion about legal institutions and economic development and growth.

3. Nearly three decades ago, Marge Schuler did pathbreaking work on legal empowerment for women in developing countries. Many in my generation learned from her seminal work, modestly entitled *Empowerment and the Law: Strategies of Third World Women* (1986). A handful of international NGOs and bilateral donors funded field work on legal empowerment for two decades before the United Nations claimed it through a high-level panel and a multitude of assertions about its perceived value.

4. Their article mentioned US assistance in Africa only in passing, and it did not even acknowledge significant British rule of law assistance at that time. James Goldston's chapter corrects that oversight.

Contributors

Louis-Alexandre Berg has designed, managed, and evaluated justice-sector reform, police assistance, and conflict-mitigation programs as an adviser to the World Bank, the US Agency for International for International Development, the United States Institute of Peace, and the United Nations Development Programme. His research explores the effects of foreign aid on governance, justice, and security, especially in countries affected by violence and conflict. He holds a PhD from Georgetown University and a master's from Princeton University.

Deval Desai is a research associate at SOAS, University of London. He also advises the United Nations on rule of law issues in the post-2015 agenda and was appointed by the United Nations as an expert on the rule of law and legal empowerment. He previously worked at the World Bank, where he helped establish a justice and conflict program. He has published widely on rule of law reform, justice and conflict, and governance and extractive industries. He is a member of the Bar of England and Wales.

Todd Foglesong is a senior research associate with the Program in Criminal Justice Policy and Management and an adjunct lecturer in public policy at Harvard Kennedy School. There, he coordinates the "Justice Systems Workshop" and supervises the work of a team of researchers collaborating with the governments of Bangladesh, Ethiopia, Jamaica, Nigeria, and Sierra Leone to design and use indicators that advance domestic ideas about improvements in justice and safety.

James A. Goldston is the executive director of the Open Society Justice Initiative. He formerly served as coordinator of prosecutions and senior trial attorney in the Office of the Prosecutor at the International Criminal Court. He also previously worked at the European Roma Rights Centre, the Organization for Security and Co-operation in Europe, the Office of the United States Attorney for the Southern District of New York, and Human Rights Watch. Goldston graduated from Columbia College and Harvard Law School and has taught at Columbia Law School and Central European University.

Margaux Hall works in Sierra Leone with the Justice Reform Group of the World Bank. She is also the Center for Reproductive Rights Fellow at Columbia Law School, where her research focuses on health-care law and fiduciary law. Her publications include "Avoiding Adaptation Apartheid: Climate Change Adaptation and Human Rights Law" (*Yale Journal of International Law*), "Answering the Millennium Call for the Right to Maternal Health" (*Yale Human Rights and Development Law Journal*), and "A Fiduciary Theory of Health Entitlements" (*Cardozo Law Review*). She holds a JD from Harvard Law School and a BS from Stanford University.

Haider Ala Hamoudi is an associate professor of law and the associate dean of research and faculty development at the University of Pittsburgh School of Law. He has worked on a number of projects in the rule of law field, primarily in the Middle East. In 2003–2004, he served as a legal advisor to the Finance Committee of the Iraq Governing Council, as well as a program manager for a project aimed at improving legal education in Iraq. In 2009, he worked in Baghdad with the University of Utah under a contract with the US Embassy. His most recent publication is *Negotiating in Civil Conflict: Constitutional Construction and Imperfect Bargaining in Iraq*. Hamoudi received his JD and JSD from Columbia Law School.

Deborah Isser is senior counsel and program manager of the Justice for the Poor program at the World Bank, where she leads work on justice in fragile and conflict-affected states. Previously, she served in policy roles at the United States Institute of Peace, the Office of the High Representative in Bosnia and Herzegovina, and the United States Mission to the United Nations. Among her publications is *Customary Justice and the Rule of Law in War-Torn Societies*. She has served as adjunct faculty at Georgetown University Law Center and George Washington University Law School. She holds degrees from Harvard Law School and the Fletcher School of Law and Diplomacy.

Erik G. Jensen is a professor at Stanford Law School, director of the law school's Rule of Law Program, and an affiliated faculty member at the Center on Democracy, Development, and the Rule of Law at Stanford's Freeman Spogli Institute for International Studies. His teaching and research activities explore various dimensions of reform aimed at strengthening the rule of law. Jensen is coeditor of the widely renowned book *Beyond Common Knowledge: Empirical Approaches to the Rule of Law*. He holds a JD from the William Mitchell College of Law and an LLM from the London School of Economics.

David Marshall is chief of the Global Issues Section of the New York Office of the United Nations Office of the High Commissioner for Human Rights. With a background in criminal law and international human rights, he has been working on criminal justice reform issues for more than twenty years. He has extensive field experience in postconflict states, including Afghanistan, Iraq, Kosovo, Nepal, and South Sudan. In 2011, he was appointed head of the United Nations' Justice and Corrections Standing Capacity, a rapidly deployable entity charged with developing justice strategies in new peacekeeping missions. He is a graduate of the University of Leeds and Harvard Law School.

Vivek Maru is the chief executive officer of Namati, which is building a movement of grassroots legal advocates around the world. Previously, he served as senior counsel in the Justice Reform Group of the World Bank. Prior to that, he co-founded the Sierra Leonean organization Timap for Justice.

Nicholas Menzies is senior counsel in the Justice Reform Group of the World Bank. There, he works on institutional reform of the formal justice sector and on mainstreaming justice into development programming with the Justice for the Poor program. Previously, he worked on land and natural resources issues in Australia, on legal empowerment and access-to-justice issues in Cambodia, and on policy issues in Papua New Guinea. He holds a BA and an LLB from the University of Sydney and a master's degree from the Hertie School of Governance.

Doug Porter is an adviser to the World Bank's Justice Practice Group. He is also an adjunct professor of international politics and security studies at the Australian National University. His work in conflict-affected countries includes assignments in Cambodia, Kenya, Malawi, Pakistan, the Philippines, Timor-Leste, Uganda, Vietnam, and Zambia. Porter is the author of several books, including *Development Beyond Neoliberalism? Governance, Poverty Reduction and Political Economy* and *Winning the Peace: New Institutions, Neo-patrimonialism and Post-conflict in Cambodia*. He holds a PhD from the Australian National University.

Mareike Schomerus is a research fellow at the London School of Economics, where she is investigating the dynamics of violent conflict and its resolution, the violence of democratization, civilian security, and the impact of living in militarized situations on personal lives. She has a particular interest in how knowledge is created, shared, and shaped. Over the past few years, Schomerus has conducted extensive fieldwork in South Sudan. Her most recent publication is the edited volume *The Borderlands of South Sudan: Authority and Identity in Contemporary and Historical Perspectives*.

Michael Woolcock is the lead social development specialist with the World Bank's Development Research Group and a lecturer in public policy at Harvard Kennedy School. His research draws on a range of methods to study the role of social institutions in the survival and mobility strategies of marginalized groups, and the way in which these institutions are shaped by the development process. He is a co-founder of the World Bank's Justice for the Poor program. Prior to joining the World Bank in 1998, Woolcock taught at Brown University and the University of Queensland. He holds an MA and a PhD from Brown University.